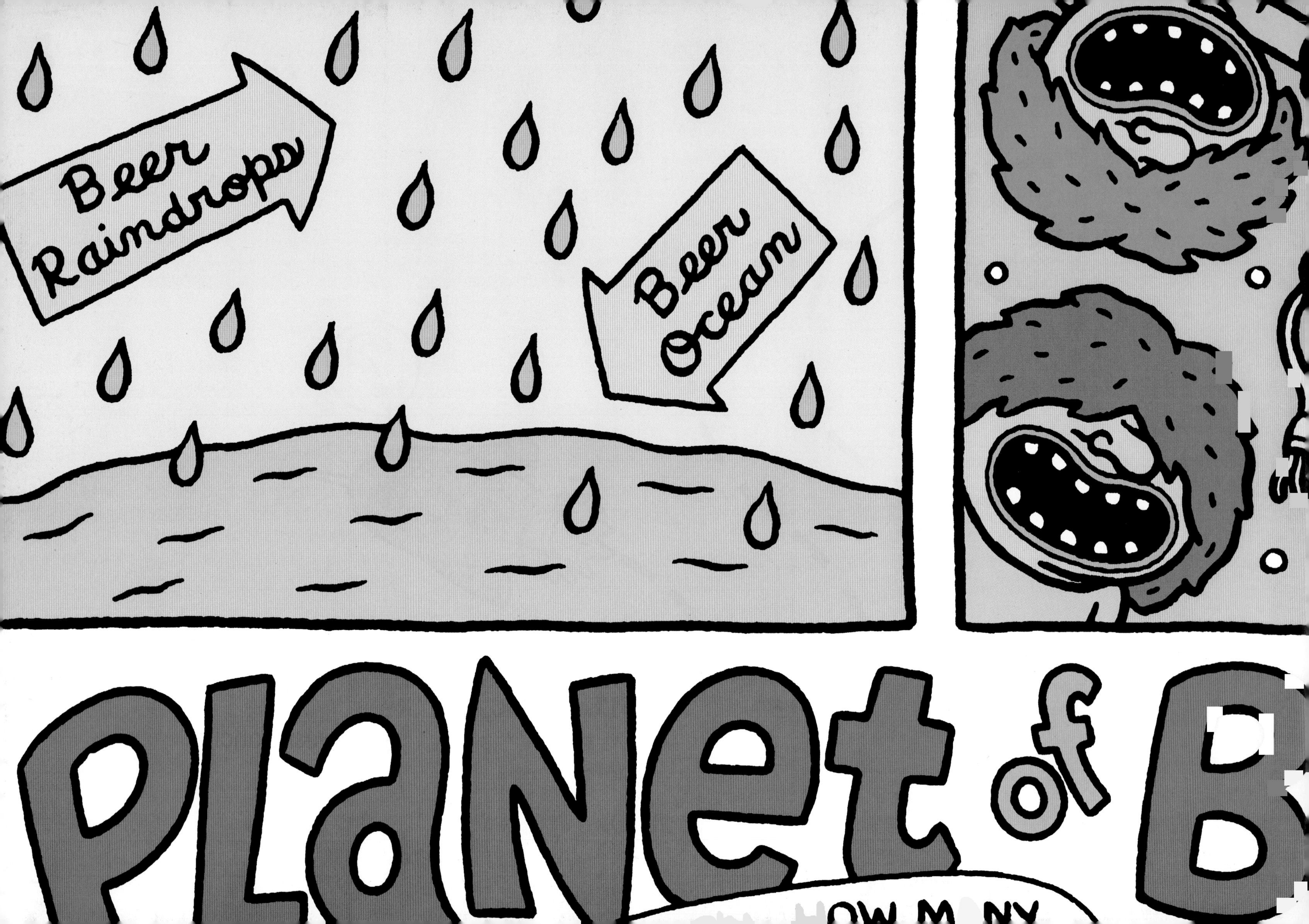
Beer Raindrops
Beer Ocean
PLANET of B

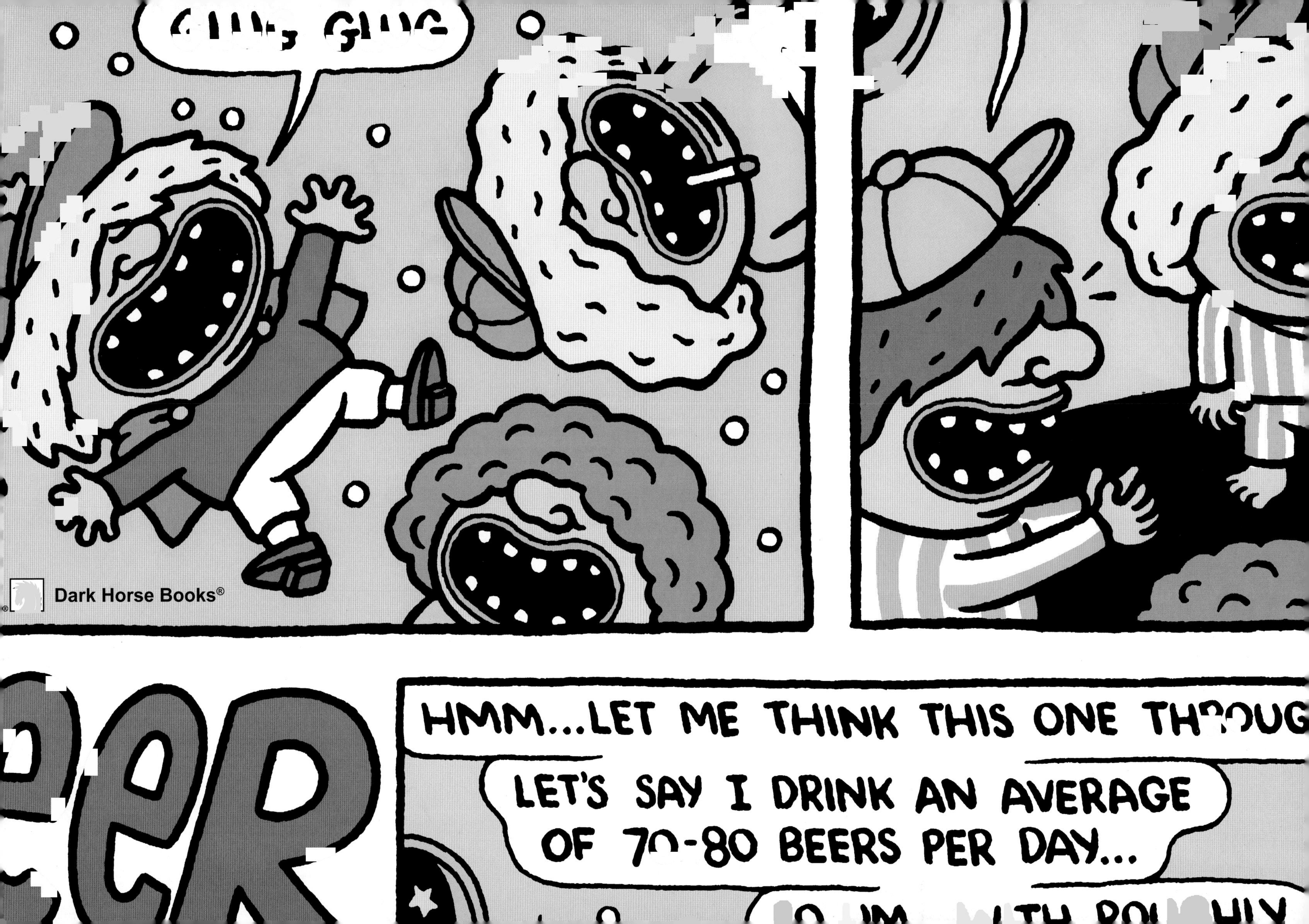
GLUG GLUG
Dark Horse Books®
HMM...LET ME THINK THIS ONE THROUG
LET'S SAY I DRINK AN AVERAGE OF 70-80 BEERS PER DAY...

Editor **SHAWNA GORE**
Assistant **JEMIAH JEFFERSON**
Designers **BRIAN SENDELBACH**
           with **HEIDI WHITCOMB**
Publisher **MIKE RICHARDSON**

Published by Dark Horse Books
A division of Dark Horse Comics, Inc.
10956 SE Main Street
Milwaukie OR 97222

darkhorse.com
First edition: March 2009
ISBN 978-1-59582-256-7

10 9 8 7 6 5 4 3 2 1

Printed in China

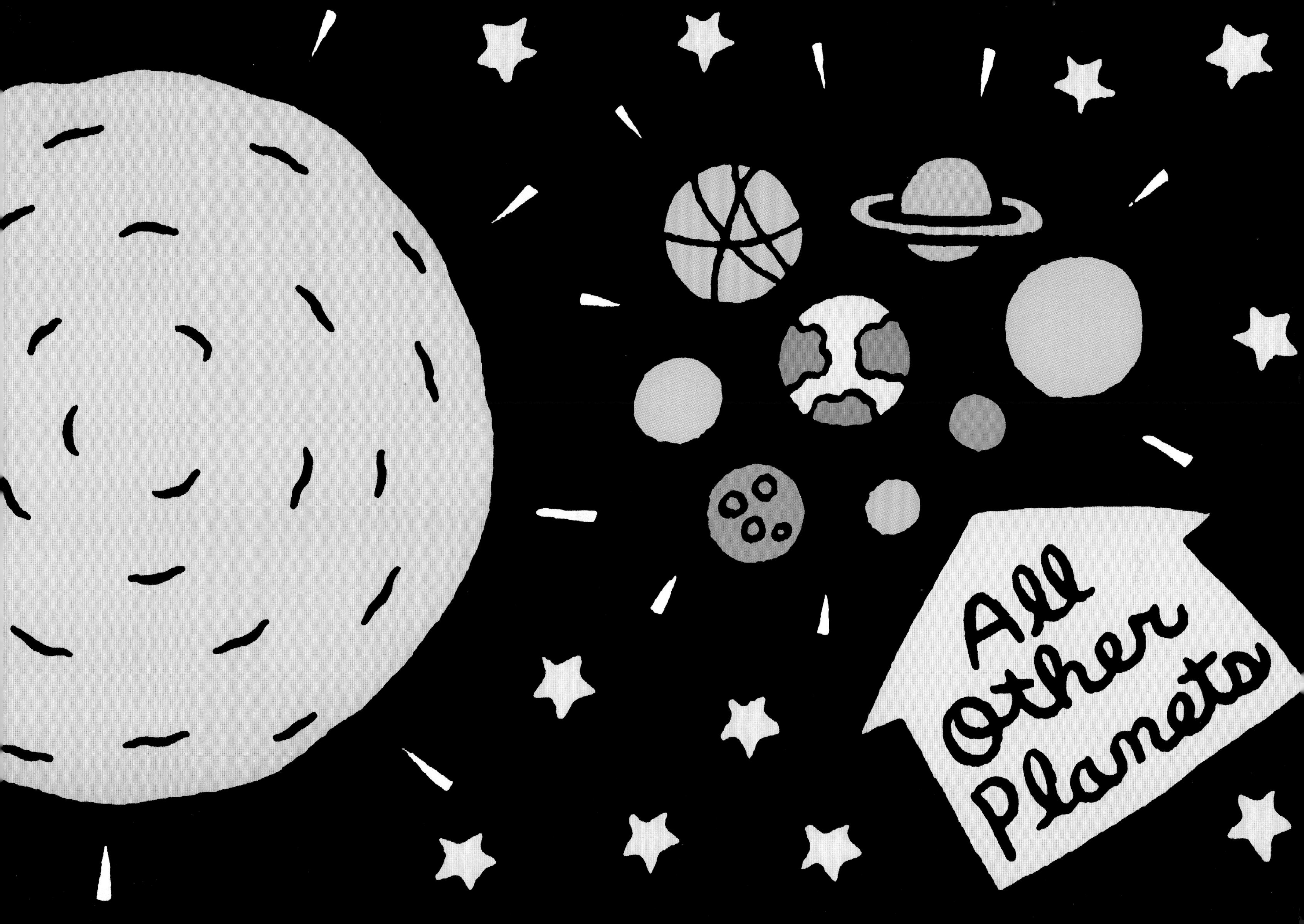
All Other Planets

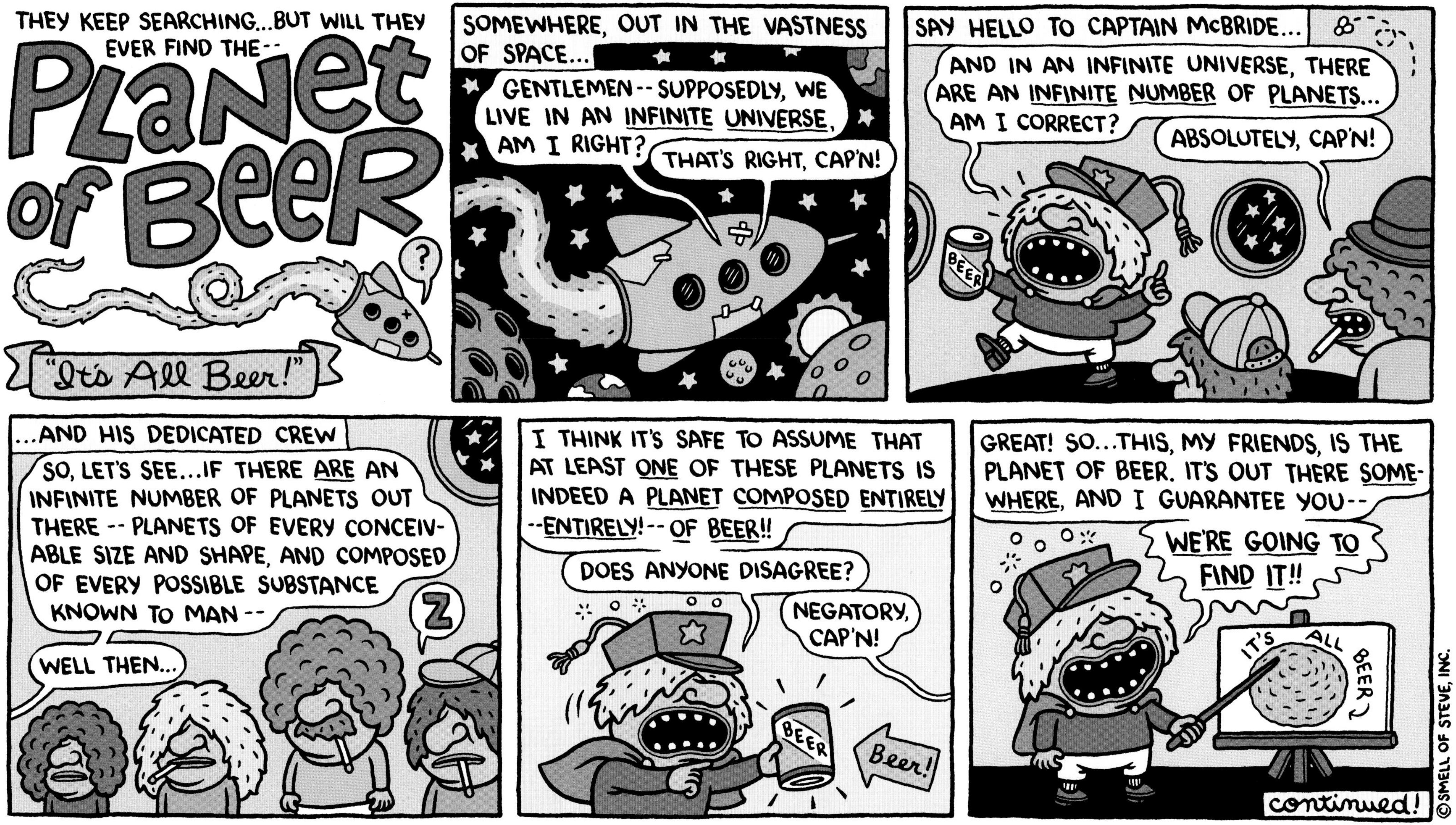
THEY KEEP SEARCHING...BUT WILL THEY EVER FIND THE--
PLANET OF BEER
"It's All Beer!"
SOMEWHERE, OUT IN THE VASTNESS OF SPACE...
GENTLEMEN--SUPPOSEDLY, WE LIVE IN AN INFINITE UNIVERSE, AM I RIGHT?
THAT'S RIGHT, CAP'N!
SAY HELLO TO CAPTAIN McBRIDE...
AND IN AN INFINITE UNIVERSE, THERE ARE AN INFINITE NUMBER OF PLANETS... AM I CORRECT?
ABSOLUTELY, CAP'N!
BEER
...AND HIS DEDICATED CREW
SO, LET'S SEE...IF THERE ARE AN INFINITE NUMBER OF PLANETS OUT THERE -- PLANETS OF EVERY CONCEIVABLE SIZE AND SHAPE, AND COMPOSED OF EVERY POSSIBLE SUBSTANCE KNOWN TO MAN--
Z
WELL THEN...
I THINK IT'S SAFE TO ASSUME THAT AT LEAST ONE OF THESE PLANETS IS INDEED A PLANET COMPOSED ENTIRELY --ENTIRELY!-- OF BEER!!
DOES ANYONE DISAGREE?
NEGATORY, CAP'N!
BEER
Beer!
GREAT! SO...THIS, MY FRIENDS, IS THE PLANET OF BEER. IT'S OUT THERE SOMEWHERE, AND I GUARANTEE YOU--
WE'RE GOING TO FIND IT!!
IT'S ALL BEER
continued!
©SMELL OF STEVE, INC.

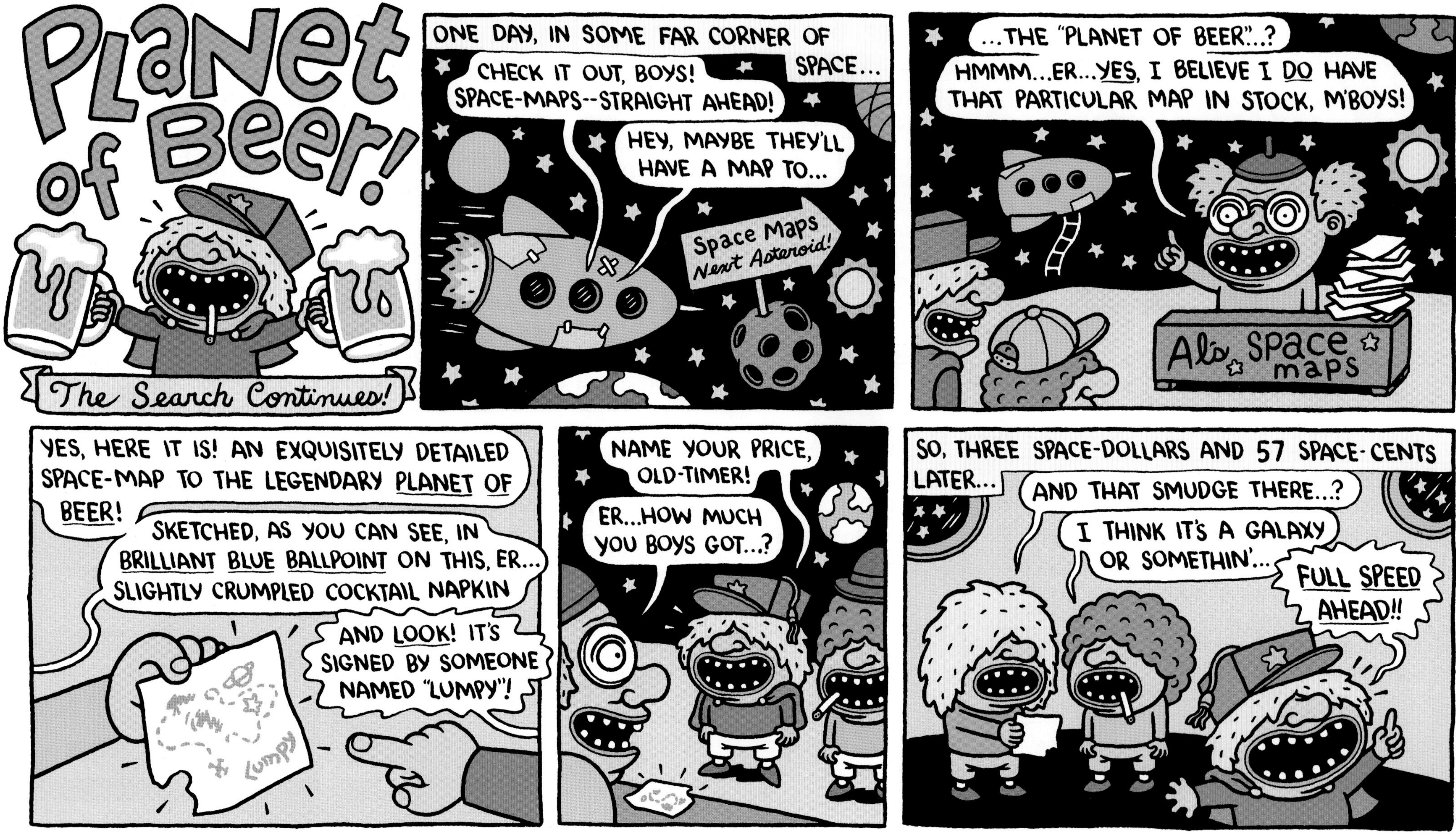
Planet of Beer!
The Search Continues!
ONE DAY, IN SOME FAR CORNER OF SPACE...
CHECK IT OUT, BOYS! SPACE-MAPS--STRAIGHT AHEAD!
HEY, MAYBE THEY'LL HAVE A MAP TO...
Space Maps Next Asteroid!
...THE "PLANET OF BEER"...?
HMMM...ER...YES, I BELIEVE I DO HAVE THAT PARTICULAR MAP IN STOCK, M'BOYS!
Al's Space maps
YES, HERE IT IS! AN EXQUISITELY DETAILED SPACE-MAP TO THE LEGENDARY PLANET OF BEER!
SKETCHED, AS YOU CAN SEE, IN BRILLIANT BLUE BALLPOINT ON THIS, ER... SLIGHTLY CRUMPLED COCKTAIL NAPKIN
AND LOOK! IT'S SIGNED BY SOMEONE NAMED "LUMPY"!
Lumpy
NAME YOUR PRICE, OLD-TIMER!
ER...HOW MUCH YOU BOYS GOT...?
SO, THREE SPACE-DOLLARS AND 57 SPACE-CENTS LATER...
AND THAT SMUDGE THERE...?
I THINK IT'S A GALAXY OR SOMETHIN'...
FULL SPEED AHEAD!!

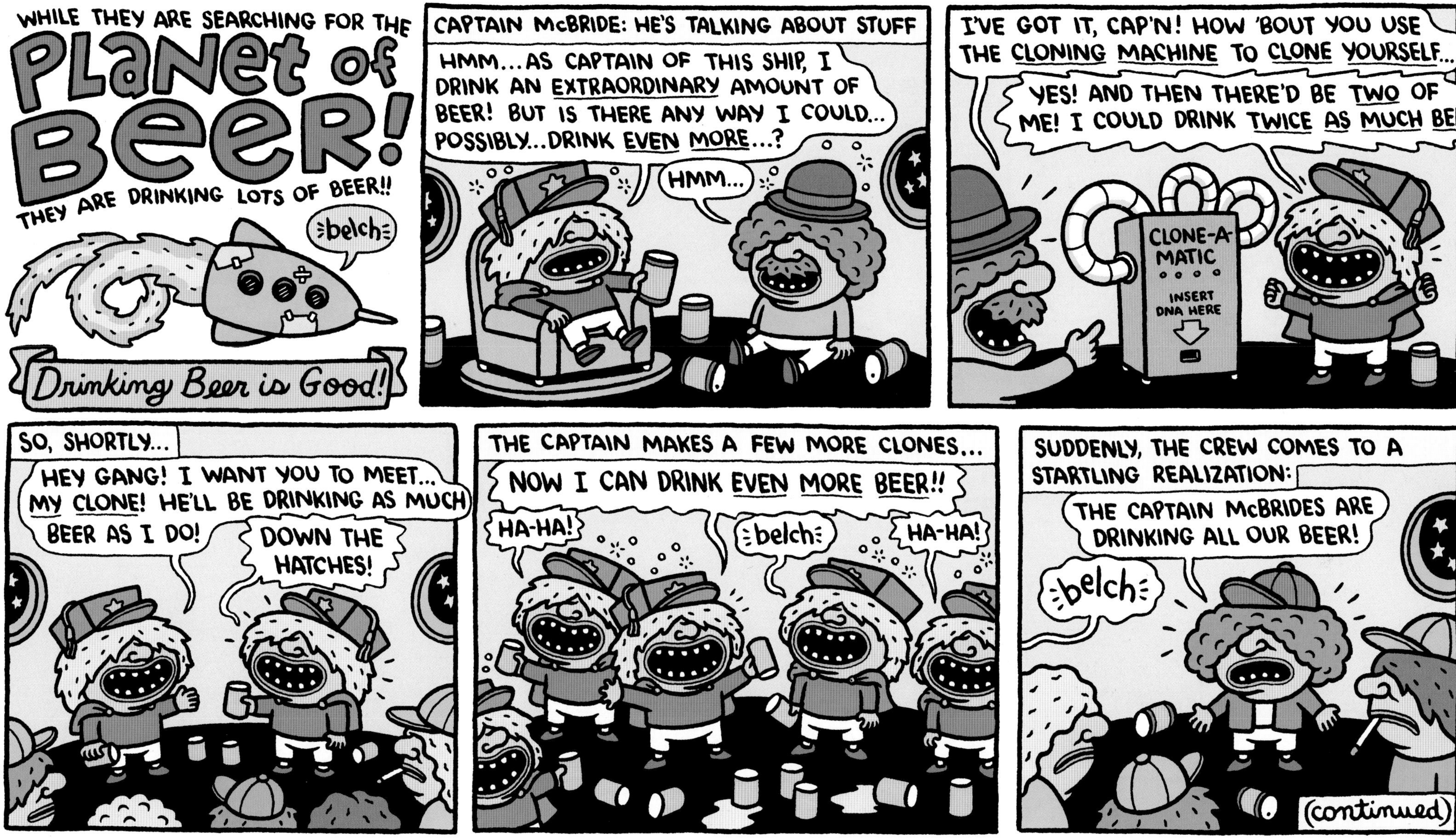
WHILE THEY ARE SEARCHING FOR THE
PLANET of BEER!
THEY ARE DRINKING LOTS OF BEER!!
belch
Drinking Beer is Good!
CAPTAIN McBRIDE: HE'S TALKING ABOUT STUFF
HMM...AS CAPTAIN OF THIS SHIP, I DRINK AN EXTRAORDINARY AMOUNT OF BEER! BUT IS THERE ANY WAY I COULD... POSSIBLY...DRINK EVEN MORE...?
HMM...
I'VE GOT IT, CAP'N! HOW 'BOUT YOU USE THE CLONING MACHINE TO CLONE YOURSELF...
YES! AND THEN THERE'D BE TWO OF ME! I COULD DRINK TWICE AS MUCH BEER!
CLONE-A-MATIC
INSERT DNA HERE
SO, SHORTLY...
HEY GANG! I WANT YOU TO MEET... MY CLONE! HE'LL BE DRINKING AS MUCH BEER AS I DO!
DOWN THE HATCHES!
THE CAPTAIN MAKES A FEW MORE CLONES...
NOW I CAN DRINK EVEN MORE BEER!!
HA-HA!
belch
HA-HA!
SUDDENLY, THE CREW COMES TO A STARTLING REALIZATION:
THE CAPTAIN McBRIDES ARE DRINKING ALL OUR BEER!
belch
(continued)

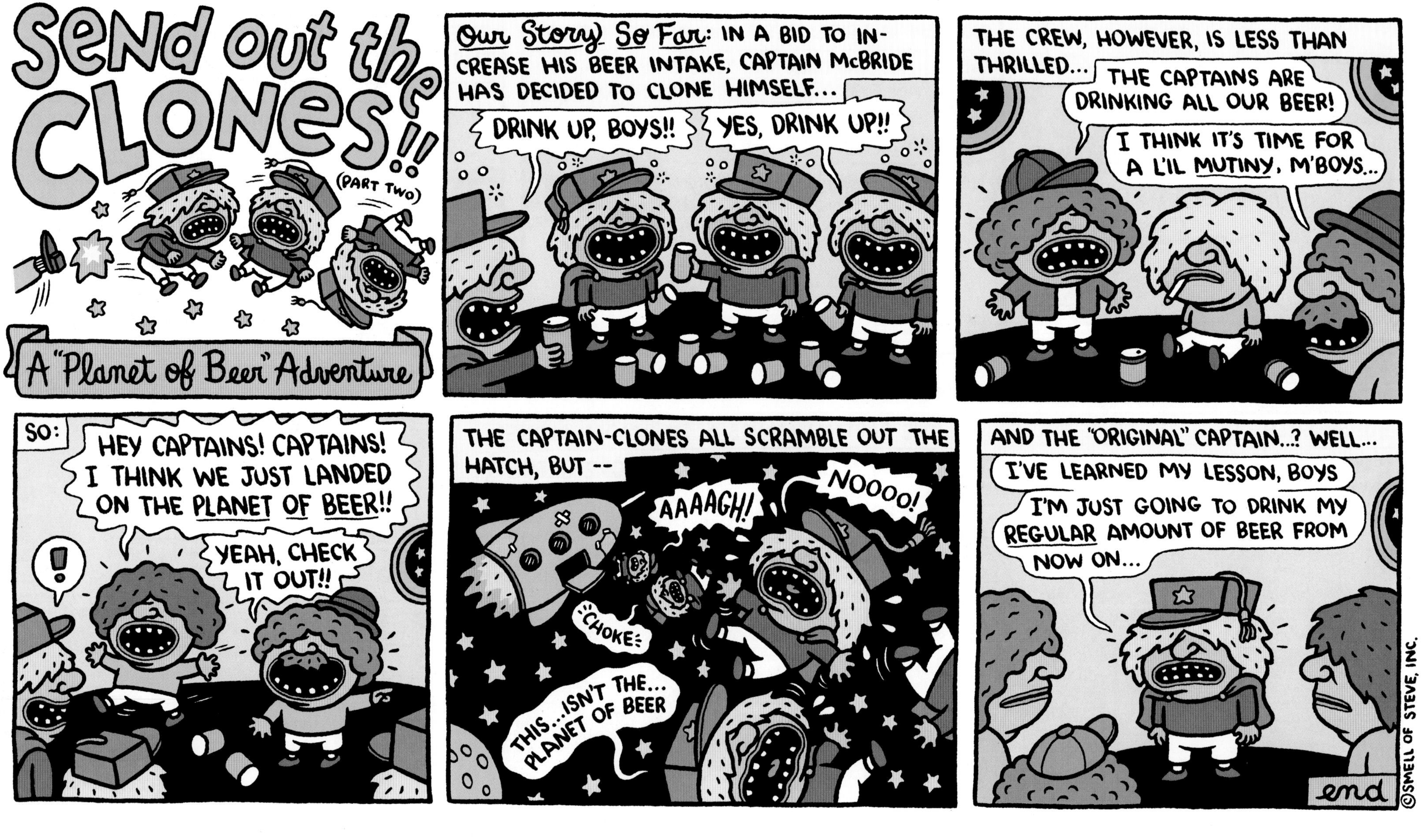
Send out the CLONES!!
(PART TWO)
A "Planet of Beer" Adventure
Our Story So Far: IN A BID TO INCREASE HIS BEER INTAKE, CAPTAIN McBRIDE HAS DECIDED TO CLONE HIMSELF...
DRINK UP, BOYS!!
YES, DRINK UP!!
THE CREW, HOWEVER, IS LESS THAN THRILLED...
THE CAPTAINS ARE DRINKING ALL OUR BEER!
I THINK IT'S TIME FOR A L'IL MUTINY, M'BOYS...
SO:
HEY CAPTAINS! CAPTAINS! I THINK WE JUST LANDED ON THE PLANET OF BEER!!
!
YEAH, CHECK IT OUT!!
THE CAPTAIN-CLONES ALL SCRAMBLE OUT THE HATCH, BUT --
AAAAGH!
NOOOO!
CHOKE
THIS...ISN'T THE... PLANET OF BEER
AND THE "ORIGINAL" CAPTAIN...? WELL...
I'VE LEARNED MY LESSON, BOYS
I'M JUST GOING TO DRINK MY REGULAR AMOUNT OF BEER FROM NOW ON...
end
©SMELL OF STEVE, INC.

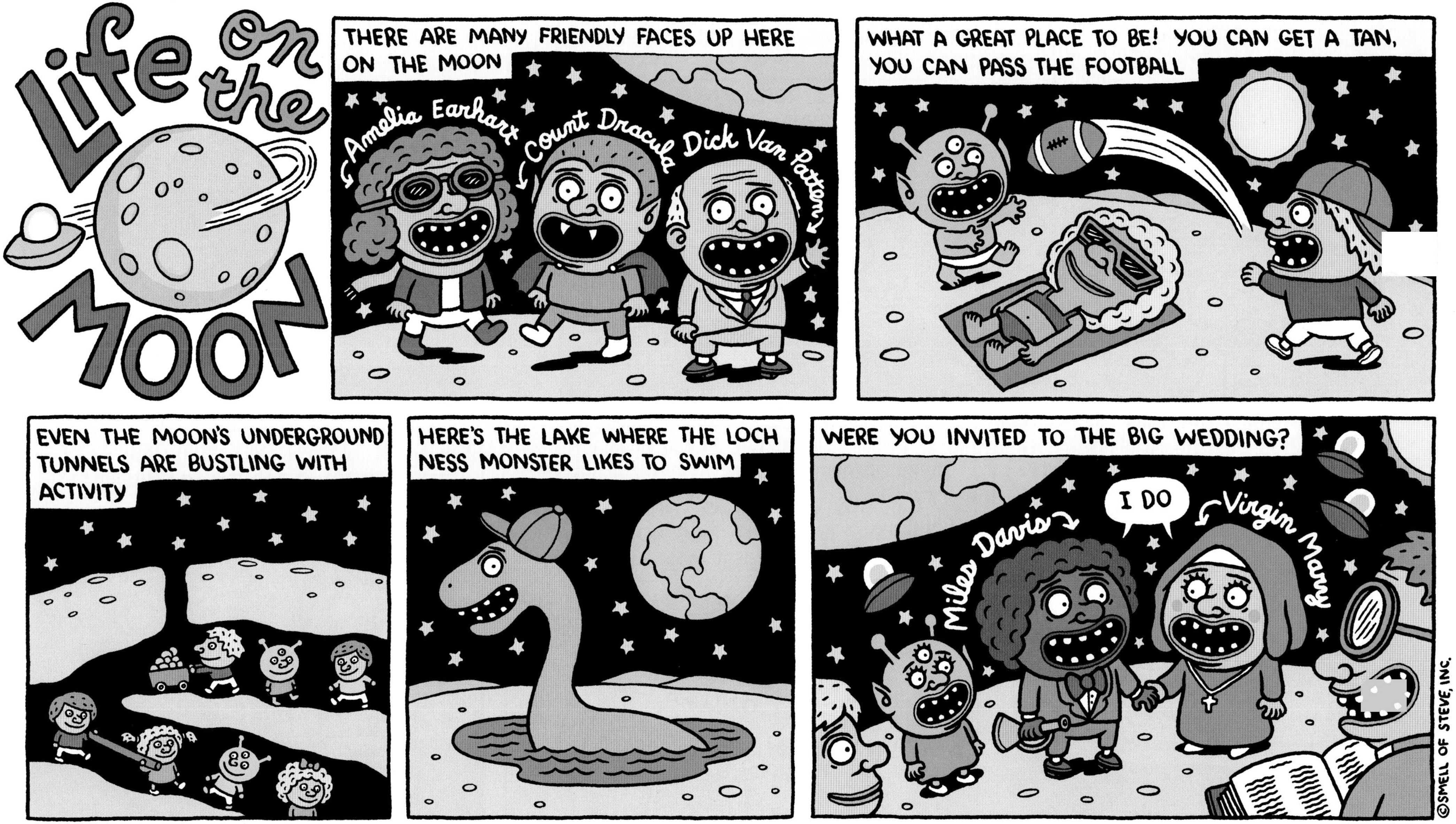
Life on the MOON
THERE ARE MANY FRIENDLY FACES UP HERE ON THE MOON
Amelia Earhart
Count Dracula
Dick Van Patten
WHAT A GREAT PLACE TO BE! YOU CAN GET A TAN, YOU CAN PASS THE FOOTBALL
EVEN THE MOON'S UNDERGROUND TUNNELS ARE BUSTLING WITH ACTIVITY
HERE'S THE LAKE WHERE THE LOCH NESS MONSTER LIKES TO SWIM
WERE YOU INVITED TO THE BIG WEDDING?
I DO
Miles Davis
Virgin Mary
©SMELL OF STEVE, INC.

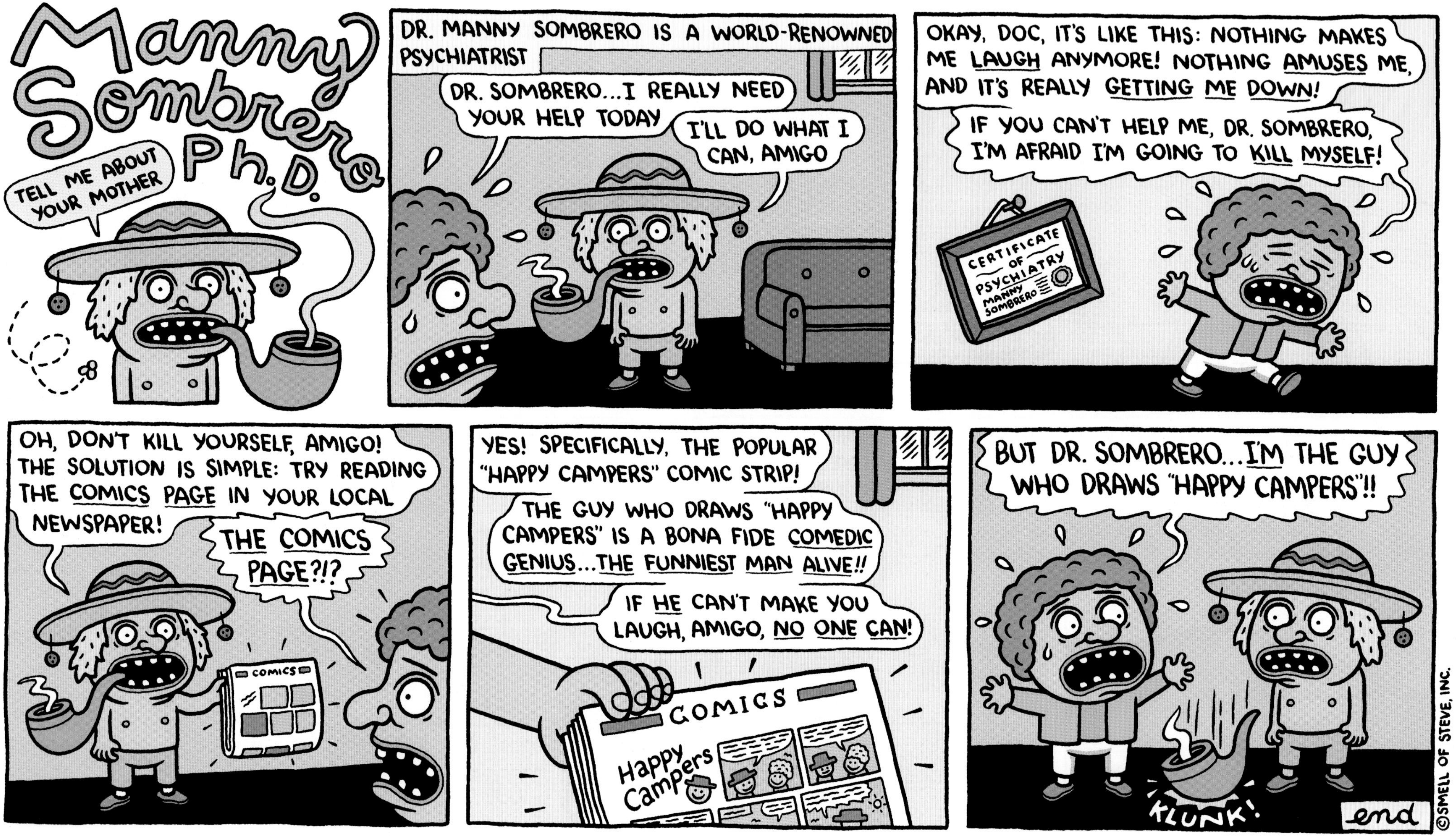
Manny Sombrero Ph.D.
TELL ME ABOUT YOUR MOTHER
DR. MANNY SOMBRERO IS A WORLD-RENOWNED PSYCHIATRIST
DR. SOMBRERO...I REALLY NEED YOUR HELP TODAY
I'LL DO WHAT I CAN, AMIGO
OKAY, DOC, IT'S LIKE THIS: NOTHING MAKES ME LAUGH ANYMORE! NOTHING AMUSES ME, AND IT'S REALLY GETTING ME DOWN!
IF YOU CAN'T HELP ME, DR. SOMBRERO, I'M AFRAID I'M GOING TO KILL MYSELF!
CERTIFICATE OF PSYCHIATRY MANNY SOMBRERO
OH, DON'T KILL YOURSELF, AMIGO! THE SOLUTION IS SIMPLE: TRY READING THE COMICS PAGE IN YOUR LOCAL NEWSPAPER!
THE COMICS PAGE?!?
COMICS
YES! SPECIFICALLY, THE POPULAR "HAPPY CAMPERS" COMIC STRIP!
THE GUY WHO DRAWS "HAPPY CAMPERS" IS A BONA FIDE COMEDIC GENIUS...THE FUNNIEST MAN ALIVE!!
IF HE CAN'T MAKE YOU LAUGH, AMIGO, NO ONE CAN!
COMICS
Happy Campers
BUT DR. SOMBRERO...I'M THE GUY WHO DRAWS "HAPPY CAMPERS"!!
KLUNK!
end
©SMELL OF STEVE, INC.

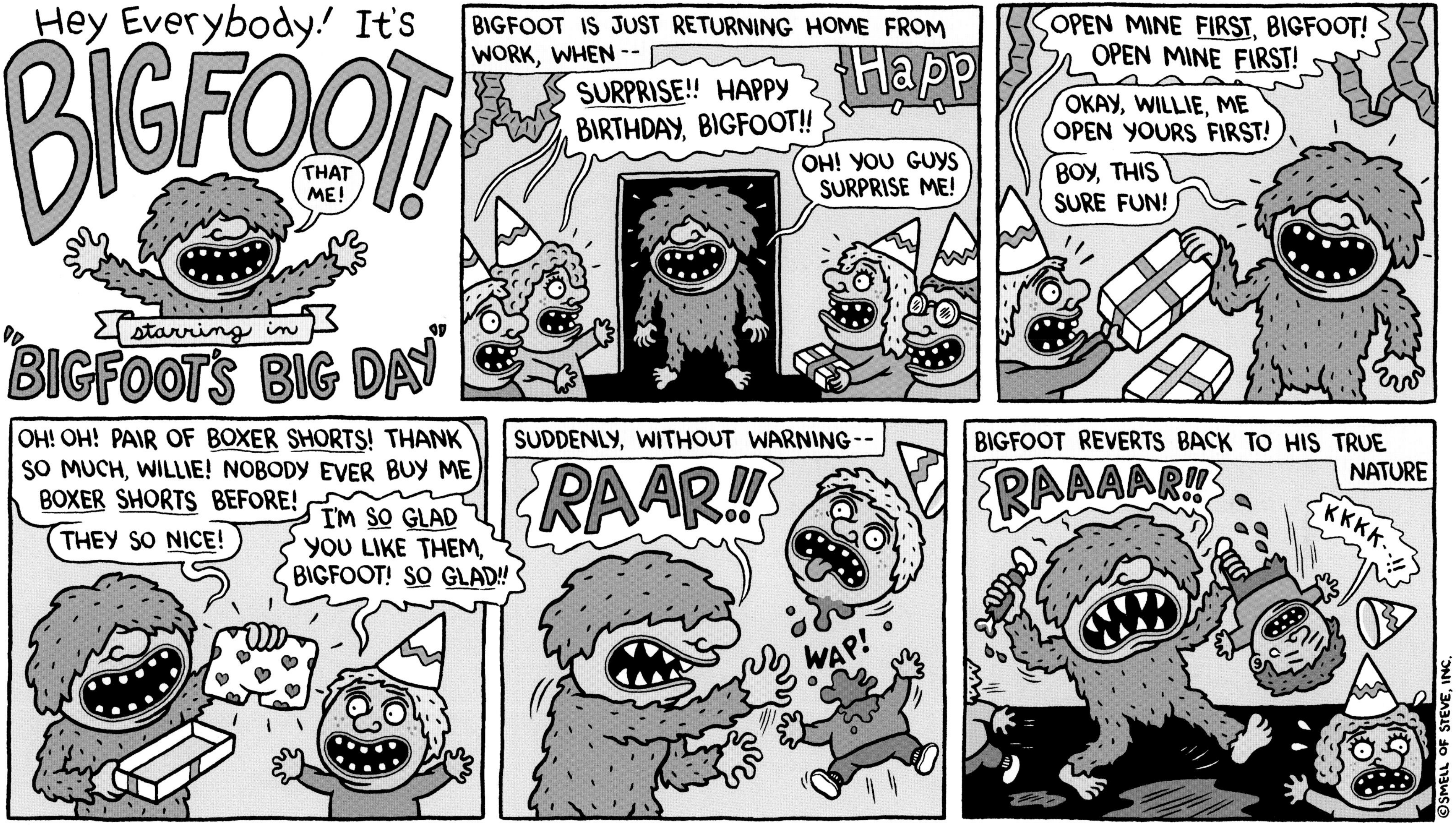
Hey Everybody! It's
BIGFOOT!
THAT ME!
starring in
"BIGFOOT'S BIG DAY"
BIGFOOT IS JUST RETURNING HOME FROM WORK, WHEN --
Happ
SURPRISE!! HAPPY BIRTHDAY, BIGFOOT!!
OH! YOU GUYS SURPRISE ME!
OPEN MINE FIRST, BIGFOOT! OPEN MINE FIRST!
OKAY, WILLIE, ME OPEN YOURS FIRST!
BOY, THIS SURE FUN!
OH! OH! PAIR OF BOXER SHORTS! THANK SO MUCH, WILLIE! NOBODY EVER BUY ME BOXER SHORTS BEFORE!
THEY SO NICE!
I'M SO GLAD YOU LIKE THEM, BIGFOOT! SO GLAD!!
SUDDENLY, WITHOUT WARNING--
RAAR!!
WAP!
BIGFOOT REVERTS BACK TO HIS TRUE NATURE
RAAAAR!!
KKKK--!!
©SMELL OF STEVE, INC.

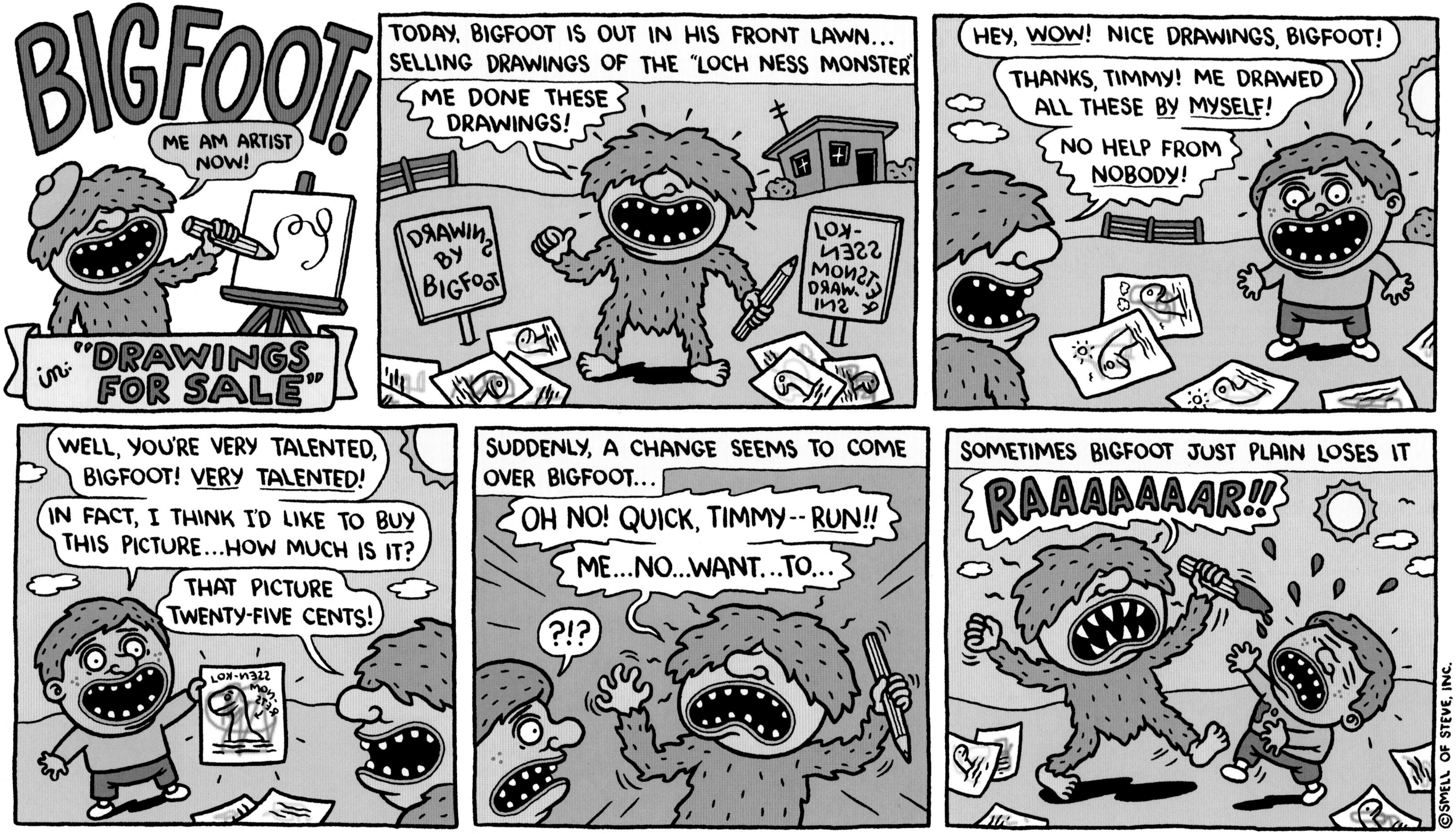
BIGFOOT!
ME AM ARTIST NOW!
in: "DRAWINGS FOR SALE"
TODAY, BIGFOOT IS OUT IN HIS FRONT LAWN... SELLING DRAWINGS OF THE "LOCH NESS MONSTER"
ME DONE THESE DRAWINGS!
DRAWINGS BY BIGFOOT
HEY, WOW! NICE DRAWINGS, BIGFOOT!
THANKS, TIMMY! ME DRAWED ALL THESE BY MYSELF!
NO HELP FROM NOBODY!
WELL, YOU'RE VERY TALENTED, BIGFOOT! VERY TALENTED!
IN FACT, I THINK I'D LIKE TO BUY THIS PICTURE...HOW MUCH IS IT?
THAT PICTURE TWENTY-FIVE CENTS!
SUDDENLY, A CHANGE SEEMS TO COME OVER BIGFOOT...
OH NO! QUICK, TIMMY-- RUN!!
ME...NO...WANT...TO...
?!?
SOMETIMES BIGFOOT JUST PLAIN LOSES IT
RAAAAAAAR!!
©SMELL OF STEVE, INC.

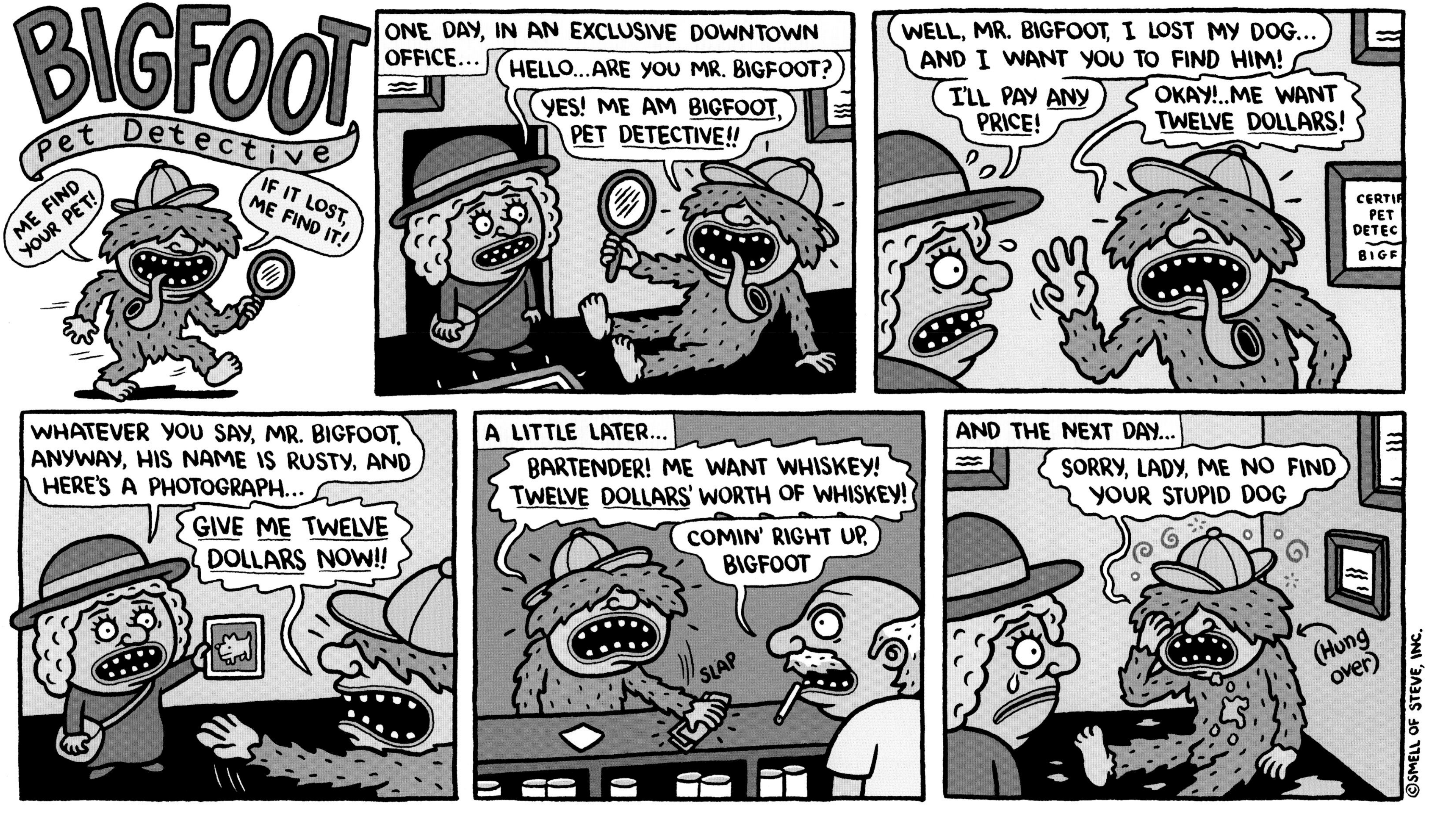
BIGFOOT
Pet Detective
ME FIND YOUR PET!
IF IT LOST, ME FIND IT!
ONE DAY, IN AN EXCLUSIVE DOWNTOWN OFFICE...
HELLO...ARE YOU MR. BIGFOOT?
YES! ME AM BIGFOOT, PET DETECTIVE!!
WELL, MR. BIGFOOT, I LOST MY DOG... AND I WANT YOU TO FIND HIM!
I'LL PAY ANY PRICE!
OKAY!..ME WANT TWELVE DOLLARS!
CERTIF PET DETEC BIGF
WHATEVER YOU SAY, MR. BIGFOOT. ANYWAY, HIS NAME IS RUSTY, AND HERE'S A PHOTOGRAPH...
GIVE ME TWELVE DOLLARS NOW!!
A LITTLE LATER...
BARTENDER! ME WANT WHISKEY! TWELVE DOLLARS' WORTH OF WHISKEY!
SLAP
COMIN' RIGHT UP, BIGFOOT
AND THE NEXT DAY...
SORRY, LADY, ME NO FIND YOUR STUPID DOG
(Hung over)
©SMELL OF STEVE, INC.

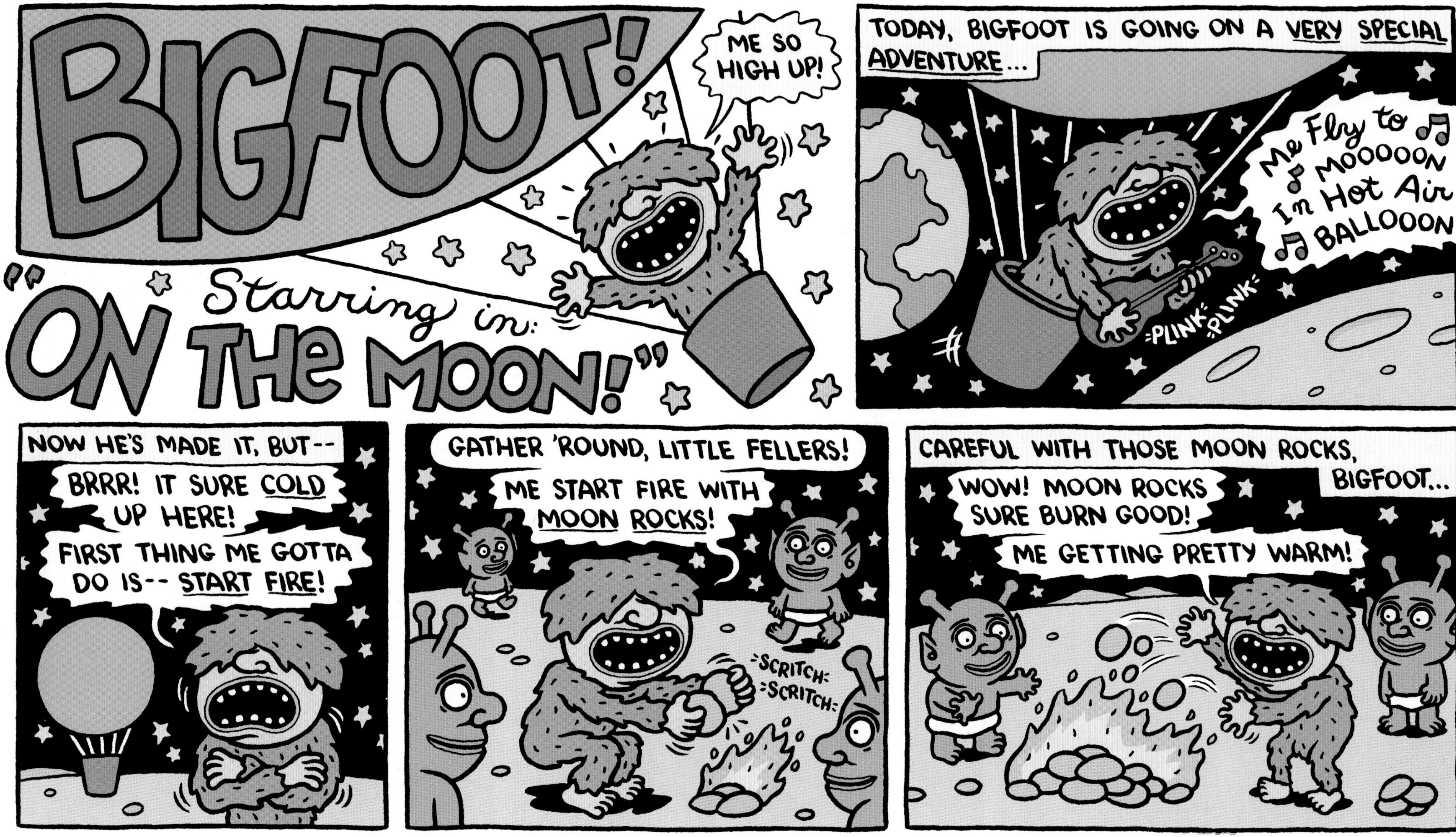
BIGFOOT!
Starring in:
"ON THE MOON!"
ME SO HIGH UP!
TODAY, BIGFOOT IS GOING ON A VERY SPECIAL ADVENTURE...
Me Fly to MOOOOON In Hot Air BALLOOON
PLINK PLINK
NOW HE'S MADE IT, BUT--
BRRR! IT SURE COLD UP HERE!
FIRST THING ME GOTTA DO IS-- START FIRE!
GATHER 'ROUND, LITTLE FELLERS!
ME START FIRE WITH MOON ROCKS!
SCRITCH SCRITCH
CAREFUL WITH THOSE MOON ROCKS, BIGFOOT...
WOW! MOON ROCKS SURE BURN GOOD!
ME GETTING PRETTY WARM!

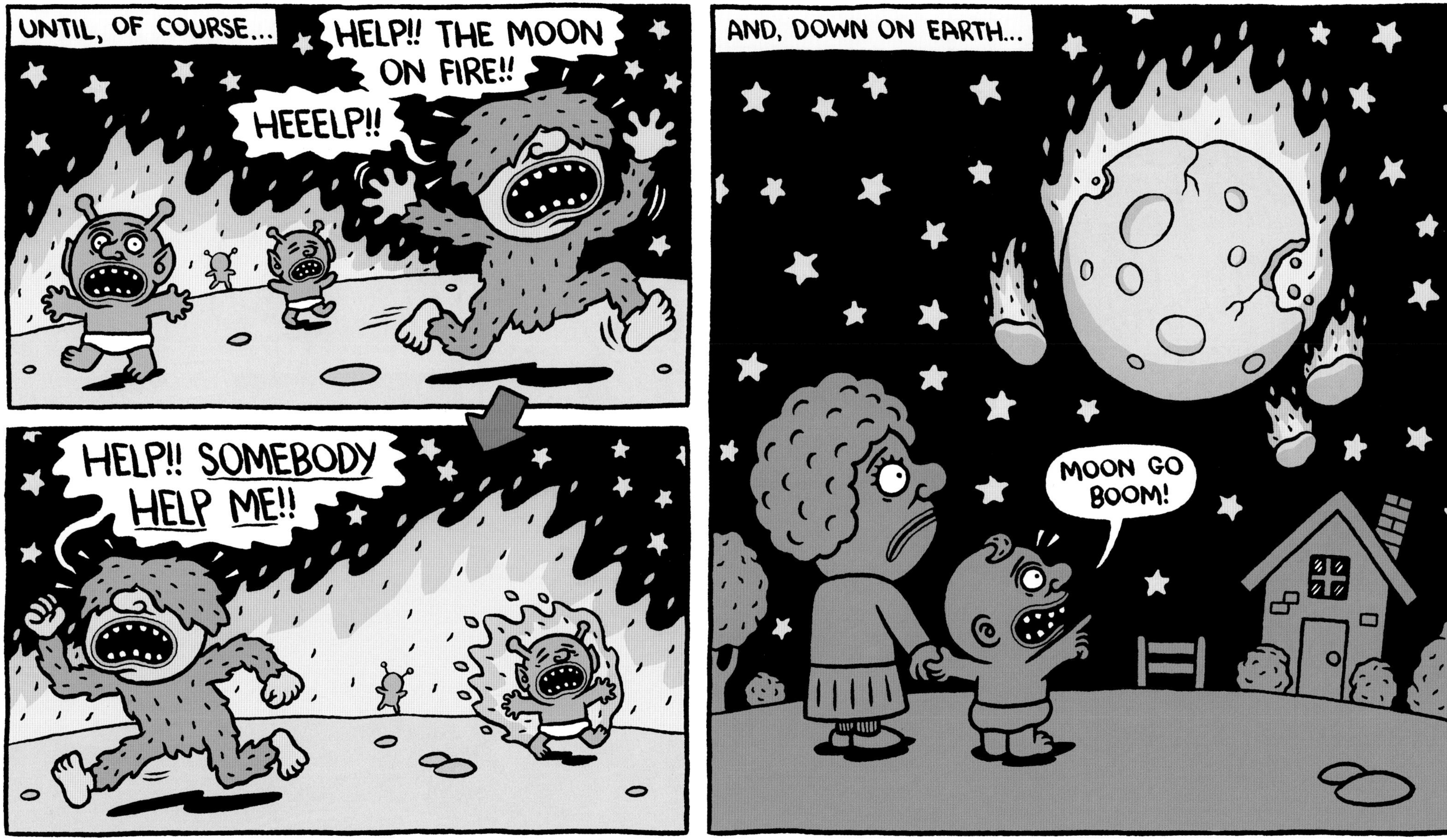

UNTIL, OF COURSE...
HELP!! THE MOON ON FIRE!!
HEEELP!!
HELP!! SOMEBODY HELP ME!!
AND, DOWN ON EARTH...
MOON GO BOOM!

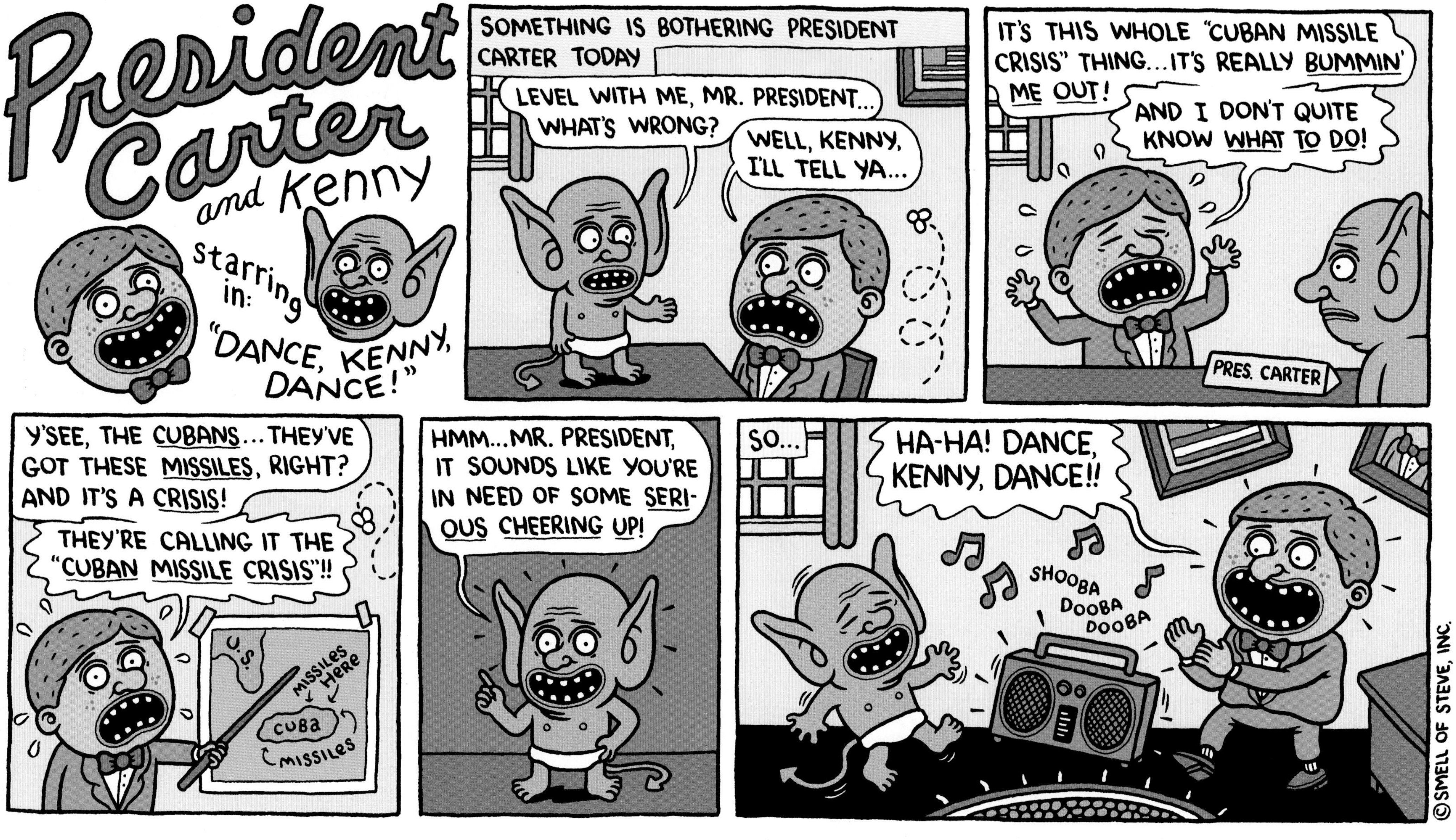
President Carter and Kenny
starring in: "DANCE, KENNY, DANCE!"
SOMETHING IS BOTHERING PRESIDENT CARTER TODAY
LEVEL WITH ME, MR. PRESIDENT... WHAT'S WRONG?
WELL, KENNY, I'LL TELL YA...
IT'S THIS WHOLE "CUBAN MISSILE CRISIS" THING... IT'S REALLY BUMMIN' ME OUT!
AND I DON'T QUITE KNOW WHAT TO DO!
PRES. CARTER
Y'SEE, THE CUBANS... THEY'VE GOT THESE MISSILES, RIGHT? AND IT'S A CRISIS!
THEY'RE CALLING IT THE "CUBAN MISSILE CRISIS"!!
U.S.
MISSILES HERE
CUBA
MISSILES
HMM... MR. PRESIDENT, IT SOUNDS LIKE YOU'RE IN NEED OF SOME SERIOUS CHEERING UP!
SO...
HA-HA! DANCE, KENNY, DANCE!!
SHOOBA DOOBA DOOBA
©SMELL OF STEVE, INC.

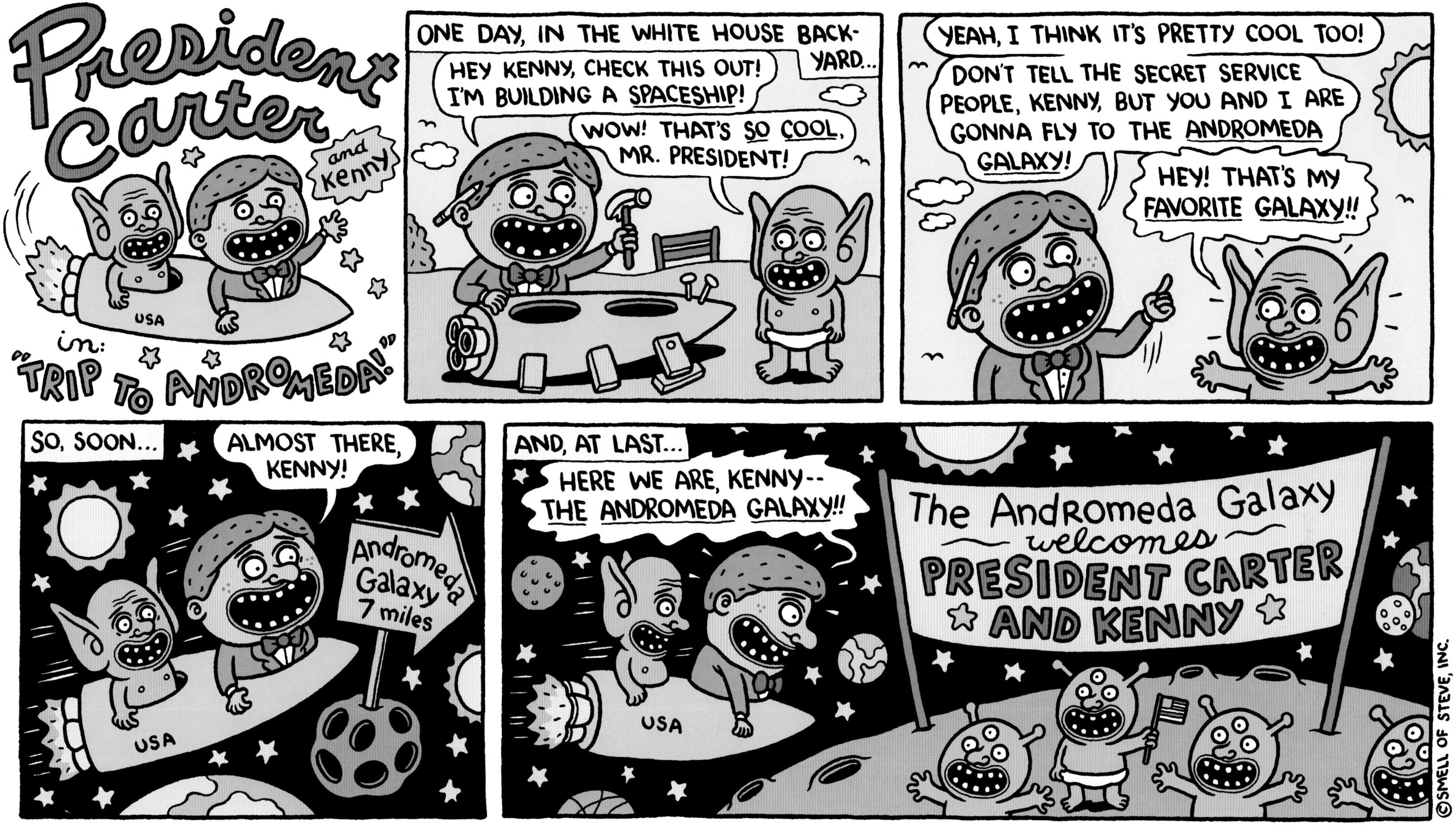
President Carter
and Kenny
USA
in: "TRIP TO ANDROMEDA!"
ONE DAY, IN THE WHITE HOUSE BACK-YARD...
HEY KENNY, CHECK THIS OUT! I'M BUILDING A SPACESHIP!
WOW! THAT'S SO COOL, MR. PRESIDENT!
YEAH, I THINK IT'S PRETTY COOL TOO!
DON'T TELL THE SECRET SERVICE PEOPLE, KENNY, BUT YOU AND I ARE GONNA FLY TO THE ANDROMEDA GALAXY!
HEY! THAT'S MY FAVORITE GALAXY!!
SO, SOON...
ALMOST THERE, KENNY!
Andromeda Galaxy 7 miles
USA
AND, AT LAST...
HERE WE ARE, KENNY-- THE ANDROMEDA GALAXY!!
The Andromeda Galaxy welcomes PRESIDENT CARTER AND KENNY
USA
©SMELL OF STEVE, INC.

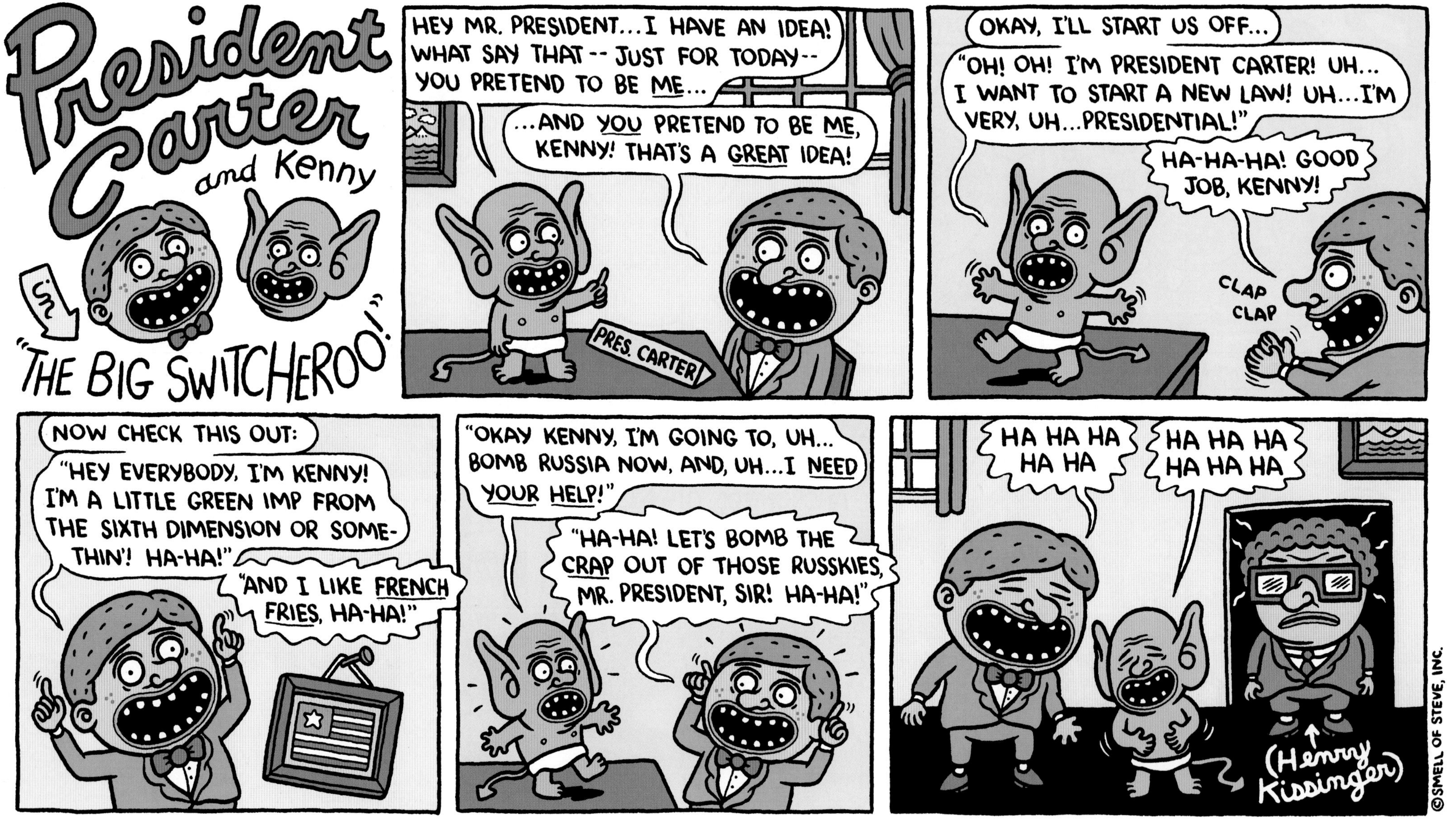
President Carter and Kenny
in
"THE BIG SWITCHEROO!"
HEY MR. PRESIDENT... I HAVE AN IDEA! WHAT SAY THAT -- JUST FOR TODAY -- YOU PRETEND TO BE ME...
...AND YOU PRETEND TO BE ME, KENNY! THAT'S A GREAT IDEA!
PRES. CARTER
OKAY, I'LL START US OFF...
"OH! OH! I'M PRESIDENT CARTER! UH... I WANT TO START A NEW LAW! UH... I'M VERY, UH... PRESIDENTIAL!"
HA-HA-HA! GOOD JOB, KENNY!
CLAP CLAP
NOW CHECK THIS OUT:
"HEY EVERYBODY, I'M KENNY! I'M A LITTLE GREEN IMP FROM THE SIXTH DIMENSION OR SOME-THIN'! HA-HA!"
"AND I LIKE FRENCH FRIES, HA-HA!"
"OKAY KENNY, I'M GOING TO, UH... BOMB RUSSIA NOW, AND, UH... I NEED YOUR HELP!"
"HA-HA! LET'S BOMB THE CRAP OUT OF THOSE RUSSKIES, MR. PRESIDENT, SIR! HA-HA!"
HA HA HA HA HA
HA HA HA HA HA HA
(Henry Kissinger)
©SMELL OF STEVE, INC.

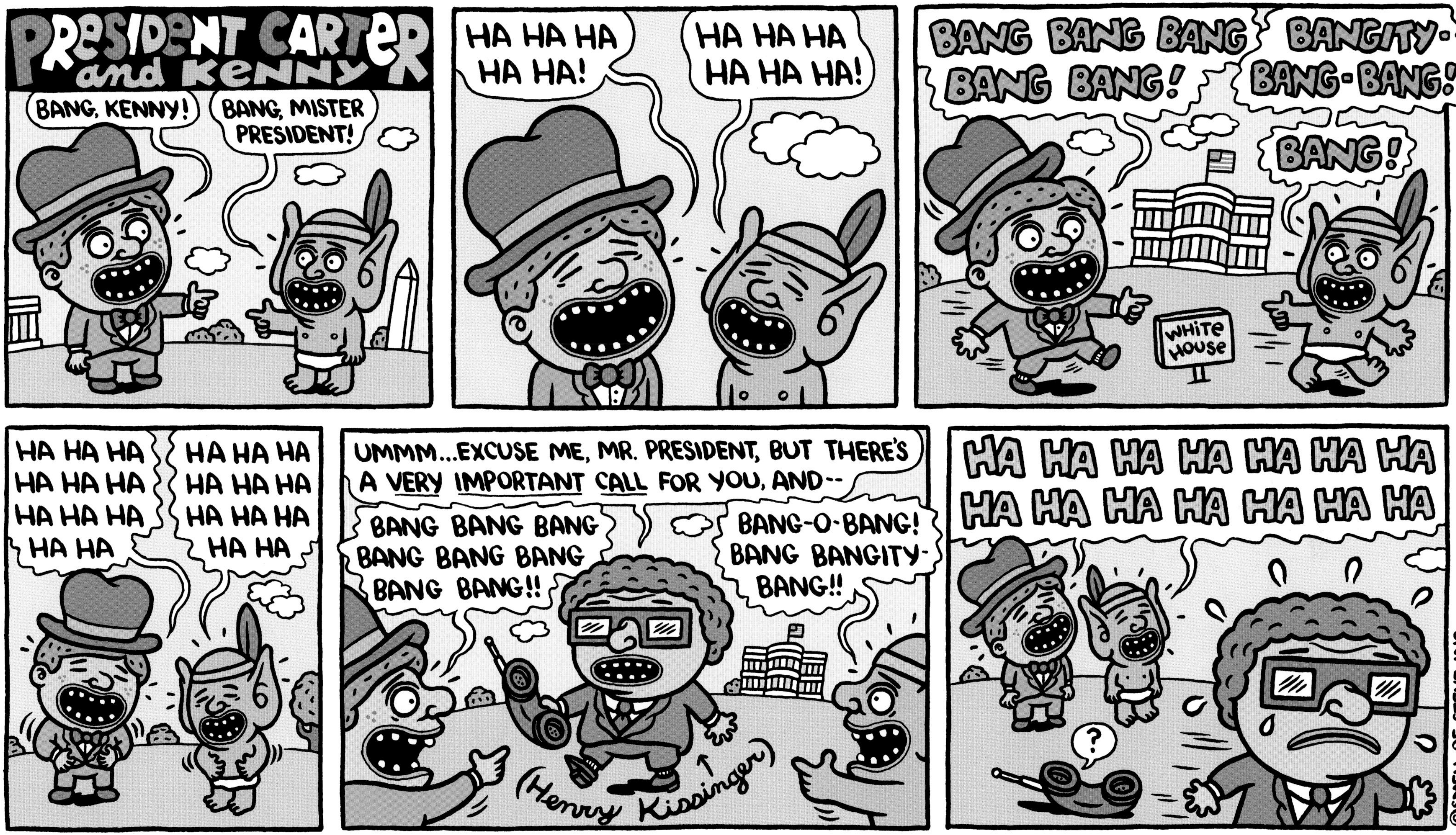
PRESIDENT CARTER and KENNY
BANG, KENNY!
BANG, MISTER PRESIDENT!
HA HA HA HA HA!
HA HA HA HA HA HA!
BANG BANG BANG BANG BANG!
BANGITY-BANG-BANG!
WHITE HOUSE
BANG!
HA HA HA HA HA HA HA HA HA HA HA
HA HA HA HA HA HA HA HA HA HA HA
UMMM...EXCUSE ME, MR. PRESIDENT, BUT THERE'S A VERY IMPORTANT CALL FOR YOU, AND--
BANG BANG BANG BANG BANG BANG BANG BANG!!
BANG-O-BANG! BANG BANGITY-BANG!!
(Henry Kissinger)
HA HA HA HA HA HA HA HA HA HA HA HA HA HA
?
©SMELL OF STEVE, INC.

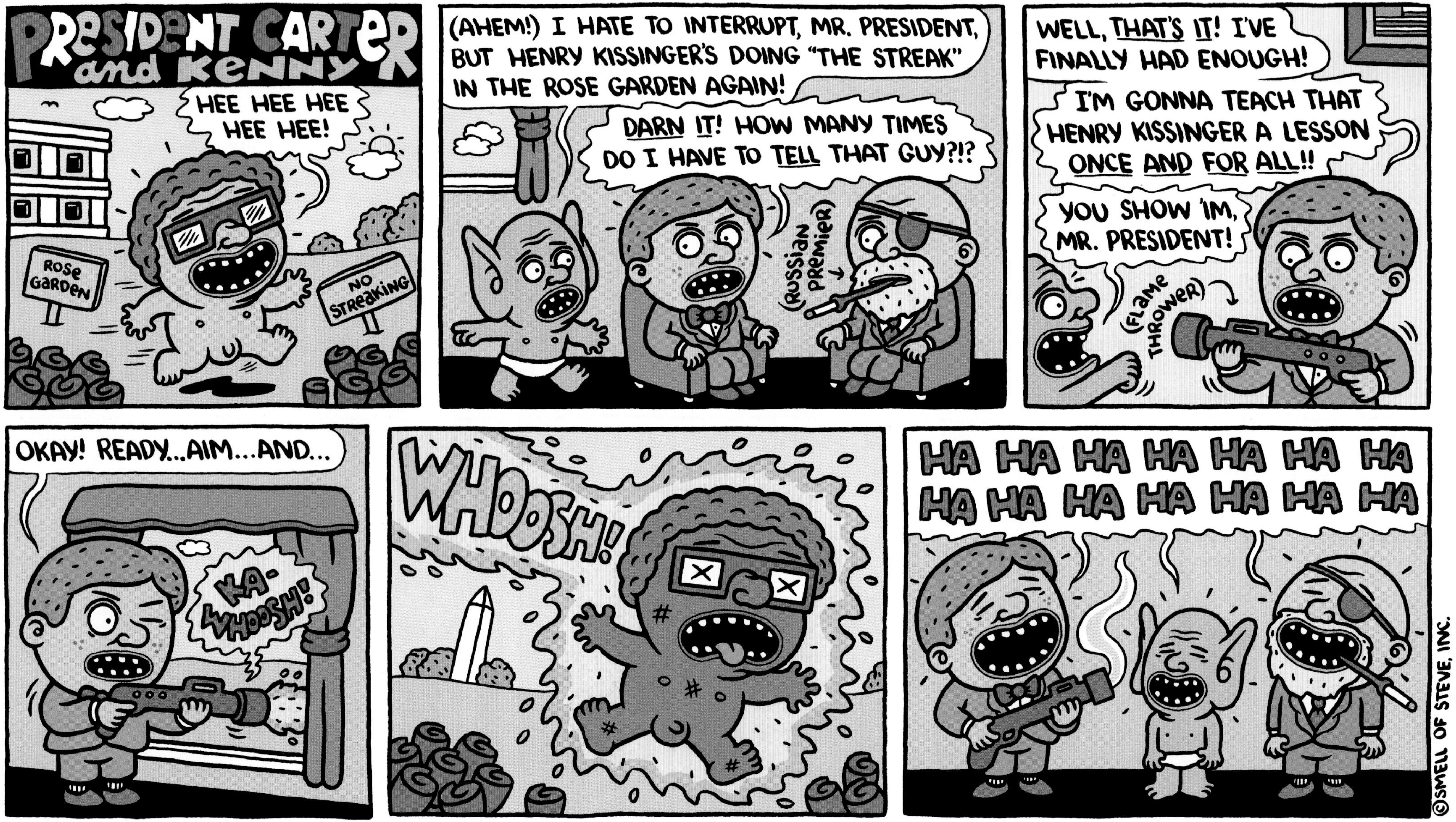
PRESIDENT CARTER and KENNY
HEE HEE HEE HEE HEE!
ROSE GARDEN
NO STREAKING
(AHEM!) I HATE TO INTERRUPT, MR. PRESIDENT, BUT HENRY KISSINGER'S DOING "THE STREAK" IN THE ROSE GARDEN AGAIN!
DARN IT! HOW MANY TIMES DO I HAVE TO TELL THAT GUY?!?
(RUSSIAN PREMIER)
WELL, THAT'S IT! I'VE FINALLY HAD ENOUGH!
I'M GONNA TEACH THAT HENRY KISSINGER A LESSON ONCE AND FOR ALL!!
YOU SHOW 'IM, MR. PRESIDENT!
(FLAME THROWER)
OKAY! READY...AIM...AND...
KA-WHOOSH!
WHOOSH!
HA HA HA HA HA HA HA HA HA HA HA HA HA HA
©SMELL OF STEVE, INC.

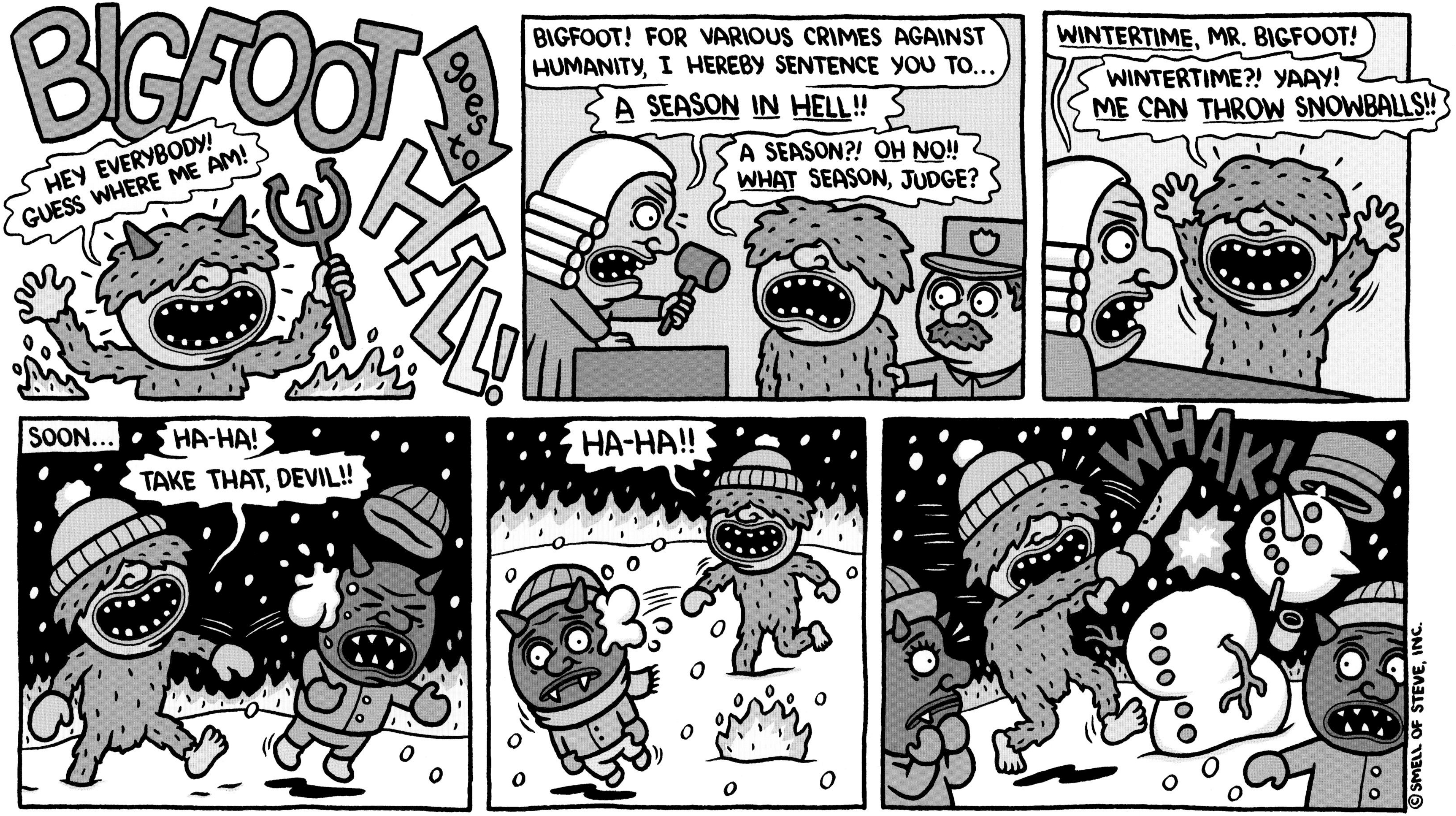
BIGFOOT goes to HELL!
HEY EVERYBODY! GUESS WHERE ME AM!
BIGFOOT! FOR VARIOUS CRIMES AGAINST HUMANITY, I HEREBY SENTENCE YOU TO...
A SEASON IN HELL!!
A SEASON?! OH NO!! WHAT SEASON, JUDGE?
WINTERTIME, MR. BIGFOOT!
WINTERTIME?! YAAY! ME CAN THROW SNOWBALLS!!
SOON...
HA-HA!
TAKE THAT, DEVIL!!
HA-HA!!
WHAK!
©SMELL OF STEVE, INC.

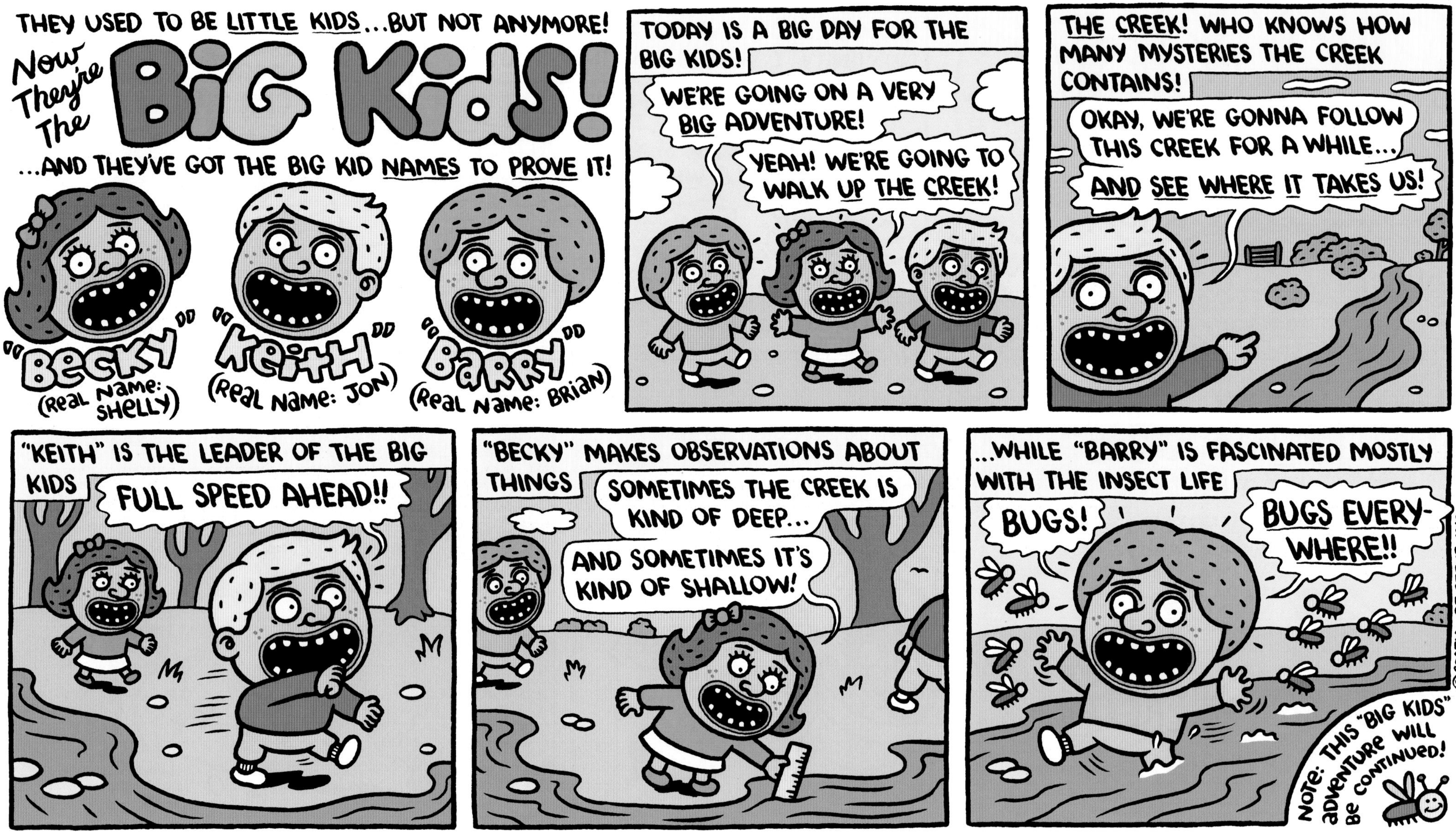
THEY USED TO BE LITTLE KIDS...BUT NOT ANYMORE!
Now They're The BIG KIDS!
...AND THEY'VE GOT THE BIG KID NAMES TO PROVE IT!
"BECKY" (Real Name: SHELLY)
"KEITH" (Real Name: JON)
"BARRY" (Real Name: BRIAN)
TODAY IS A BIG DAY FOR THE BIG KIDS!
WE'RE GOING ON A VERY BIG ADVENTURE!
YEAH! WE'RE GOING TO WALK UP THE CREEK!
THE CREEK! WHO KNOWS HOW MANY MYSTERIES THE CREEK CONTAINS!
OKAY, WE'RE GONNA FOLLOW THIS CREEK FOR A WHILE...
AND SEE WHERE IT TAKES US!
"KEITH" IS THE LEADER OF THE BIG KIDS
FULL SPEED AHEAD!!
"BECKY" MAKES OBSERVATIONS ABOUT THINGS
SOMETIMES THE CREEK IS KIND OF DEEP...
AND SOMETIMES IT'S KIND OF SHALLOW!
...WHILE "BARRY" IS FASCINATED MOSTLY WITH THE INSECT LIFE
BUGS!
BUGS EVERY-WHERE!!
NOTE: THIS "BIG KIDS" ADVENTURE WILL BE CONTINUED!
©SMELL OF STEVE, INC.

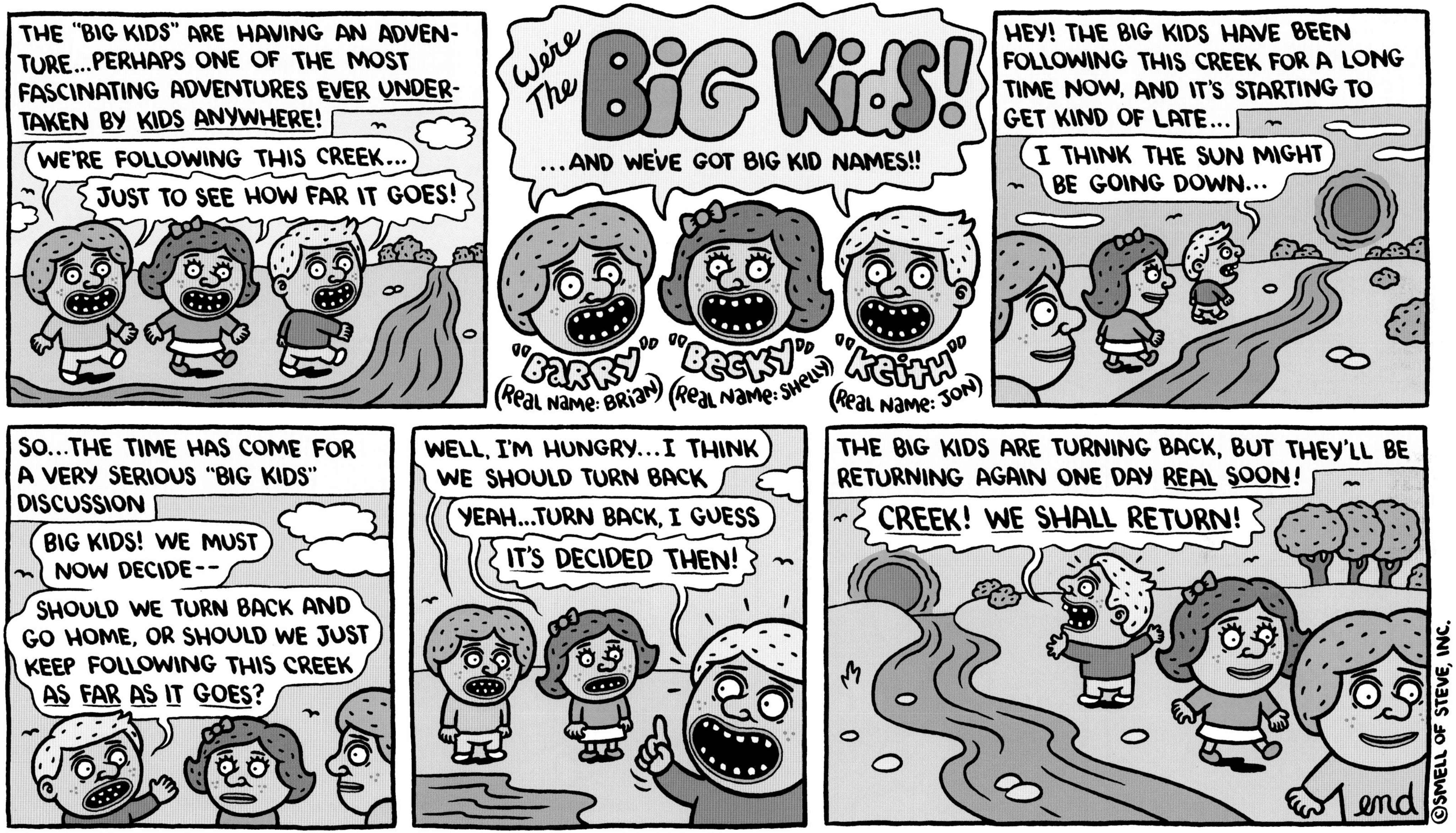
THE "BIG KIDS" ARE HAVING AN ADVENTURE...PERHAPS ONE OF THE MOST FASCINATING ADVENTURES EVER UNDERTAKEN BY KIDS ANYWHERE!
WE'RE FOLLOWING THIS CREEK...
JUST TO SEE HOW FAR IT GOES!
We're The BIG KIDS!
...AND WE'VE GOT BIG KID NAMES!!
"BARRY" (Real Name: BRIAN)
"BECKY" (Real Name: SHELLY)
"KEITH" (Real Name: JON)
HEY! THE BIG KIDS HAVE BEEN FOLLOWING THIS CREEK FOR A LONG TIME NOW, AND IT'S STARTING TO GET KIND OF LATE...
I THINK THE SUN MIGHT BE GOING DOWN...
SO...THE TIME HAS COME FOR A VERY SERIOUS "BIG KIDS" DISCUSSION
BIG KIDS! WE MUST NOW DECIDE--
SHOULD WE TURN BACK AND GO HOME, OR SHOULD WE JUST KEEP FOLLOWING THIS CREEK AS FAR AS IT GOES?
WELL, I'M HUNGRY...I THINK WE SHOULD TURN BACK
YEAH...TURN BACK, I GUESS
IT'S DECIDED THEN!
THE BIG KIDS ARE TURNING BACK, BUT THEY'LL BE RETURNING AGAIN ONE DAY REAL SOON!
CREEK! WE SHALL RETURN!
end
©SMELL OF STEVE, INC.

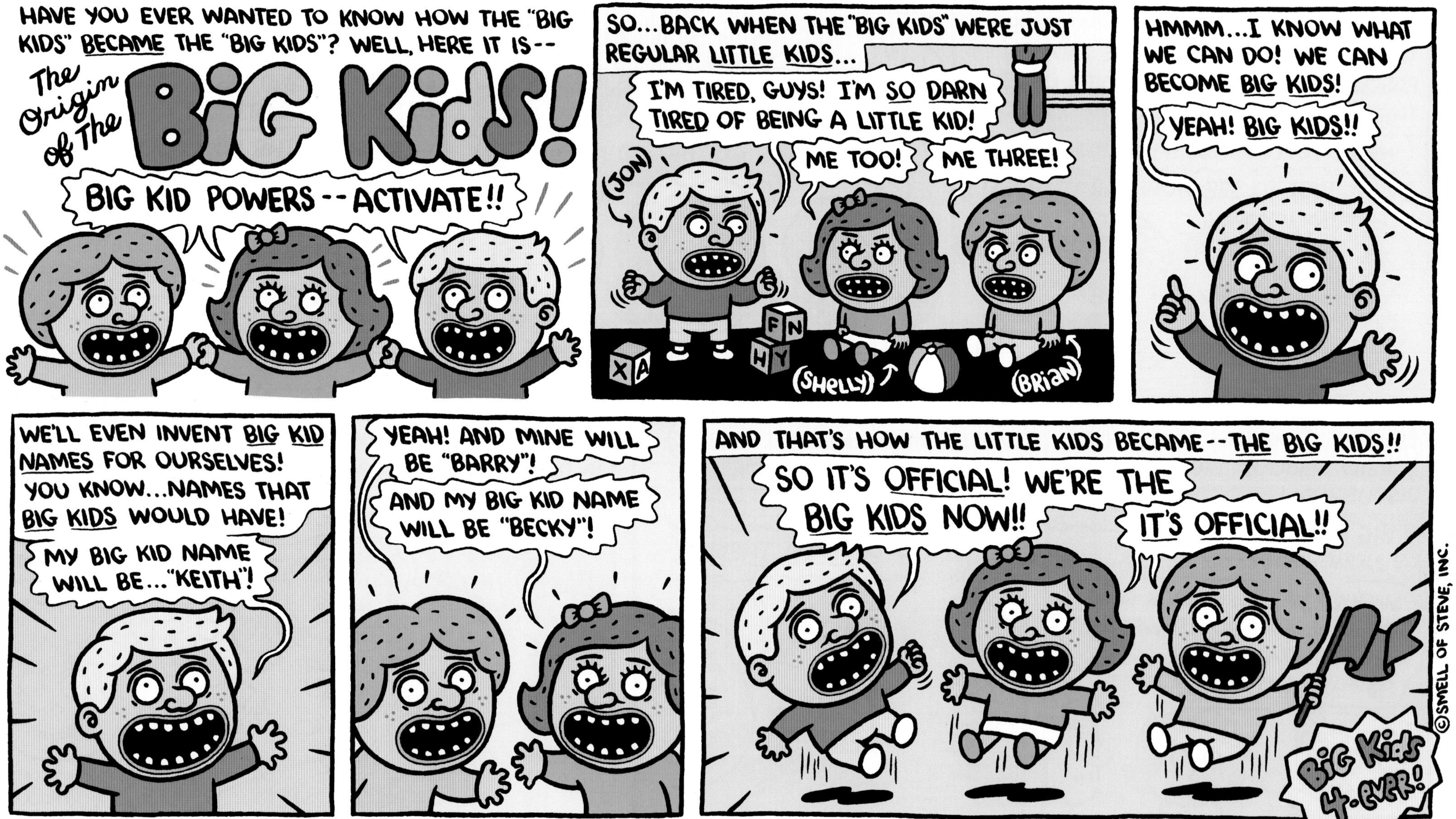
HAVE YOU EVER WANTED TO KNOW HOW THE "BIG KIDS" BECAME THE "BIG KIDS"? WELL, HERE IT IS--
The Origin of The BiG KidS!
BIG KID POWERS--ACTIVATE!!
SO...BACK WHEN THE "BIG KIDS" WERE JUST REGULAR LITTLE KIDS...
I'M TIRED, GUYS! I'M SO DARN TIRED OF BEING A LITTLE KID!
ME TOO!
ME THREE!
(JON)
(SHELLY)
(BRIAN)
HMMM...I KNOW WHAT WE CAN DO! WE CAN BECOME BIG KIDS!
YEAH! BIG KIDS!!
WE'LL EVEN INVENT BIG KID NAMES FOR OURSELVES! YOU KNOW...NAMES THAT BIG KIDS WOULD HAVE!
MY BIG KID NAME WILL BE..."KEITH"!
YEAH! AND MINE WILL BE "BARRY"!
AND MY BIG KID NAME WILL BE "BECKY"!
AND THAT'S HOW THE LITTLE KIDS BECAME--THE BIG KIDS!!
SO IT'S OFFICIAL! WE'RE THE BIG KIDS NOW!!
IT'S OFFICIAL!!
BiG KidS 4-EVER!
©SMELL OF STEVE, INC.

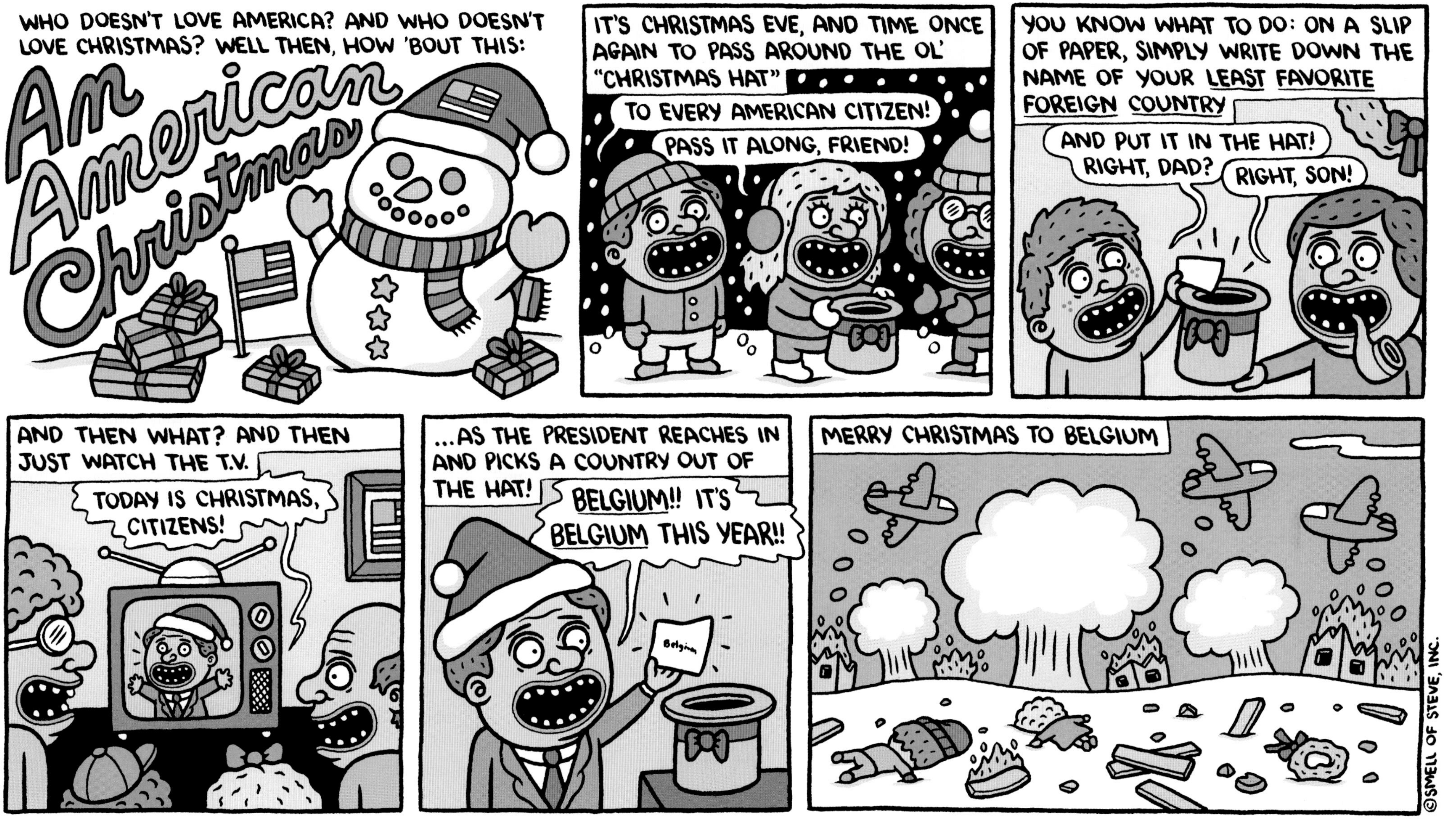
WHO DOESN'T LOVE AMERICA? AND WHO DOESN'T LOVE CHRISTMAS? WELL THEN, HOW 'BOUT THIS:
An American Christmas
IT'S CHRISTMAS EVE, AND TIME ONCE AGAIN TO PASS AROUND THE OL' "CHRISTMAS HAT"
TO EVERY AMERICAN CITIZEN!
PASS IT ALONG, FRIEND!
YOU KNOW WHAT TO DO: ON A SLIP OF PAPER, SIMPLY WRITE DOWN THE NAME OF YOUR LEAST FAVORITE FOREIGN COUNTRY
AND PUT IT IN THE HAT! RIGHT, DAD?
RIGHT, SON!
AND THEN WHAT? AND THEN JUST WATCH THE T.V.
TODAY IS CHRISTMAS, CITIZENS!
...AS THE PRESIDENT REACHES IN AND PICKS A COUNTRY OUT OF THE HAT!
BELGIUM!! IT'S BELGIUM THIS YEAR!!
Belgium
MERRY CHRISTMAS TO BELGIUM
©SMELL OF STEVE, INC.

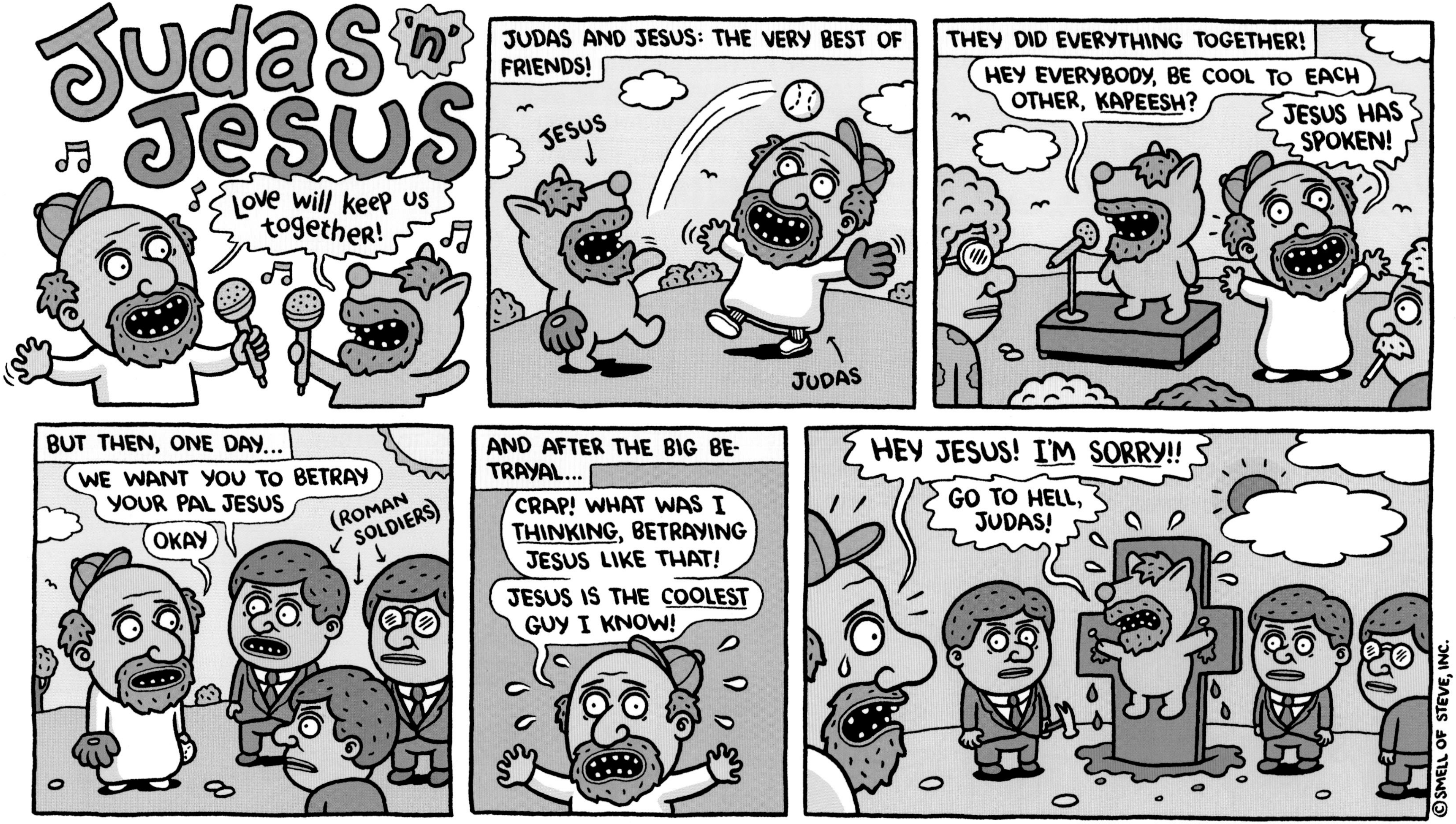
Judas 'n' Jesus
Love will keep us together!
JUDAS AND JESUS: THE VERY BEST OF FRIENDS!
JESUS
JUDAS
THEY DID EVERYTHING TOGETHER!
HEY EVERYBODY, BE COOL TO EACH OTHER, KAPEESH?
JESUS HAS SPOKEN!
BUT THEN, ONE DAY...
WE WANT YOU TO BETRAY YOUR PAL JESUS
OKAY
(ROMAN SOLDIERS)
AND AFTER THE BIG BE-TRAYAL...
CRAP! WHAT WAS I THINKING, BETRAYING JESUS LIKE THAT!
JESUS IS THE COOLEST GUY I KNOW!
HEY JESUS! I'M SORRY!!
GO TO HELL, JUDAS!
©SMELL OF STEVE, INC.

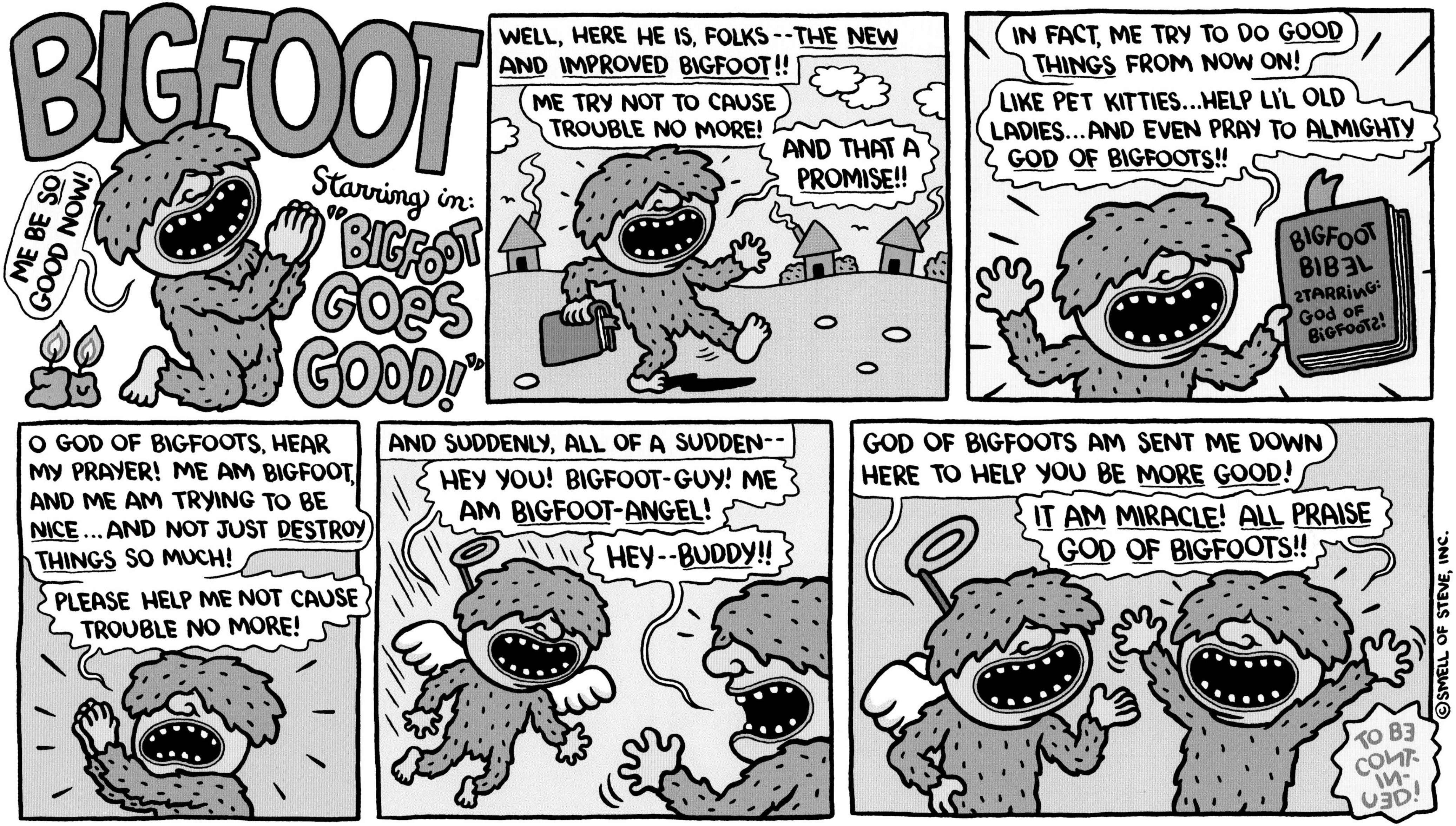
BIGFOOT
ME BE SO GOOD NOW!
Starring in: "BIGFOOT GOES GOOD!"
WELL, HERE HE IS, FOLKS--THE NEW AND IMPROVED BIGFOOT!!
ME TRY NOT TO CAUSE TROUBLE NO MORE!
AND THAT A PROMISE!!
IN FACT, ME TRY TO DO GOOD THINGS FROM NOW ON!
LIKE PET KITTIES...HELP LI'L OLD LADIES...AND EVEN PRAY TO ALMIGHTY GOD OF BIGFOOTS!!
BIGFOOT BIBEL STARRING: God of BIGFOOTS!
O GOD OF BIGFOOTS, HEAR MY PRAYER! ME AM BIGFOOT, AND ME AM TRYING TO BE NICE... AND NOT JUST DESTROY THINGS SO MUCH!
PLEASE HELP ME NOT CAUSE TROUBLE NO MORE!
AND SUDDENLY, ALL OF A SUDDEN--
HEY YOU! BIGFOOT-GUY! ME AM BIGFOOT-ANGEL!
HEY--BUDDY!!
GOD OF BIGFOOTS AM SENT ME DOWN HERE TO HELP YOU BE MORE GOOD!
IT AM MIRACLE! ALL PRAISE GOD OF BIGFOOTS!!
TO BE CONT-IN-UED!
©SMELL OF STEVE, INC.

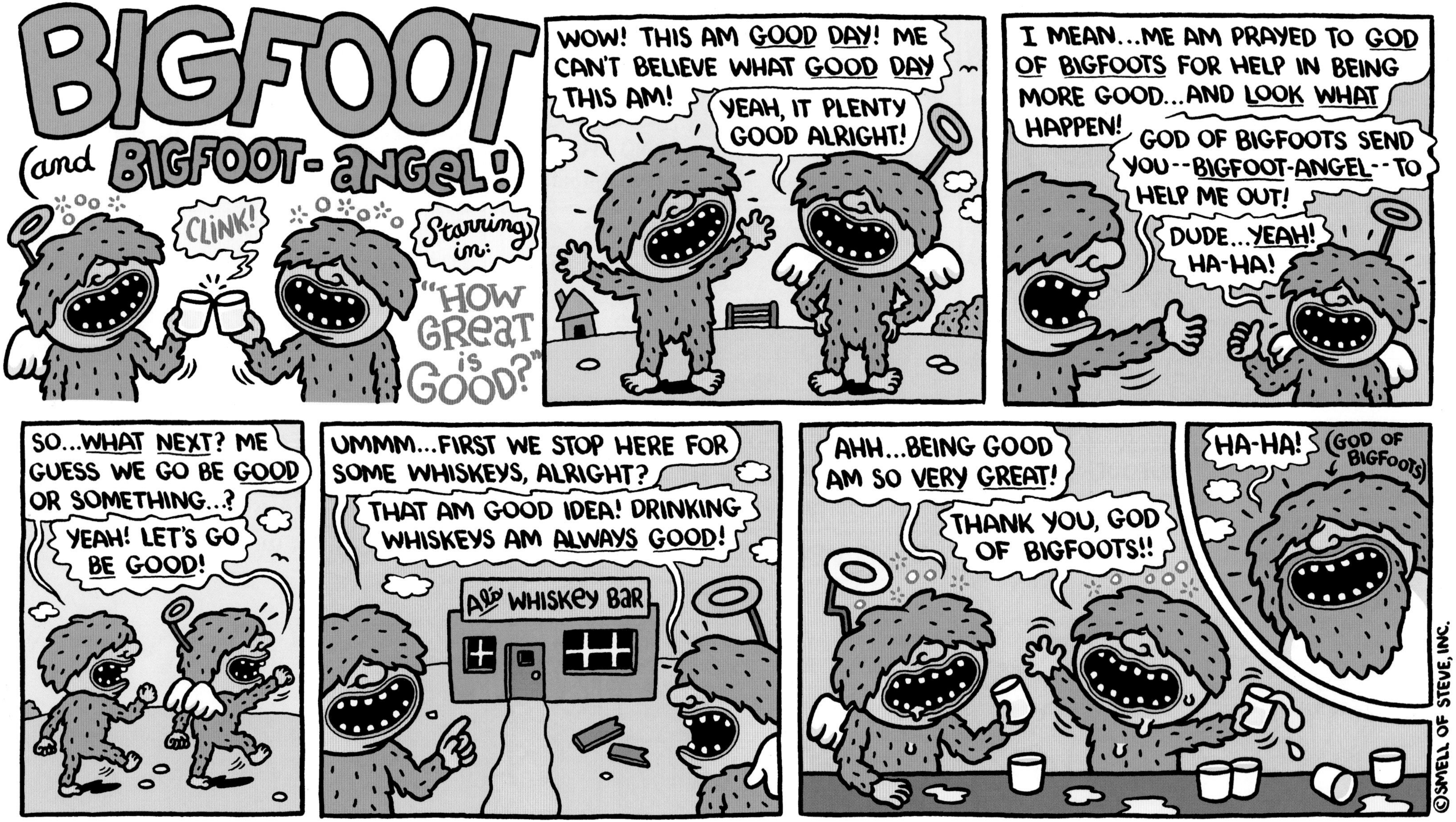
BIGFOOT
(and BIGFOOT-ANGEL!)
CLINK!
Starring in:
"HOW GREAT is GOOD?"
WOW! THIS AM GOOD DAY! ME CAN'T BELIEVE WHAT GOOD DAY THIS AM!
YEAH, IT PLENTY GOOD ALRIGHT!
I MEAN...ME AM PRAYED TO GOD OF BIGFOOTS FOR HELP IN BEING MORE GOOD...AND LOOK WHAT HAPPEN!
GOD OF BIGFOOTS SEND YOU--BIGFOOT-ANGEL--TO HELP ME OUT!
DUDE...YEAH! HA-HA!
SO...WHAT NEXT? ME GUESS WE GO BE GOOD OR SOMETHING...?
YEAH! LET'S GO BE GOOD!
UMMM...FIRST WE STOP HERE FOR SOME WHISKEYS, ALRIGHT?
THAT AM GOOD IDEA! DRINKING WHISKEYS AM ALWAYS GOOD!
AL'S WHISKEY BAR
AHH...BEING GOOD AM SO VERY GREAT!
THANK YOU, GOD OF BIGFOOTS!!
HA-HA!
(GOD OF BIGFOOTS)
©SMELL OF STEVE, INC.

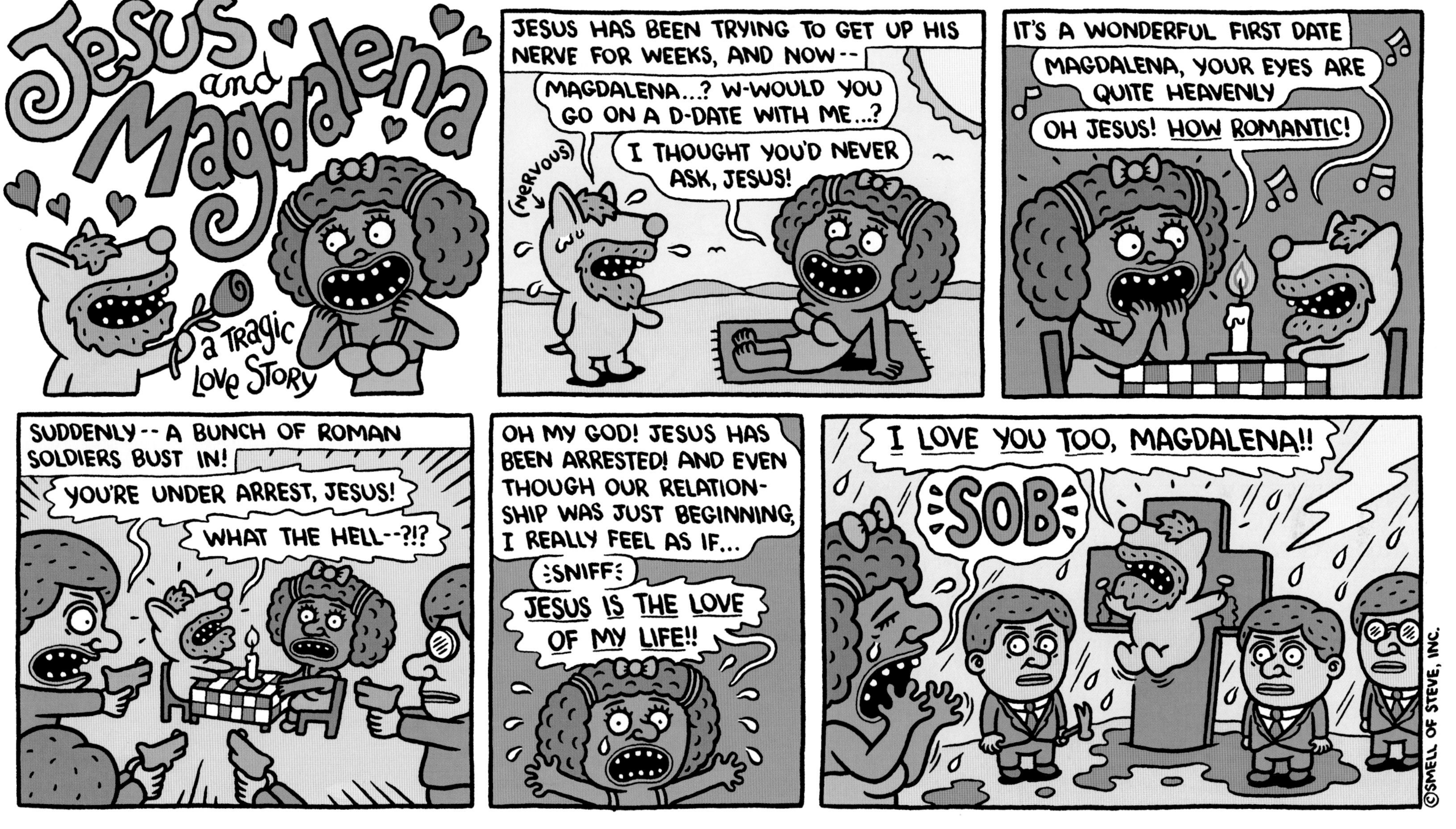
JESUS and MAGDALENA
a TRAGIC LOVE STORY
JESUS HAS BEEN TRYING TO GET UP HIS NERVE FOR WEEKS, AND NOW--
MAGDALENA...? W-WOULD YOU GO ON A D-DATE WITH ME...?
(NERVOUS)
I THOUGHT YOU'D NEVER ASK, JESUS!
IT'S A WONDERFUL FIRST DATE
MAGDALENA, YOUR EYES ARE QUITE HEAVENLY
OH JESUS! HOW ROMANTIC!
SUDDENLY-- A BUNCH OF ROMAN SOLDIERS BUST IN!
YOU'RE UNDER ARREST, JESUS!
WHAT THE HELL--?!?
OH MY GOD! JESUS HAS BEEN ARRESTED! AND EVEN THOUGH OUR RELATIONSHIP WAS JUST BEGINNING, I REALLY FEEL AS IF...
SNIFF
JESUS IS THE LOVE OF MY LIFE!!
I LOVE YOU TOO, MAGDALENA!!
SOB
©SMELL OF STEVE, INC.

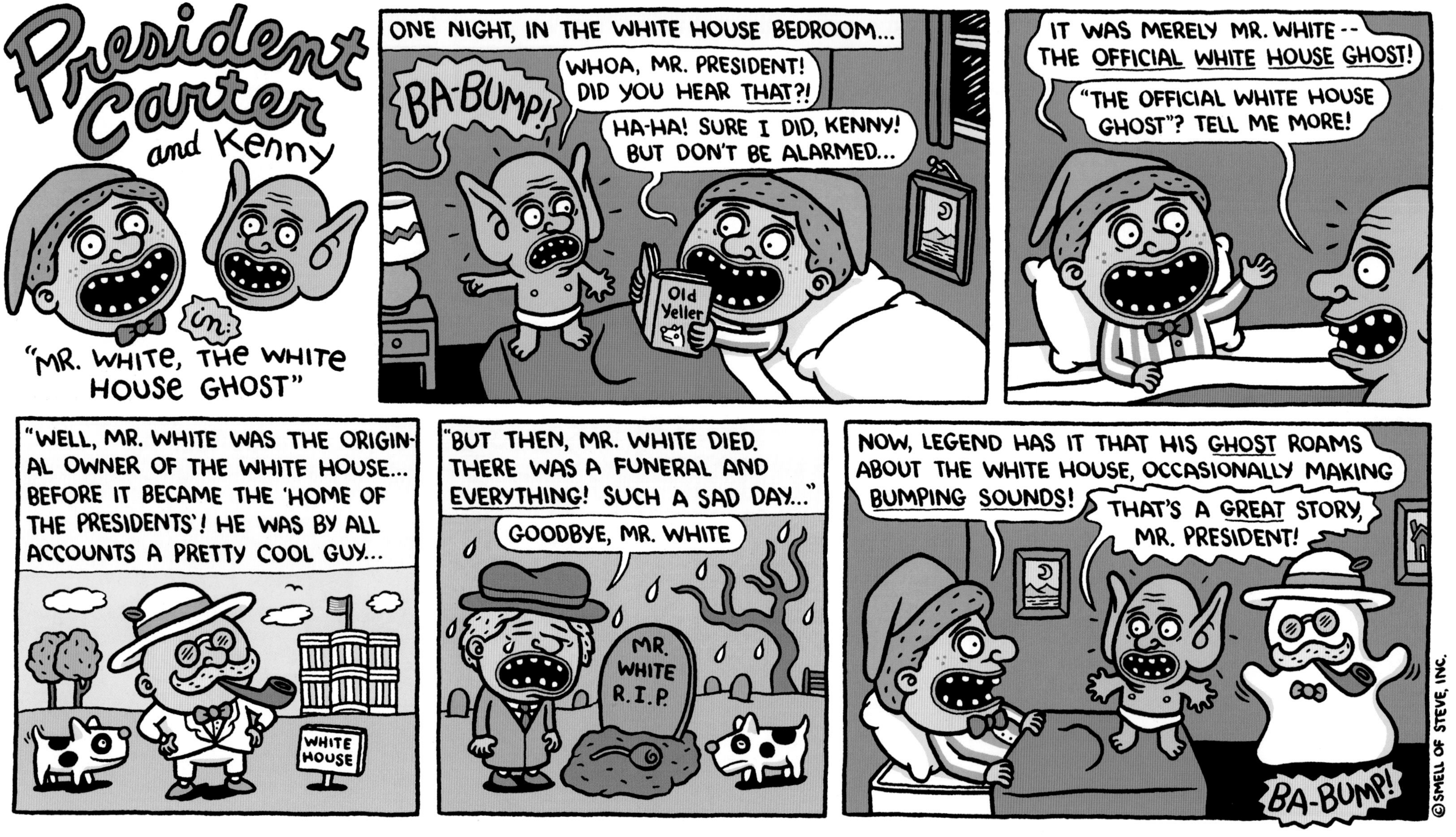
President Carter and Kenny
in:
"MR. WHITE, THE WHITE HOUSE GHOST"
ONE NIGHT, IN THE WHITE HOUSE BEDROOM...
BA-BUMP!
WHOA, MR. PRESIDENT! DID YOU HEAR THAT?!
HA-HA! SURE I DID, KENNY! BUT DON'T BE ALARMED...
Old Yeller
IT WAS MERELY MR. WHITE -- THE OFFICIAL WHITE HOUSE GHOST!
"THE OFFICIAL WHITE HOUSE GHOST"? TELL ME MORE!
"WELL, MR. WHITE WAS THE ORIGINAL OWNER OF THE WHITE HOUSE... BEFORE IT BECAME THE 'HOME OF THE PRESIDENTS'! HE WAS BY ALL ACCOUNTS A PRETTY COOL GUY...
WHITE HOUSE
"BUT THEN, MR. WHITE DIED. THERE WAS A FUNERAL AND EVERYTHING! SUCH A SAD DAY..."
GOODBYE, MR. WHITE
MR. WHITE R.I.P.
NOW, LEGEND HAS IT THAT HIS GHOST ROAMS ABOUT THE WHITE HOUSE, OCCASIONALLY MAKING BUMPING SOUNDS!
THAT'S A GREAT STORY, MR. PRESIDENT!
BA-BUMP!
©SMELL OF STEVE, INC.

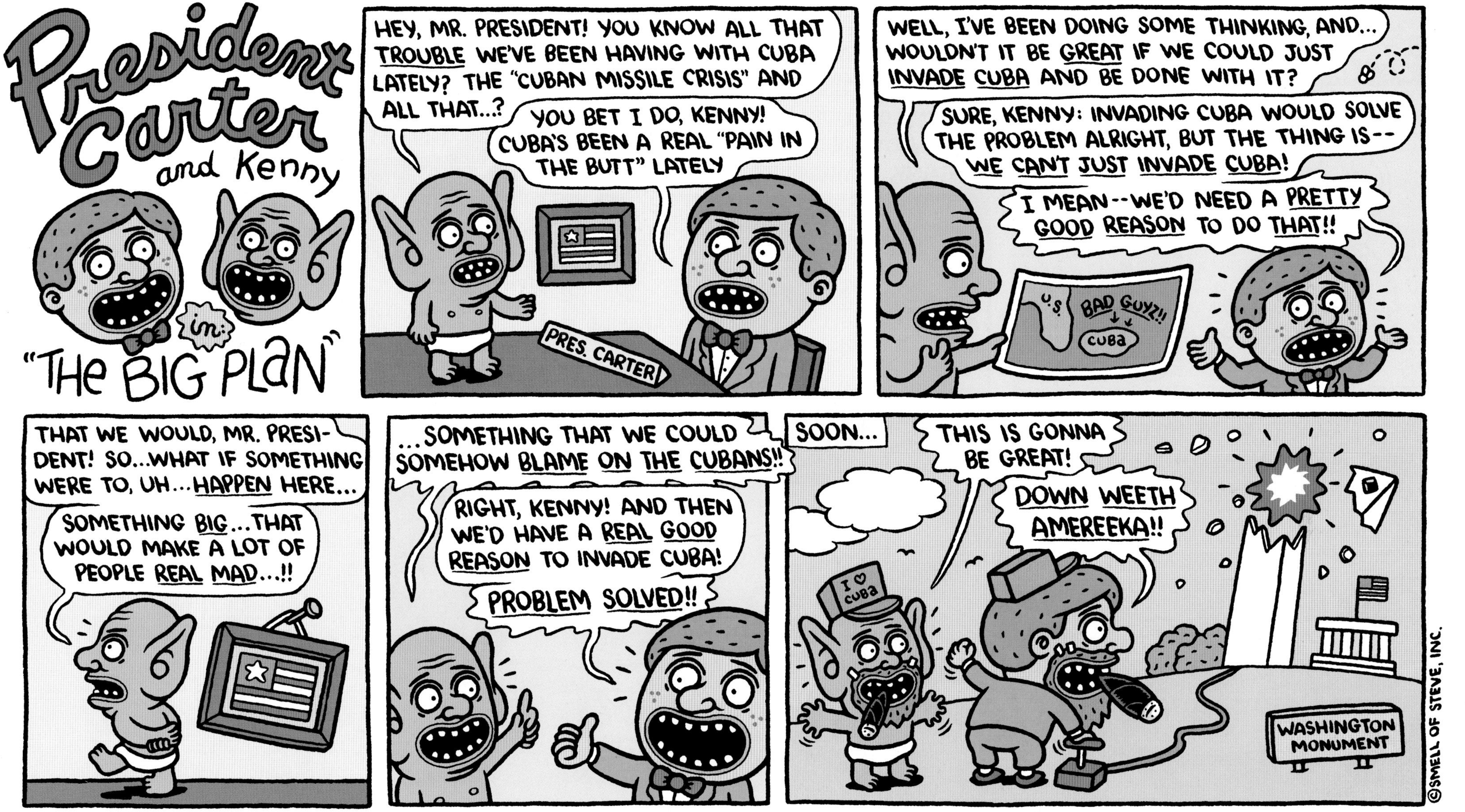
President Carter and Kenny in: "The BIG PLAN"
HEY, MR. PRESIDENT! YOU KNOW ALL THAT TROUBLE WE'VE BEEN HAVING WITH CUBA LATELY? THE "CUBAN MISSILE CRISIS" AND ALL THAT...?
YOU BET I DO, KENNY! CUBA'S BEEN A REAL "PAIN IN THE BUTT" LATELY
PRES. CARTER
WELL, I'VE BEEN DOING SOME THINKING, AND... WOULDN'T IT BE GREAT IF WE COULD JUST INVADE CUBA AND BE DONE WITH IT?
SURE, KENNY: INVADING CUBA WOULD SOLVE THE PROBLEM ALRIGHT, BUT THE THING IS-- WE CAN'T JUST INVADE CUBA!
I MEAN--WE'D NEED A PRETTY GOOD REASON TO DO THAT!!
U.S.
BAD GUYZ!!
CUBA
THAT WE WOULD, MR. PRESI-DENT! SO...WHAT IF SOMETHING WERE TO, UH...HAPPEN HERE...
SOMETHING BIG...THAT WOULD MAKE A LOT OF PEOPLE REAL MAD...!!
...SOMETHING THAT WE COULD SOMEHOW BLAME ON THE CUBANS!!
RIGHT, KENNY! AND THEN WE'D HAVE A REAL GOOD REASON TO INVADE CUBA!
PROBLEM SOLVED!!
SOON...
THIS IS GONNA BE GREAT!
DOWN WEETH AMEREEKA!!
I ♡ CUBA
WASHINGTON MONUMENT
©SMELL OF STEVE, INC.

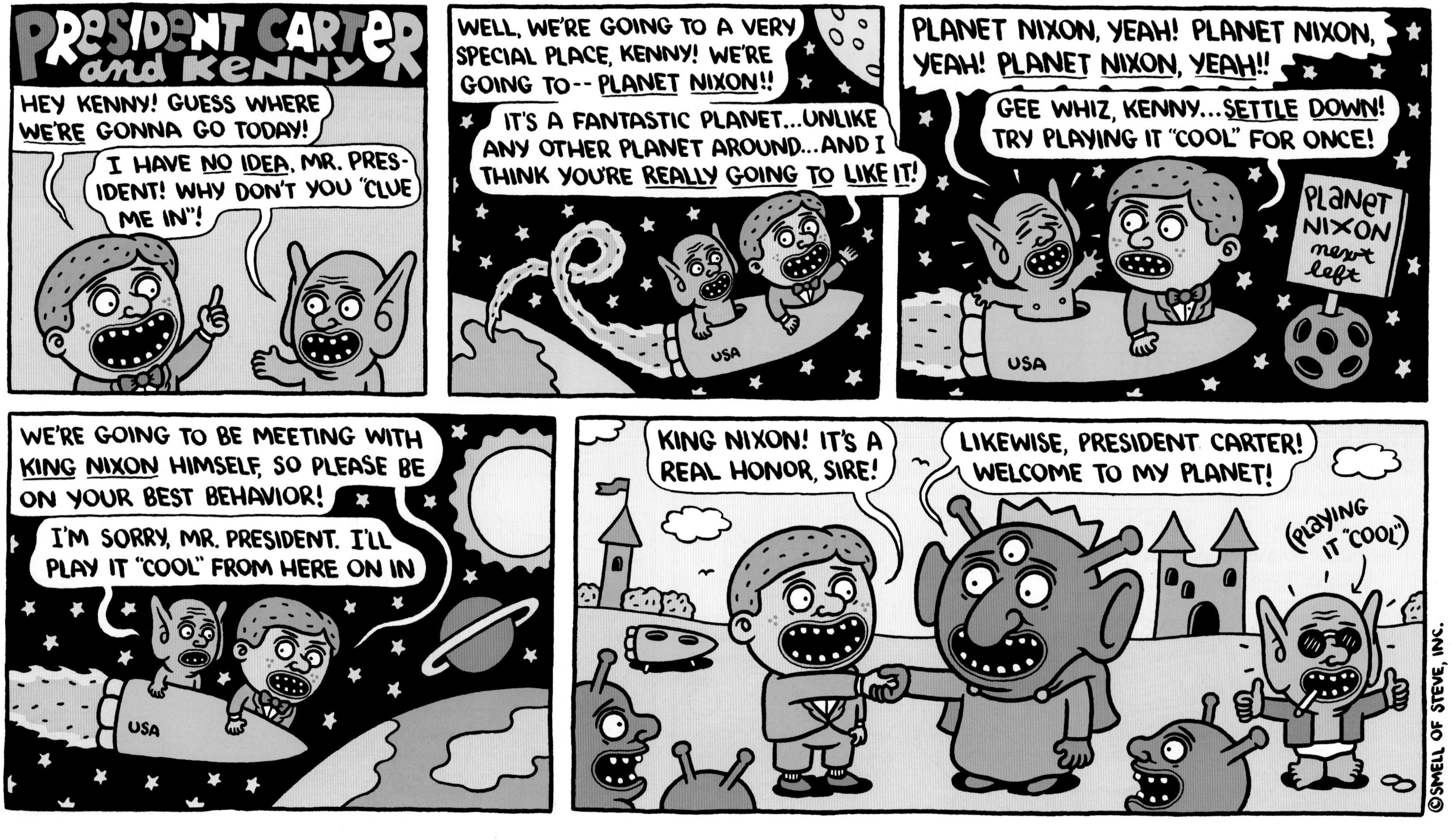

PRESIDENT CARTER and KENNY
HEY KENNY! GUESS WHERE WE'RE GONNA GO TODAY!
I HAVE NO IDEA, MR. PRESIDENT! WHY DON'T YOU "CLUE ME IN"!
WELL, WE'RE GOING TO A VERY SPECIAL PLACE, KENNY! WE'RE GOING TO-- PLANET NIXON!!
IT'S A FANTASTIC PLANET...UNLIKE ANY OTHER PLANET AROUND...AND I THINK YOU'RE REALLY GOING TO LIKE IT!
USA
PLANET NIXON, YEAH! PLANET NIXON, YEAH! PLANET NIXON, YEAH!!
GEE WHIZ, KENNY...SETTLE DOWN! TRY PLAYING IT "COOL" FOR ONCE!
PLANET NIXON next left
USA
WE'RE GOING TO BE MEETING WITH KING NIXON HIMSELF, SO PLEASE BE ON YOUR BEST BEHAVIOR!
I'M SORRY, MR. PRESIDENT. I'LL PLAY IT "COOL" FROM HERE ON IN
USA
KING NIXON! IT'S A REAL HONOR, SIRE!
LIKEWISE, PRESIDENT CARTER! WELCOME TO MY PLANET!
(PLAYING IT "COOL")
©SMELL OF STEVE, INC.

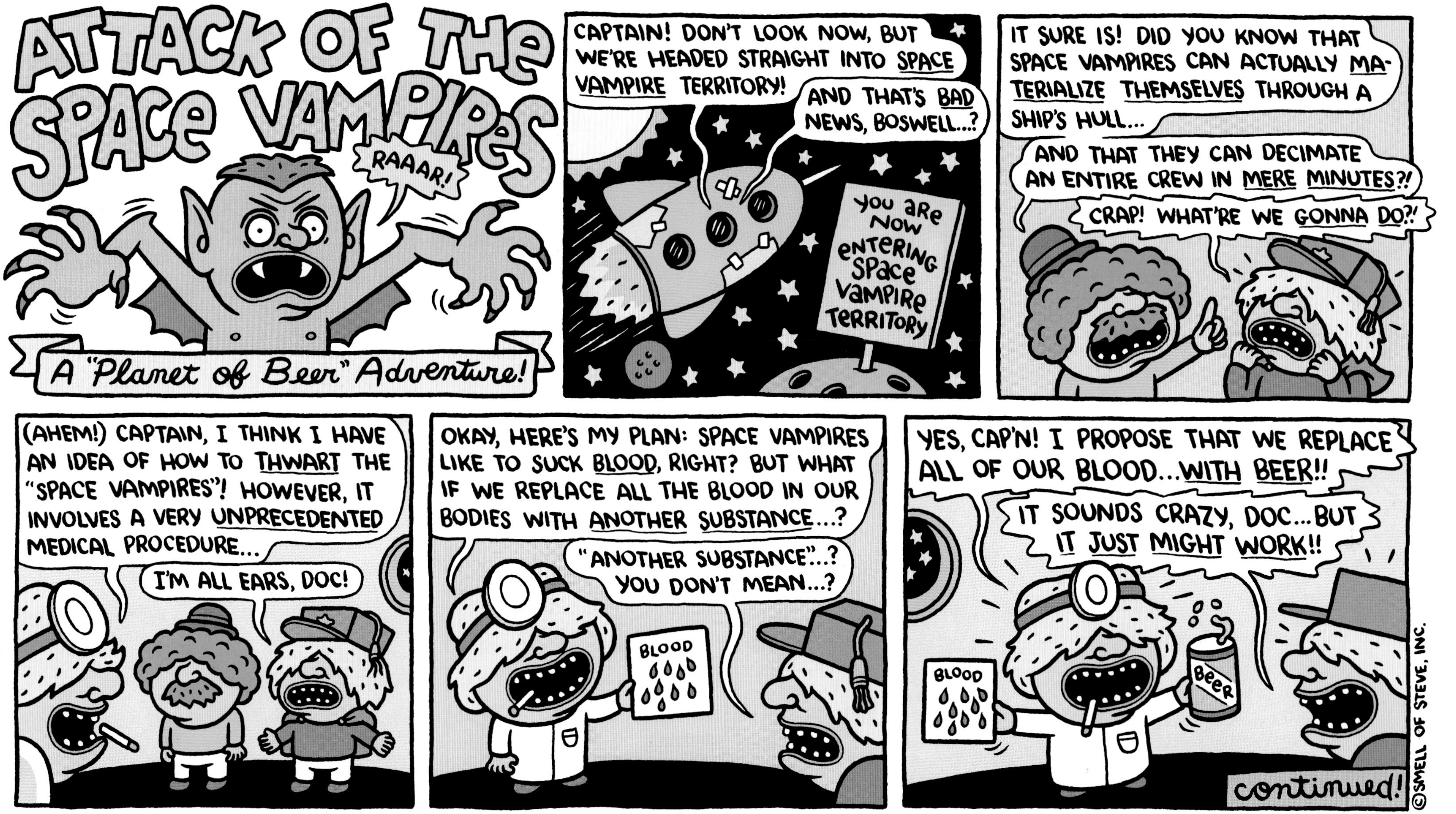
ATTACK OF THE SPACE VAMPIRES
RAAAR!
A "Planet of Beer" Adventure!
CAPTAIN! DON'T LOOK NOW, BUT WE'RE HEADED STRAIGHT INTO SPACE VAMPIRE TERRITORY!
AND THAT'S BAD NEWS, BOSWELL...?
YOU ARE NOW ENTERING SPACE VAMPIRE TERRITORY
IT SURE IS! DID YOU KNOW THAT SPACE VAMPIRES CAN ACTUALLY MA-TERIALIZE THEMSELVES THROUGH A SHIP'S HULL...
AND THAT THEY CAN DECIMATE AN ENTIRE CREW IN MERE MINUTES?!
CRAP! WHAT'RE WE GONNA DO?!
(AHEM!) CAPTAIN, I THINK I HAVE AN IDEA OF HOW TO THWART THE "SPACE VAMPIRES"! HOWEVER, IT INVOLVES A VERY UNPRECEDENTED MEDICAL PROCEDURE...
I'M ALL EARS, DOC!
OKAY, HERE'S MY PLAN: SPACE VAMPIRES LIKE TO SUCK BLOOD, RIGHT? BUT WHAT IF WE REPLACE ALL THE BLOOD IN OUR BODIES WITH ANOTHER SUBSTANCE...?
"ANOTHER SUBSTANCE"...? YOU DON'T MEAN...?
BLOOD
YES, CAP'N! I PROPOSE THAT WE REPLACE ALL OF OUR BLOOD...WITH BEER!!
IT SOUNDS CRAZY, DOC...BUT IT JUST MIGHT WORK!!
BLOOD
BEER
continued!
©SMELL OF STEVE, INC.

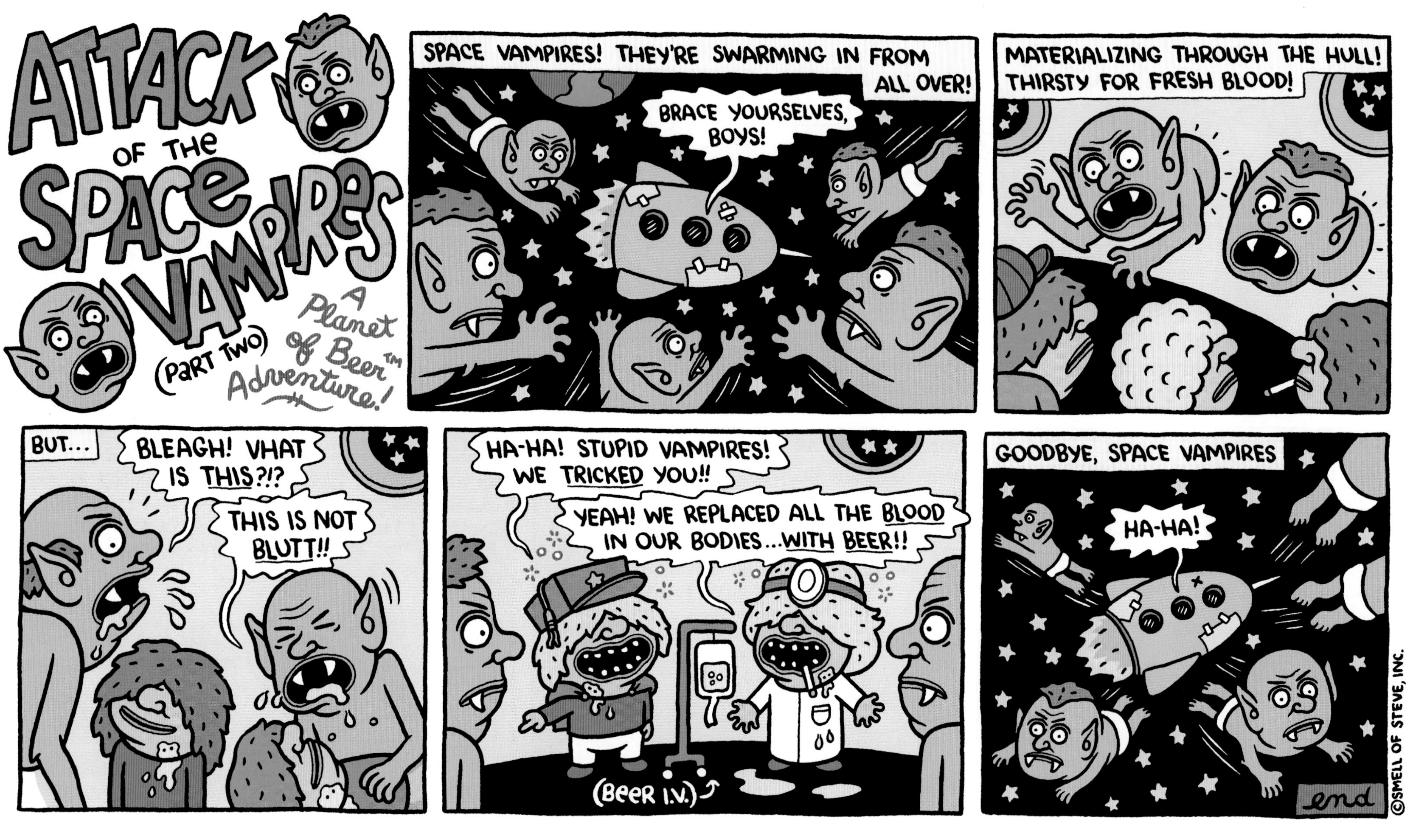
ATTACK OF THE SPACE VAMPIRES
(PART TWO)
A Planet of Beer™ Adventure!
SPACE VAMPIRES! THEY'RE SWARMING IN FROM ALL OVER!
BRACE YOURSELVES, BOYS!
MATERIALIZING THROUGH THE HULL! THIRSTY FOR FRESH BLOOD!
BUT...
BLEAGH! VHAT IS THIS?!?
THIS IS NOT BLUTT!!
HA-HA! STUPID VAMPIRES! WE TRICKED YOU!!
YEAH! WE REPLACED ALL THE BLOOD IN OUR BODIES...WITH BEER!!
(BEER I.V.)
GOODBYE, SPACE VAMPIRES
HA-HA!
end
©SMELL OF STEVE, INC.

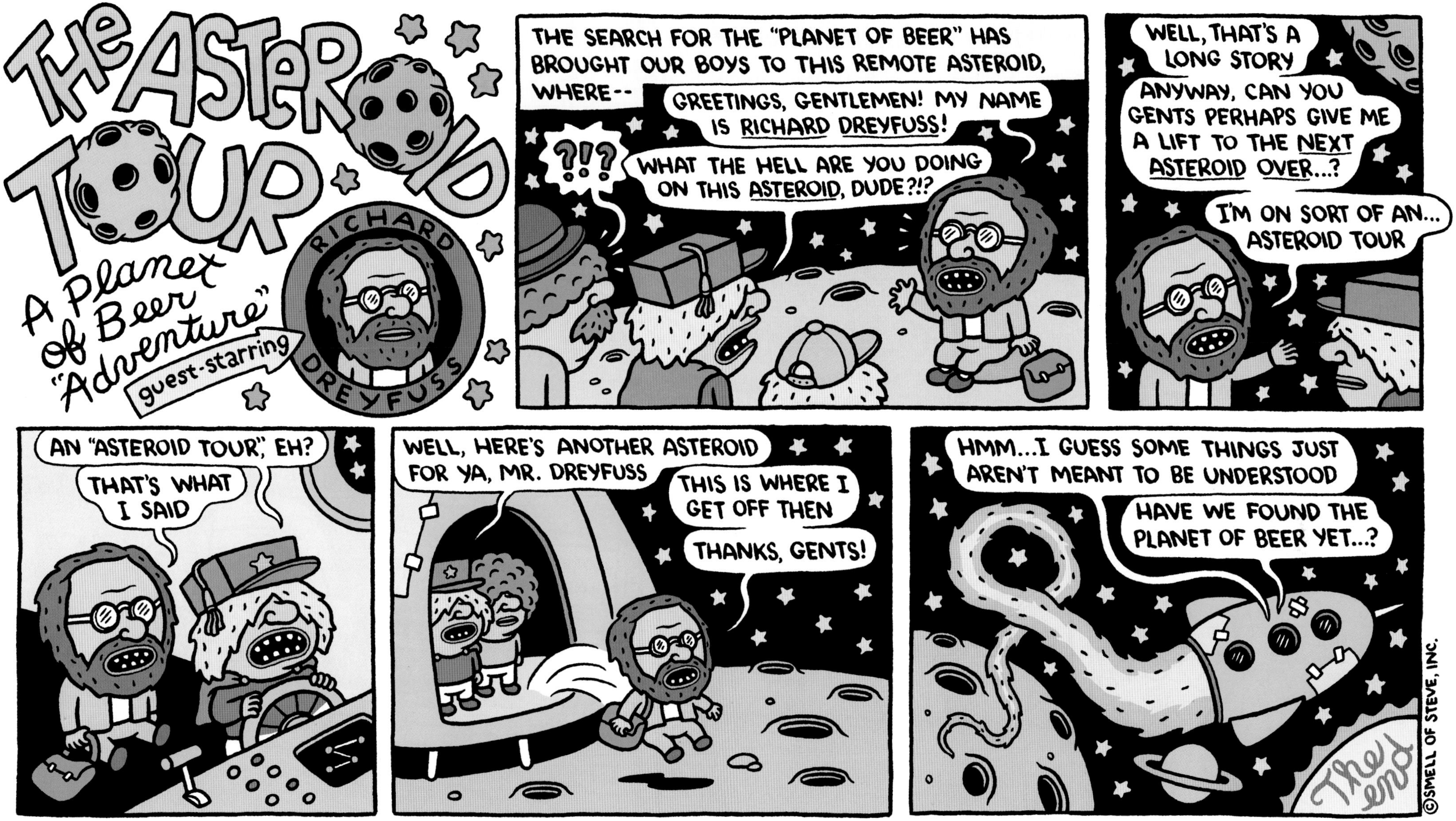
The Asteroid Tour
A Planet of Beer "Adventure"
guest-starring
RICHARD DREYFUSS
THE SEARCH FOR THE "PLANET OF BEER" HAS BROUGHT OUR BOYS TO THIS REMOTE ASTEROID, WHERE--
GREETINGS, GENTLEMEN! MY NAME IS RICHARD DREYFUSS!
?!?
WHAT THE HELL ARE YOU DOING ON THIS ASTEROID, DUDE?!?
WELL, THAT'S A LONG STORY
ANYWAY, CAN YOU GENTS PERHAPS GIVE ME A LIFT TO THE NEXT ASTEROID OVER...?
I'M ON SORT OF AN... ASTEROID TOUR
AN "ASTEROID TOUR", EH?
THAT'S WHAT I SAID
WELL, HERE'S ANOTHER ASTEROID FOR YA, MR. DREYFUSS
THIS IS WHERE I GET OFF THEN
THANKS, GENTS!
HMM...I GUESS SOME THINGS JUST AREN'T MEANT TO BE UNDERSTOOD
HAVE WE FOUND THE PLANET OF BEER YET...?
The end
©SMELL OF STEVE, INC.

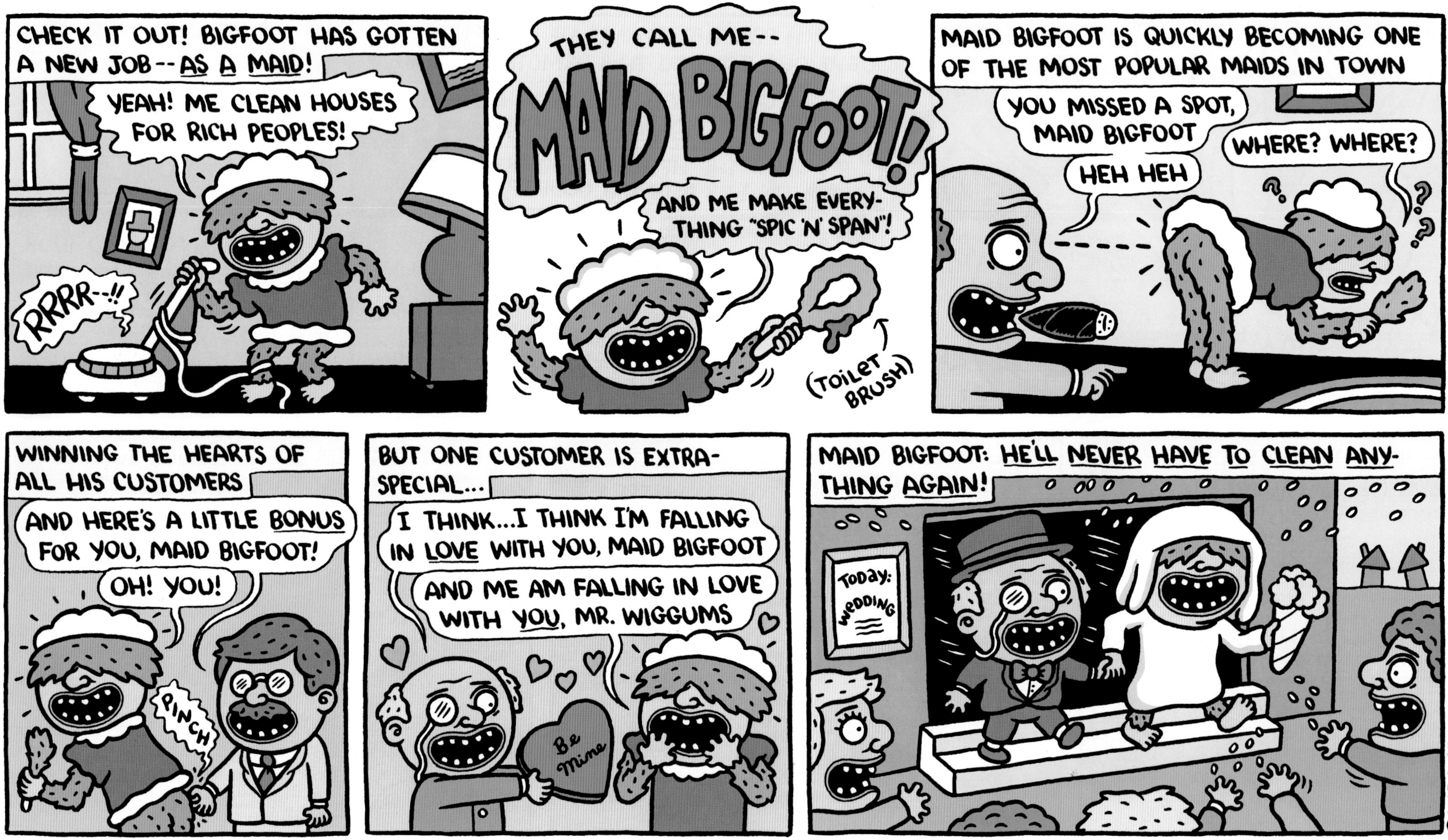
CHECK IT OUT! BIGFOOT HAS GOTTEN A NEW JOB--AS A MAID!
YEAH! ME CLEAN HOUSES FOR RICH PEOPLES!
RRRR--!!
THEY CALL ME--
MAID BIGFOOT!
AND ME MAKE EVERY-THING "SPIC 'N' SPAN"!
(TOILET BRUSH)
MAID BIGFOOT IS QUICKLY BECOMING ONE OF THE MOST POPULAR MAIDS IN TOWN
YOU MISSED A SPOT, MAID BIGFOOT
HEH HEH
WHERE? WHERE?
WINNING THE HEARTS OF ALL HIS CUSTOMERS
AND HERE'S A LITTLE BONUS FOR YOU, MAID BIGFOOT!
OH! YOU!
PINCH
BUT ONE CUSTOMER IS EXTRA-SPECIAL...
I THINK...I THINK I'M FALLING IN LOVE WITH YOU, MAID BIGFOOT
AND ME AM FALLING IN LOVE WITH YOU, MR. WIGGUMS
Be Mine
MAID BIGFOOT: HE'LL NEVER HAVE TO CLEAN ANY-THING AGAIN!
TODAY: WEDDING

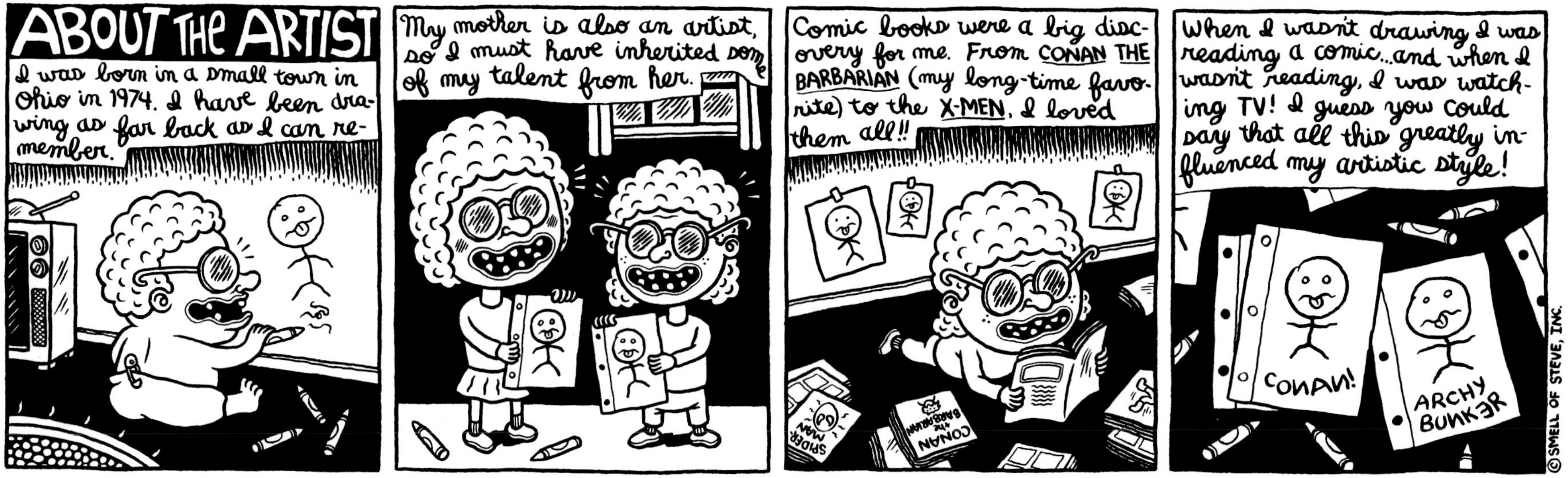
ABOUT THE ARTIST
I was born in a small town in Ohio in 1974. I have been drawing as far back as I can remember.
My mother is also an artist, so I must have inherited some of my talent from her.
Comic books were a big discovery for me. From CONAN THE BARBARIAN (my long-time favorite) to the X-MEN, I loved them all!!
When I wasn't drawing I was reading a comic...and when I wasn't reading, I was watching TV! I guess you could say that all this greatly influenced my artistic style!
CONAN!
ARCHY BUNKER
©SMELL OF STEVE, INC.

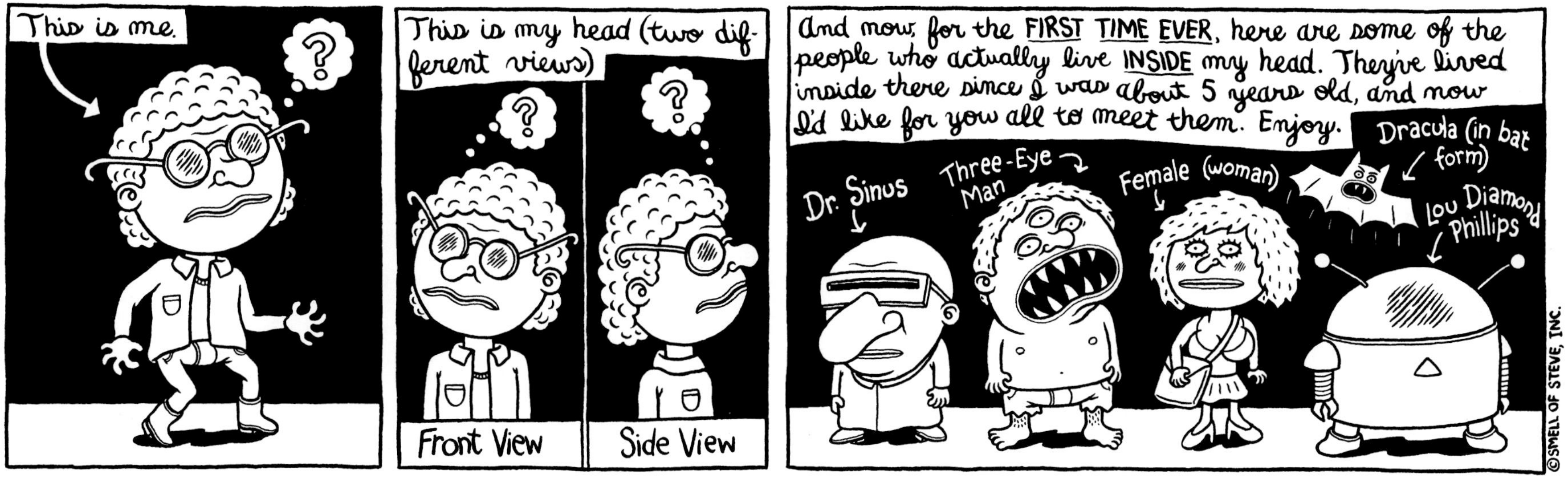
This is me.
This is my head (two different views)
Front View
Side View
And now, for the FIRST TIME EVER, here are some of the people who actually live INSIDE my head. They've lived inside there since I was about 5 years old, and now I'd like for you all to meet them. Enjoy.
Dr. Sinus
Three-Eye Man
Female (woman)
Dracula (in bat form)
Lou Diamond Phillips
©SMELL OF STEVE, INC.

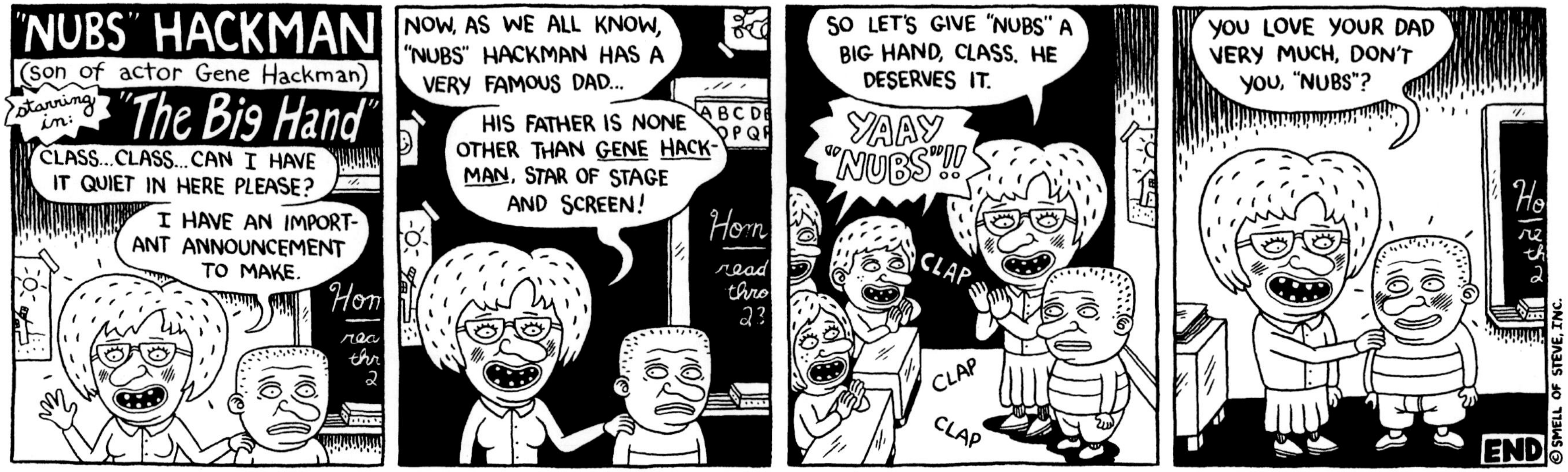
"NUBS" HACKMAN
(son of actor Gene Hackman)
starring in: "The Big Hand"
CLASS...CLASS...CAN I HAVE IT QUIET IN HERE PLEASE?
I HAVE AN IMPORTANT ANNOUNCEMENT TO MAKE.
NOW, AS WE ALL KNOW, "NUBS" HACKMAN HAS A VERY FAMOUS DAD...
HIS FATHER IS NONE OTHER THAN GENE HACKMAN, STAR OF STAGE AND SCREEN!
SO LET'S GIVE "NUBS" A BIG HAND, CLASS. HE DESERVES IT.
YAAY "NUBS"!!
CLAP
CLAP
CLAP
YOU LOVE YOUR DAD VERY MUCH, DON'T YOU, "NUBS"?
END
©SMELL OF STEVE, INC.

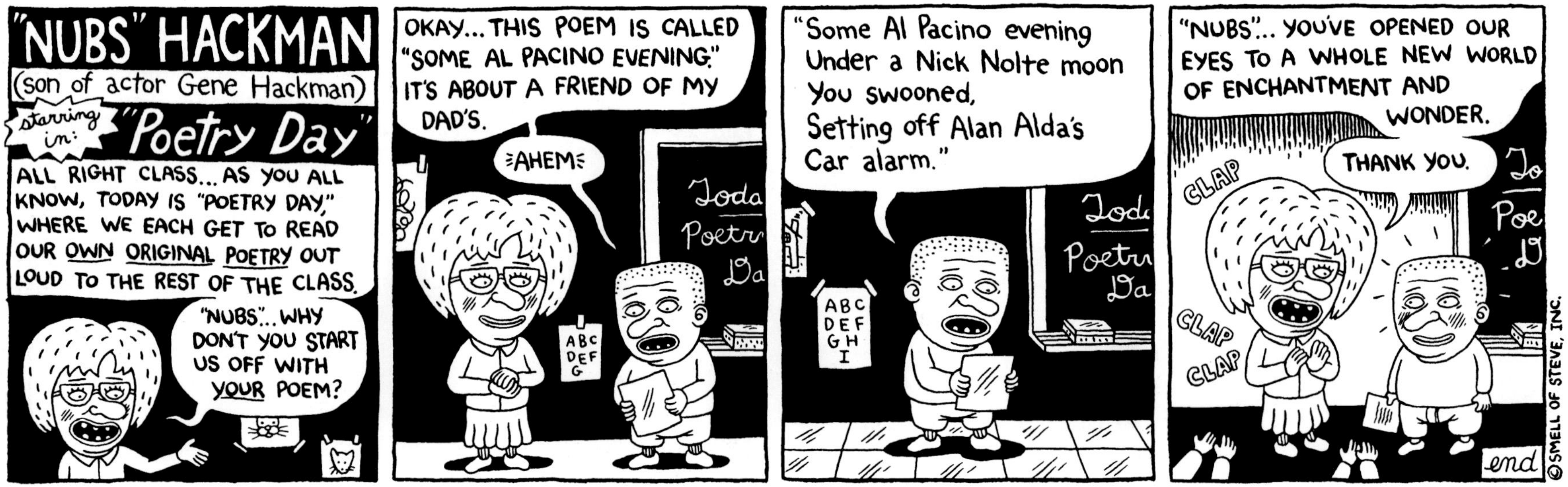
"NUBS" HACKMAN
(son of actor Gene Hackman)
starring in: "Poetry Day"
ALL RIGHT CLASS... AS YOU ALL KNOW, TODAY IS "POETRY DAY," WHERE WE EACH GET TO READ OUR OWN ORIGINAL POETRY OUT LOUD TO THE REST OF THE CLASS.
"NUBS"... WHY DON'T YOU START US OFF WITH YOUR POEM?
OKAY... THIS POEM IS CALLED "SOME AL PACINO EVENING." IT'S ABOUT A FRIEND OF MY DAD'S.
AHEM
"Some Al Pacino evening
Under a Nick Nolte moon
You swooned,
Setting off Alan Alda's
Car alarm."
"NUBS"... YOU'VE OPENED OUR EYES TO A WHOLE NEW WORLD OF ENCHANTMENT AND WONDER.
THANK YOU.
CLAP
CLAP
CLAP
end
©SMELL OF STEVE, INC.

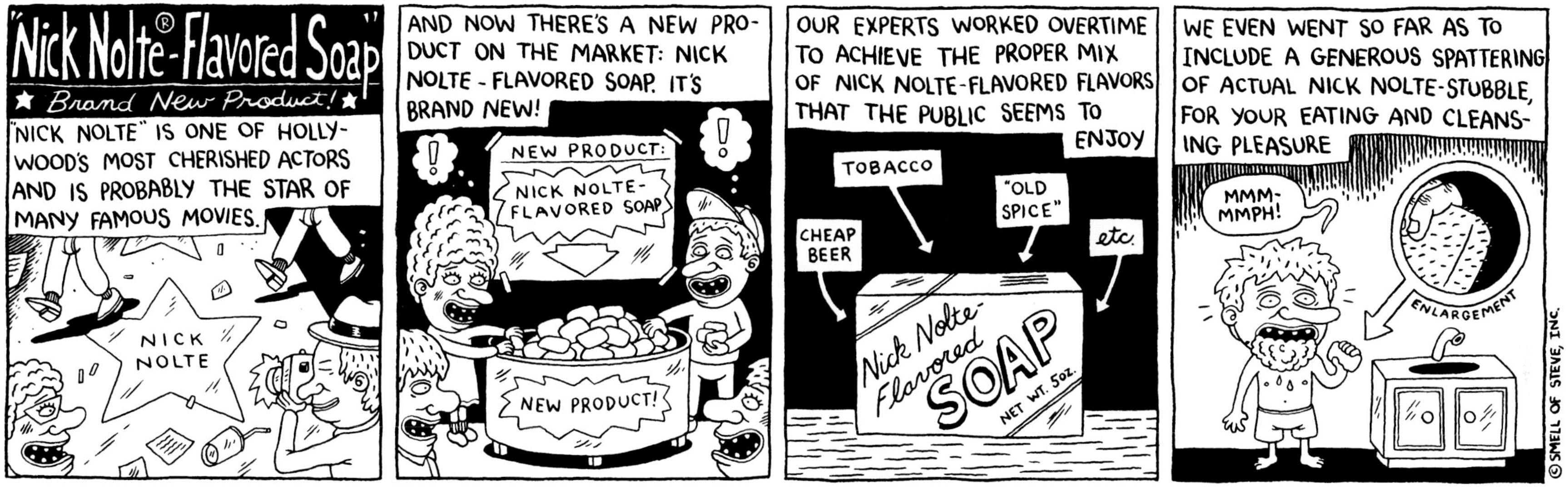
"Nick Nolte® -Flavored Soap"
★ Brand New Product! ★
"NICK NOLTE" IS ONE OF HOLLYWOOD'S MOST CHERISHED ACTORS AND IS PROBABLY THE STAR OF MANY FAMOUS MOVIES.
NICK NOLTE
AND NOW THERE'S A NEW PRODUCT ON THE MARKET: NICK NOLTE - FLAVORED SOAP. IT'S BRAND NEW!
!
NEW PRODUCT:
NICK NOLTE-FLAVORED SOAP
!
NEW PRODUCT!
OUR EXPERTS WORKED OVERTIME TO ACHIEVE THE PROPER MIX OF NICK NOLTE-FLAVORED FLAVORS THAT THE PUBLIC SEEMS TO ENJOY
TOBACCO
"OLD SPICE"
CHEAP BEER
etc.
Nick Nolte-Flavored SOAP
NET WT. 5oz.
WE EVEN WENT SO FAR AS TO INCLUDE A GENEROUS SPATTERING OF ACTUAL NICK NOLTE-STUBBLE, FOR YOUR EATING AND CLEANSING PLEASURE
MMM-MMPH!
ENLARGEMENT
© SMELL OF STEVE, INC.

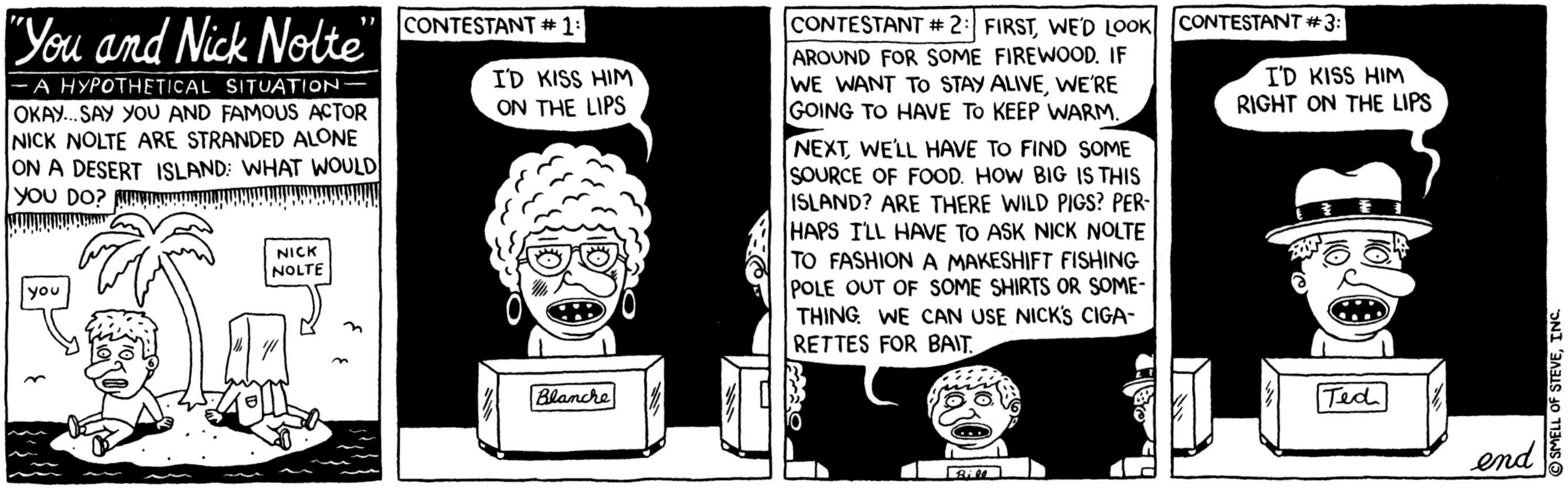
"You and Nick Nolte"
— A HYPOTHETICAL SITUATION —
OKAY...SAY YOU AND FAMOUS ACTOR NICK NOLTE ARE STRANDED ALONE ON A DESERT ISLAND: WHAT WOULD YOU DO?
YOU
NICK NOLTE
CONTESTANT # 1:
I'D KISS HIM ON THE LIPS
Blanche
CONTESTANT # 2:
FIRST, WE'D LOOK AROUND FOR SOME FIREWOOD. IF WE WANT TO STAY ALIVE, WE'RE GOING TO HAVE TO KEEP WARM.
NEXT, WE'LL HAVE TO FIND SOME SOURCE OF FOOD. HOW BIG IS THIS ISLAND? ARE THERE WILD PIGS? PERHAPS I'LL HAVE TO ASK NICK NOLTE TO FASHION A MAKESHIFT FISHING POLE OUT OF SOME SHIRTS OR SOMETHING. WE CAN USE NICK'S CIGARETTES FOR BAIT.
CONTESTANT # 3:
I'D KISS HIM RIGHT ON THE LIPS
Ted
end
© SMELL OF STEVE, INC.

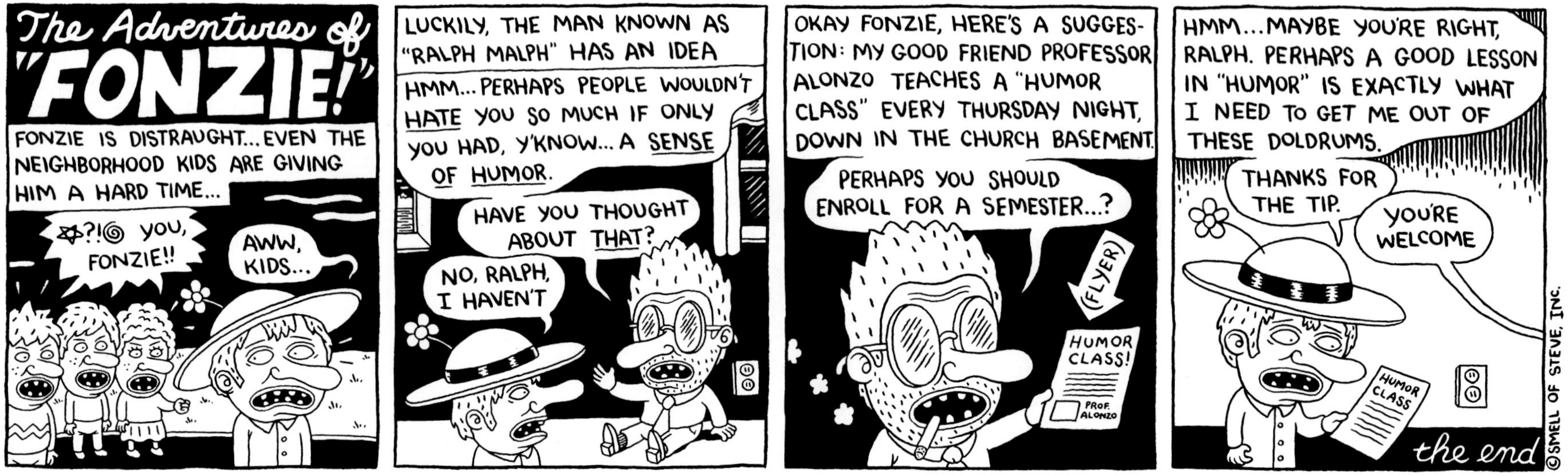
The Adventures of
"FONZIE!"
FONZIE IS DISTRAUGHT... EVEN THE NEIGHBORHOOD KIDS ARE GIVING HIM A HARD TIME...
?! YOU, FONZIE!!
AWW, KIDS...
LUCKILY, THE MAN KNOWN AS "RALPH MALPH" HAS AN IDEA
HMM... PERHAPS PEOPLE WOULDN'T HATE YOU SO MUCH IF ONLY YOU HAD, Y'KNOW... A SENSE OF HUMOR.
HAVE YOU THOUGHT ABOUT THAT?
NO, RALPH, I HAVEN'T
OKAY FONZIE, HERE'S A SUGGESTION: MY GOOD FRIEND PROFESSOR ALONZO TEACHES A "HUMOR CLASS" EVERY THURSDAY NIGHT, DOWN IN THE CHURCH BASEMENT.
PERHAPS YOU SHOULD ENROLL FOR A SEMESTER...?
(FLYER)
HUMOR CLASS!
PROF. ALONZO
HMM... MAYBE YOU'RE RIGHT, RALPH. PERHAPS A GOOD LESSON IN "HUMOR" IS EXACTLY WHAT I NEED TO GET ME OUT OF THESE DOLDRUMS.
THANKS FOR THE TIP.
YOU'RE WELCOME
HUMOR CLASS
the end
©SMELL OF STEVE, INC.

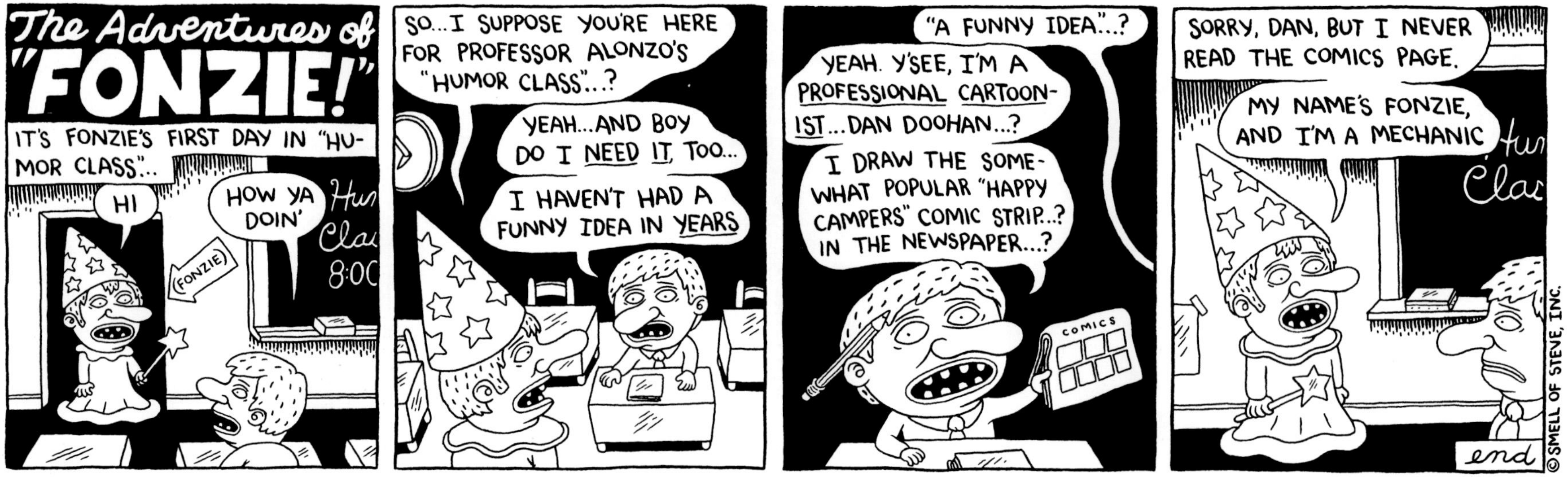
The Adventures of
"FONZIE!"
IT'S FONZIE'S FIRST DAY IN "HUMOR CLASS"...
HI
HOW YA DOIN'
(FONZIE)
Hu Cla 8:00
SO... I SUPPOSE YOU'RE HERE FOR PROFESSOR ALONZO'S "HUMOR CLASS"...?
YEAH... AND BOY DO I NEED IT, TOO...
I HAVEN'T HAD A FUNNY IDEA IN YEARS
"A FUNNY IDEA"...?
YEAH. Y'SEE, I'M A PROFESSIONAL CARTOONIST... DAN DOOHAN...?
I DRAW THE SOMEWHAT POPULAR "HAPPY CAMPERS" COMIC STRIP...? IN THE NEWSPAPER...?
COMICS
SORRY, DAN, BUT I NEVER READ THE COMICS PAGE.
MY NAME'S FONZIE, AND I'M A MECHANIC
end
©SMELL OF STEVE, INC.

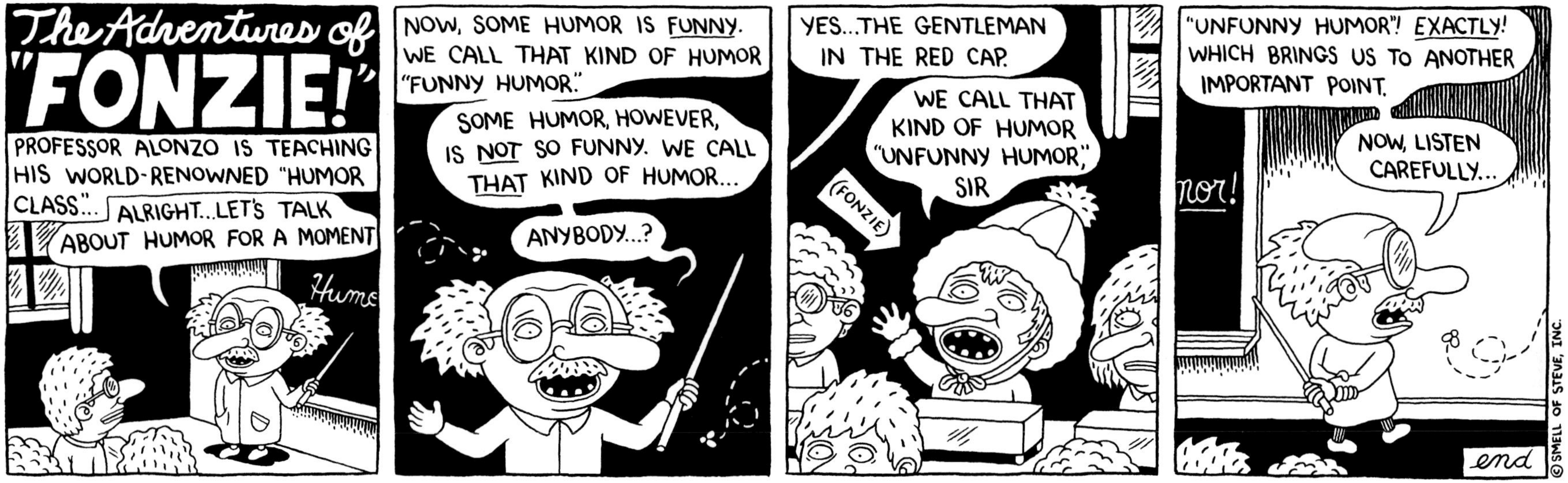
The Adventures of "FONZIE!"
PROFESSOR ALONZO IS TEACHING HIS WORLD-RENOWNED "HUMOR CLASS"...
ALRIGHT...LET'S TALK ABOUT HUMOR FOR A MOMENT
Hum
NOW, SOME HUMOR IS FUNNY. WE CALL THAT KIND OF HUMOR "FUNNY HUMOR."
SOME HUMOR, HOWEVER, IS NOT SO FUNNY. WE CALL THAT KIND OF HUMOR...
ANYBODY...?
YES...THE GENTLEMAN IN THE RED CAP.
WE CALL THAT KIND OF HUMOR "UNFUNNY HUMOR," SIR
(FONZIE)
"UNFUNNY HUMOR"! EXACTLY! WHICH BRINGS US TO ANOTHER IMPORTANT POINT.
NOW, LISTEN CAREFULLY...
mor!
end
©SMELL OF STEVE, INC.

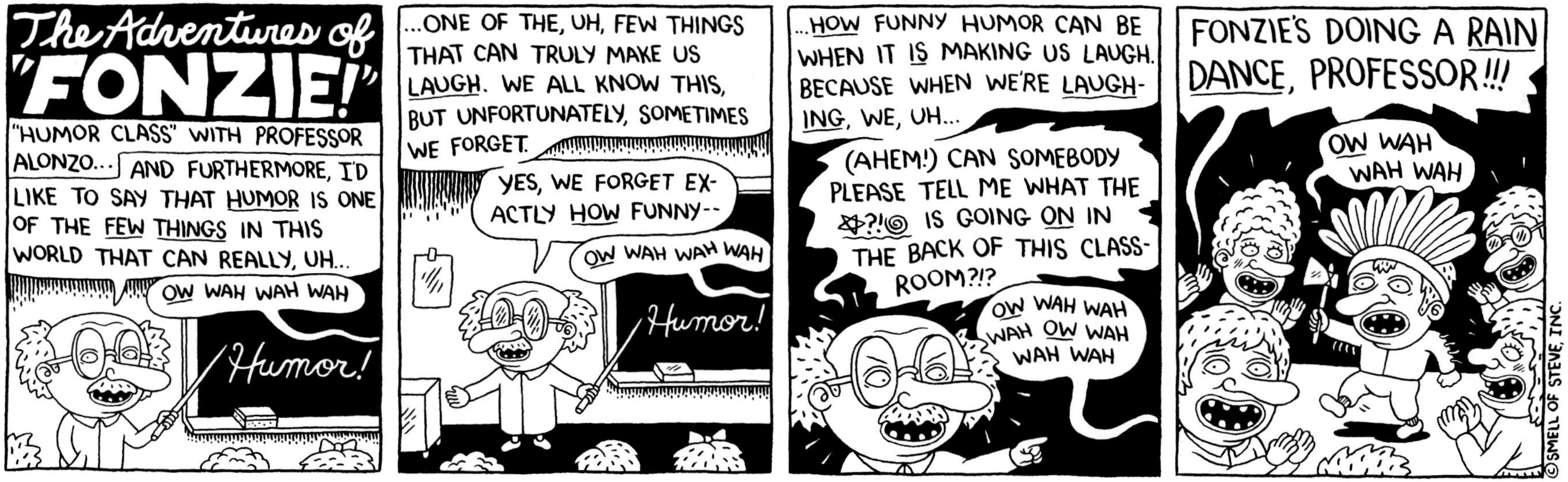
The Adventures of "FONZIE!"
"HUMOR CLASS" WITH PROFESSOR ALONZO...
AND FURTHERMORE, I'D LIKE TO SAY THAT HUMOR IS ONE OF THE FEW THINGS IN THIS WORLD THAT CAN REALLY, UH...
OW WAH WAH WAH
Humor!
...ONE OF THE, UH, FEW THINGS THAT CAN TRULY MAKE US LAUGH. WE ALL KNOW THIS, BUT UNFORTUNATELY, SOMETIMES WE FORGET.
YES, WE FORGET EXACTLY HOW FUNNY--
OW WAH WAH WAH
Humor!
...HOW FUNNY HUMOR CAN BE WHEN IT IS MAKING US LAUGH. BECAUSE WHEN WE'RE LAUGHING, WE, UH...
(AHEM!) CAN SOMEBODY PLEASE TELL ME WHAT THE ✡?!◎ IS GOING ON IN THE BACK OF THIS CLASSROOM?!?
OW WAH WAH WAH OW WAH WAH WAH
FONZIE'S DOING A RAIN DANCE, PROFESSOR!!!
OW WAH WAH WAH
©SMELL OF STEVE, INC.

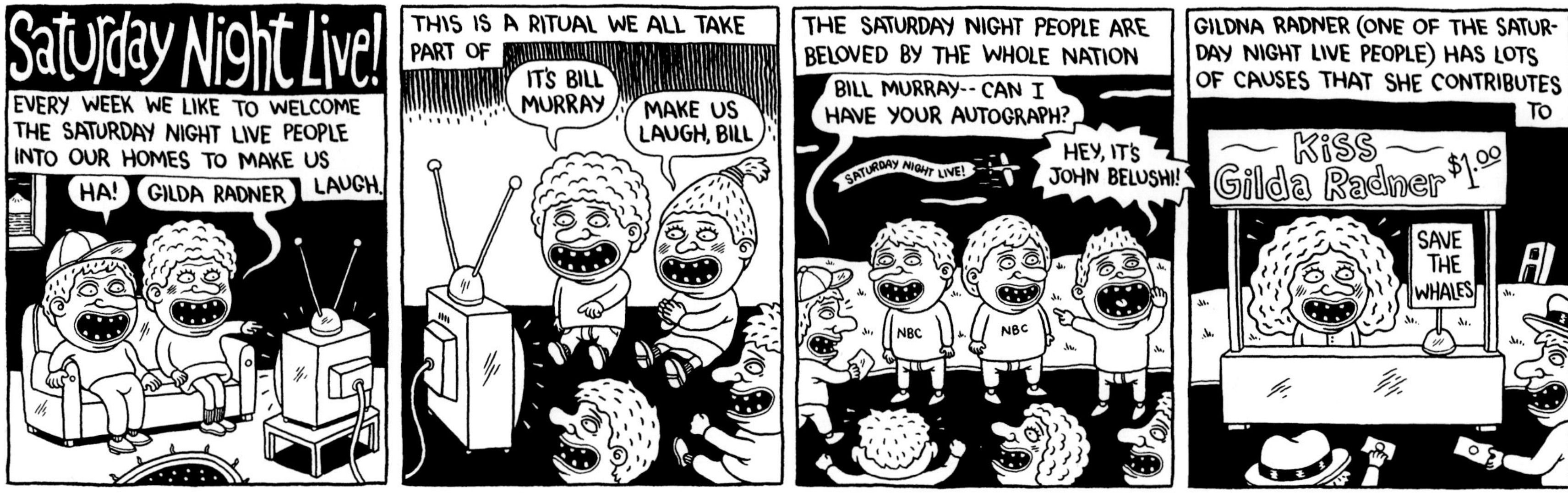
Saturday Night Live!
EVERY WEEK WE LIKE TO WELCOME THE SATURDAY NIGHT LIVE PEOPLE INTO OUR HOMES TO MAKE US LAUGH.
HA!
GILDA RADNER
THIS IS A RITUAL WE ALL TAKE PART OF
IT'S BILL MURRAY
MAKE US LAUGH, BILL
THE SATURDAY NIGHT PEOPLE ARE BELOVED BY THE WHOLE NATION
BILL MURRAY-- CAN I HAVE YOUR AUTOGRAPH?
SATURDAY NIGHT LIVE!
HEY, IT'S JOHN BELUSHI!
NBC
NBC
GILDNA RADNER (ONE OF THE SATURDAY NIGHT LIVE PEOPLE) HAS LOTS OF CAUSES THAT SHE CONTRIBUTES TO
KISS Gilda Radner $1.00
SAVE THE WHALES

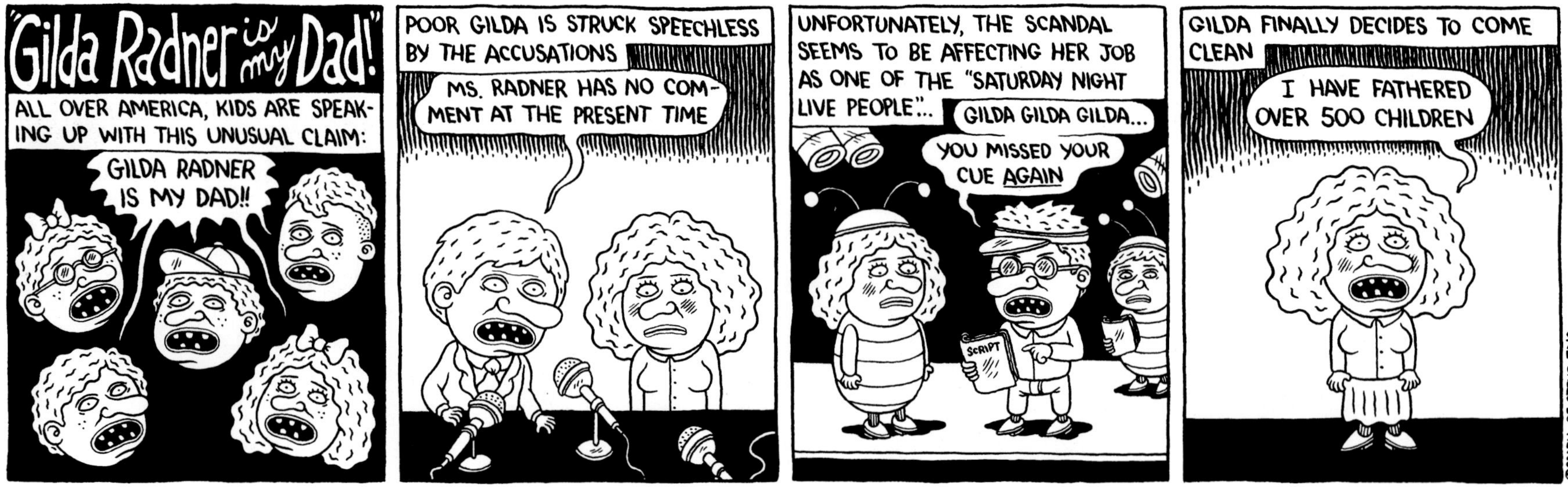
"Gilda Radner is my Dad!"
ALL OVER AMERICA, KIDS ARE SPEAKING UP WITH THIS UNUSUAL CLAIM:
GILDA RADNER IS MY DAD!!
POOR GILDA IS STRUCK SPEECHLESS BY THE ACCUSATIONS
MS. RADNER HAS NO COMMENT AT THE PRESENT TIME
UNFORTUNATELY, THE SCANDAL SEEMS TO BE AFFECTING HER JOB AS ONE OF THE "SATURDAY NIGHT LIVE PEOPLE"...
GILDA GILDA GILDA...
YOU MISSED YOUR CUE AGAIN
SCRIPT
GILDA FINALLY DECIDES TO COME CLEAN
I HAVE FATHERED OVER 500 CHILDREN

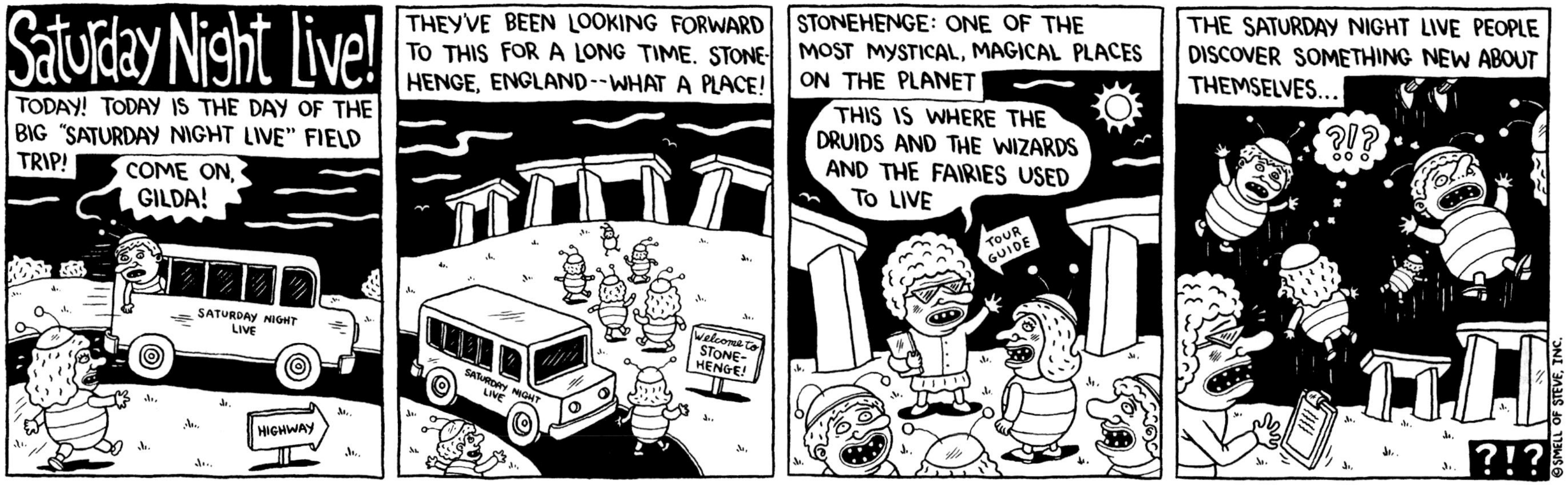
Saturday Night Live!
TODAY! TODAY IS THE DAY OF THE BIG "SATURDAY NIGHT LIVE" FIELD TRIP!
COME ON, GILDA!
SATURDAY NIGHT LIVE
HIGHWAY
THEY'VE BEEN LOOKING FORWARD TO THIS FOR A LONG TIME. STONEHENGE, ENGLAND--WHAT A PLACE!
SATURDAY NIGHT LIVE
Welcome to STONEHENGE!
STONEHENGE: ONE OF THE MOST MYSTICAL, MAGICAL PLACES ON THE PLANET
THIS IS WHERE THE DRUIDS AND THE WIZARDS AND THE FAIRIES USED TO LIVE
TOUR GUIDE
THE SATURDAY NIGHT LIVE PEOPLE DISCOVER SOMETHING NEW ABOUT THEMSELVES...
?!?
?!?
©SMELL OF STEVE, INC.

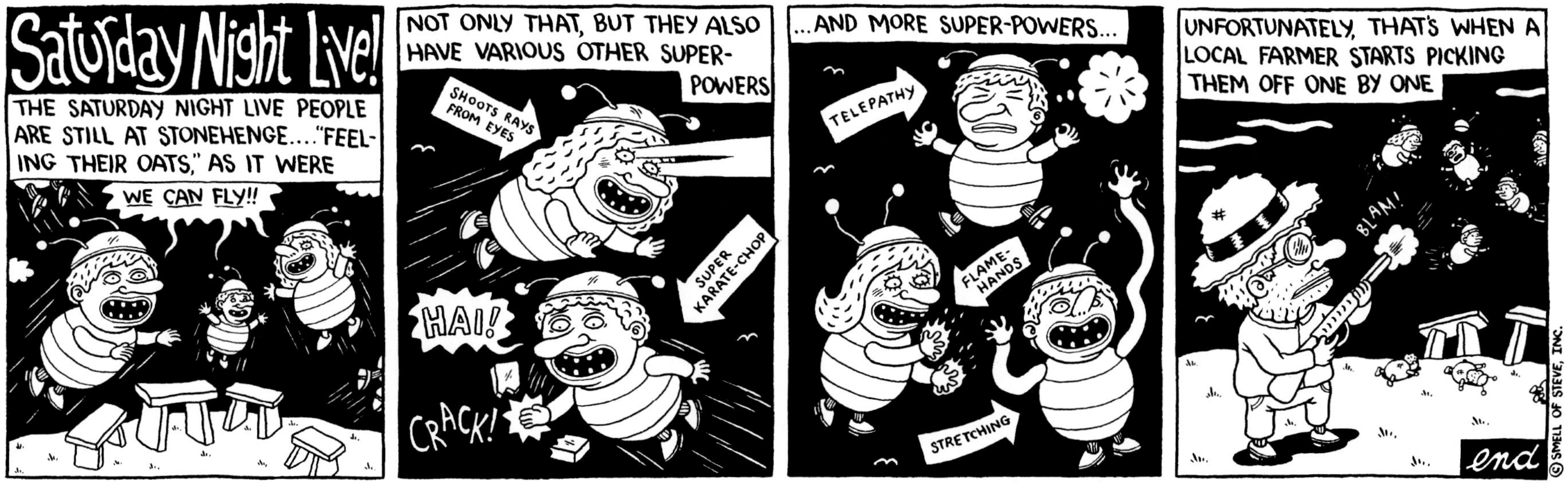
Saturday Night Live!
THE SATURDAY NIGHT LIVE PEOPLE ARE STILL AT STONEHENGE...."FEELING THEIR OATS," AS IT WERE
WE CAN FLY!!
NOT ONLY THAT, BUT THEY ALSO HAVE VARIOUS OTHER SUPER-POWERS
SHOOTS RAYS FROM EYES
SUPER KARATE-CHOP
HAI!
CRACK!
...AND MORE SUPER-POWERS...
TELEPATHY
FLAME-HANDS
STRETCHING
UNFORTUNATELY, THAT'S WHEN A LOCAL FARMER STARTS PICKING THEM OFF ONE BY ONE
BLAM!
end
©SMELL OF STEVE, INC.

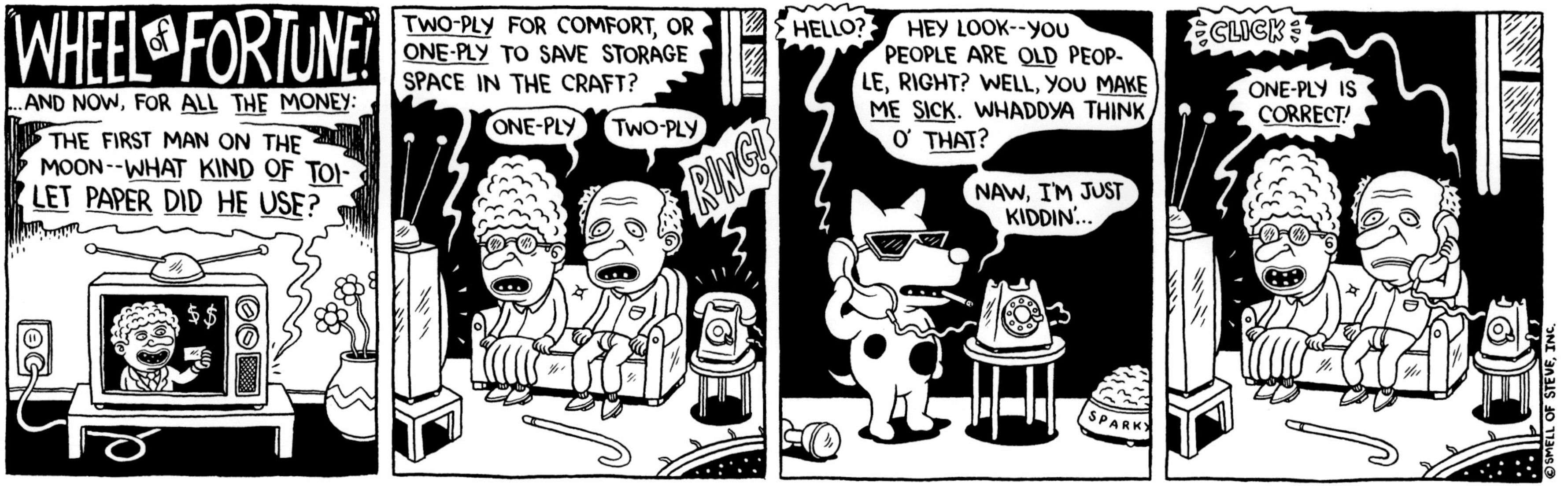
"WHEEL of FORTUNE!"
...AND NOW, FOR ALL THE MONEY:
THE FIRST MAN ON THE MOON--WHAT KIND OF TOI-LET PAPER DID HE USE?
TWO-PLY FOR COMFORT, OR ONE-PLY TO SAVE STORAGE SPACE IN THE CRAFT?
ONE-PLY
TWO-PLY
RING!
HELLO?
HEY LOOK--YOU PEOPLE ARE OLD PEOP-LE, RIGHT? WELL, YOU MAKE ME SICK. WHADDYA THINK O' THAT?
NAW, I'M JUST KIDDIN'...
SPARKY
CLICK
ONE-PLY IS CORRECT!
©SMELL OF STEVE, INC.

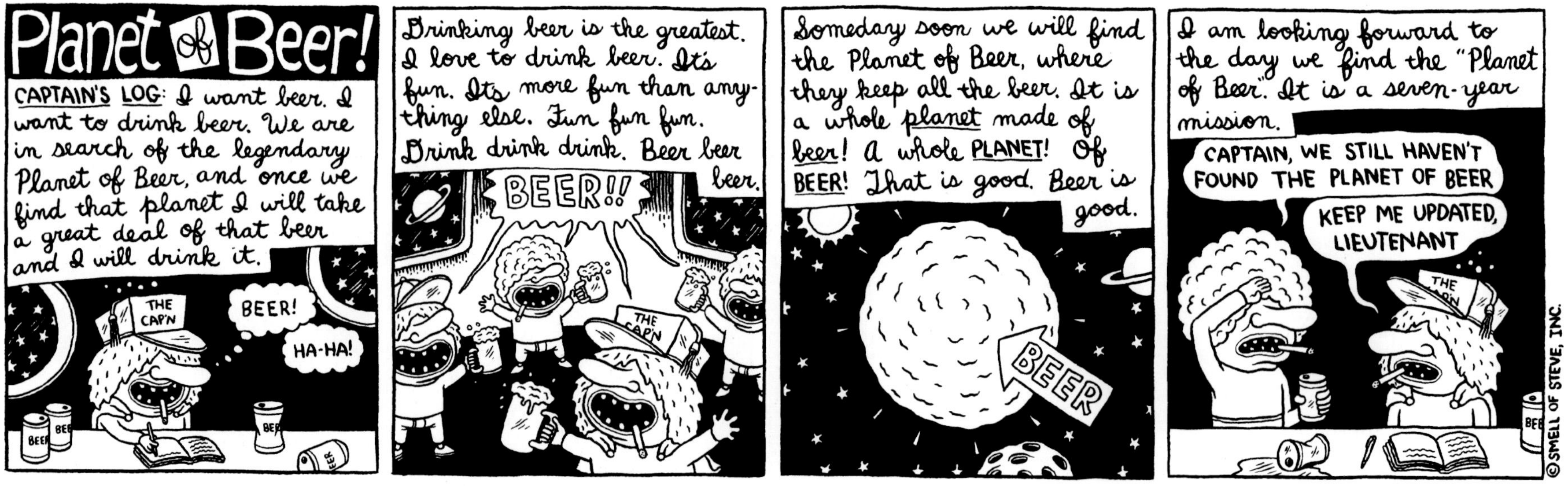
Planet of Beer!
CAPTAIN'S LOG: I want beer. I want to drink beer. We are in search of the legendary Planet of Beer, and once we find that planet I will take a great deal of that beer and I will drink it.
THE CAP'N
BEER!
HA-HA!
Drinking beer is the greatest. I love to drink beer. It's fun. It's more fun than any-thing else. Fun fun fun. Drink drink drink. Beer beer beer.
BEER!!
THE CAP'N
Someday soon we will find the Planet of Beer, where they keep all the beer. It is a whole planet made of beer! A whole PLANET! Of BEER! That is good. Beer is good.
BEER
I am looking forward to the day we find the "Planet of Beer". It is a seven-year mission.
CAPTAIN, WE STILL HAVEN'T FOUND THE PLANET OF BEER
KEEP ME UPDATED, LIEUTENANT
©SMELL OF STEVE, INC.

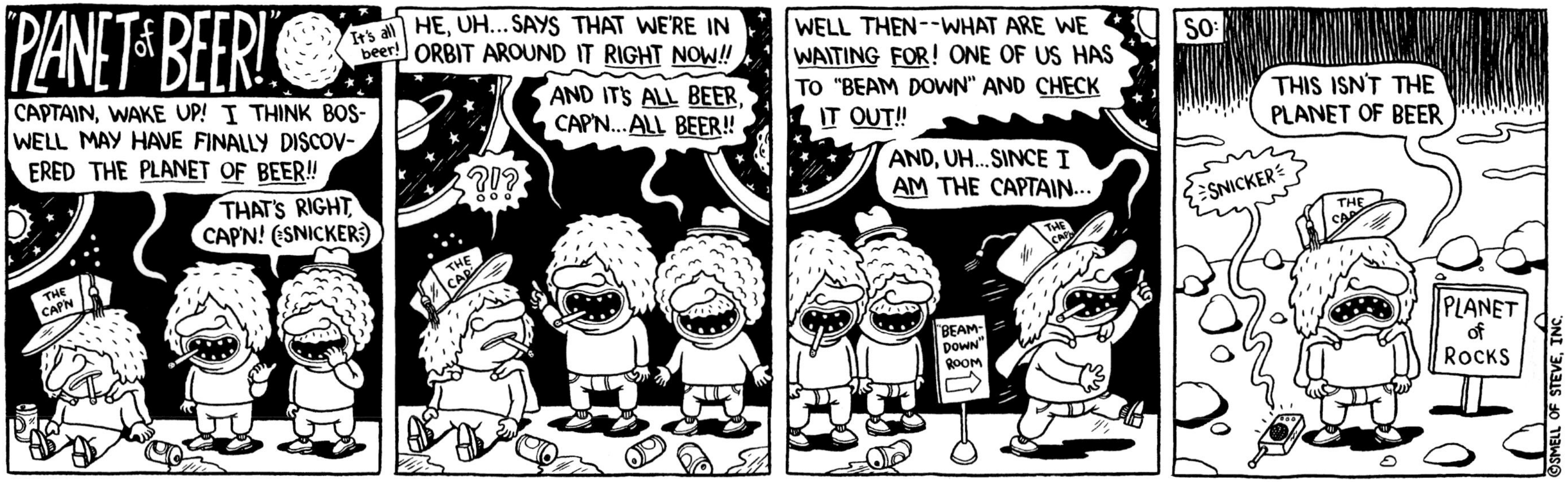
"PLANET of BEER!"
It's all beer!
CAPTAIN, WAKE UP! I THINK BOSWELL MAY HAVE FINALLY DISCOVERED THE PLANET OF BEER!!
THE CAP'N
THAT'S RIGHT, CAP'N! (SNICKER)
HE, UH...SAYS THAT WE'RE IN ORBIT AROUND IT RIGHT NOW!!
AND IT'S ALL BEER, CAP'N...ALL BEER!!
?!?
THE CAP'N
WELL THEN--WHAT ARE WE WAITING FOR! ONE OF US HAS TO "BEAM DOWN" AND CHECK IT OUT!!
AND, UH...SINCE I AM THE CAPTAIN...
THE CAP'N
"BEAM-DOWN" ROOM
SO:
THIS ISN'T THE PLANET OF BEER
SNICKER
THE CAP'N
PLANET of ROCKS
©SMELL OF STEVE, INC.

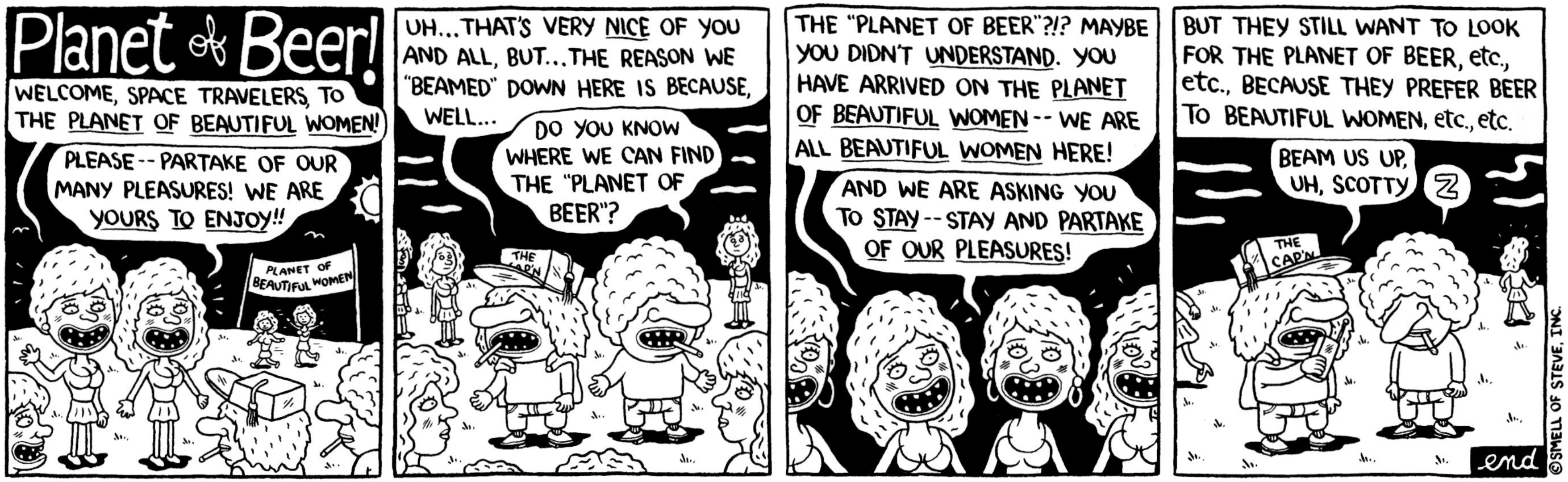
Planet of Beer!
WELCOME, SPACE TRAVELERS, TO THE PLANET OF BEAUTIFUL WOMEN!
PLEASE--PARTAKE OF OUR MANY PLEASURES! WE ARE YOURS TO ENJOY!!
PLANET OF BEAUTIFUL WOMEN
UH...THAT'S VERY NICE OF YOU AND ALL, BUT...THE REASON WE "BEAMED" DOWN HERE IS BECAUSE, WELL...
DO YOU KNOW WHERE WE CAN FIND THE "PLANET OF BEER"?
THE CAP'N
THE "PLANET OF BEER"?!? MAYBE YOU DIDN'T UNDERSTAND. YOU HAVE ARRIVED ON THE PLANET OF BEAUTIFUL WOMEN--WE ARE ALL BEAUTIFUL WOMEN HERE!
AND WE ARE ASKING YOU TO STAY--STAY AND PARTAKE OF OUR PLEASURES!
BUT THEY STILL WANT TO LOOK FOR THE PLANET OF BEER, etc., etc., BECAUSE THEY PREFER BEER TO BEAUTIFUL WOMEN, etc., etc.
BEAM US UP, UH, SCOTTY
Z
THE CAP'N
end
©SMELL OF STEVE, INC.

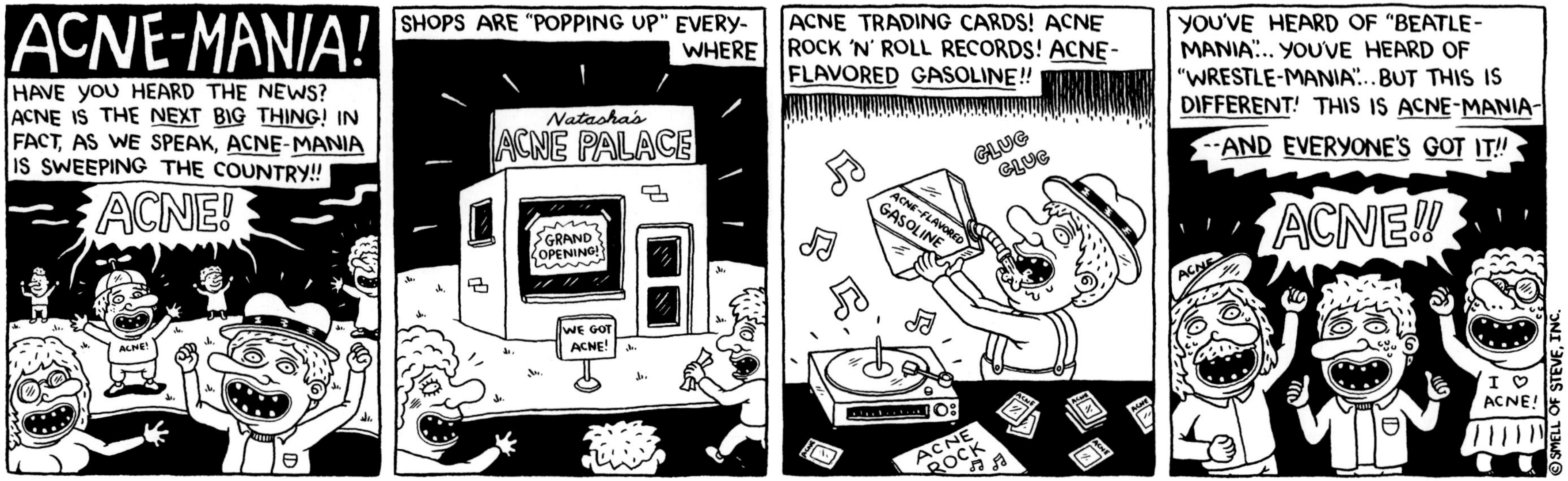
ACNE-MANIA!
HAVE YOU HEARD THE NEWS? ACNE IS THE NEXT BIG THING! IN FACT, AS WE SPEAK, ACNE-MANIA IS SWEEPING THE COUNTRY!!
ACNE!
ACNE!
SHOPS ARE "POPPING UP" EVERYWHERE
Natasha's ACNE PALACE
GRAND OPENING!
WE GOT ACNE!
ACNE TRADING CARDS! ACNE ROCK 'N' ROLL RECORDS! ACNE-FLAVORED GASOLINE!!
GLUG GLUG
ACNE-FLAVORED GASOLINE
ACNE ROCK
YOU'VE HEARD OF "BEATLE-MANIA"... YOU'VE HEARD OF "WRESTLE-MANIA"... BUT THIS IS DIFFERENT! THIS IS ACNE-MANIA-
--AND EVERYONE'S GOT IT!!
ACNE!!
ACNE
I ♡ ACNE!
© SMELL OF STEVE, INC.

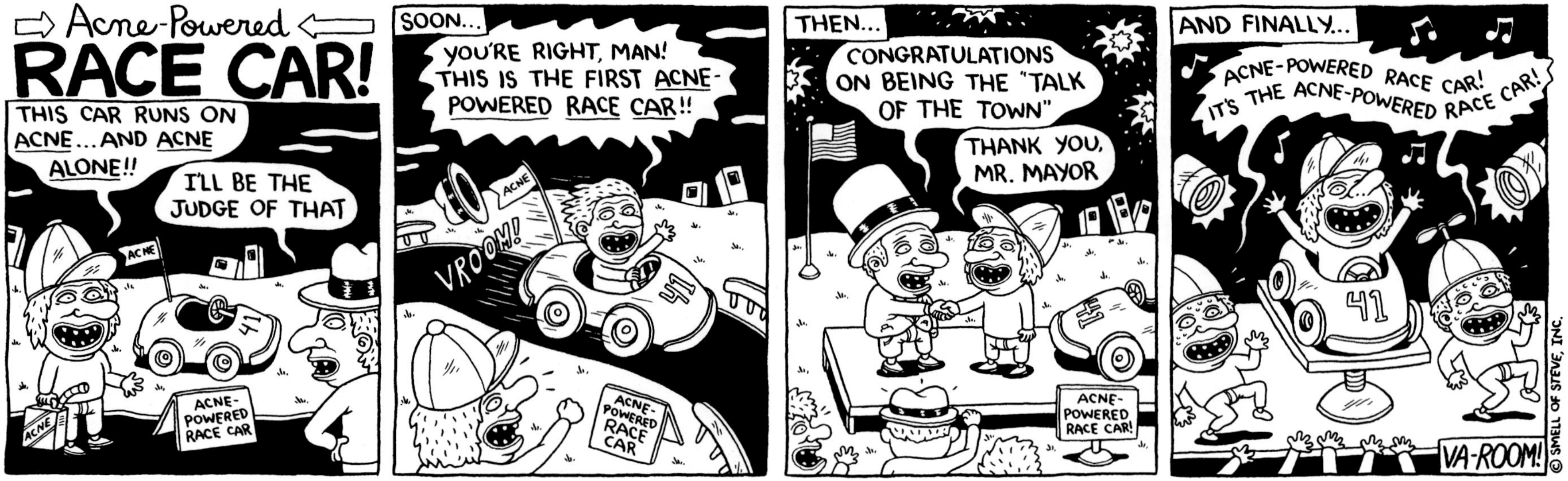
Acne-Powered RACE CAR!
THIS CAR RUNS ON ACNE... AND ACNE ALONE!!
I'LL BE THE JUDGE OF THAT
ACNE
ACNE
41
ACNE-POWERED RACE CAR
SOON...
YOU'RE RIGHT, MAN! THIS IS THE FIRST ACNE-POWERED RACE CAR!!
ACNE
VROOM!
41
ACNE-POWERED RACE CAR
THEN...
CONGRATULATIONS ON BEING THE "TALK OF THE TOWN"
THANK YOU, MR. MAYOR
ACNE-POWERED RACE CAR!
AND FINALLY...
ACNE-POWERED RACE CAR! IT'S THE ACNE-POWERED RACE CAR!
41
VA-ROOM!
© SMELL OF STEVE, INC.

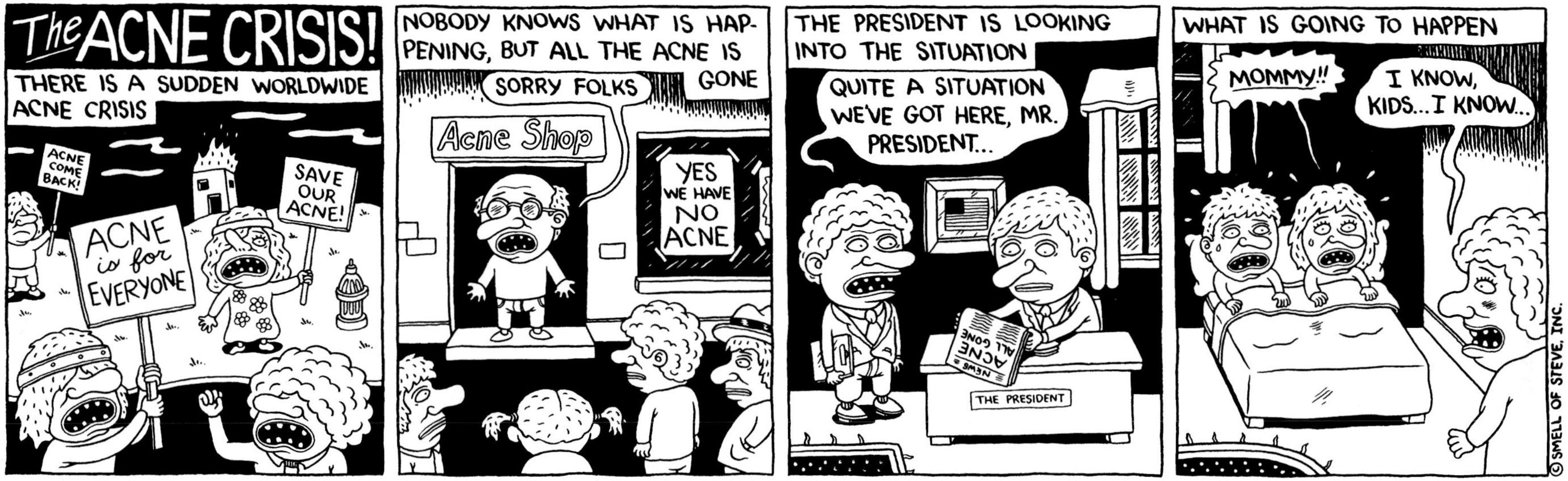
The ACNE CRISIS!
THERE IS A SUDDEN WORLDWIDE ACNE CRISIS
ACNE COME BACK!
SAVE OUR ACNE!
ACNE is for EVERYONE
NOBODY KNOWS WHAT IS HAPPENING, BUT ALL THE ACNE IS GONE
SORRY FOLKS
Acne Shop
YES WE HAVE NO ACNE
THE PRESIDENT IS LOOKING INTO THE SITUATION
QUITE A SITUATION WE'VE GOT HERE, MR. PRESIDENT...
NEWS ACNE ALL GONE
THE PRESIDENT
WHAT IS GOING TO HAPPEN
MOMMY!!
I KNOW, KIDS... I KNOW...
©SMELL OF STEVE, INC.

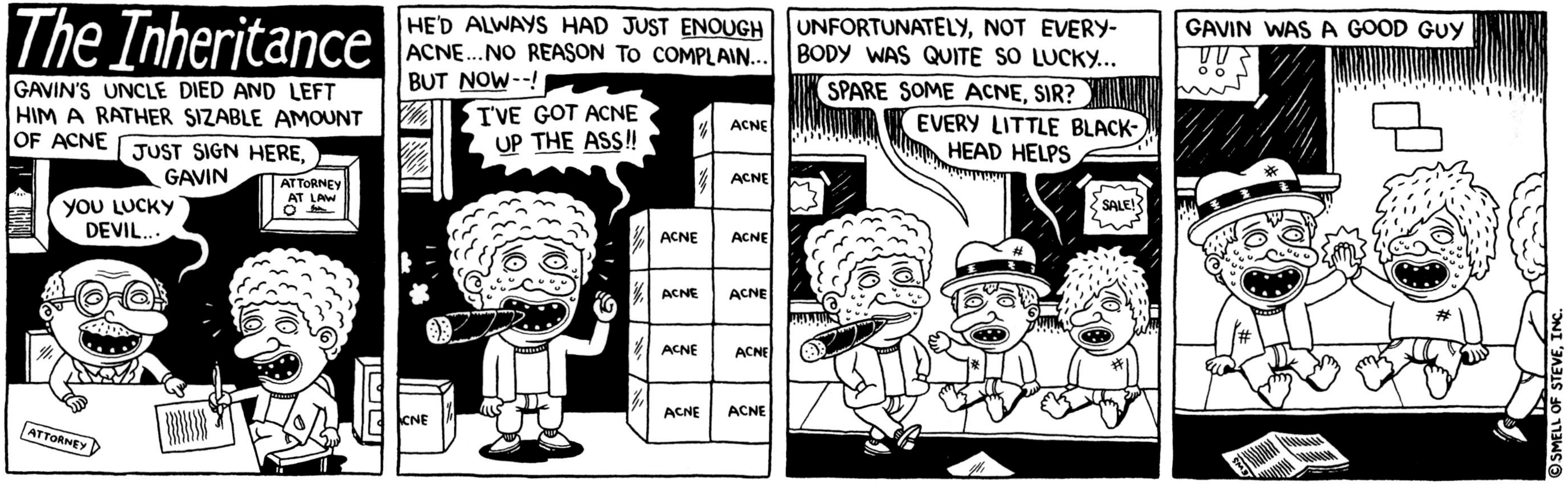
The Inheritance
GAVIN'S UNCLE DIED AND LEFT HIM A RATHER SIZABLE AMOUNT OF ACNE
JUST SIGN HERE, GAVIN
YOU LUCKY DEVIL...
ATTORNEY AT LAW
ATTORNEY
HE'D ALWAYS HAD JUST ENOUGH ACNE... NO REASON TO COMPLAIN... BUT NOW--!
I'VE GOT ACNE UP THE ASS!!
ACNE
UNFORTUNATELY, NOT EVERYBODY WAS QUITE SO LUCKY...
SPARE SOME ACNE, SIR?
EVERY LITTLE BLACKHEAD HELPS
SALE!
GAVIN WAS A GOOD GUY
©SMELL OF STEVE, INC.

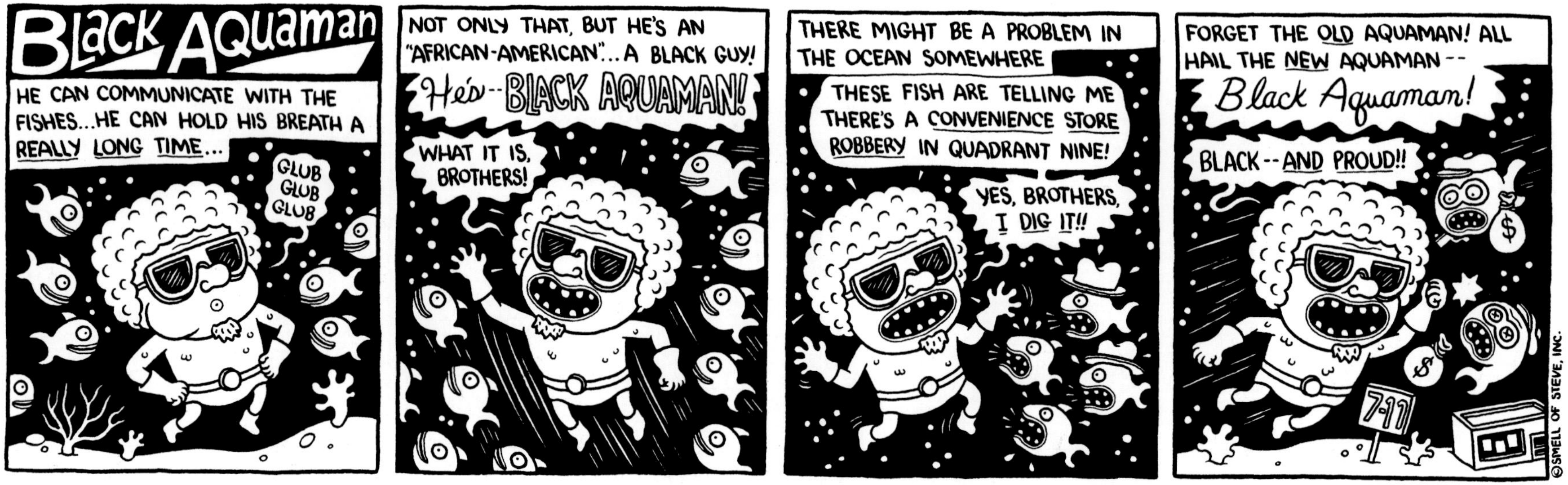
Black Aquaman
HE CAN COMMUNICATE WITH THE FISHES...HE CAN HOLD HIS BREATH A REALLY LONG TIME...
GLUB GLUB GLUB
NOT ONLY THAT, BUT HE'S AN "AFRICAN-AMERICAN"... A BLACK GUY!
He's--BLACK AQUAMAN!
WHAT IT IS, BROTHERS!
THERE MIGHT BE A PROBLEM IN THE OCEAN SOMEWHERE
THESE FISH ARE TELLING ME THERE'S A CONVENIENCE STORE ROBBERY IN QUADRANT NINE!
YES, BROTHERS, I DIG IT!!
FORGET THE OLD AQUAMAN! ALL HAIL THE NEW AQUAMAN--
Black Aquaman!
BLACK--AND PROUD!!
7-11
©SMELL OF STEVE, INC.

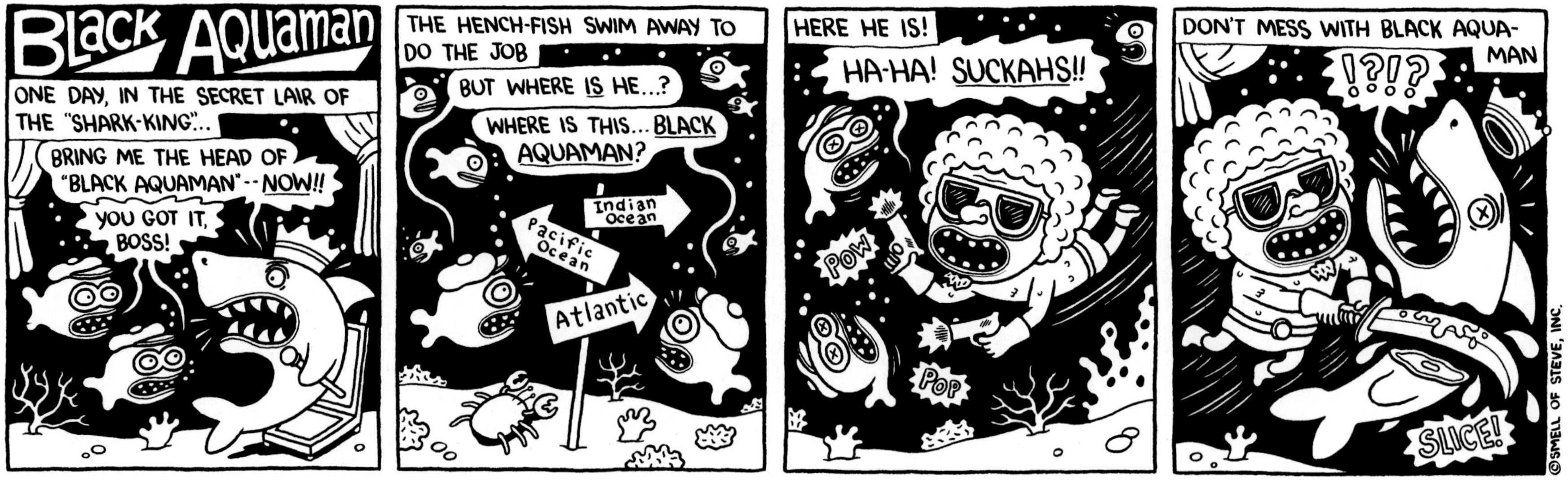
Black Aquaman
ONE DAY, IN THE SECRET LAIR OF THE "SHARK-KING"...
BRING ME THE HEAD OF "BLACK AQUAMAN"--NOW!!
YOU GOT IT, BOSS!
THE HENCH-FISH SWIM AWAY TO DO THE JOB
BUT WHERE IS HE...?
WHERE IS THIS... BLACK AQUAMAN?
Indian Ocean
Pacific Ocean
Atlantic
HERE HE IS!
HA-HA! SUCKAHS!!
POW
POP
DON'T MESS WITH BLACK AQUA-MAN
!?!?
SLICE!
©SMELL OF STEVE, INC.

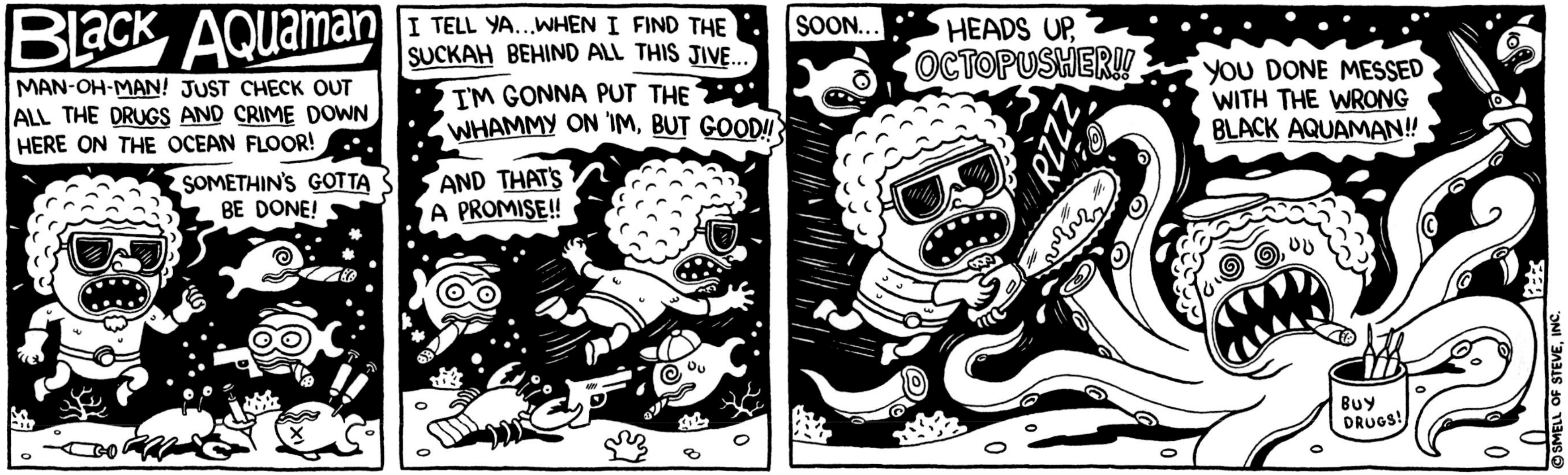
Black Aquaman
MAN-OH-MAN! JUST CHECK OUT ALL THE DRUGS AND CRIME DOWN HERE ON THE OCEAN FLOOR!
SOMETHIN'S GOTTA BE DONE!
I TELL YA...WHEN I FIND THE SUCKAH BEHIND ALL THIS JIVE...
I'M GONNA PUT THE WHAMMY ON 'IM, BUT GOOD!!
AND THAT'S A PROMISE!!
SOON...
HEADS UP, OCTOPUSHER!!
RZZZ
YOU DONE MESSED WITH THE WRONG BLACK AQUAMAN!!
BUY DRUGS!
©SMELL OF STEVE, INC.

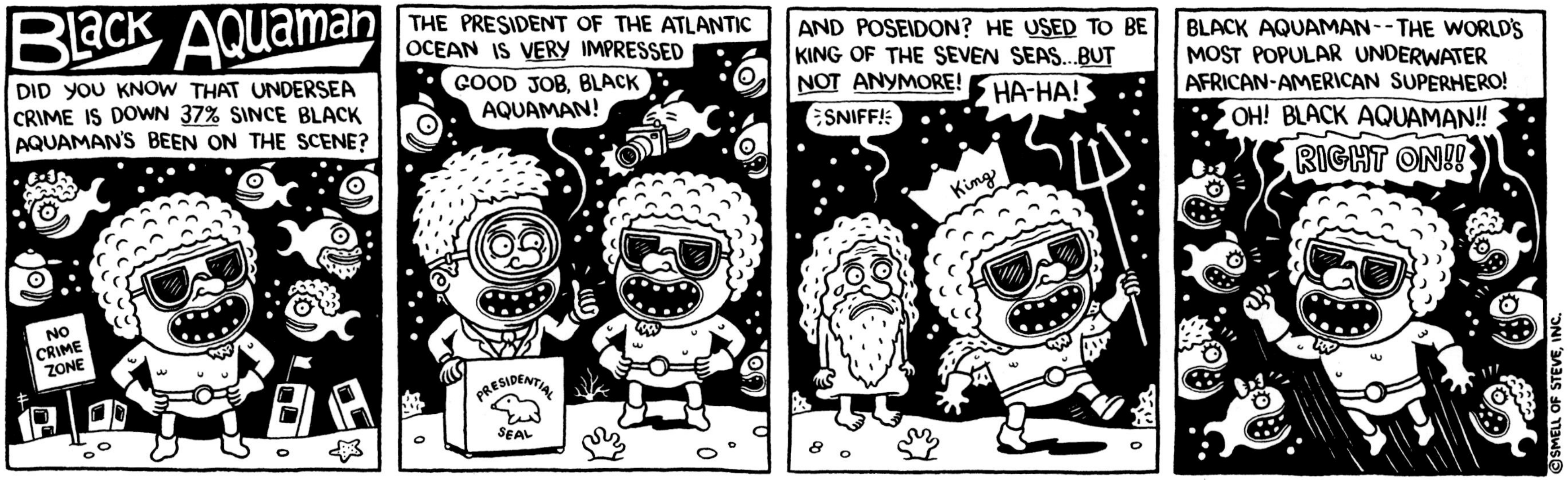
Black Aquaman
DID YOU KNOW THAT UNDERSEA CRIME IS DOWN 37% SINCE BLACK AQUAMAN'S BEEN ON THE SCENE?
NO CRIME ZONE
THE PRESIDENT OF THE ATLANTIC OCEAN IS VERY IMPRESSED
GOOD JOB, BLACK AQUAMAN!
PRESIDENTIAL SEAL
AND POSEIDON? HE USED TO BE KING OF THE SEVEN SEAS...BUT NOT ANYMORE!
HA-HA!
SNIFF!
King
BLACK AQUAMAN--THE WORLD'S MOST POPULAR UNDERWATER AFRICAN-AMERICAN SUPERHERO!
OH! BLACK AQUAMAN!!
RIGHT ON!!
©SMELL OF STEVE, INC.

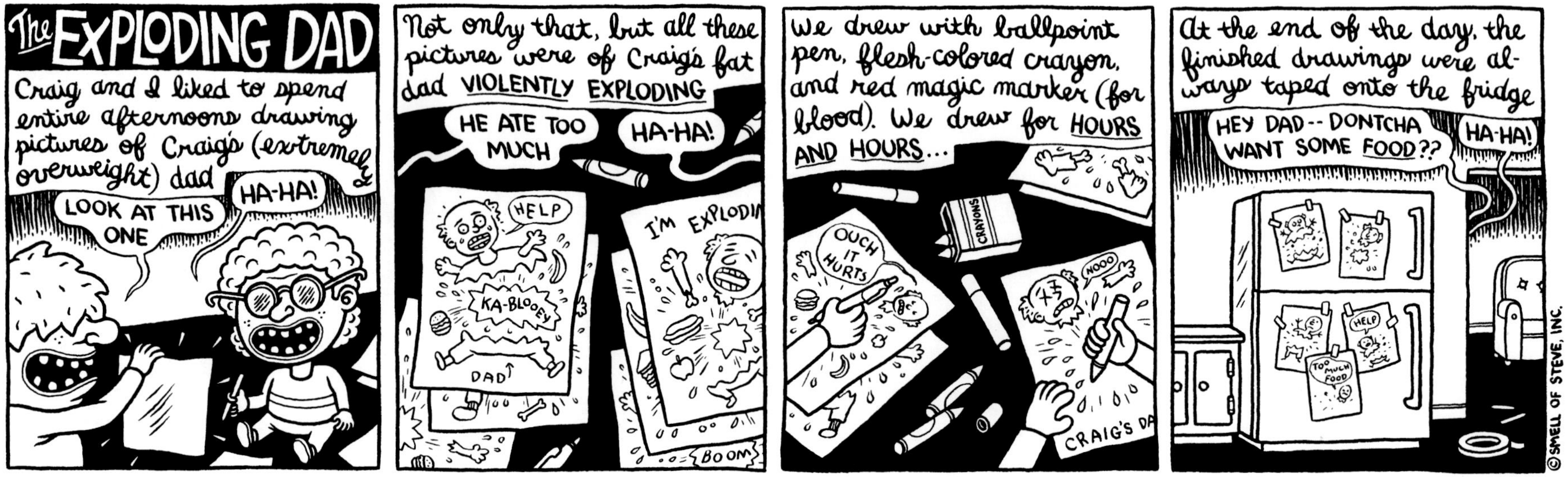
The EXPLODING DAD
Craig and I liked to spend entire afternoons drawing pictures of Craig's (extremely overweight) dad
LOOK AT THIS ONE
HA-HA!
Not only that, but all these pictures were of Craig's fat dad VIOLENTLY EXPLODING
HE ATE TOO MUCH
HA-HA!
HELP
KA-BLOOEY
DAD
BOOM
We drew with ballpoint pen, flesh-colored crayon, and red magic marker (for blood). We drew for HOURS AND HOURS...
OUCH IT HURTS
CRAYONS
NOOO
At the end of the day, the finished drawings were always taped onto the fridge
HEY DAD -- DONTCHA WANT SOME FOOD??
HA-HA!
HELP
TOO MUCH FOOD
©SMELL OF STEVE, INC.

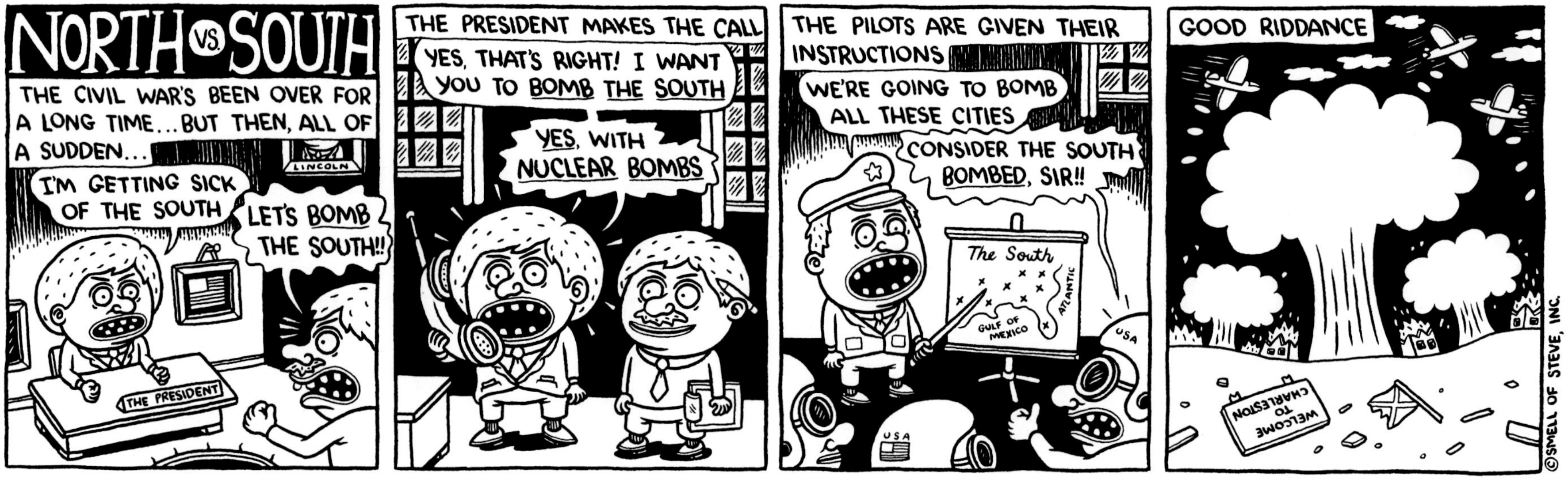
NORTH VS. SOUTH
THE CIVIL WAR'S BEEN OVER FOR A LONG TIME... BUT THEN, ALL OF A SUDDEN...
LINCOLN
I'M GETTING SICK OF THE SOUTH
LET'S BOMB THE SOUTH!!
THE PRESIDENT
THE PRESIDENT MAKES THE CALL
YES, THAT'S RIGHT! I WANT YOU TO BOMB THE SOUTH
YES, WITH NUCLEAR BOMBS
THE PILOTS ARE GIVEN THEIR INSTRUCTIONS
WE'RE GOING TO BOMB ALL THESE CITIES
CONSIDER THE SOUTH BOMBED, SIR!!
The South
GULF OF MEXICO
ATLANTIC
USA
GOOD RIDDANCE
WELCOME TO CHARLESTON
©SMELL OF STEVE, INC.

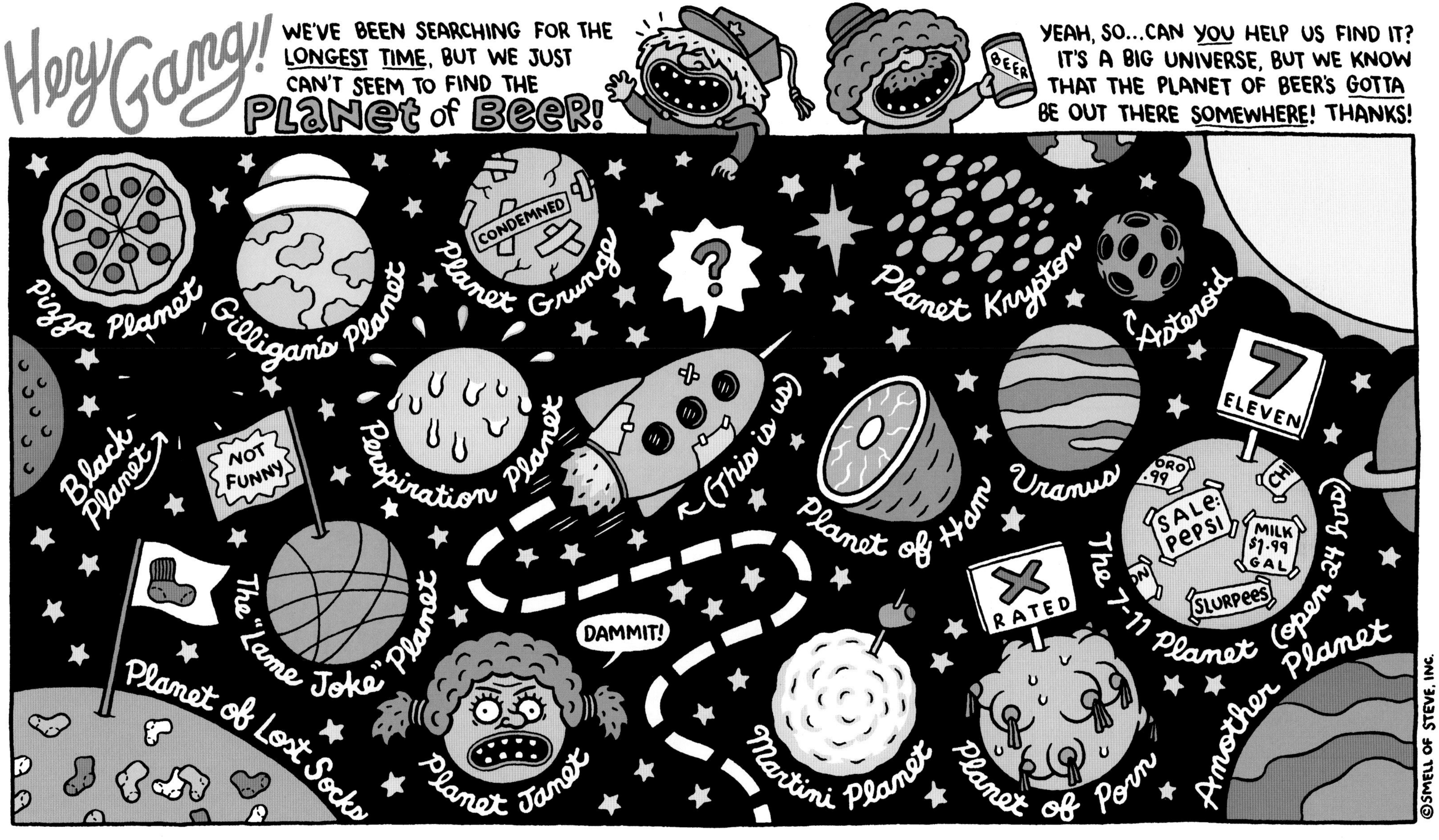
Hey Gang!
WE'VE BEEN SEARCHING FOR THE LONGEST TIME, BUT WE JUST CAN'T SEEM TO FIND THE PLANET of BEER!
YEAH, SO...CAN YOU HELP US FIND IT? IT'S A BIG UNIVERSE, BUT WE KNOW THAT THE PLANET OF BEER'S GOTTA BE OUT THERE SOMEWHERE! THANKS!
BEER
Pizza Planet
Gilligan's Planet
CONDEMNED
Planet Grunge
?
Planet Krypton
Asteroid
Black Planet
NOT FUNNY
Perspiration Planet
(This is us)
Planet of Ham
Uranus
7 ELEVEN
SALE: PEPSI
MILK $1.99 GAL
SLURPEES
The 7-11 Planet (open 24 hrs)
The "Lame Joke" Planet
DAMMIT!
X RATED
Planet of Lost Socks
Planet Janet
Martini Planet
Planet of Porn
Another Planet
©SMELL OF STEVE, INC.

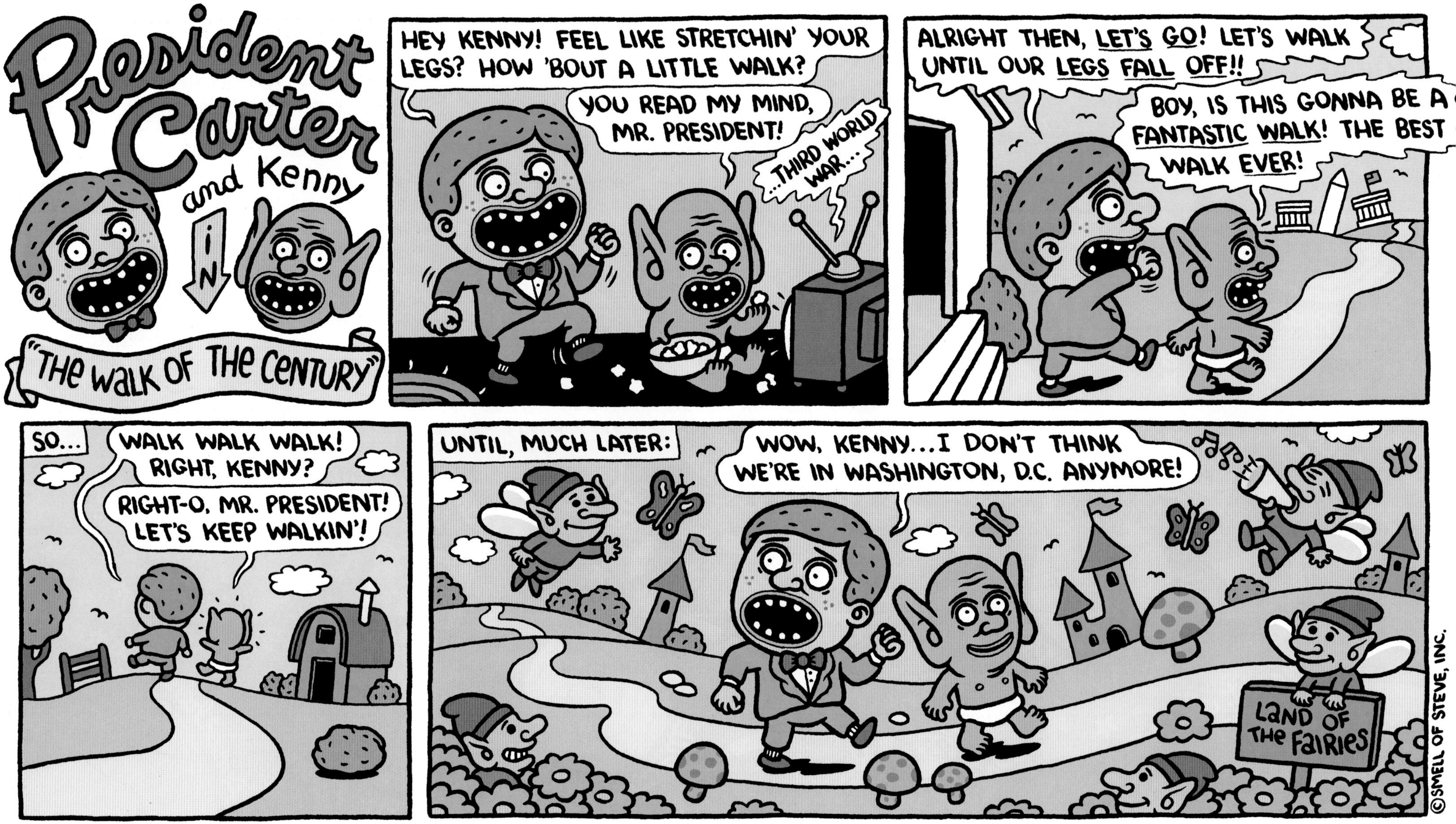
President Carter and Kenny in
"The Walk of the Century"
HEY KENNY! FEEL LIKE STRETCHIN' YOUR LEGS? HOW 'BOUT A LITTLE WALK?
YOU READ MY MIND, MR. PRESIDENT!
...THIRD WORLD WAR...
ALRIGHT THEN, LET'S GO! LET'S WALK UNTIL OUR LEGS FALL OFF!!
BOY, IS THIS GONNA BE A FANTASTIC WALK! THE BEST WALK EVER!
SO...
WALK WALK WALK! RIGHT, KENNY?
RIGHT-O, MR. PRESIDENT! LET'S KEEP WALKIN'!
UNTIL, MUCH LATER:
WOW, KENNY...I DON'T THINK WE'RE IN WASHINGTON, D.C. ANYMORE!
LAND OF THE FAIRIES
©SMELL OF STEVE, INC.

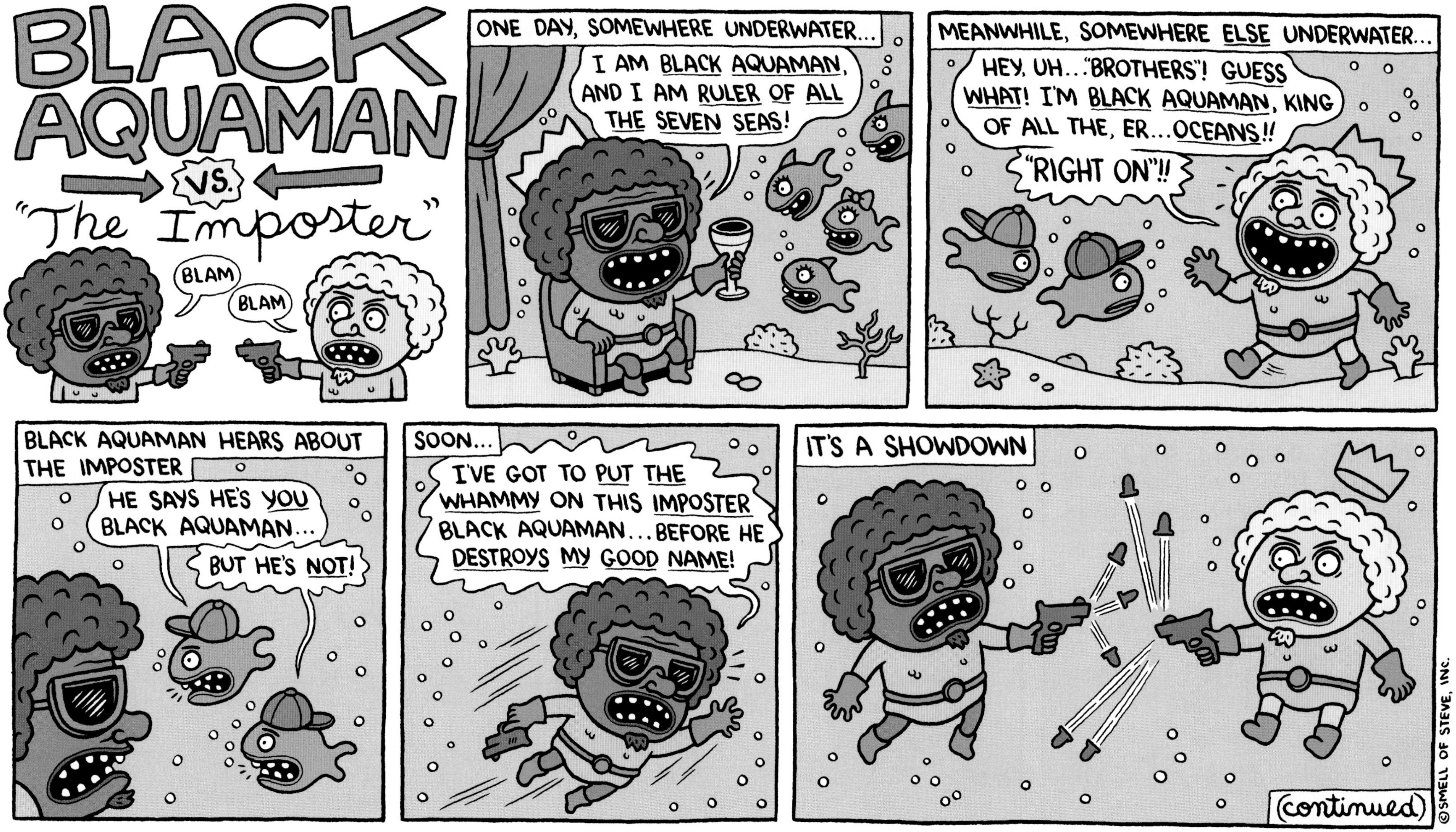
BLACK AQUAMAN
VS.
"The Imposter"
BLAM
BLAM
ONE DAY, SOMEWHERE UNDERWATER...
I AM BLACK AQUAMAN, AND I AM RULER OF ALL THE SEVEN SEAS!
MEANWHILE, SOMEWHERE ELSE UNDERWATER...
HEY, UH..."BROTHERS"! GUESS WHAT! I'M BLACK AQUAMAN, KING OF ALL THE, ER...OCEANS!!
"RIGHT ON"!!
BLACK AQUAMAN HEARS ABOUT THE IMPOSTER
HE SAYS HE'S YOU BLACK AQUAMAN...
BUT HE'S NOT!
SOON...
I'VE GOT TO PUT THE WHAMMY ON THIS IMPOSTER BLACK AQUAMAN...BEFORE HE DESTROYS MY GOOD NAME!
IT'S A SHOWDOWN
(continued)
©SMELL OF STEVE, INC.

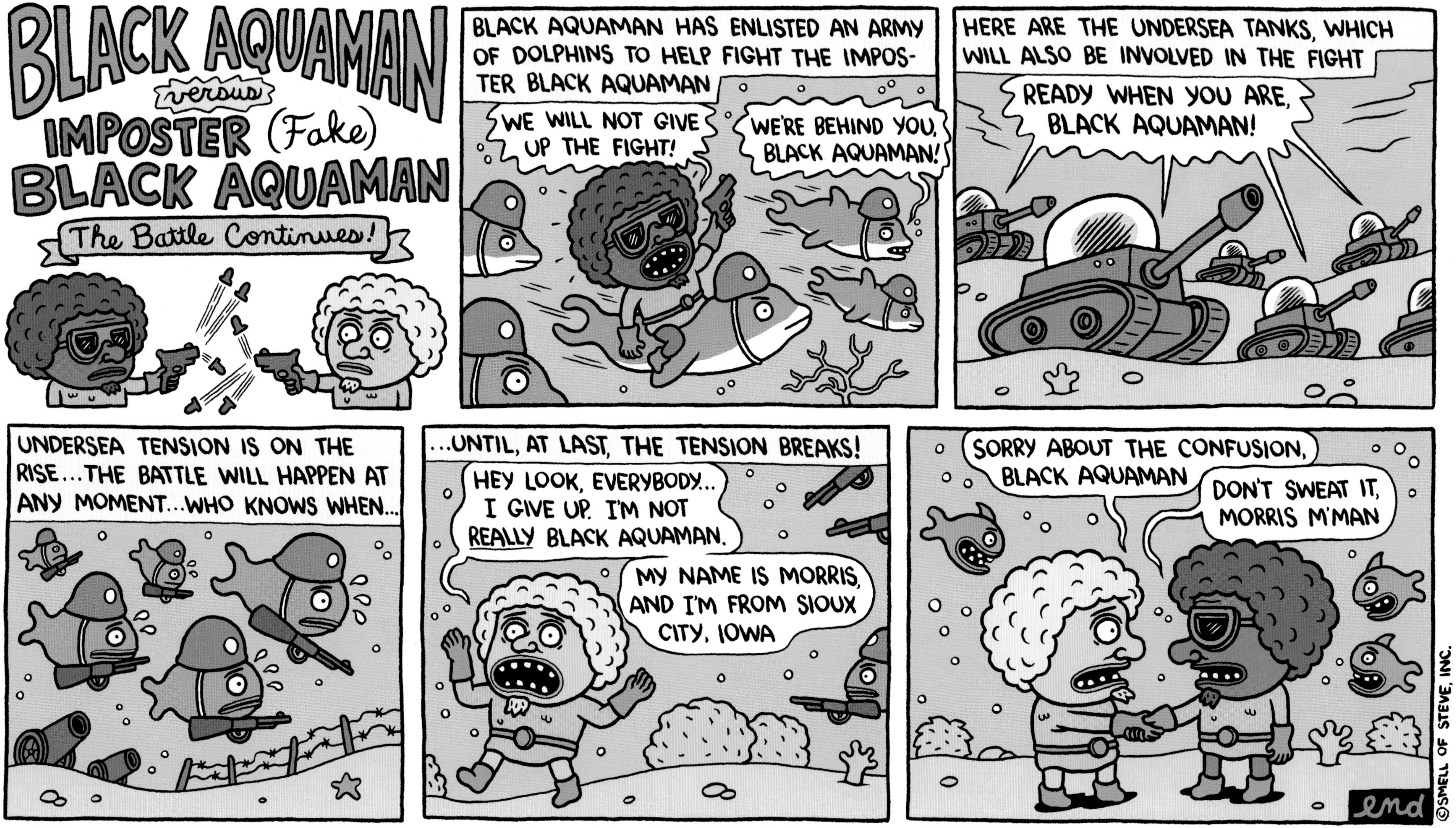
BLACK AQUAMAN
versus
IMPOSTER (Fake) BLACK AQUAMAN
The Battle Continues!
BLACK AQUAMAN HAS ENLISTED AN ARMY OF DOLPHINS TO HELP FIGHT THE IMPOSTER BLACK AQUAMAN
WE WILL NOT GIVE UP THE FIGHT!
WE'RE BEHIND YOU, BLACK AQUAMAN!
HERE ARE THE UNDERSEA TANKS, WHICH WILL ALSO BE INVOLVED IN THE FIGHT
READY WHEN YOU ARE, BLACK AQUAMAN!
UNDERSEA TENSION IS ON THE RISE...THE BATTLE WILL HAPPEN AT ANY MOMENT...WHO KNOWS WHEN...
...UNTIL, AT LAST, THE TENSION BREAKS!
HEY LOOK, EVERYBODY... I GIVE UP. I'M NOT REALLY BLACK AQUAMAN.
MY NAME IS MORRIS, AND I'M FROM SIOUX CITY, IOWA
SORRY ABOUT THE CONFUSION, BLACK AQUAMAN
DON'T SWEAT IT, MORRIS M'MAN
end
©SMELL OF STEVE, INC.

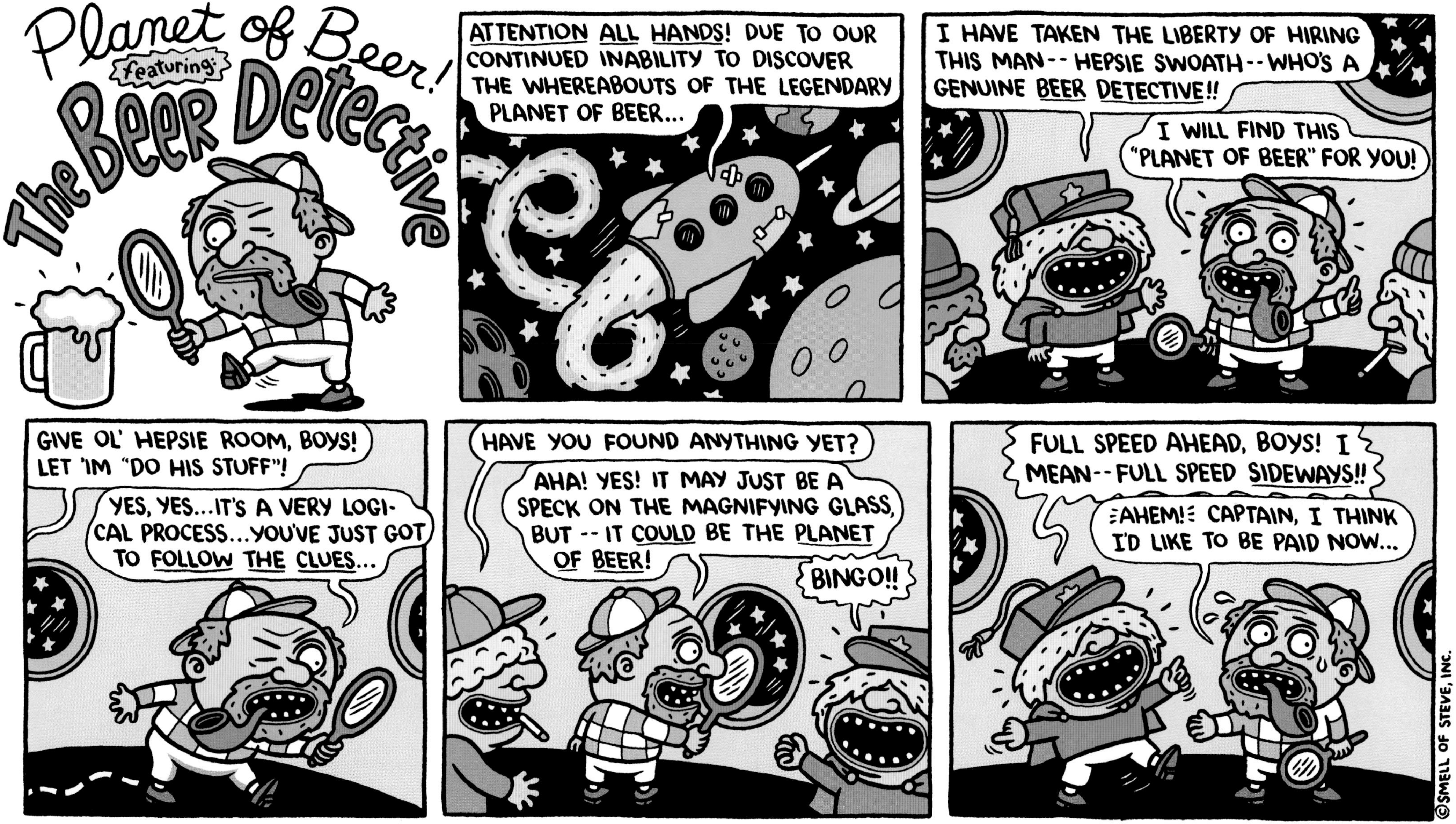
Planet of Beer!
featuring:
The Beer Detective
ATTENTION ALL HANDS! DUE TO OUR CONTINUED INABILITY TO DISCOVER THE WHEREABOUTS OF THE LEGENDARY PLANET OF BEER...
I HAVE TAKEN THE LIBERTY OF HIRING THIS MAN-- HEPSIE SWOATH--WHO'S A GENUINE BEER DETECTIVE!!
I WILL FIND THIS "PLANET OF BEER" FOR YOU!
GIVE OL' HEPSIE ROOM, BOYS! LET 'IM "DO HIS STUFF"!
YES, YES...IT'S A VERY LOGI-CAL PROCESS...YOU'VE JUST GOT TO FOLLOW THE CLUES...
HAVE YOU FOUND ANYTHING YET?
AHA! YES! IT MAY JUST BE A SPECK ON THE MAGNIFYING GLASS, BUT -- IT COULD BE THE PLANET OF BEER!
BINGO!!
FULL SPEED AHEAD, BOYS! I MEAN--FULL SPEED SIDEWAYS!!
AHEM! CAPTAIN, I THINK I'D LIKE TO BE PAID NOW...
©SMELL OF STEVE, INC.

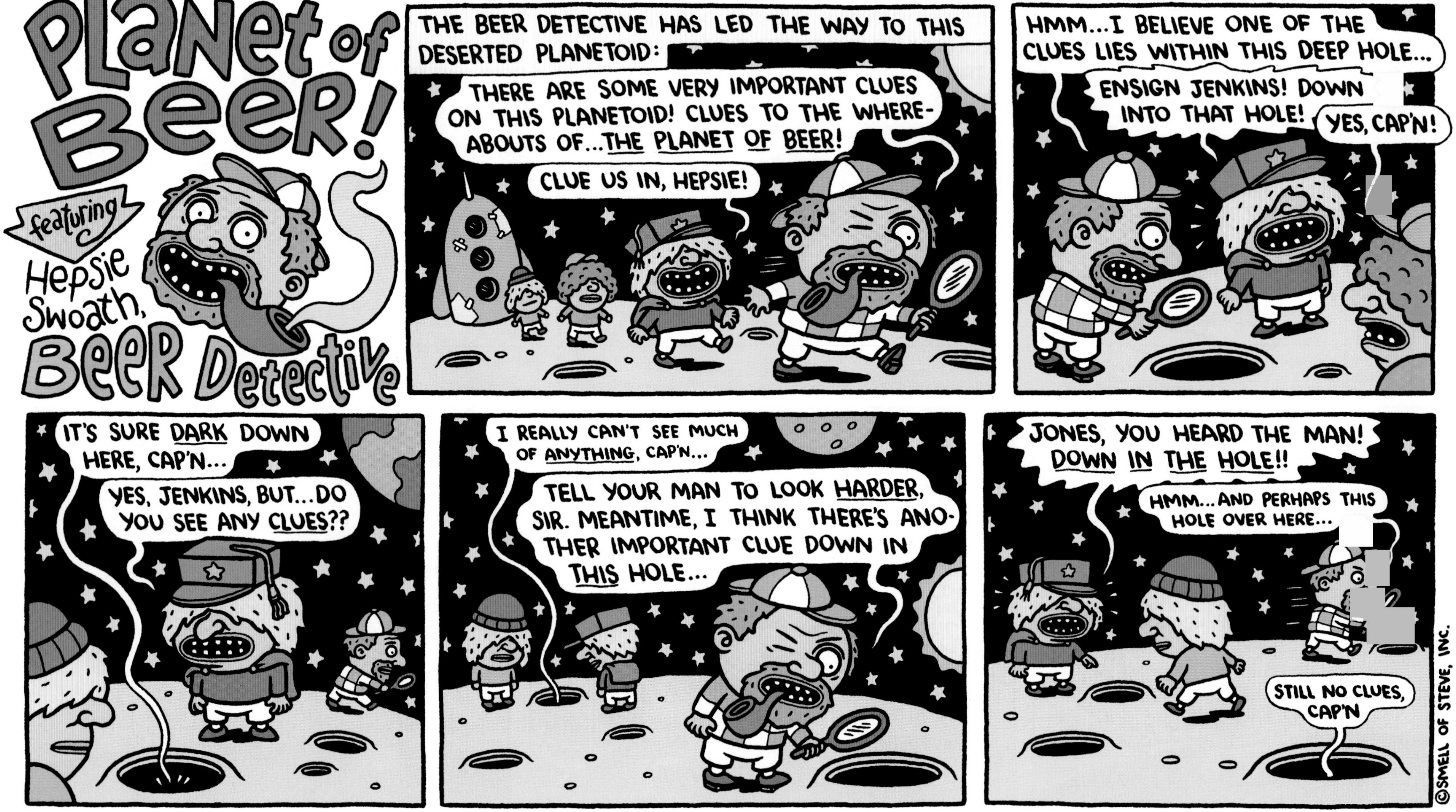
PLANET of BEER!
featuring
Hepsie Swoath,
BEER Detective
THE BEER DETECTIVE HAS LED THE WAY TO THIS DESERTED PLANETOID:
THERE ARE SOME VERY IMPORTANT CLUES ON THIS PLANETOID! CLUES TO THE WHERE-ABOUTS OF...THE PLANET OF BEER!
CLUE US IN, HEPSIE!
HMM...I BELIEVE ONE OF THE CLUES LIES WITHIN THIS DEEP HOLE...
ENSIGN JENKINS! DOWN INTO THAT HOLE!
YES, CAP'N!
IT'S SURE DARK DOWN HERE, CAP'N...
YES, JENKINS, BUT...DO YOU SEE ANY CLUES??
I REALLY CAN'T SEE MUCH OF ANYTHING, CAP'N...
TELL YOUR MAN TO LOOK HARDER, SIR. MEANTIME, I THINK THERE'S ANO-THER IMPORTANT CLUE DOWN IN THIS HOLE...
JONES, YOU HEARD THE MAN! DOWN IN THE HOLE!!
HMM...AND PERHAPS THIS HOLE OVER HERE...
STILL NO CLUES, CAP'N
©SMELL OF STEVE, INC.

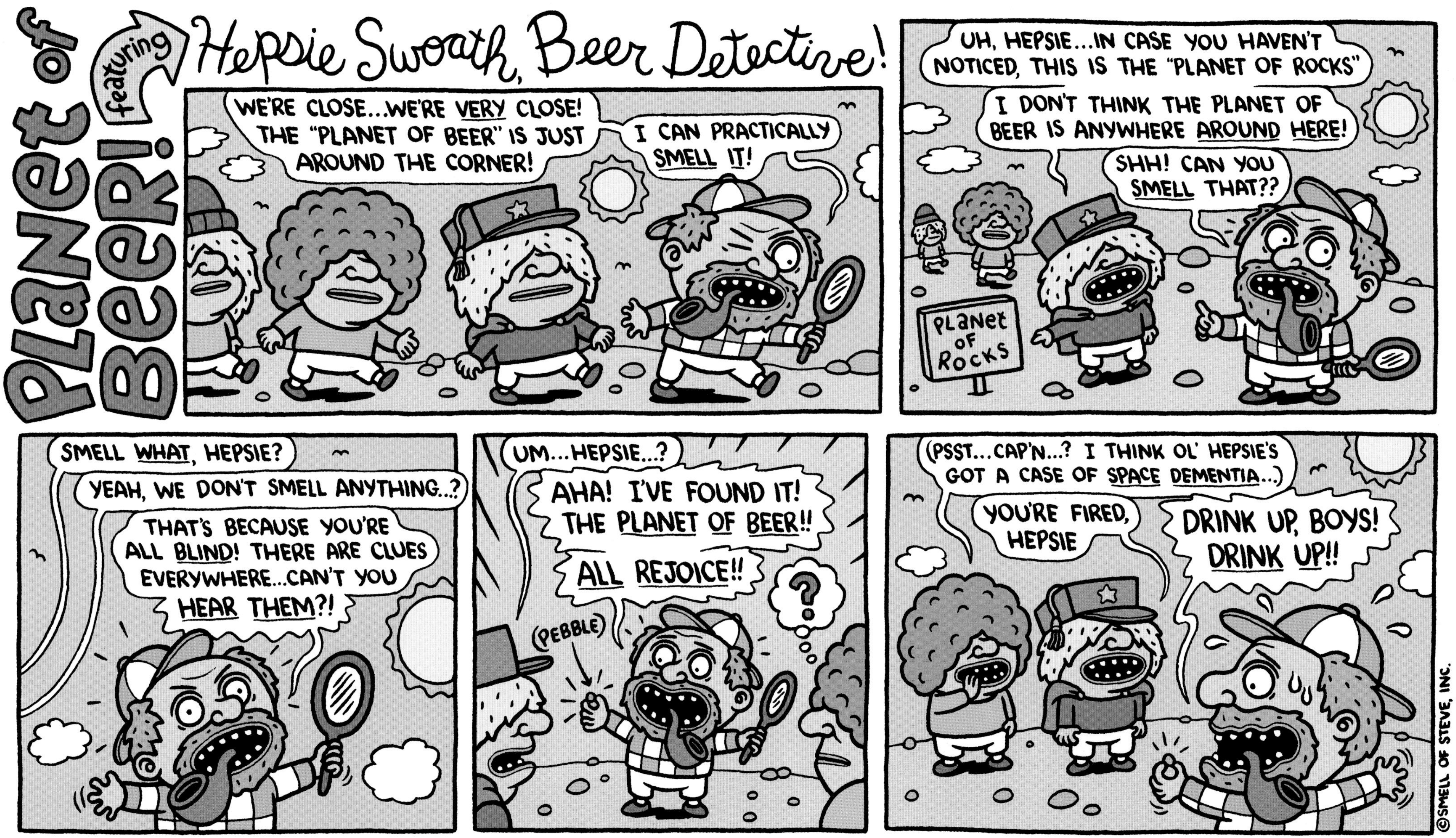
PLANET OF BEER!
featuring
Hepsie Swoath, Beer Detective!
WE'RE CLOSE...WE'RE VERY CLOSE! THE "PLANET OF BEER" IS JUST AROUND THE CORNER!
I CAN PRACTICALLY SMELL IT!
UH, HEPSIE...IN CASE YOU HAVEN'T NOTICED, THIS IS THE "PLANET OF ROCKS"
I DON'T THINK THE PLANET OF BEER IS ANYWHERE AROUND HERE!
SHH! CAN YOU SMELL THAT??
PLANET OF ROCKS
SMELL WHAT, HEPSIE?
YEAH, WE DON'T SMELL ANYTHING...?
THAT'S BECAUSE YOU'RE ALL BLIND! THERE ARE CLUES EVERYWHERE...CAN'T YOU HEAR THEM?!
UM...HEPSIE...?
AHA! I'VE FOUND IT! THE PLANET OF BEER!!
ALL REJOICE!!
(PEBBLE)
?
(PSST...CAP'N...? I THINK OL' HEPSIE'S GOT A CASE OF SPACE DEMENTIA...)
YOU'RE FIRED, HEPSIE
DRINK UP, BOYS! DRINK UP!!
©SMELL OF STEVE, INC.

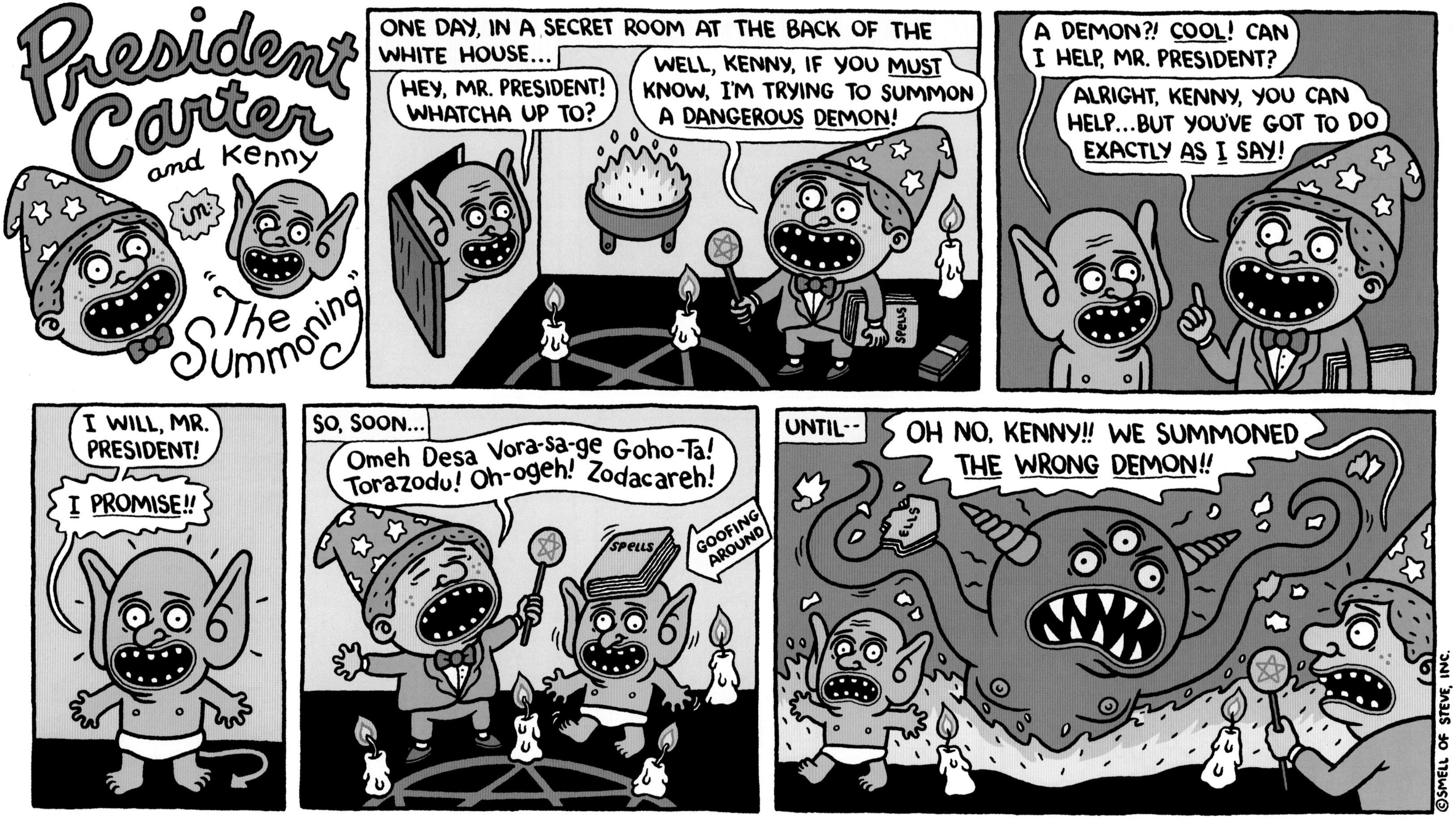
President Carter and Kenny in: "The Summoning"
ONE DAY, IN A SECRET ROOM AT THE BACK OF THE WHITE HOUSE...
HEY, MR. PRESIDENT! WHATCHA UP TO?
WELL, KENNY, IF YOU MUST KNOW, I'M TRYING TO SUMMON A DANGEROUS DEMON!
SPELLS
A DEMON?! COOL! CAN I HELP, MR. PRESIDENT?
ALRIGHT, KENNY, YOU CAN HELP...BUT YOU'VE GOT TO DO EXACTLY AS I SAY!
I WILL, MR. PRESIDENT!
I PROMISE!!
SO, SOON...
Omeh Desa Vora-sa-ge Goho-Ta! Torazodu! Oh-ogeh! Zodacareh!
SPELLS
GOOFING AROUND
UNTIL--
OH NO, KENNY!! WE SUMMONED THE WRONG DEMON!!
©SMELL OF STEVE, INC.

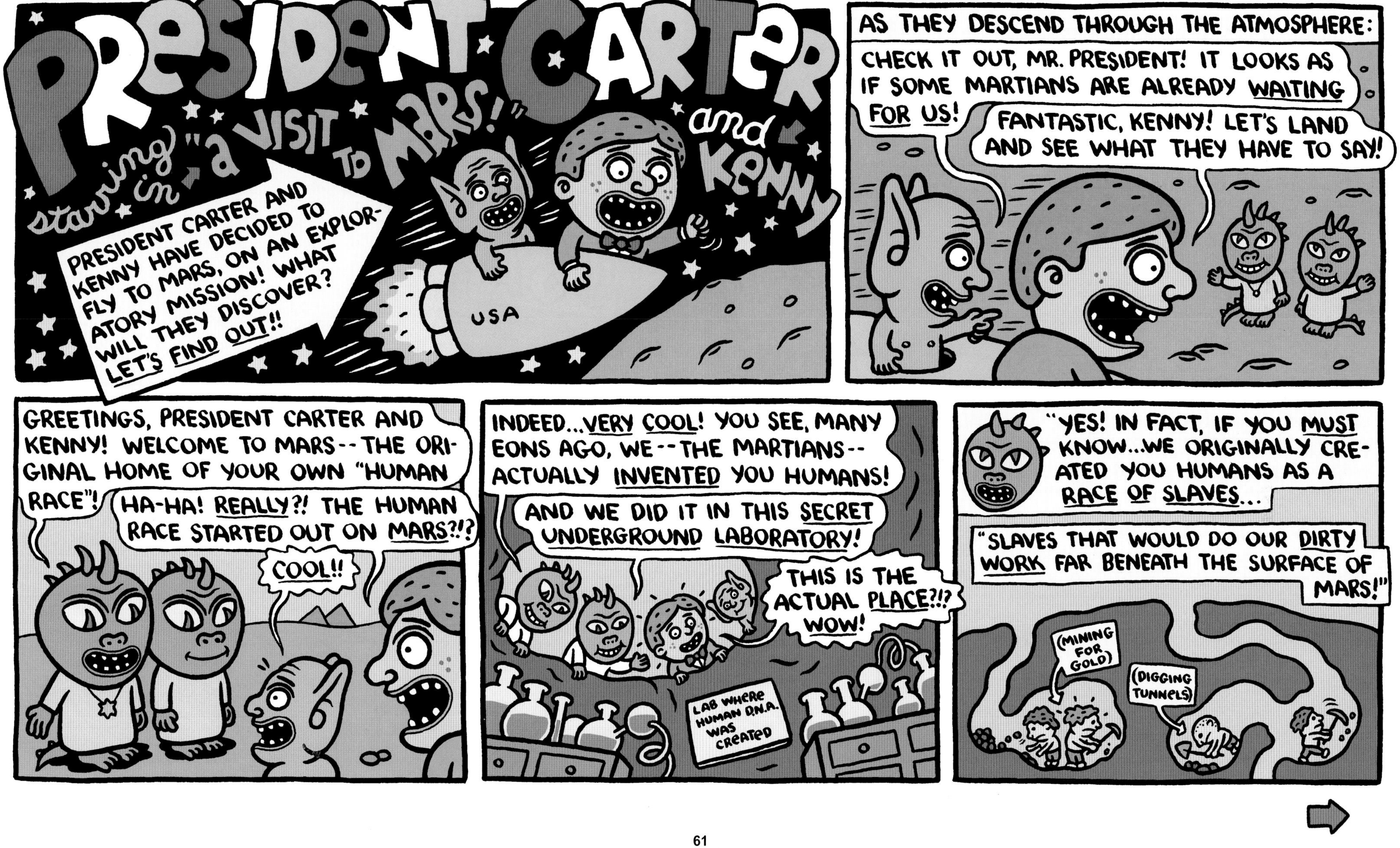
PRESIDENT CARTER and KENNY
starring in "a VISIT TO MARS!"
PRESIDENT CARTER AND KENNY HAVE DECIDED TO FLY TO MARS, ON AN EXPLORATORY MISSION! WHAT WILL THEY DISCOVER? LET'S FIND OUT!!
USA
AS THEY DESCEND THROUGH THE ATMOSPHERE:
CHECK IT OUT, MR. PRESIDENT! IT LOOKS AS IF SOME MARTIANS ARE ALREADY WAITING FOR US!
FANTASTIC, KENNY! LET'S LAND AND SEE WHAT THEY HAVE TO SAY!
GREETINGS, PRESIDENT CARTER AND KENNY! WELCOME TO MARS--THE ORIGINAL HOME OF YOUR OWN "HUMAN RACE"!
HA-HA! REALLY?! THE HUMAN RACE STARTED OUT ON MARS?!?
COOL!!
INDEED...VERY COOL! YOU SEE, MANY EONS AGO, WE--THE MARTIANS--ACTUALLY INVENTED YOU HUMANS!
AND WE DID IT IN THIS SECRET UNDERGROUND LABORATORY!
THIS IS THE ACTUAL PLACE?!? WOW!
LAB WHERE HUMAN D.N.A. WAS CREATED
"YES! IN FACT, IF YOU MUST KNOW...WE ORIGINALLY CREATED YOU HUMANS AS A RACE OF SLAVES...
"SLAVES THAT WOULD DO OUR DIRTY WORK FAR BENEATH THE SURFACE OF MARS!"
(MINING FOR GOLD)
(DIGGING TUNNELS)

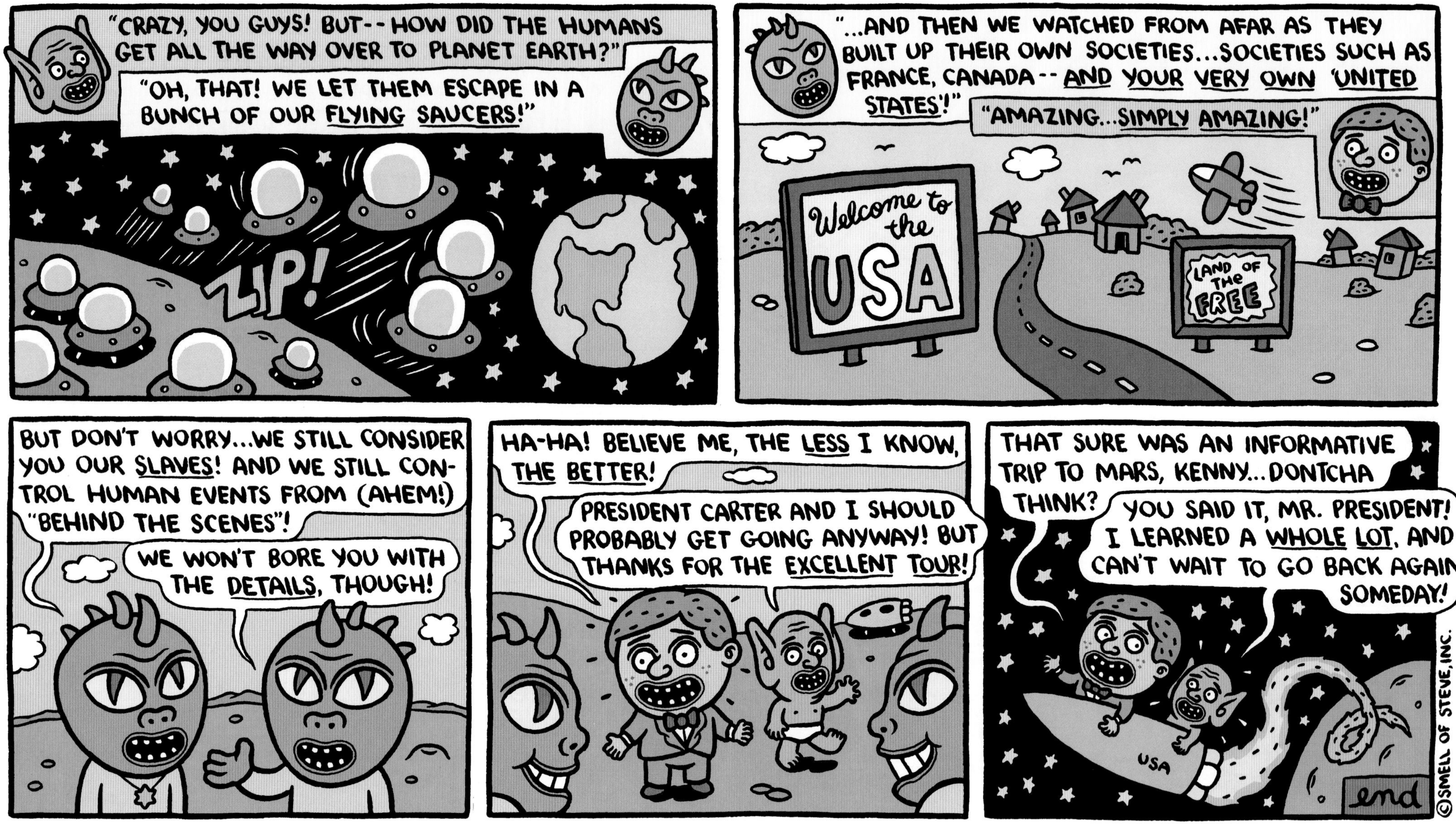
"CRAZY, YOU GUYS! BUT-- HOW DID THE HUMANS GET ALL THE WAY OVER TO PLANET EARTH?"
"OH, THAT! WE LET THEM ESCAPE IN A BUNCH OF OUR FLYING SAUCERS!"
ZIP!
"...AND THEN WE WATCHED FROM AFAR AS THEY BUILT UP THEIR OWN SOCIETIES...SOCIETIES SUCH AS FRANCE, CANADA-- AND YOUR VERY OWN 'UNITED STATES'!"
"AMAZING...SIMPLY AMAZING!"
Welcome to the USA
LAND OF THE FREE
BUT DON'T WORRY...WE STILL CONSIDER YOU OUR SLAVES! AND WE STILL CONTROL HUMAN EVENTS FROM (AHEM!) "BEHIND THE SCENES"!
WE WON'T BORE YOU WITH THE DETAILS, THOUGH!
HA-HA! BELIEVE ME, THE LESS I KNOW, THE BETTER!
PRESIDENT CARTER AND I SHOULD PROBABLY GET GOING ANYWAY! BUT THANKS FOR THE EXCELLENT TOUR!
THAT SURE WAS AN INFORMATIVE TRIP TO MARS, KENNY...DONTCHA THINK?
YOU SAID IT, MR. PRESIDENT! I LEARNED A WHOLE LOT, AND CAN'T WAIT TO GO BACK AGAIN SOMEDAY!
USA
end
©SMELL OF STEVE, INC.

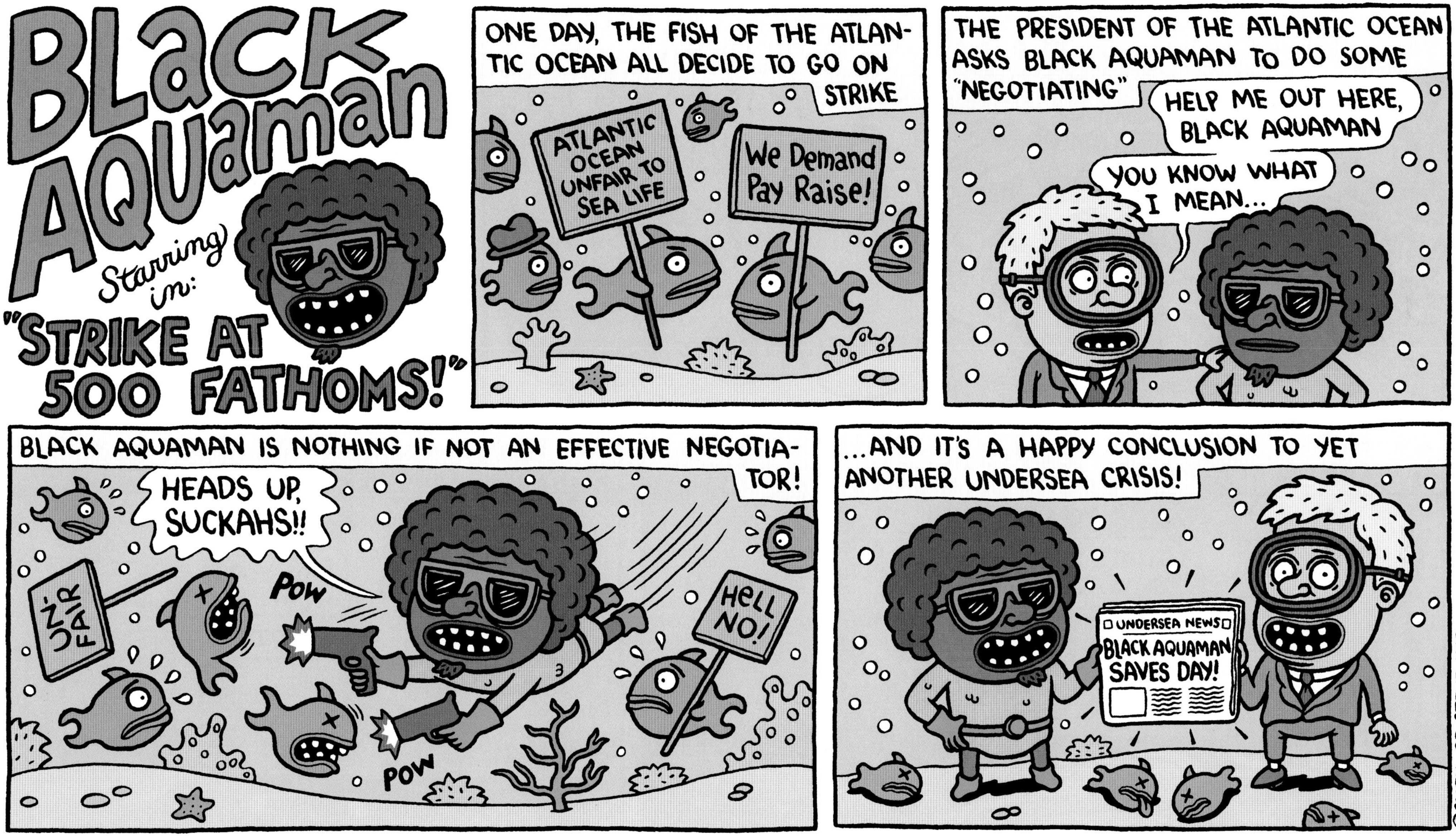
BLACK AQUAMAN
Starring in:
"STRIKE AT 500 FATHOMS!"
ONE DAY, THE FISH OF THE ATLANTIC OCEAN ALL DECIDE TO GO ON STRIKE
ATLANTIC OCEAN UNFAIR TO SEA LIFE
We Demand Pay Raise!
THE PRESIDENT OF THE ATLANTIC OCEAN ASKS BLACK AQUAMAN TO DO SOME "NEGOTIATING"
HELP ME OUT HERE, BLACK AQUAMAN
YOU KNOW WHAT I MEAN...
BLACK AQUAMAN IS NOTHING IF NOT AN EFFECTIVE NEGOTIATOR!
HEADS UP, SUCKAHS!!
UN-FAIR
POW
POW
HELL NO!
...AND IT'S A HAPPY CONCLUSION TO YET ANOTHER UNDERSEA CRISIS!
UNDERSEA NEWS
BLACK AQUAMAN SAVES DAY!

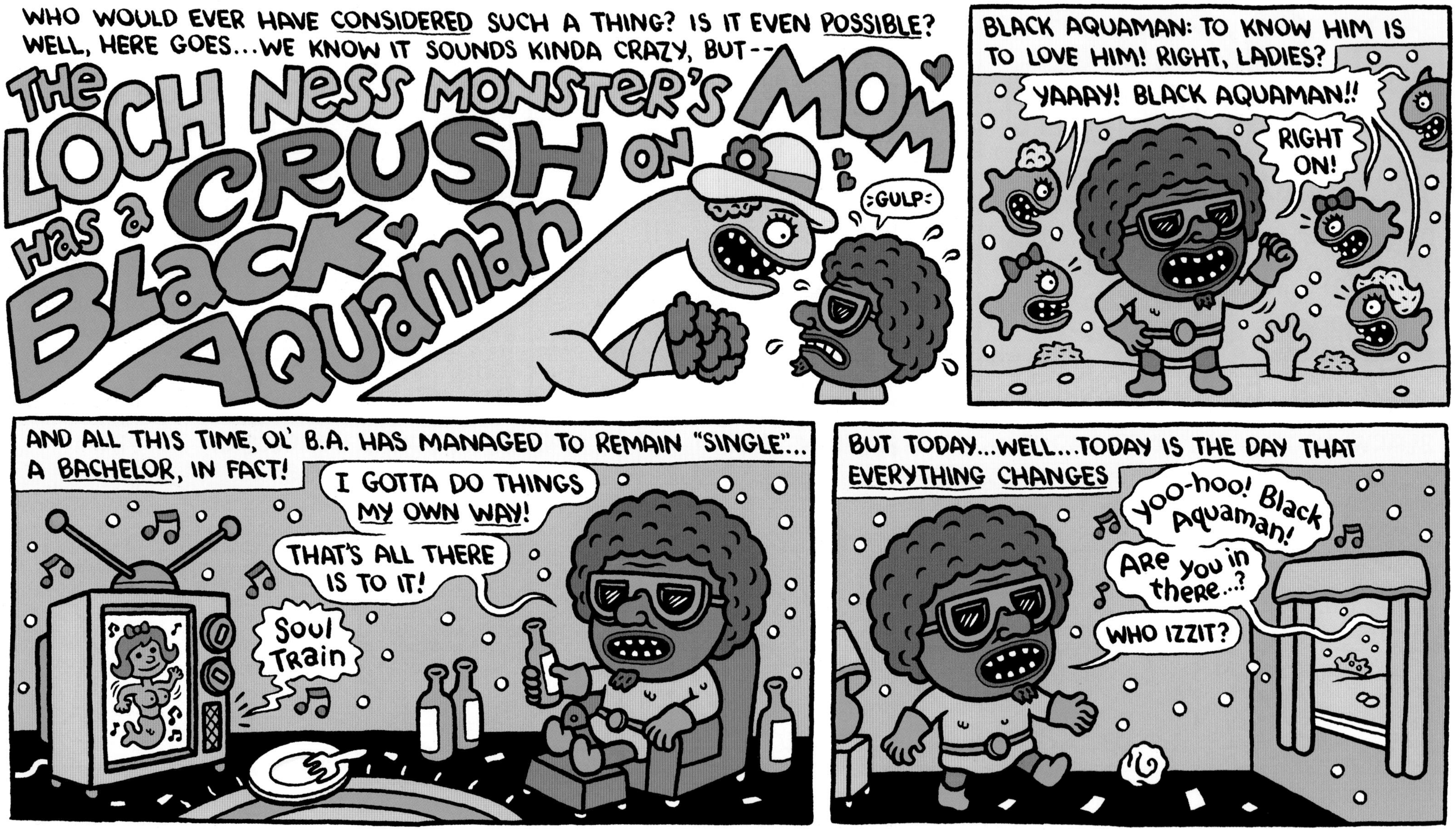
WHO WOULD EVER HAVE CONSIDERED SUCH A THING? IS IT EVEN POSSIBLE? WELL, HERE GOES...WE KNOW IT SOUNDS KINDA CRAZY, BUT--
THE LOCH NESS MONSTER'S MOM HAS A CRUSH ON BLACK AQUAMAN
GULP
BLACK AQUAMAN: TO KNOW HIM IS TO LOVE HIM! RIGHT, LADIES?
YAAAY! BLACK AQUAMAN!!
RIGHT ON!
AND ALL THIS TIME, OL' B.A. HAS MANAGED TO REMAIN "SINGLE"... A BACHELOR, IN FACT!
I GOTTA DO THINGS MY OWN WAY!
THAT'S ALL THERE IS TO IT!
Soul Train
BUT TODAY...WELL...TODAY IS THE DAY THAT EVERYTHING CHANGES
Yoo-hoo! Black Aquaman!
Are you in there...?
WHO IZZIT?

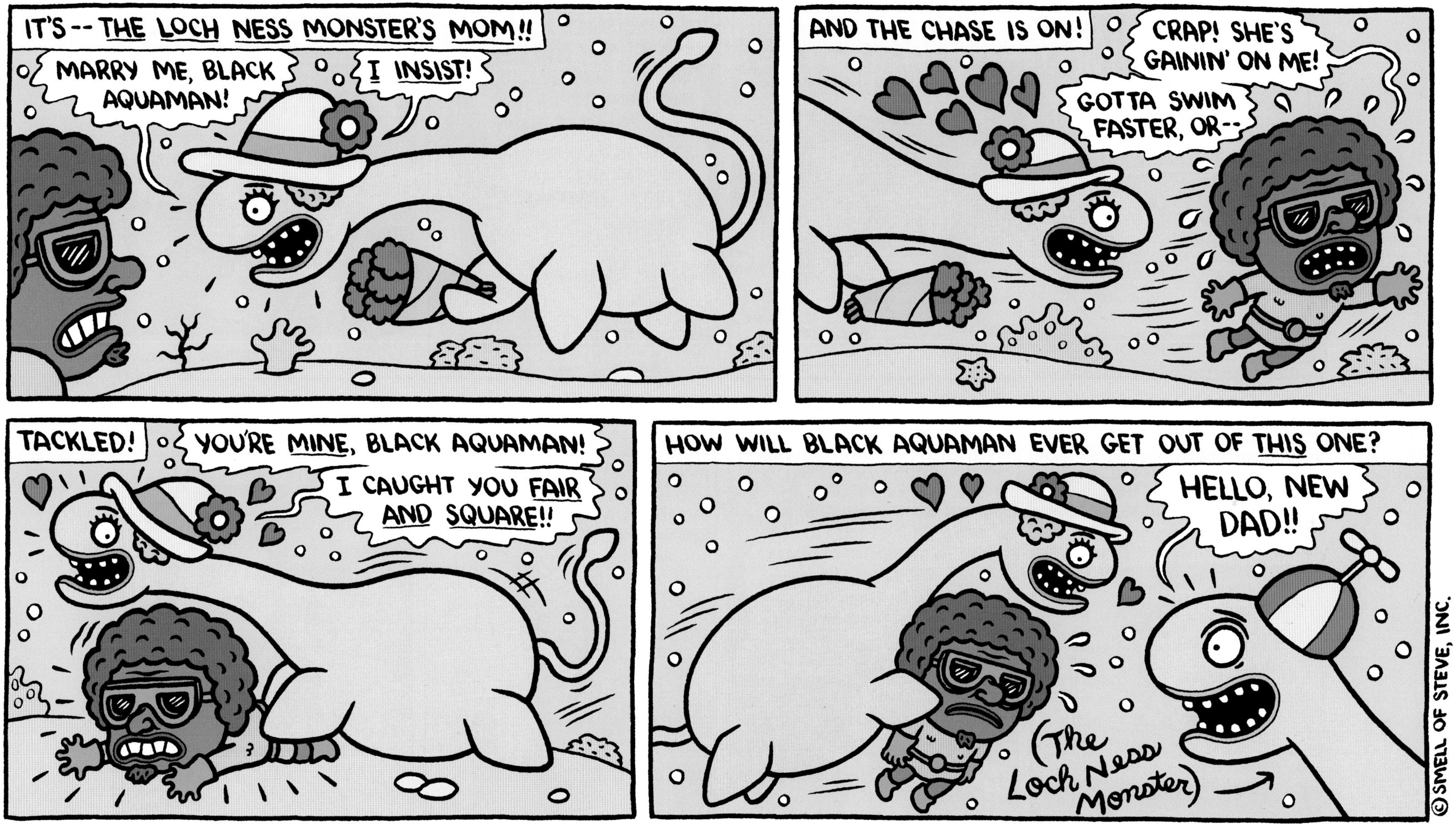
IT'S -- THE LOCH NESS MONSTER'S MOM!!
MARRY ME, BLACK AQUAMAN!
I INSIST!
AND THE CHASE IS ON!
CRAP! SHE'S GAININ' ON ME!
GOTTA SWIM FASTER, OR--
TACKLED!
YOU'RE MINE, BLACK AQUAMAN!
I CAUGHT YOU FAIR AND SQUARE!!
HOW WILL BLACK AQUAMAN EVER GET OUT OF THIS ONE?
HELLO, NEW DAD!!
(The Loch Ness Monster)
©SMELL OF STEVE, INC.

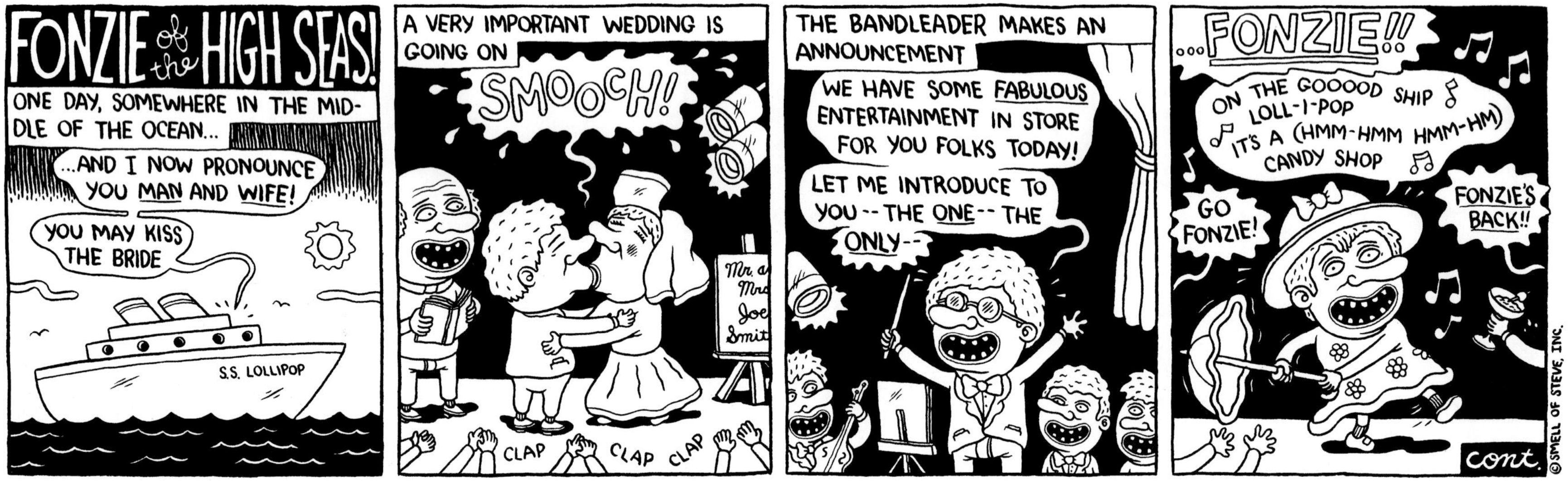
FONZIE of the HIGH SEAS!
ONE DAY, SOMEWHERE IN THE MIDDLE OF THE OCEAN...
...AND I NOW PRONOUNCE YOU MAN AND WIFE!
YOU MAY KISS THE BRIDE
S.S. LOLLIPOP
A VERY IMPORTANT WEDDING IS GOING ON
SMOOCH!
CLAP CLAP CLAP
THE BANDLEADER MAKES AN ANNOUNCEMENT
WE HAVE SOME FABULOUS ENTERTAINMENT IN STORE FOR YOU FOLKS TODAY!
LET ME INTRODUCE TO YOU -- THE ONE -- THE ONLY --
...FONZIE!!
ON THE GOOOOD SHIP LOLL-I-POP IT'S A (HMM-HMM HMM-HM) CANDY SHOP
GO FONZIE!
FONZIE'S BACK!!
cont.
© SMELL OF STEVE, INC.

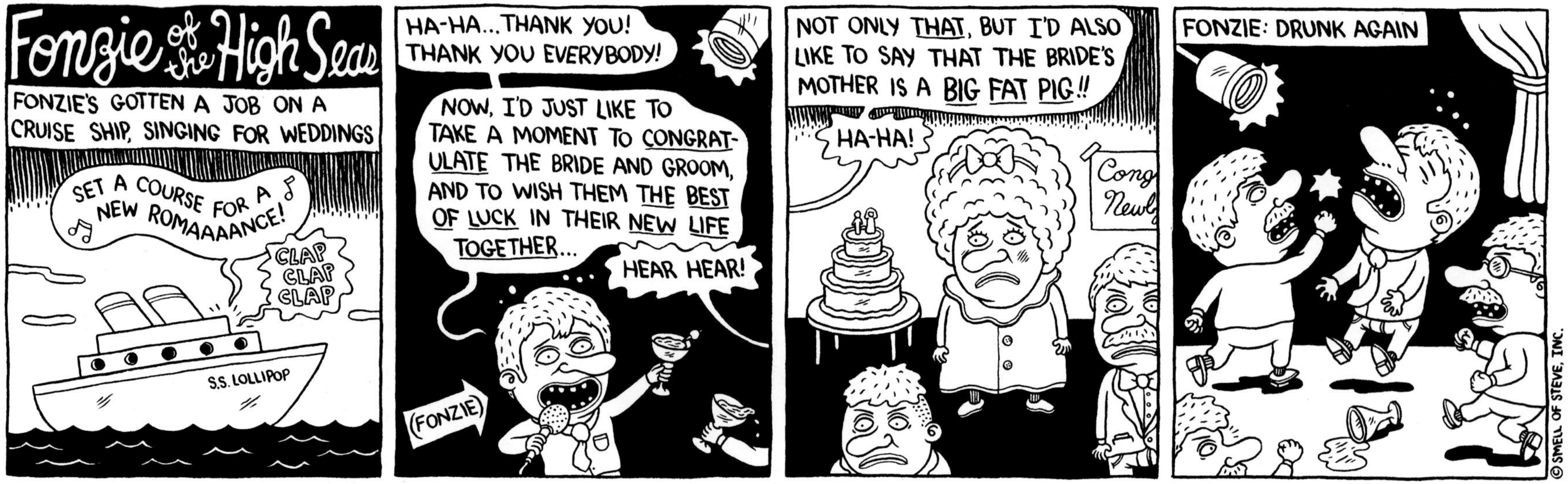
Fonzie of the High Seas
FONZIE'S GOTTEN A JOB ON A CRUISE SHIP, SINGING FOR WEDDINGS
SET A COURSE FOR A NEW ROMAAAANCE!
CLAP CLAP CLAP
S.S. LOLLIPOP
HA-HA... THANK YOU! THANK YOU EVERYBODY!
NOW, I'D JUST LIKE TO TAKE A MOMENT TO CONGRATULATE THE BRIDE AND GROOM, AND TO WISH THEM THE BEST OF LUCK IN THEIR NEW LIFE TOGETHER...
HEAR HEAR!
(FONZIE)
NOT ONLY THAT, BUT I'D ALSO LIKE TO SAY THAT THE BRIDE'S MOTHER IS A BIG FAT PIG!!
HA-HA!
FONZIE: DRUNK AGAIN
© SMELL OF STEVE, INC.

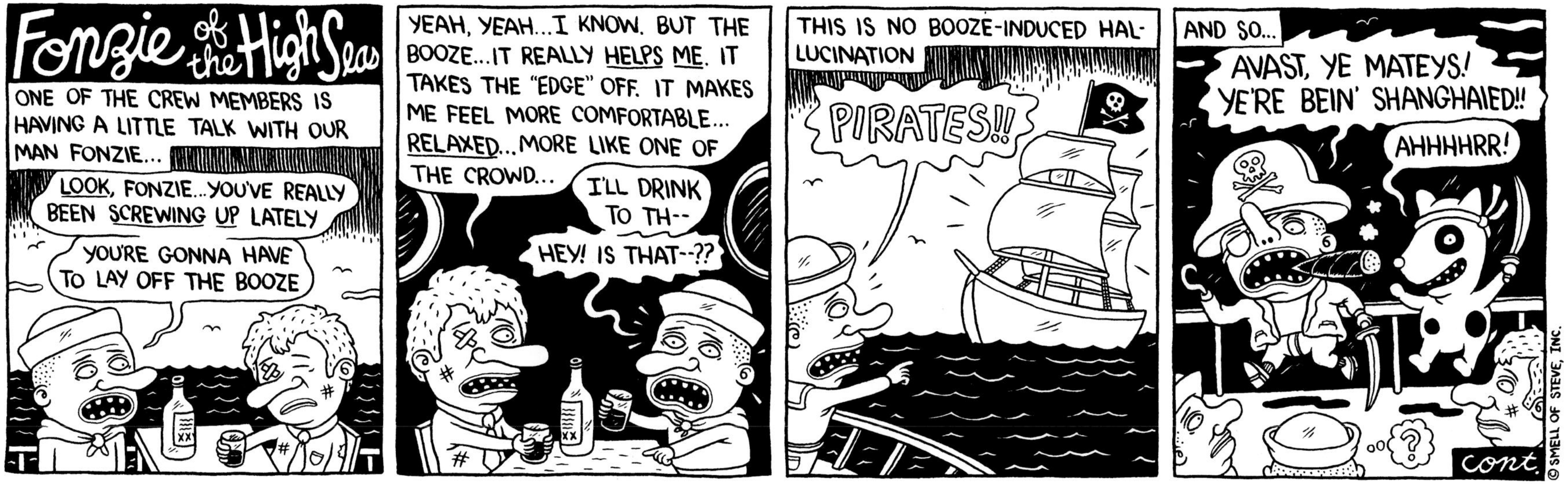
Fonzie of the High Seas
ONE OF THE CREW MEMBERS IS HAVING A LITTLE TALK WITH OUR MAN FONZIE...
LOOK, FONZIE...YOU'VE REALLY BEEN SCREWING UP LATELY
YOU'RE GONNA HAVE TO LAY OFF THE BOOZE
XX
YEAH, YEAH...I KNOW. BUT THE BOOZE...IT REALLY HELPS ME. IT TAKES THE "EDGE" OFF. IT MAKES ME FEEL MORE COMFORTABLE... RELAXED...MORE LIKE ONE OF THE CROWD...
I'LL DRINK TO TH--
HEY! IS THAT--??
XX
THIS IS NO BOOZE-INDUCED HAL-LUCINATION
PIRATES!!
AND SO...
AVAST, YE MATEYS! YE'RE BEIN' SHANGHAIED!!
AHHHHRR!
?
cont.
© SMELL OF STEVE, INC.

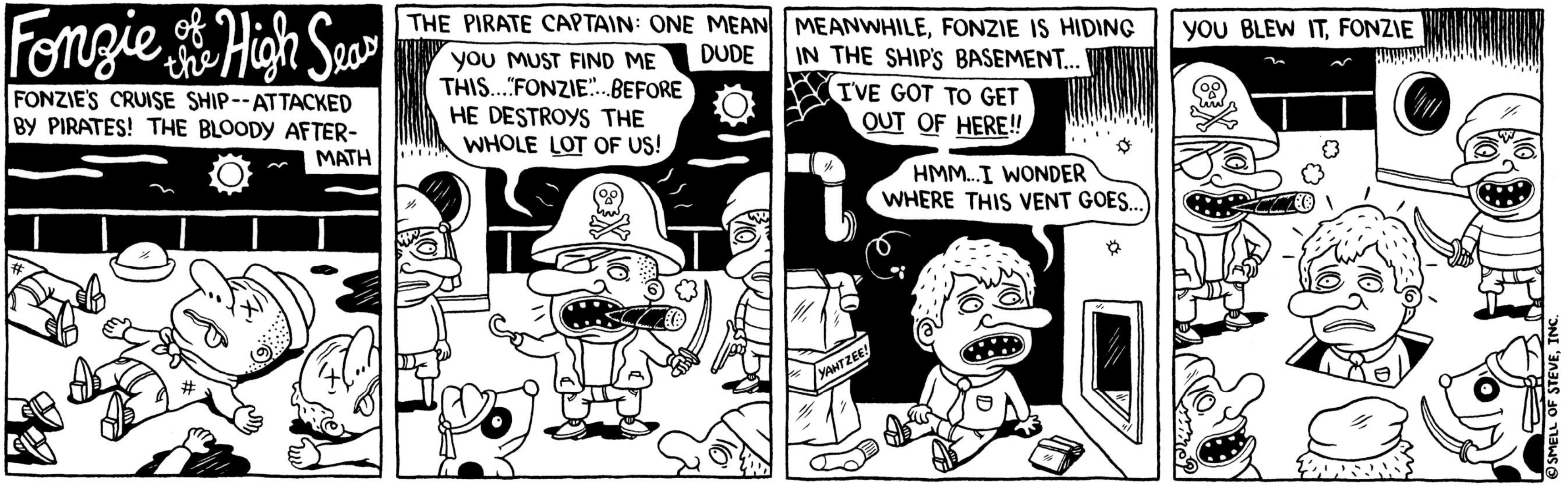
Fonzie of the High Seas
FONZIE'S CRUISE SHIP--ATTACKED BY PIRATES! THE BLOODY AFTER-MATH
THE PIRATE CAPTAIN: ONE MEAN DUDE
YOU MUST FIND ME THIS..."FONZIE"...BEFORE HE DESTROYS THE WHOLE LOT OF US!
MEANWHILE, FONZIE IS HIDING IN THE SHIP'S BASEMENT...
I'VE GOT TO GET OUT OF HERE!!
HMM...I WONDER WHERE THIS VENT GOES...
YAHTZEE!
YOU BLEW IT, FONZIE
© SMELL OF STEVE, INC.

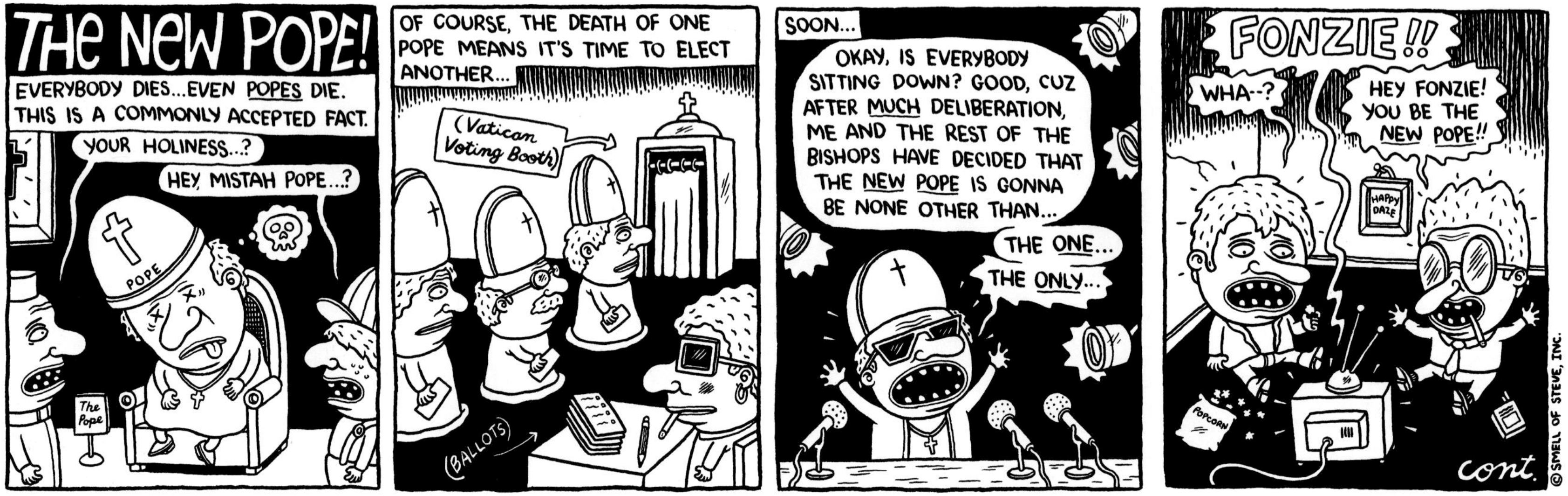

THE NEW POPE!
EVERYBODY DIES...EVEN POPES DIE. THIS IS A COMMONLY ACCEPTED FACT.
YOUR HOLINESS...?
HEY, MISTAH POPE...?
POPE
The Pope
OF COURSE, THE DEATH OF ONE POPE MEANS IT'S TIME TO ELECT ANOTHER...
(Vatican Voting Booth)
(BALLOTS)
SOON...
OKAY, IS EVERYBODY SITTING DOWN? GOOD, CUZ AFTER MUCH DELIBERATION, ME AND THE REST OF THE BISHOPS HAVE DECIDED THAT THE NEW POPE IS GONNA BE NONE OTHER THAN...
THE ONE...
THE ONLY...
FONZIE!!
WHA--?
HEY FONZIE! YOU BE THE NEW POPE!!
HAPPY DAZE
POPCORN
cont.
©SMELL OF STEVE, INC.

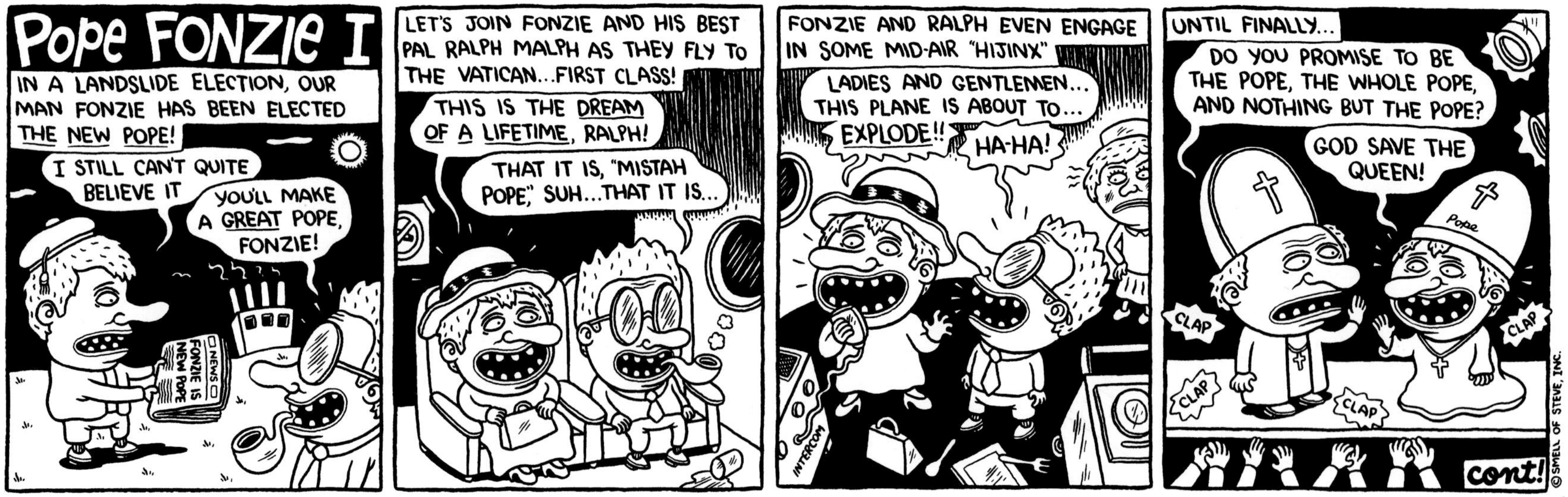

Pope FONZIE I
IN A LANDSLIDE ELECTION, OUR MAN FONZIE HAS BEEN ELECTED THE NEW POPE!
I STILL CAN'T QUITE BELIEVE IT
YOU'LL MAKE A GREAT POPE, FONZIE!
NEWS
FONZIE IS NEW POPE
LET'S JOIN FONZIE AND HIS BEST PAL RALPH MALPH AS THEY FLY TO THE VATICAN...FIRST CLASS!
THIS IS THE DREAM OF A LIFETIME, RALPH!
THAT IT IS, "MISTAH POPE," SUH...THAT IT IS...
FONZIE AND RALPH EVEN ENGAGE IN SOME MID-AIR "HIJINX"
LADIES AND GENTLEMEN... THIS PLANE IS ABOUT TO... EXPLODE!!
HA-HA!
INTERCOM
UNTIL FINALLY...
DO YOU PROMISE TO BE THE POPE, THE WHOLE POPE, AND NOTHING BUT THE POPE?
GOD SAVE THE QUEEN!
Pope
CLAP
CLAP
CLAP
CLAP
cont!
©SMELL OF STEVE, INC.

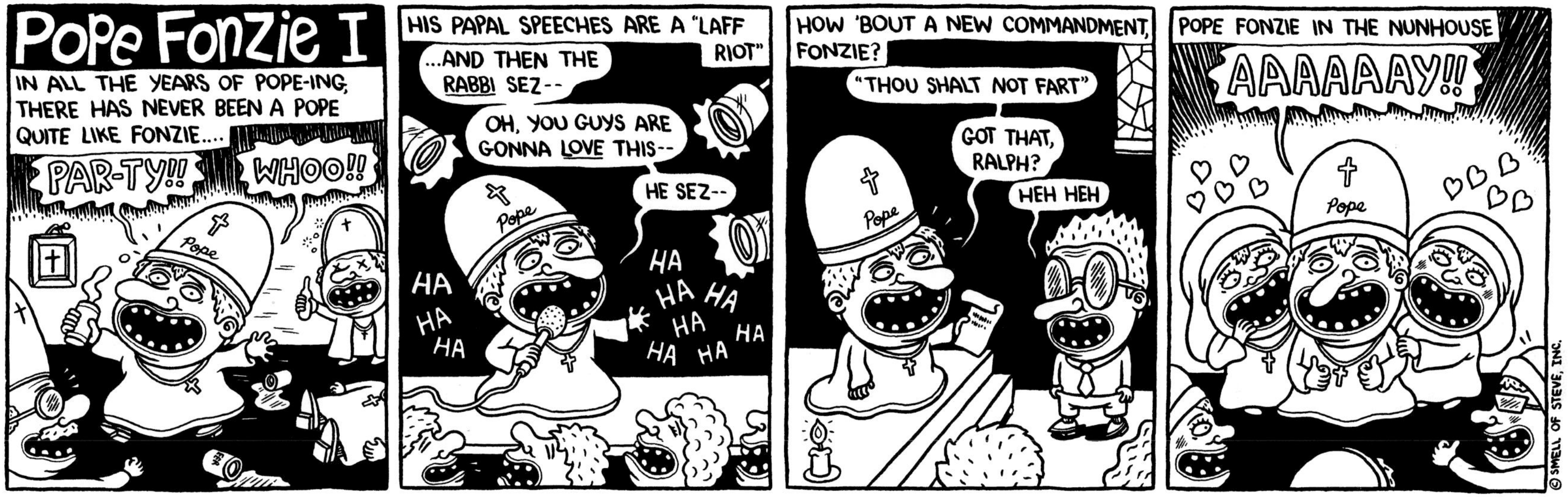
Pope Fonzie I
IN ALL THE YEARS OF POPE-ING, THERE HAS NEVER BEEN A POPE QUITE LIKE FONZIE....
PAR-TY!!
WHOO!!
Pope
HIS PAPAL SPEECHES ARE A "LAFF RIOT"
...AND THEN THE RABBI SEZ--
OH, YOU GUYS ARE GONNA LOVE THIS--
HE SEZ--
HA HA HA
HA HA HA HA HA HA HA HA
Pope
HOW 'BOUT A NEW COMMANDMENT, FONZIE?
"THOU SHALT NOT FART"
GOT THAT, RALPH?
HEH HEH
Pope
POPE FONZIE IN THE NUNHOUSE
AAAAAAY!!
Pope
© SMELL OF STEVE, INC.

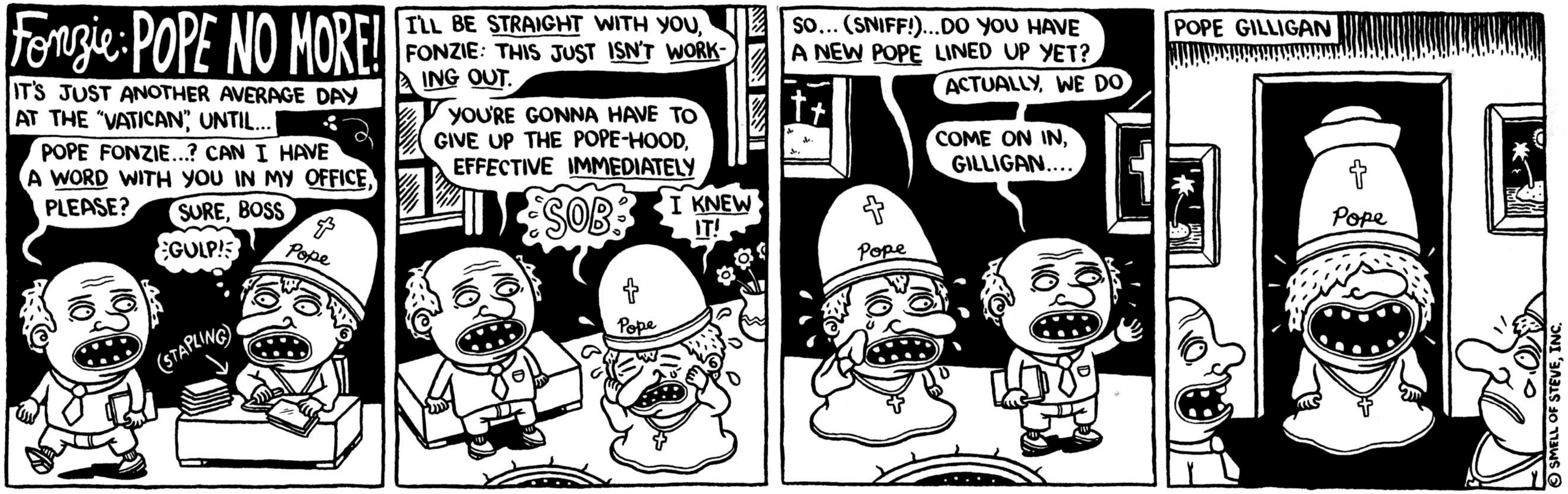
Fonzie: POPE NO MORE!
IT'S JUST ANOTHER AVERAGE DAY AT THE "VATICAN," UNTIL...
POPE FONZIE...? CAN I HAVE A WORD WITH YOU IN MY OFFICE, PLEASE?
SURE, BOSS
GULP!
Pope
(STAPLING)
I'LL BE STRAIGHT WITH YOU, FONZIE: THIS JUST ISN'T WORKING OUT.
YOU'RE GONNA HAVE TO GIVE UP THE POPE-HOOD, EFFECTIVE IMMEDIATELY
SOB
I KNEW IT!
Pope
SO... (SNIFF!)...DO YOU HAVE A NEW POPE LINED UP YET?
ACTUALLY, WE DO
COME ON IN, GILLIGAN....
Pope
POPE GILLIGAN
Pope
© SMELL OF STEVE, INC.

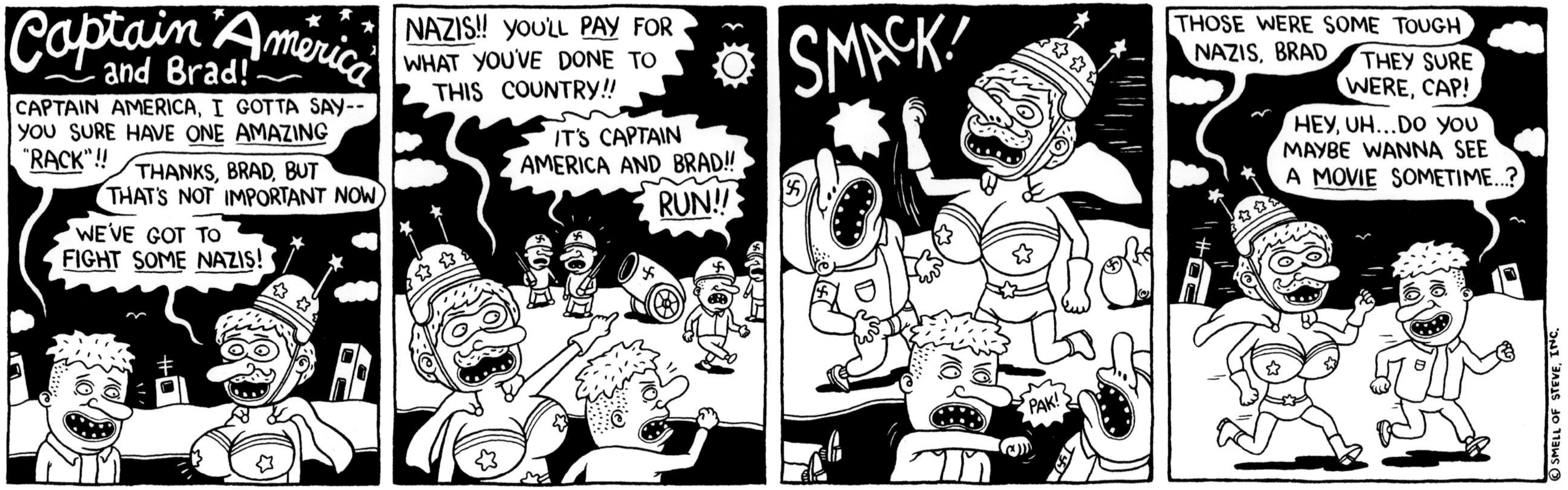
Captain America and Brad!
CAPTAIN AMERICA, I GOTTA SAY-- YOU SURE HAVE ONE AMAZING "RACK"!!
THANKS, BRAD, BUT THAT'S NOT IMPORTANT NOW
WE'VE GOT TO FIGHT SOME NAZIS!
NAZIS!! YOU'LL PAY FOR WHAT YOU'VE DONE TO THIS COUNTRY!!
IT'S CAPTAIN AMERICA AND BRAD!!
RUN!!
SMACK!
PAK!
THOSE WERE SOME TOUGH NAZIS, BRAD
THEY SURE WERE, CAP!
HEY, UH...DO YOU MAYBE WANNA SEE A MOVIE SOMETIME...?
© SMELL OF STEVE, INC.

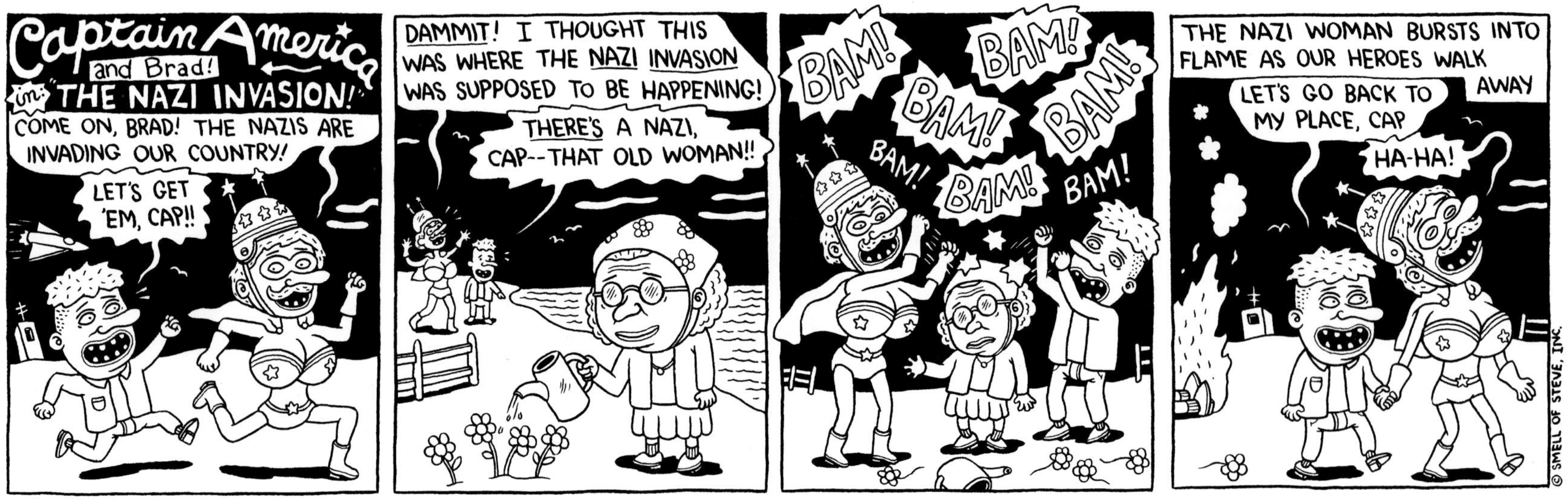
Captain America and Brad! in: "THE NAZI INVASION!"
COME ON, BRAD! THE NAZIS ARE INVADING OUR COUNTRY!
LET'S GET 'EM, CAP!!
DAMMIT! I THOUGHT THIS WAS WHERE THE NAZI INVASION WAS SUPPOSED TO BE HAPPENING!
THERE'S A NAZI, CAP--THAT OLD WOMAN!!
BAM!
BAM!
BAM!
BAM!
BAM!
BAM!
BAM!
THE NAZI WOMAN BURSTS INTO FLAME AS OUR HEROES WALK AWAY
LET'S GO BACK TO MY PLACE, CAP
HA-HA!
© SMELL OF STEVE, INC.

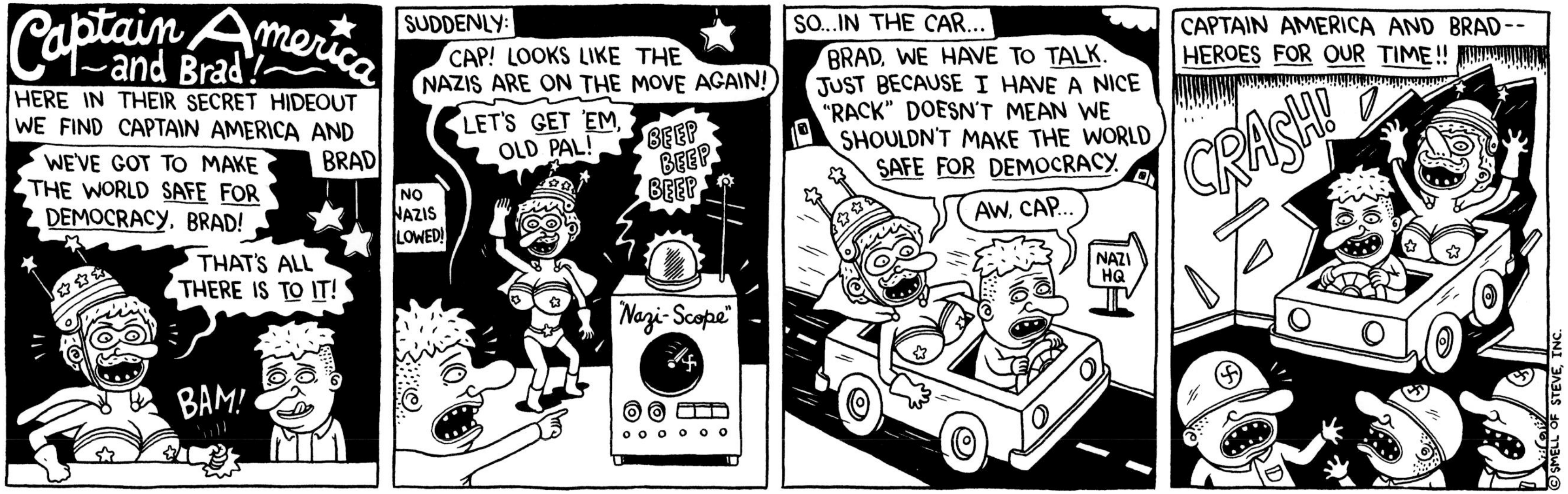
Captain America ~and Brad!~
HERE IN THEIR SECRET HIDEOUT WE FIND CAPTAIN AMERICA AND BRAD
WE'VE GOT TO MAKE THE WORLD SAFE FOR DEMOCRACY, BRAD!
THAT'S ALL THERE IS TO IT!
BAM!
SUDDENLY:
CAP! LOOKS LIKE THE NAZIS ARE ON THE MOVE AGAIN!
LET'S GET 'EM, OLD PAL!
BEEP BEEP BEEP
NO NAZIS LOWED!
"Nazi-Scope"
SO... IN THE CAR...
BRAD, WE HAVE TO TALK. JUST BECAUSE I HAVE A NICE "RACK" DOESN'T MEAN WE SHOULDN'T MAKE THE WORLD SAFE FOR DEMOCRACY.
AW, CAP...
NAZI HQ
CAPTAIN AMERICA AND BRAD-- HEROES FOR OUR TIME!!
CRASH!
© SMELL OF STEVE, INC.

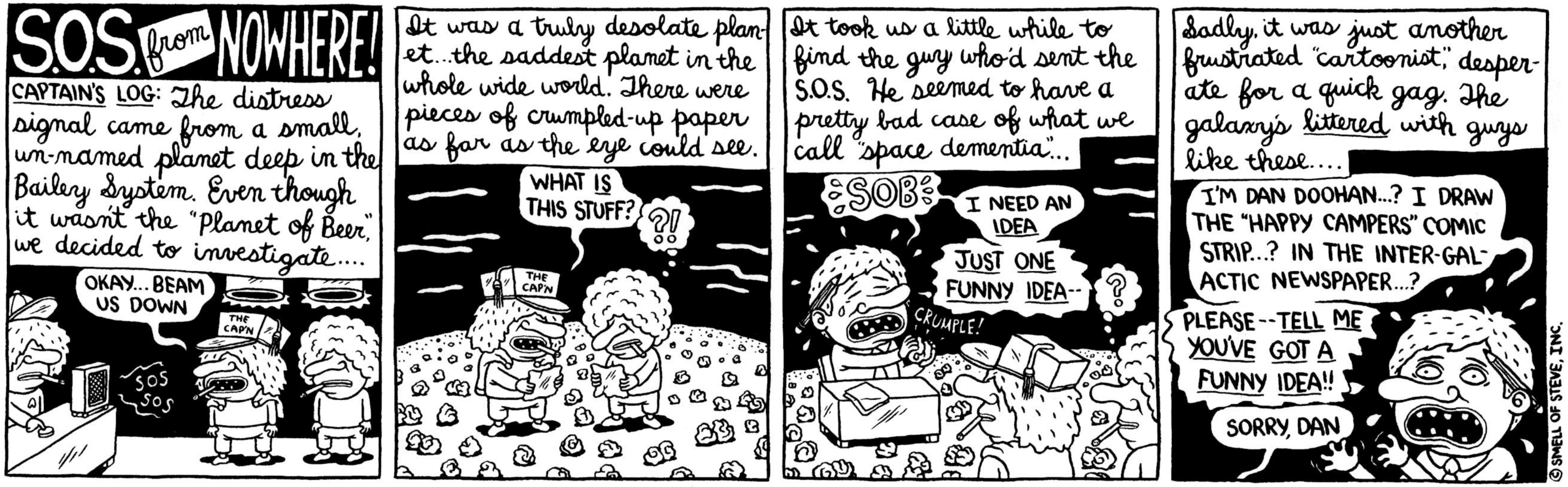
S.O.S. from NOWHERE!
CAPTAIN'S LOG: The distress signal came from a small, un-named planet deep in the Bailey System. Even though it wasn't the "Planet of Beer", we decided to investigate....
OKAY... BEAM US DOWN
SOS SOS
THE CAP'N
It was a truly desolate planet...the saddest planet in the whole wide world. There were pieces of crumpled-up paper as far as the eye could see.
WHAT IS THIS STUFF?
?!
THE CAP'N
It took us a little while to find the guy who'd sent the S.O.S. He seemed to have a pretty bad case of what we call "space dementia"...
SOB
I NEED AN IDEA
JUST ONE FUNNY IDEA--
?
CRUMPLE!
Sadly, it was just another frustrated "cartoonist," desperate for a quick gag. The galaxy's littered with guys like these....
I'M DAN DOOHAN...? I DRAW THE "HAPPY CAMPERS" COMIC STRIP...? IN THE INTER-GALACTIC NEWSPAPER...?
PLEASE--TELL ME YOU'VE GOT A FUNNY IDEA!!
SORRY, DAN
© SMELL OF STEVE, INC.

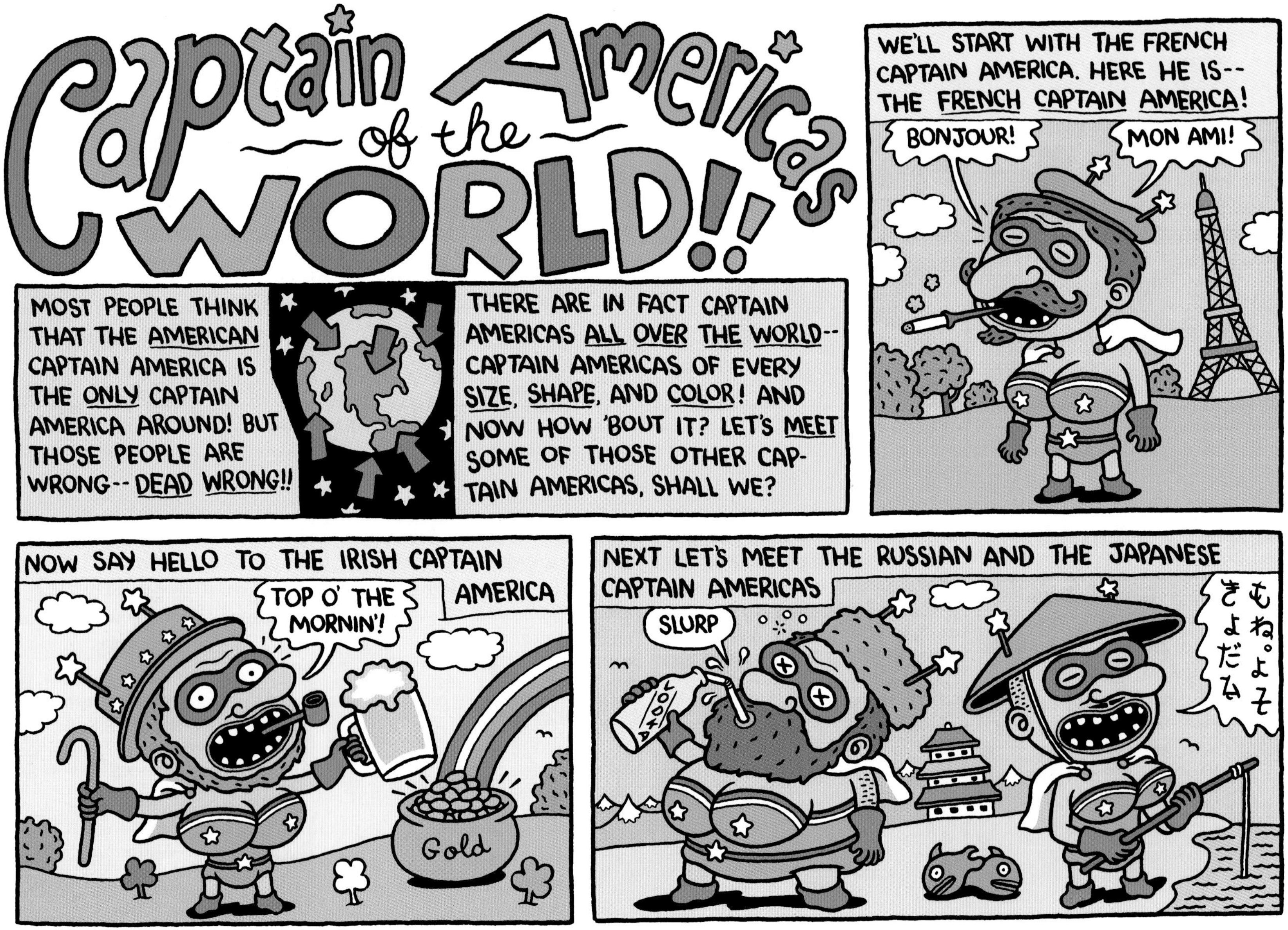
Captain Americas of the WORLD!!
MOST PEOPLE THINK THAT THE AMERICAN CAPTAIN AMERICA IS THE ONLY CAPTAIN AMERICA AROUND! BUT THOSE PEOPLE ARE WRONG-- DEAD WRONG!!
THERE ARE IN FACT CAPTAIN AMERICAS ALL OVER THE WORLD-- CAPTAIN AMERICAS OF EVERY SIZE, SHAPE, AND COLOR! AND NOW HOW 'BOUT IT? LET'S MEET SOME OF THOSE OTHER CAPTAIN AMERICAS, SHALL WE?
WE'LL START WITH THE FRENCH CAPTAIN AMERICA. HERE HE IS-- THE FRENCH CAPTAIN AMERICA!
BONJOUR!
MON AMI!
NOW SAY HELLO TO THE IRISH CAPTAIN AMERICA
TOP O' THE MORNIN'!
Gold
NEXT LET'S MEET THE RUSSIAN AND THE JAPANESE CAPTAIN AMERICAS
SLURP
VODKA
もね。よそ
きよだな

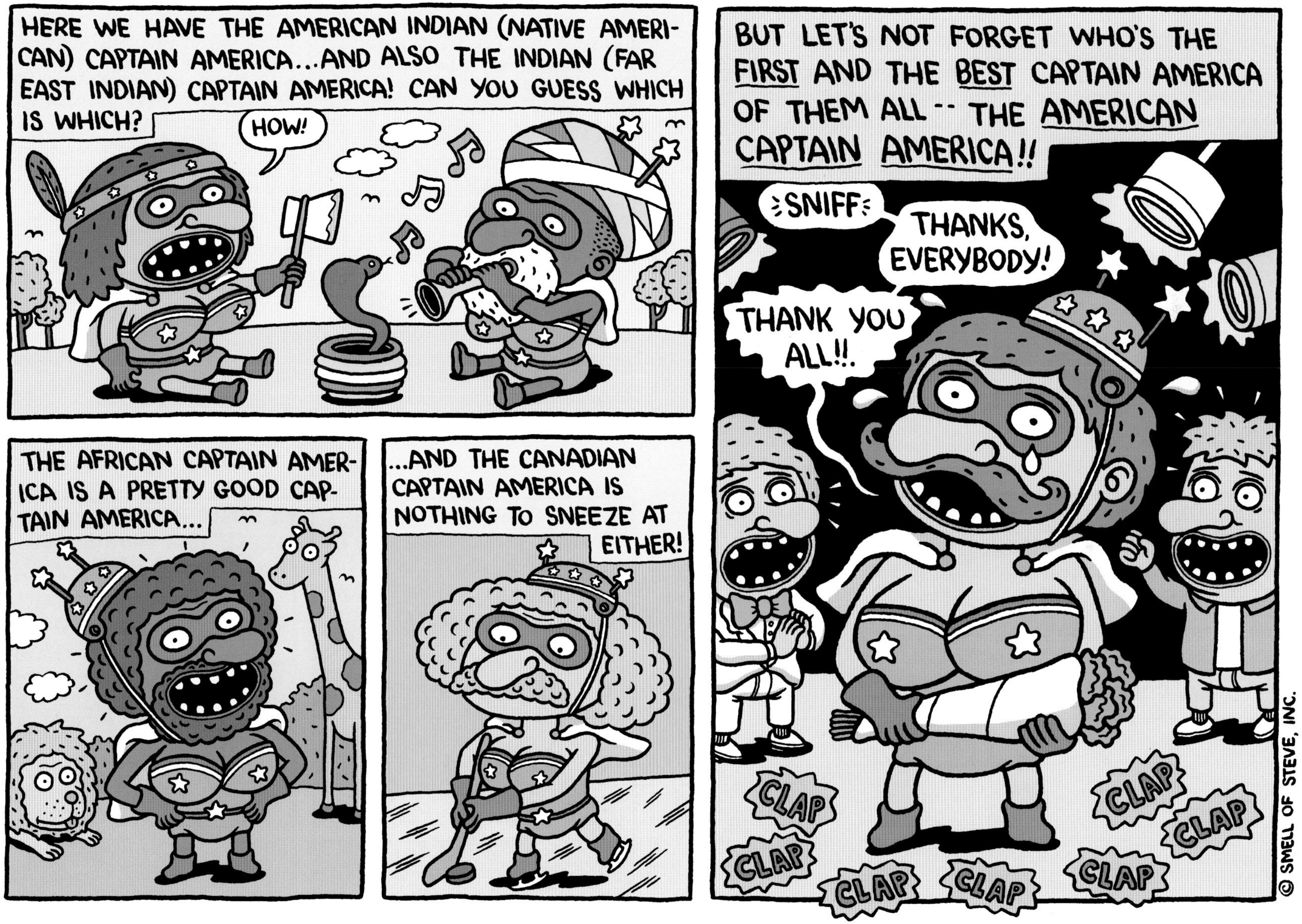
HERE WE HAVE THE AMERICAN INDIAN (NATIVE AMERICAN) CAPTAIN AMERICA...AND ALSO THE INDIAN (FAR EAST INDIAN) CAPTAIN AMERICA! CAN YOU GUESS WHICH IS WHICH?
HOW!
THE AFRICAN CAPTAIN AMERICA IS A PRETTY GOOD CAPTAIN AMERICA...
...AND THE CANADIAN CAPTAIN AMERICA IS NOTHING TO SNEEZE AT EITHER!
BUT LET'S NOT FORGET WHO'S THE FIRST AND THE BEST CAPTAIN AMERICA OF THEM ALL -- THE AMERICAN CAPTAIN AMERICA!!
SNIFF
THANKS, EVERYBODY!
THANK YOU ALL!!
CLAP
CLAP
CLAP
CLAP
CLAP
CLAP
CLAP

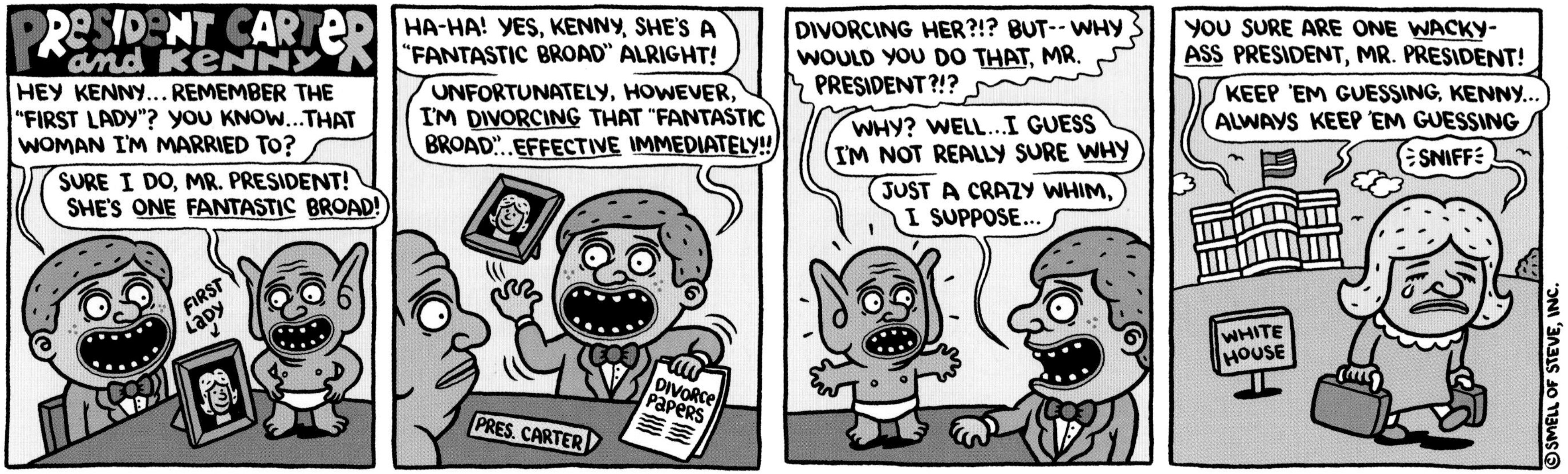
PRESIDENT CARTER and KENNY
HEY KENNY... REMEMBER THE "FIRST LADY"? YOU KNOW...THAT WOMAN I'M MARRIED TO?
SURE I DO, MR. PRESIDENT! SHE'S ONE FANTASTIC BROAD!
FIRST LADY
HA-HA! YES, KENNY, SHE'S A "FANTASTIC BROAD" ALRIGHT!
UNFORTUNATELY, HOWEVER, I'M DIVORCING THAT "FANTASTIC BROAD"...EFFECTIVE IMMEDIATELY!!
DIVORCE PAPERS
PRES. CARTER
DIVORCING HER?!? BUT-- WHY WOULD YOU DO THAT, MR. PRESIDENT?!?
WHY? WELL...I GUESS I'M NOT REALLY SURE WHY
JUST A CRAZY WHIM, I SUPPOSE...
YOU SURE ARE ONE WACKY-ASS PRESIDENT, MR. PRESIDENT!
KEEP 'EM GUESSING, KENNY... ALWAYS KEEP 'EM GUESSING
SNIFF
WHITE HOUSE
©SMELL OF STEVE, INC.

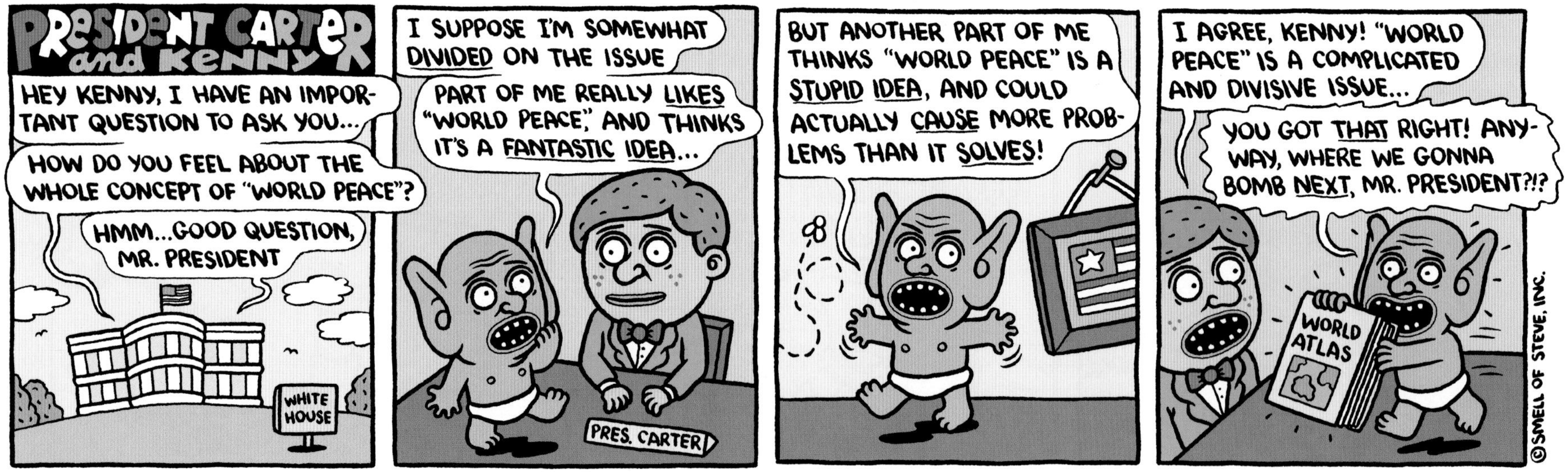
PRESIDENT CARTER and KENNY
HEY KENNY, I HAVE AN IMPORTANT QUESTION TO ASK YOU...
HOW DO YOU FEEL ABOUT THE WHOLE CONCEPT OF "WORLD PEACE"?
HMM...GOOD QUESTION, MR. PRESIDENT
WHITE HOUSE
I SUPPOSE I'M SOMEWHAT DIVIDED ON THE ISSUE
PART OF ME REALLY LIKES "WORLD PEACE," AND THINKS IT'S A FANTASTIC IDEA...
PRES. CARTER
BUT ANOTHER PART OF ME THINKS "WORLD PEACE" IS A STUPID IDEA, AND COULD ACTUALLY CAUSE MORE PROBLEMS THAN IT SOLVES!
I AGREE, KENNY! "WORLD PEACE" IS A COMPLICATED AND DIVISIVE ISSUE...
YOU GOT THAT RIGHT! ANYWAY, WHERE WE GONNA BOMB NEXT, MR. PRESIDENT?!?
WORLD ATLAS
©SMELL OF STEVE, INC.

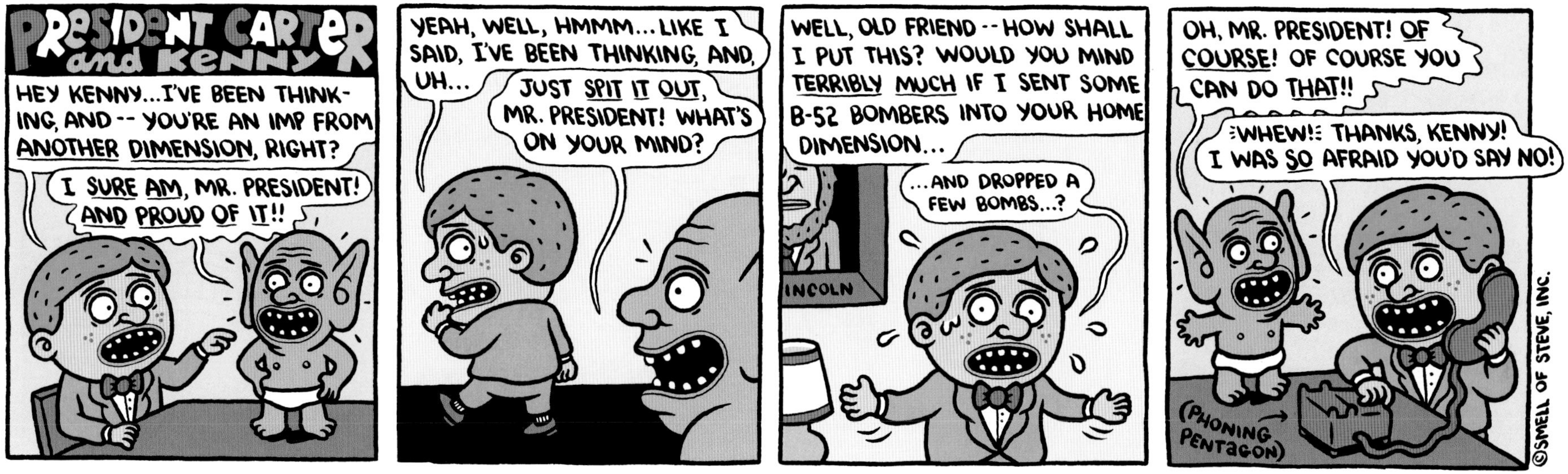
PRESIDENT CARTER and KENNY
HEY KENNY...I'VE BEEN THINKING, AND -- YOU'RE AN IMP FROM ANOTHER DIMENSION, RIGHT?
I SURE AM, MR. PRESIDENT! AND PROUD OF IT!!
YEAH, WELL, HMMM... LIKE I SAID, I'VE BEEN THINKING, AND, UH...
JUST SPIT IT OUT, MR. PRESIDENT! WHAT'S ON YOUR MIND?
WELL, OLD FRIEND -- HOW SHALL I PUT THIS? WOULD YOU MIND TERRIBLY MUCH IF I SENT SOME B-52 BOMBERS INTO YOUR HOME DIMENSION...
INCOLN
...AND DROPPED A FEW BOMBS...?
OH, MR. PRESIDENT! OF COURSE! OF COURSE YOU CAN DO THAT!!
WHEW! THANKS, KENNY! I WAS SO AFRAID YOU'D SAY NO!
(PHONING PENTAGON)
©SMELL OF STEVE, INC.

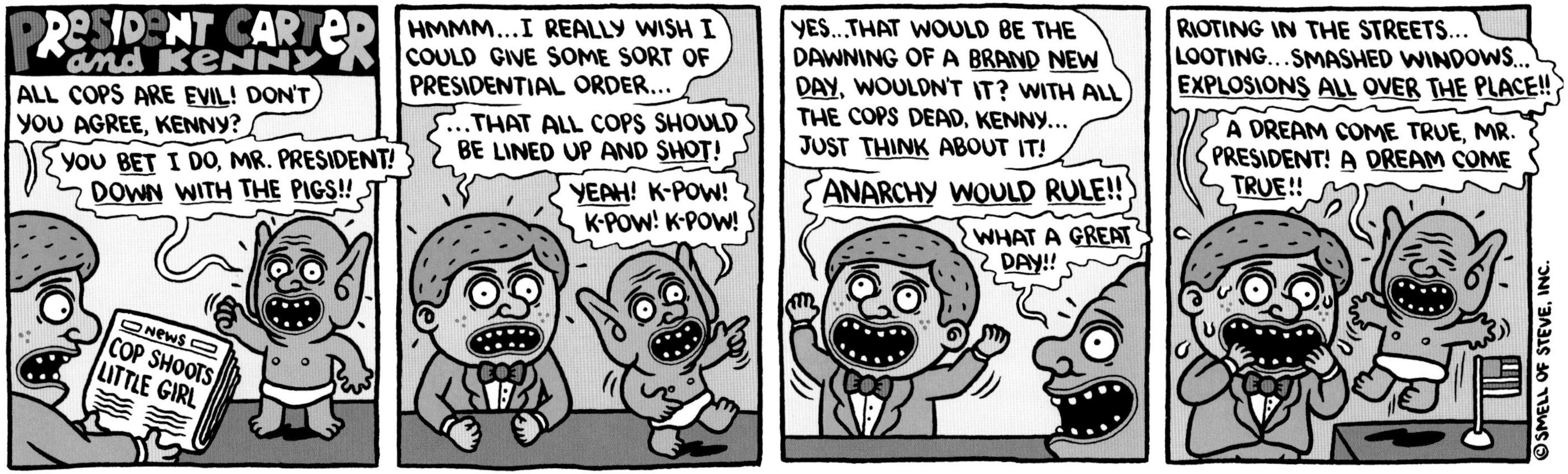
PRESIDENT CARTER and KENNY
ALL COPS ARE EVIL! DON'T YOU AGREE, KENNY?
YOU BET I DO, MR. PRESIDENT! DOWN WITH THE PIGS!!
NEWS
COP SHOOTS LITTLE GIRL
HMMM...I REALLY WISH I COULD GIVE SOME SORT OF PRESIDENTIAL ORDER...
...THAT ALL COPS SHOULD BE LINED UP AND SHOT!
YEAH! K-POW! K-POW! K-POW!
YES...THAT WOULD BE THE DAWNING OF A BRAND NEW DAY, WOULDN'T IT? WITH ALL THE COPS DEAD, KENNY... JUST THINK ABOUT IT!
ANARCHY WOULD RULE!!
WHAT A GREAT DAY!!
RIOTING IN THE STREETS... LOOTING...SMASHED WINDOWS... EXPLOSIONS ALL OVER THE PLACE!!
A DREAM COME TRUE, MR. PRESIDENT! A DREAM COME TRUE!!
©SMELL OF STEVE, INC.

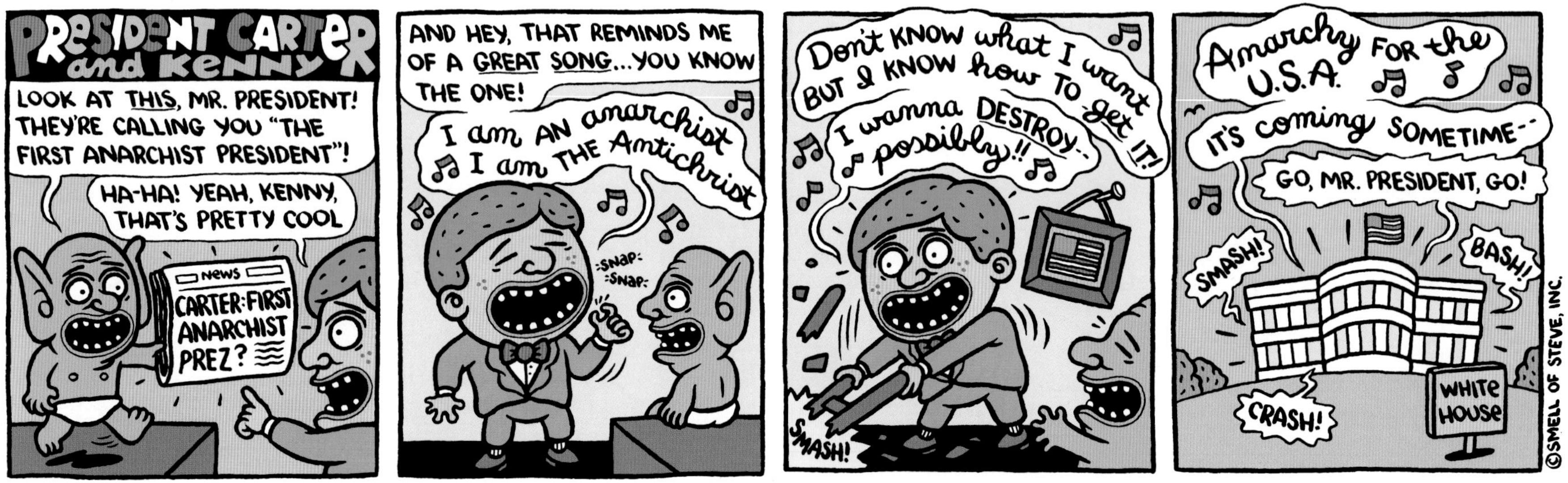
PRESIDENT CARTER and KENNY
LOOK AT THIS, MR. PRESIDENT! THEY'RE CALLING YOU "THE FIRST ANARCHIST PRESIDENT"!
HA-HA! YEAH, KENNY, THAT'S PRETTY COOL
NEWS
CARTER: FIRST ANARCHIST PREZ?
AND HEY, THAT REMINDS ME OF A GREAT SONG... YOU KNOW THE ONE!
I am AN anarchist I am THE Antichrist
SNAP SNAP
Don't KNOW what I want BUT I KNOW how TO get IT!
I wanna DESTROY... possibly!!
SMASH!
Anarchy FOR the U.S.A.
IT'S coming SOMETIME--
GO, MR. PRESIDENT, GO!
SMASH!
BASH!
CRASH!
WHITE HOUSE
©SMELL OF STEVE, INC.

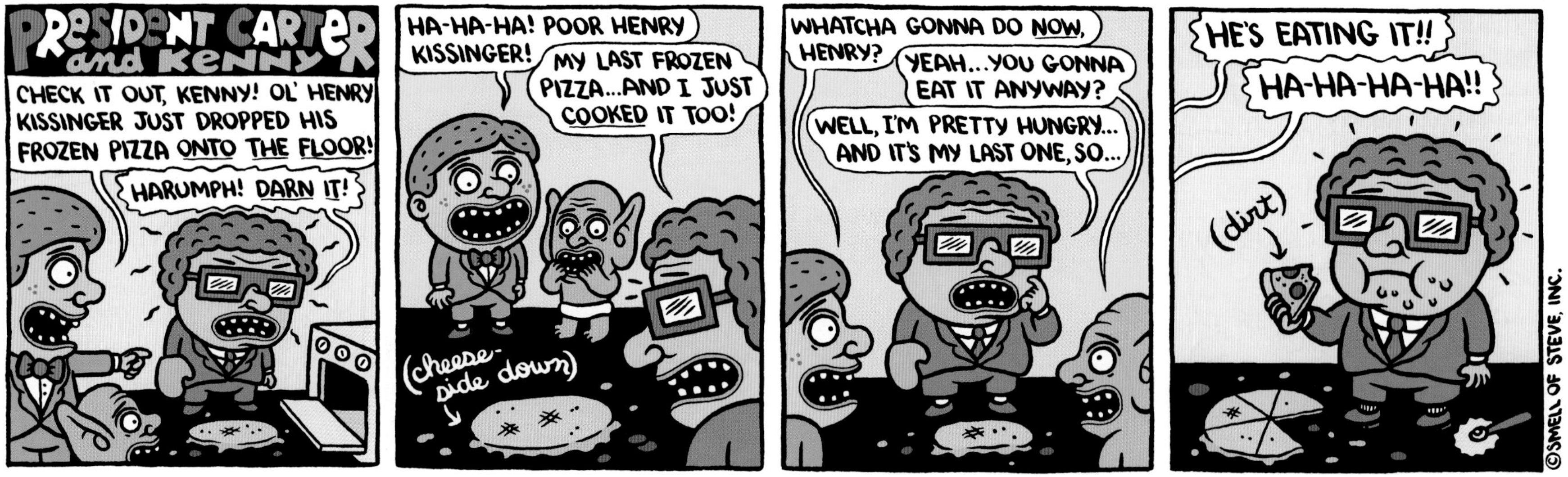
PRESIDENT CARTER and KENNY
CHECK IT OUT, KENNY! OL' HENRY KISSINGER JUST DROPPED HIS FROZEN PIZZA ONTO THE FLOOR!
HARUMPH! DARN IT!
HA-HA-HA! POOR HENRY KISSINGER!
MY LAST FROZEN PIZZA...AND I JUST COOKED IT TOO!
(cheese-side down)
WHATCHA GONNA DO NOW, HENRY?
YEAH...YOU GONNA EAT IT ANYWAY?
WELL, I'M PRETTY HUNGRY... AND IT'S MY LAST ONE, SO...
HE'S EATING IT!!
HA-HA-HA-HA!!
(dirt)
©SMELL OF STEVE, INC.

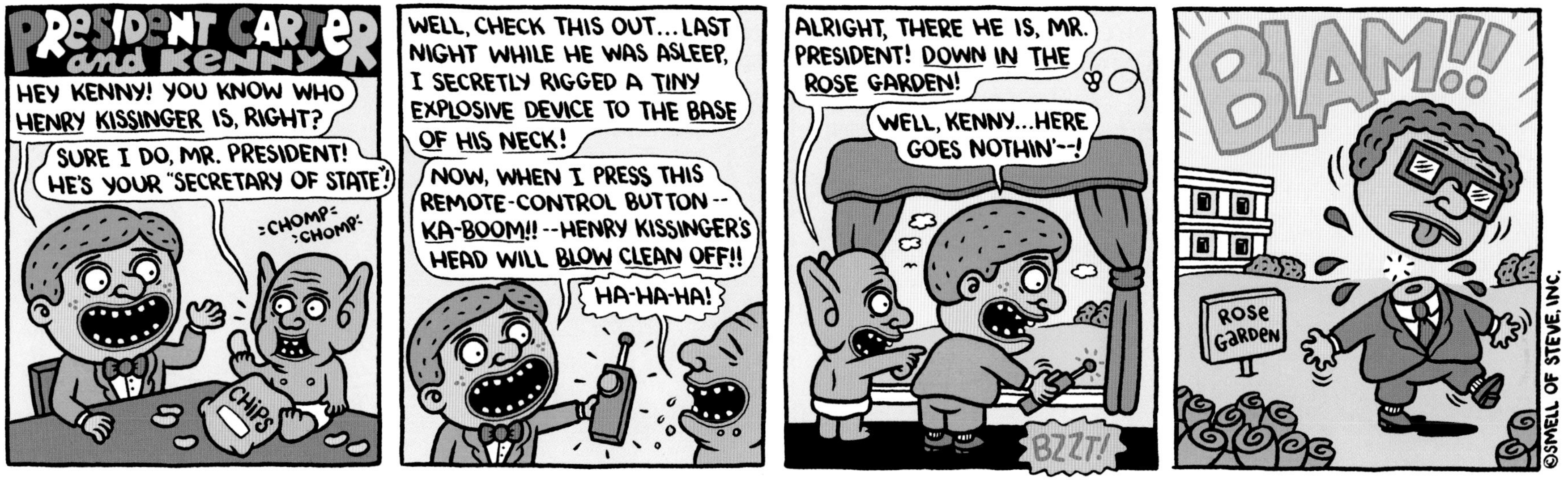
PRESIDENT CARTER and KENNY
HEY KENNY! YOU KNOW WHO HENRY KISSINGER IS, RIGHT?
SURE I DO, MR. PRESIDENT! HE'S YOUR "SECRETARY OF STATE"!
CHOMP CHOMP
CHIPS
WELL, CHECK THIS OUT... LAST NIGHT WHILE HE WAS ASLEEP, I SECRETLY RIGGED A TINY EXPLOSIVE DEVICE TO THE BASE OF HIS NECK!
NOW, WHEN I PRESS THIS REMOTE-CONTROL BUTTON -- KA-BOOM!! --HENRY KISSINGER'S HEAD WILL BLOW CLEAN OFF!!
HA-HA-HA!
ALRIGHT, THERE HE IS, MR. PRESIDENT! DOWN IN THE ROSE GARDEN!
WELL, KENNY... HERE GOES NOTHIN'--!
BZZT!
BLAM!!
ROSE GARDEN
©SMELL OF STEVE, INC.

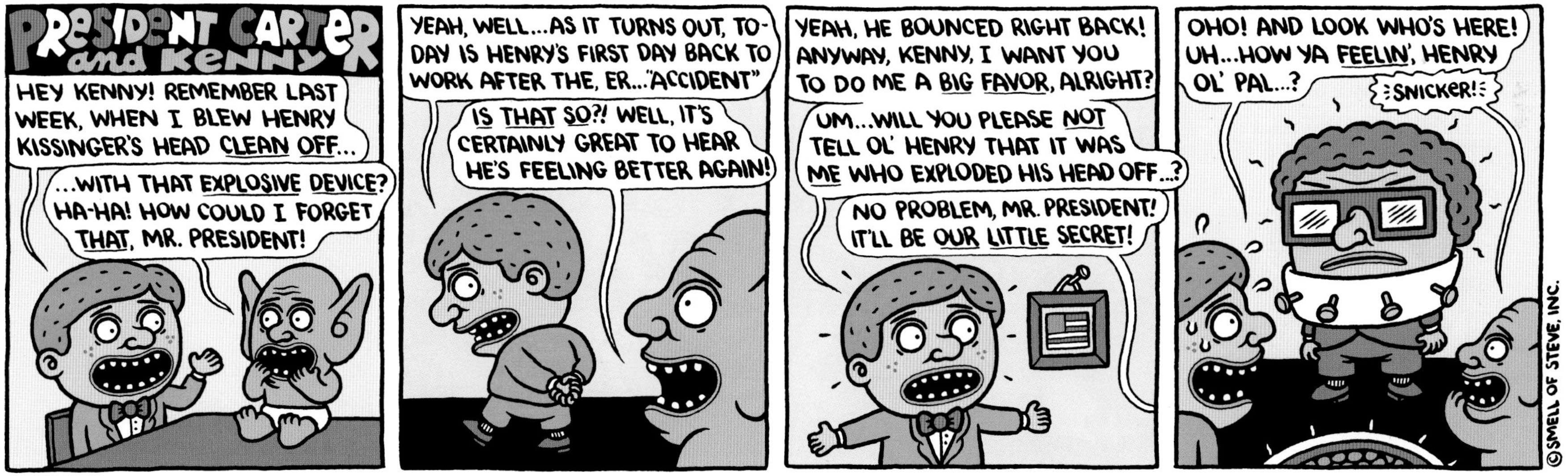
PRESIDENT CARTER and KENNY
HEY KENNY! REMEMBER LAST WEEK, WHEN I BLEW HENRY KISSINGER'S HEAD CLEAN OFF...
...WITH THAT EXPLOSIVE DEVICE? HA-HA! HOW COULD I FORGET THAT, MR. PRESIDENT!
YEAH, WELL...AS IT TURNS OUT, TODAY IS HENRY'S FIRST DAY BACK TO WORK AFTER THE, ER..."ACCIDENT"
IS THAT SO?! WELL, IT'S CERTAINLY GREAT TO HEAR HE'S FEELING BETTER AGAIN!
YEAH, HE BOUNCED RIGHT BACK! ANYWAY, KENNY, I WANT YOU TO DO ME A BIG FAVOR, ALRIGHT?
UM...WILL YOU PLEASE NOT TELL OL' HENRY THAT IT WAS ME WHO EXPLODED HIS HEAD OFF...?
NO PROBLEM, MR. PRESIDENT! IT'LL BE OUR LITTLE SECRET!
OHO! AND LOOK WHO'S HERE! UH...HOW YA FEELIN', HENRY OL' PAL...?
SNICKER!
©SMELL OF STEVE, INC.

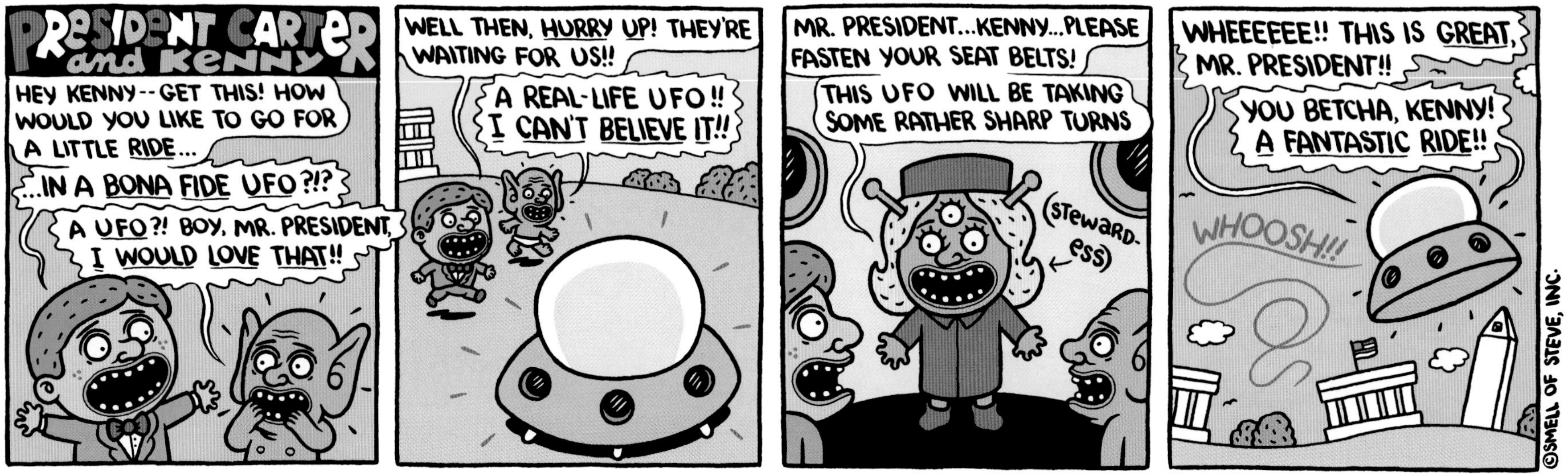
PRESIDENT CARTER and KENNY
HEY KENNY--GET THIS! HOW WOULD YOU LIKE TO GO FOR A LITTLE RIDE...
...IN A BONA FIDE UFO?!?
A UFO?! BOY, MR. PRESIDENT, I WOULD LOVE THAT!!
WELL THEN, HURRY UP! THEY'RE WAITING FOR US!!
A REAL-LIFE UFO!! I CAN'T BELIEVE IT!!
MR. PRESIDENT...KENNY...PLEASE FASTEN YOUR SEAT BELTS!
THIS UFO WILL BE TAKING SOME RATHER SHARP TURNS
(STEWARDESS)
WHEEEEEE!! THIS IS GREAT, MR. PRESIDENT!!
YOU BETCHA, KENNY! A FANTASTIC RIDE!!
WHOOSH!!!
©SMELL OF STEVE, INC.

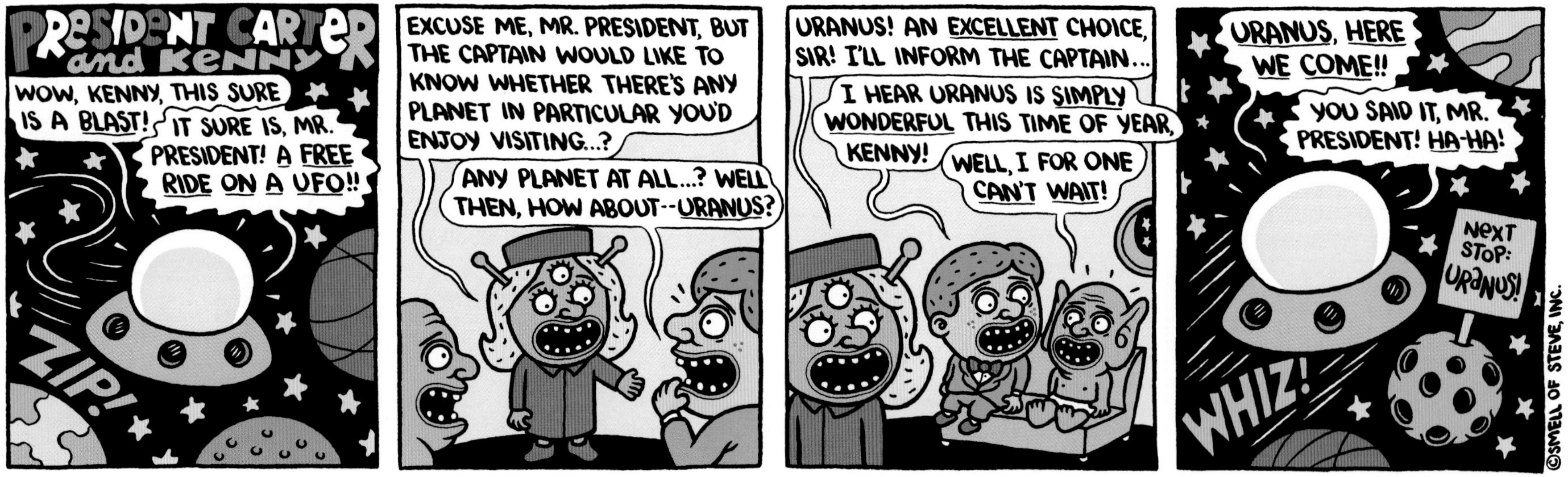
PRESIDENT CARTER and KENNY
WOW, KENNY, THIS SURE IS A BLAST!
IT SURE IS, MR. PRESIDENT! A FREE RIDE ON A UFO!!
ZIP!
EXCUSE ME, MR. PRESIDENT, BUT THE CAPTAIN WOULD LIKE TO KNOW WHETHER THERE'S ANY PLANET IN PARTICULAR YOU'D ENJOY VISITING...?
ANY PLANET AT ALL...? WELL THEN, HOW ABOUT--URANUS?
URANUS! AN EXCELLENT CHOICE, SIR! I'LL INFORM THE CAPTAIN...
I HEAR URANUS IS SIMPLY WONDERFUL THIS TIME OF YEAR, KENNY!
WELL, I FOR ONE CAN'T WAIT!
URANUS, HERE WE COME!!
YOU SAID IT, MR. PRESIDENT! HA-HA!
NEXT STOP: URANUS!
WHIZ!
©SMELL OF STEVE, INC.

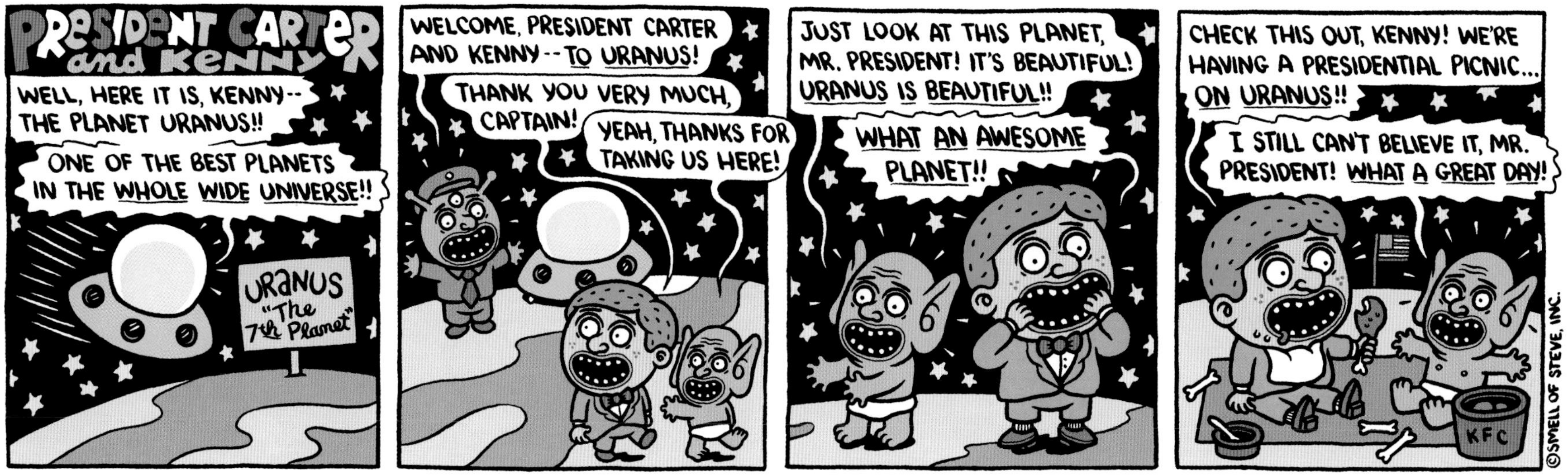
PRESIDENT CARTER and KENNY
WELL, HERE IT IS, KENNY-- THE PLANET URANUS!!
ONE OF THE BEST PLANETS IN THE WHOLE WIDE UNIVERSE!!
URANUS "The 7th Planet"
WELCOME, PRESIDENT CARTER AND KENNY--TO URANUS!
THANK YOU VERY MUCH, CAPTAIN!
YEAH, THANKS FOR TAKING US HERE!
JUST LOOK AT THIS PLANET, MR. PRESIDENT! IT'S BEAUTIFUL! URANUS IS BEAUTIFUL!!
WHAT AN AWESOME PLANET!!
CHECK THIS OUT, KENNY! WE'RE HAVING A PRESIDENTIAL PICNIC... ON URANUS!!
I STILL CAN'T BELIEVE IT, MR. PRESIDENT! WHAT A GREAT DAY!
KFC
©SMELL OF STEVE, INC.

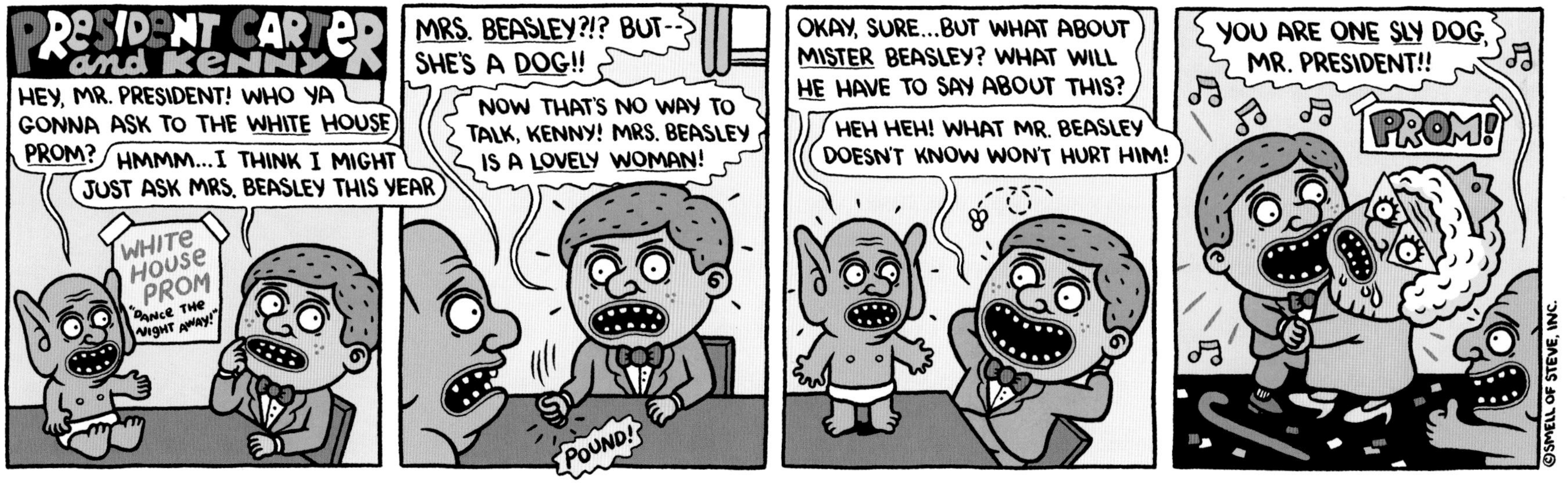
PRESIDENT CARTER and KENNY
HEY, MR. PRESIDENT! WHO YA GONNA ASK TO THE WHITE HOUSE PROM?
HMMM...I THINK I MIGHT JUST ASK MRS. BEASLEY THIS YEAR
WHITE HOUSE PROM "DANCE THE NIGHT AWAY!"
MRS. BEASLEY?!? BUT-- SHE'S A DOG!!
NOW THAT'S NO WAY TO TALK, KENNY! MRS. BEASLEY IS A LOVELY WOMAN!
POUND!
OKAY, SURE...BUT WHAT ABOUT MISTER BEASLEY? WHAT WILL HE HAVE TO SAY ABOUT THIS?
HEH HEH! WHAT MR. BEASLEY DOESN'T KNOW WON'T HURT HIM!
YOU ARE ONE SLY DOG, MR. PRESIDENT!!
PROM!
©SMELL OF STEVE, INC.

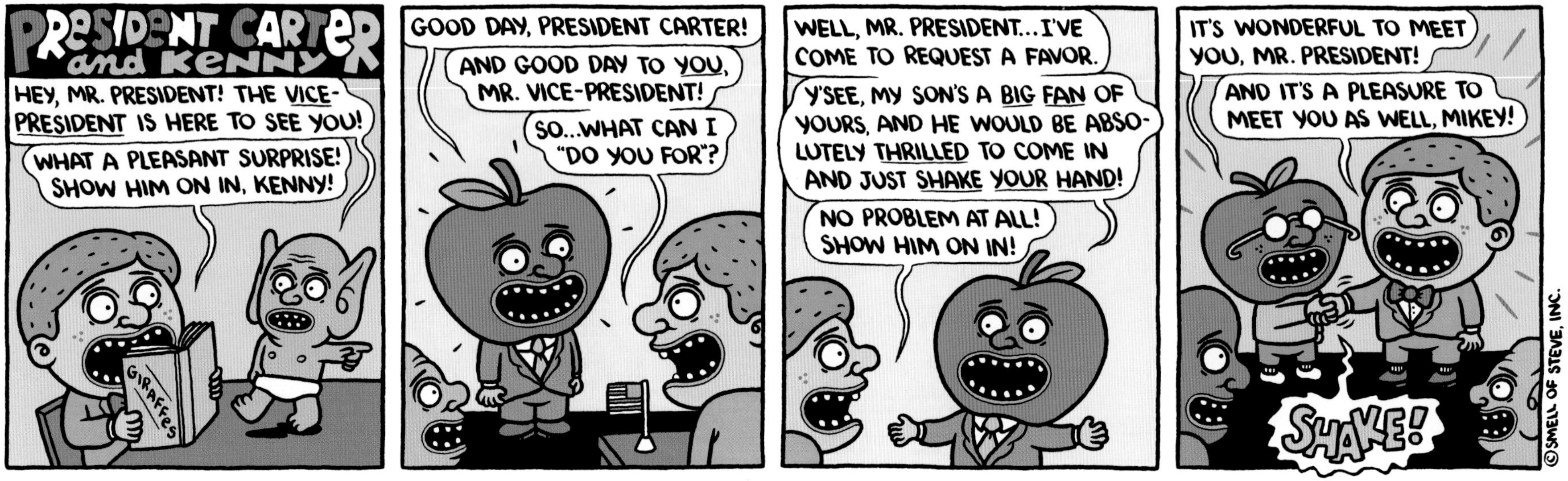
PRESIDENT CARTER and KENNY
HEY, MR. PRESIDENT! THE VICE-PRESIDENT IS HERE TO SEE YOU!
WHAT A PLEASANT SURPRISE! SHOW HIM ON IN, KENNY!
GIRAFFES
GOOD DAY, PRESIDENT CARTER!
AND GOOD DAY TO YOU, MR. VICE-PRESIDENT!
SO...WHAT CAN I "DO YOU FOR"?
WELL, MR. PRESIDENT...I'VE COME TO REQUEST A FAVOR.
Y'SEE, MY SON'S A BIG FAN OF YOURS, AND HE WOULD BE ABSOLUTELY THRILLED TO COME IN AND JUST SHAKE YOUR HAND!
NO PROBLEM AT ALL! SHOW HIM ON IN!
IT'S WONDERFUL TO MEET YOU, MR. PRESIDENT!
AND IT'S A PLEASURE TO MEET YOU AS WELL, MIKEY!
SHAKE!
©SMELL OF STEVE, INC.

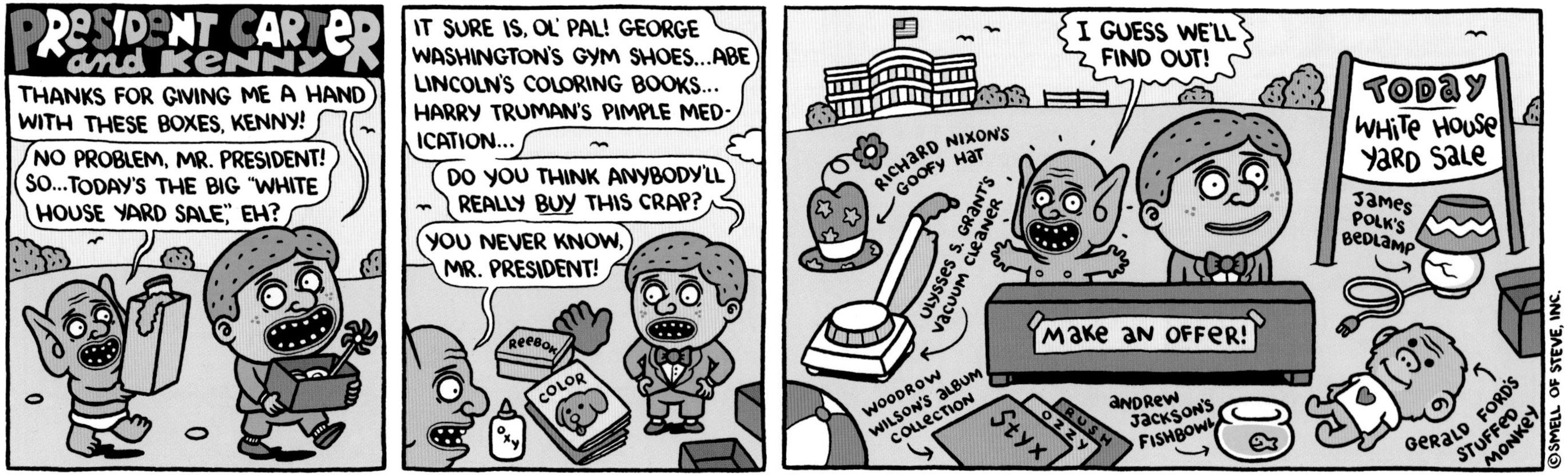
PRESIDENT CARTER and KENNY
THANKS FOR GIVING ME A HAND WITH THESE BOXES, KENNY!
NO PROBLEM, MR. PRESIDENT! SO...TODAY'S THE BIG "WHITE HOUSE YARD SALE," EH?
IT SURE IS, OL' PAL! GEORGE WASHINGTON'S GYM SHOES...ABE LINCOLN'S COLORING BOOKS...HARRY TRUMAN'S PIMPLE MEDICATION...
DO YOU THINK ANYBODY'LL REALLY BUY THIS CRAP?
YOU NEVER KNOW, MR. PRESIDENT!
REEBOK
COLOR
OXY
I GUESS WE'LL FIND OUT!
TODAY WHITE HOUSE YARD SALE
RICHARD NIXON'S GOOFY HAT
ULYSSES S. GRANT'S VACUUM CLEANER
JAMES POLK'S BEDLAMP
MAKE AN OFFER!
WOODROW WILSON'S ALBUM COLLECTION
STYX
OZZY
RUSH
ANDREW JACKSON'S FISHBOWL
GERALD FORD'S STUFFED MONKEY
©SMELL OF STEVE, INC.

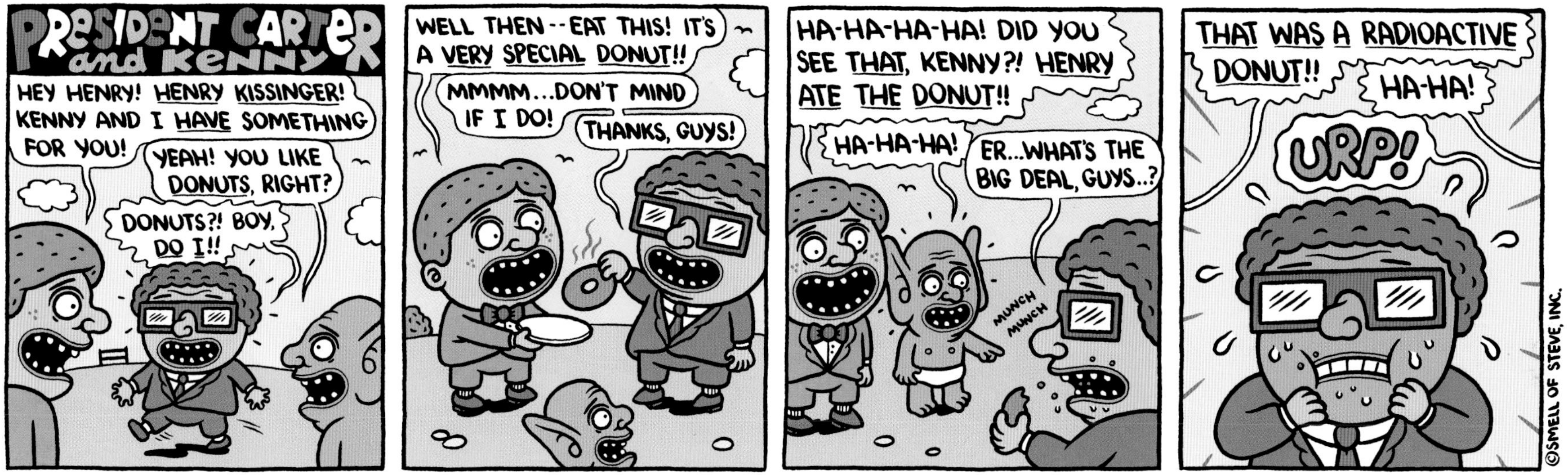
PRESIDENT CARTER and KENNY
HEY HENRY! HENRY KISSINGER! KENNY AND I HAVE SOMETHING FOR YOU!
YEAH! YOU LIKE DONUTS, RIGHT?
DONUTS?! BOY, DO I!!
WELL THEN--EAT THIS! IT'S A VERY SPECIAL DONUT!!
MMMM...DON'T MIND IF I DO!
THANKS, GUYS!
HA-HA-HA-HA! DID YOU SEE THAT, KENNY?! HENRY ATE THE DONUT!!
HA-HA-HA!
ER...WHAT'S THE BIG DEAL, GUYS...?
MUNCH MUNCH
THAT WAS A RADIOACTIVE DONUT!!
HA-HA!
URP!
©SMELL OF STEVE, INC.

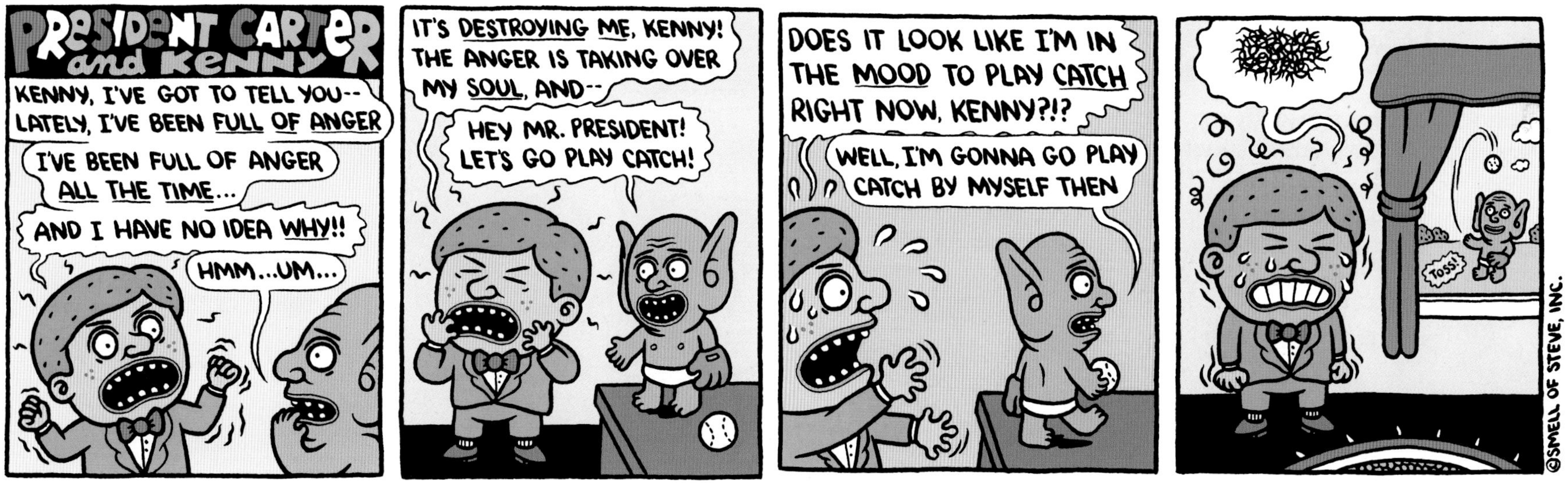
PRESIDENT CARTER and KENNY
KENNY, I'VE GOT TO TELL YOU-- LATELY, I'VE BEEN FULL OF ANGER
I'VE BEEN FULL OF ANGER ALL THE TIME...
AND I HAVE NO IDEA WHY!!
HMM...UM...
IT'S DESTROYING ME, KENNY! THE ANGER IS TAKING OVER MY SOUL, AND--
HEY MR. PRESIDENT! LET'S GO PLAY CATCH!
DOES IT LOOK LIKE I'M IN THE MOOD TO PLAY CATCH RIGHT NOW, KENNY?!?
WELL, I'M GONNA GO PLAY CATCH BY MYSELF THEN
TOSS!
©SMELL OF STEVE, INC.

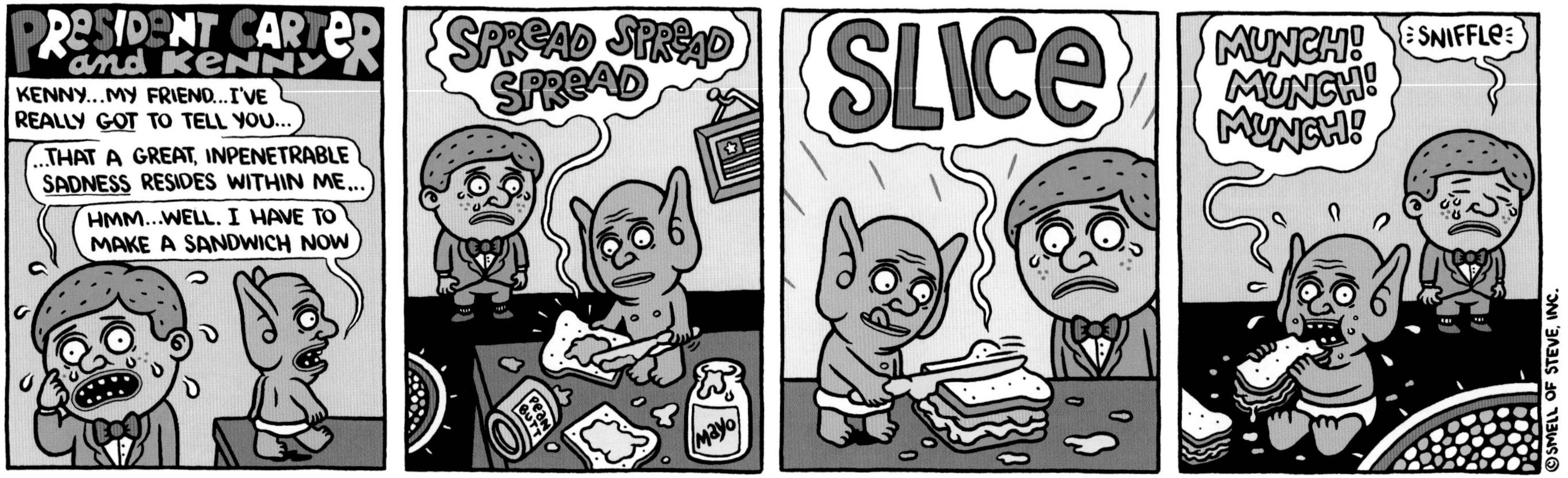
PRESIDENT CARTER and KENNY
KENNY...MY FRIEND...I'VE REALLY GOT TO TELL YOU...
...THAT A GREAT, INPENETRABLE SADNESS RESIDES WITHIN ME...
HMM...WELL. I HAVE TO MAKE A SANDWICH NOW
SPREAD SPREAD SPREAD
PEANUT BUTT
MAYO
SLICE
MUNCH! MUNCH! MUNCH!
SNIFFLE
©SMELL OF STEVE, INC.

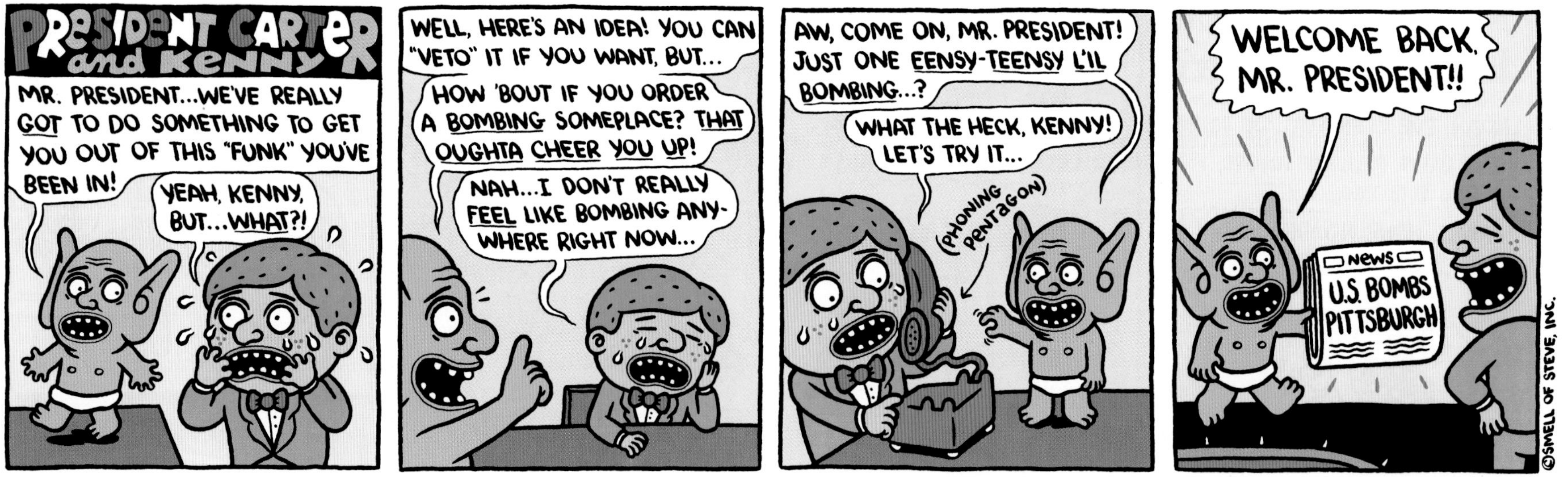
PRESIDENT CARTER and KENNY
MR. PRESIDENT...WE'VE REALLY GOT TO DO SOMETHING TO GET YOU OUT OF THIS "FUNK" YOU'VE BEEN IN!
YEAH, KENNY, BUT...WHAT?!
WELL, HERE'S AN IDEA! YOU CAN "VETO" IT IF YOU WANT, BUT...
HOW 'BOUT IF YOU ORDER A BOMBING SOMEPLACE? THAT OUGHTA CHEER YOU UP!
NAH...I DON'T REALLY FEEL LIKE BOMBING ANYWHERE RIGHT NOW...
AW, COME ON, MR. PRESIDENT! JUST ONE EENSY-TEENSY L'IL BOMBING...?
WHAT THE HECK, KENNY! LET'S TRY IT...
(PHONING PENTAGON)
WELCOME BACK, MR. PRESIDENT!!
NEWS
U.S. BOMBS PITTSBURGH
©SMELL OF STEVE, INC.

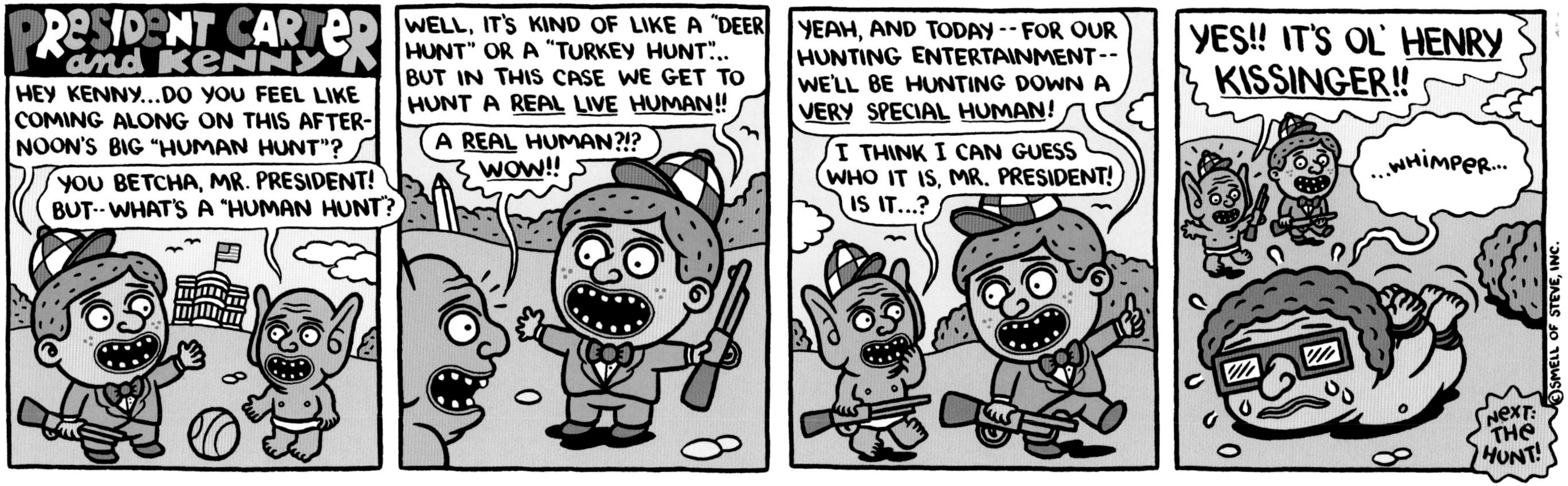
PRESIDENT CARTER and KENNY
HEY KENNY...DO YOU FEEL LIKE COMING ALONG ON THIS AFTERNOON'S BIG "HUMAN HUNT"?
YOU BETCHA, MR. PRESIDENT! BUT--WHAT'S A "HUMAN HUNT"?
WELL, IT'S KIND OF LIKE A "DEER HUNT" OR A "TURKEY HUNT"... BUT IN THIS CASE WE GET TO HUNT A REAL LIVE HUMAN!!
A REAL HUMAN?!? WOW!!
YEAH, AND TODAY--FOR OUR HUNTING ENTERTAINMENT--WE'LL BE HUNTING DOWN A VERY SPECIAL HUMAN!
I THINK I CAN GUESS WHO IT IS, MR. PRESIDENT! IS IT...?
YES!! IT'S OL' HENRY KISSINGER!!
...whimper...
NEXT: THE HUNT!
©SMELL OF STEVE, INC.

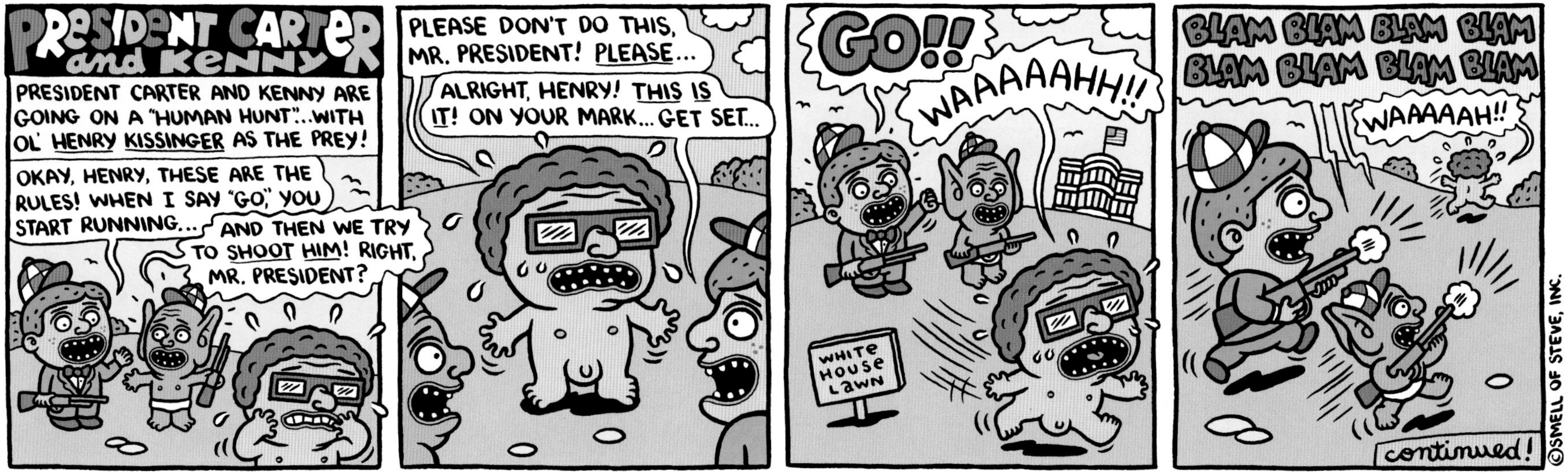
PRESIDENT CARTER and KENNY
PRESIDENT CARTER AND KENNY ARE GOING ON A "HUMAN HUNT"...WITH OL' HENRY KISSINGER AS THE PREY!
OKAY, HENRY, THESE ARE THE RULES! WHEN I SAY "GO," YOU START RUNNING...
AND THEN WE TRY TO SHOOT HIM! RIGHT, MR. PRESIDENT?
PLEASE DON'T DO THIS, MR. PRESIDENT! PLEASE...
ALRIGHT, HENRY! THIS IS IT! ON YOUR MARK... GET SET...
GO!!
WAAAAAHH!!
WHITE HOUSE LAWN
BLAM BLAM BLAM BLAM
BLAM BLAM BLAM BLAM
WAAAAAH!!
continued!
©SMELL OF STEVE, INC.

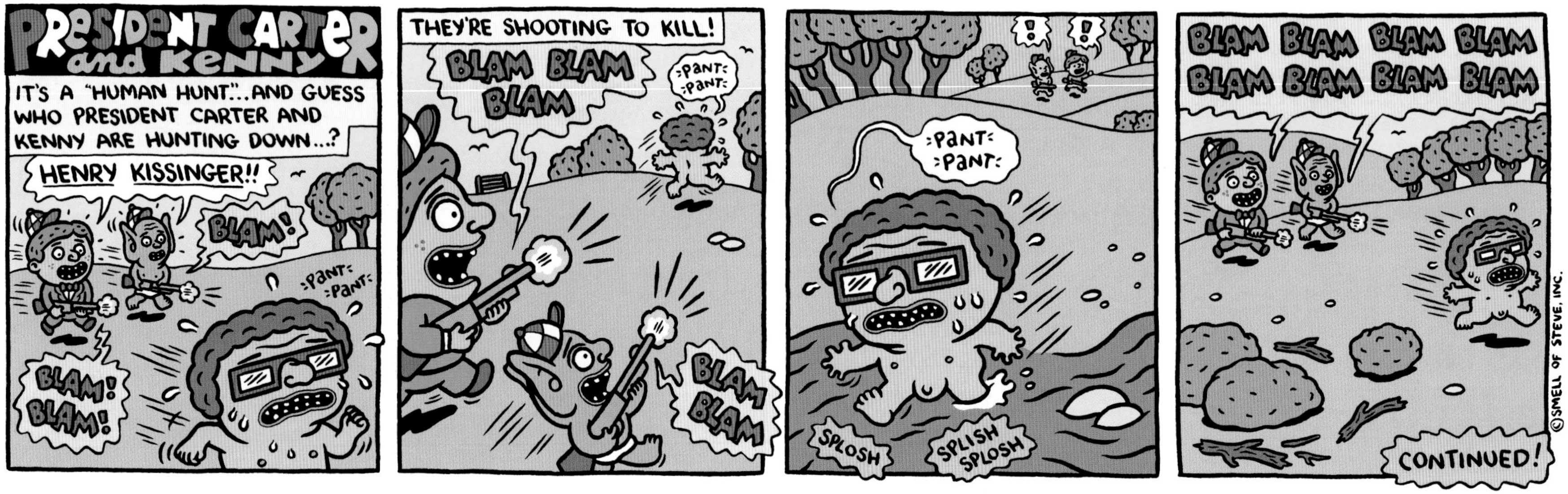
PRESIDENT CARTER and KENNY
IT'S A "HUMAN HUNT"... AND GUESS WHO PRESIDENT CARTER AND KENNY ARE HUNTING DOWN...?
HENRY KISSINGER!!
BLAM!
:PANT: :PANT:
BLAM! BLAM!
THEY'RE SHOOTING TO KILL!
BLAM BLAM BLAM
:PANT: :PANT:
BLAM BLAM
!
!
:PANT: :PANT:
SPLOSH
SPLISH SPLOSH
BLAM BLAM BLAM BLAM BLAM BLAM BLAM BLAM
CONTINUED!

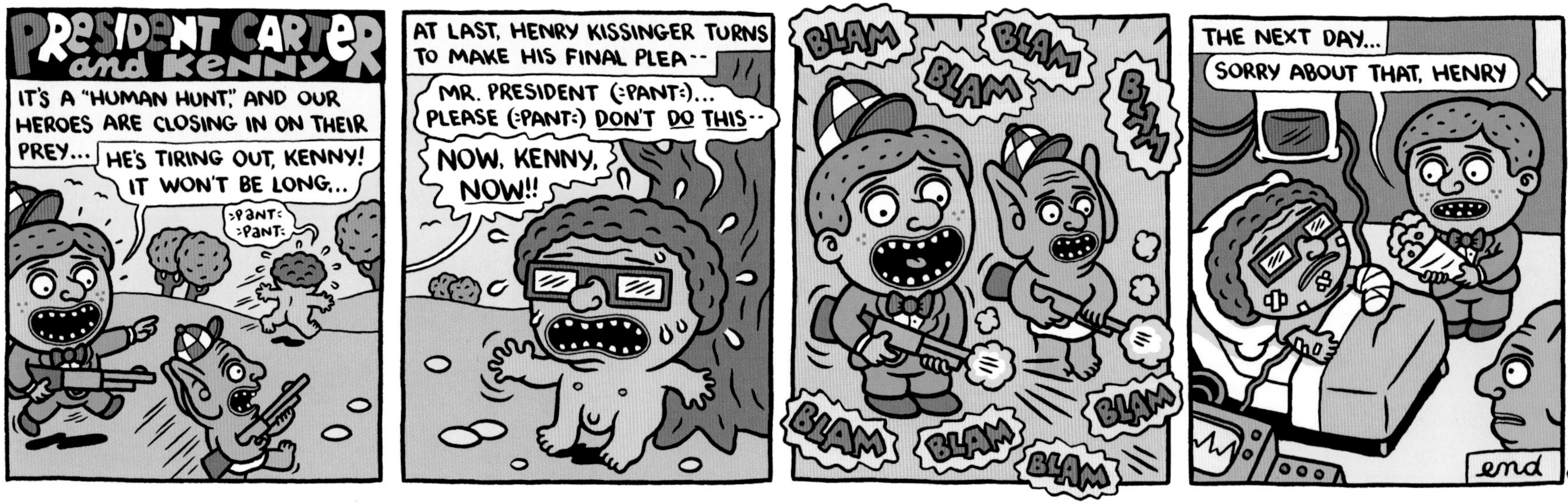
PRESIDENT CARTER and KENNY
IT'S A "HUMAN HUNT," AND OUR HEROES ARE CLOSING IN ON THEIR PREY...
HE'S TIRING OUT, KENNY! IT WON'T BE LONG...
:PANT: :PANT:
AT LAST, HENRY KISSINGER TURNS TO MAKE HIS FINAL PLEA--
MR. PRESIDENT (:PANT:)... PLEASE (:PANT:) DON'T DO THIS--
NOW, KENNY, NOW!!
BLAM
BLAM
BLAM
BLAM
BLAM
BLAM
BLAM
BLAM
THE NEXT DAY...
SORRY ABOUT THAT, HENRY
end

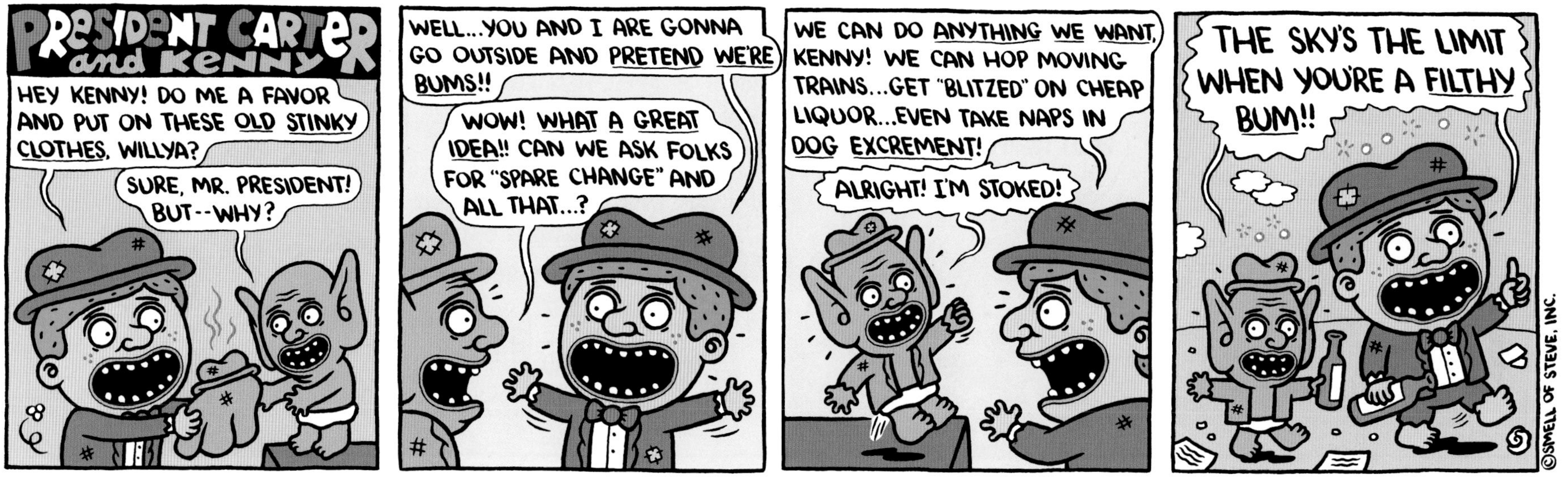
PRESIDENT CARTER and KENNY
HEY KENNY! DO ME A FAVOR AND PUT ON THESE OLD STINKY CLOTHES, WILLYA?
SURE, MR. PRESIDENT! BUT--WHY?
WELL...YOU AND I ARE GONNA GO OUTSIDE AND PRETEND WE'RE BUMS!!
WOW! WHAT A GREAT IDEA!! CAN WE ASK FOLKS FOR "SPARE CHANGE" AND ALL THAT...?
WE CAN DO ANYTHING WE WANT, KENNY! WE CAN HOP MOVING TRAINS...GET "BLITZED" ON CHEAP LIQUOR...EVEN TAKE NAPS IN DOG EXCREMENT!
ALRIGHT! I'M STOKED!
THE SKY'S THE LIMIT WHEN YOU'RE A FILTHY BUM!!
©SMELL OF STEVE, INC.

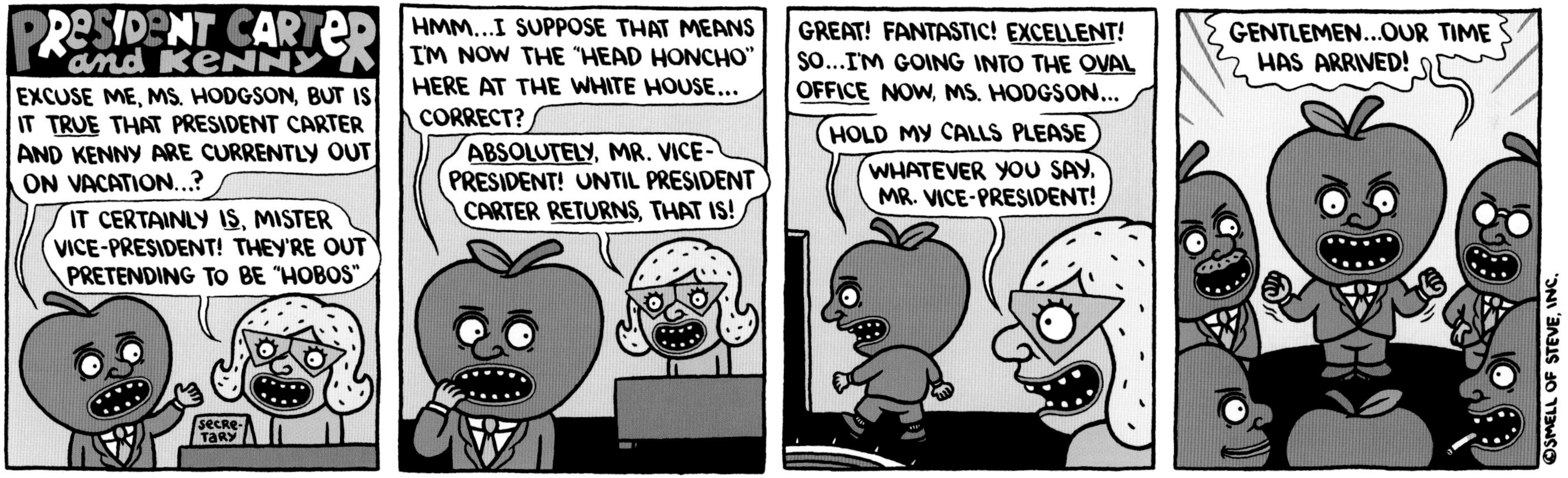
PRESIDENT CARTER and KENNY
EXCUSE ME, MS. HODGSON, BUT IS IT TRUE THAT PRESIDENT CARTER AND KENNY ARE CURRENTLY OUT ON VACATION...?
IT CERTAINLY IS, MISTER VICE-PRESIDENT! THEY'RE OUT PRETENDING TO BE "HOBOS"
SECRE-TARY
HMM...I SUPPOSE THAT MEANS I'M NOW THE "HEAD HONCHO" HERE AT THE WHITE HOUSE... CORRECT?
ABSOLUTELY, MR. VICE-PRESIDENT! UNTIL PRESIDENT CARTER RETURNS, THAT IS!
GREAT! FANTASTIC! EXCELLENT! SO...I'M GOING INTO THE OVAL OFFICE NOW, MS. HODGSON...
HOLD MY CALLS PLEASE
WHATEVER YOU SAY, MR. VICE-PRESIDENT!
GENTLEMEN...OUR TIME HAS ARRIVED!
©SMELL OF STEVE, INC.

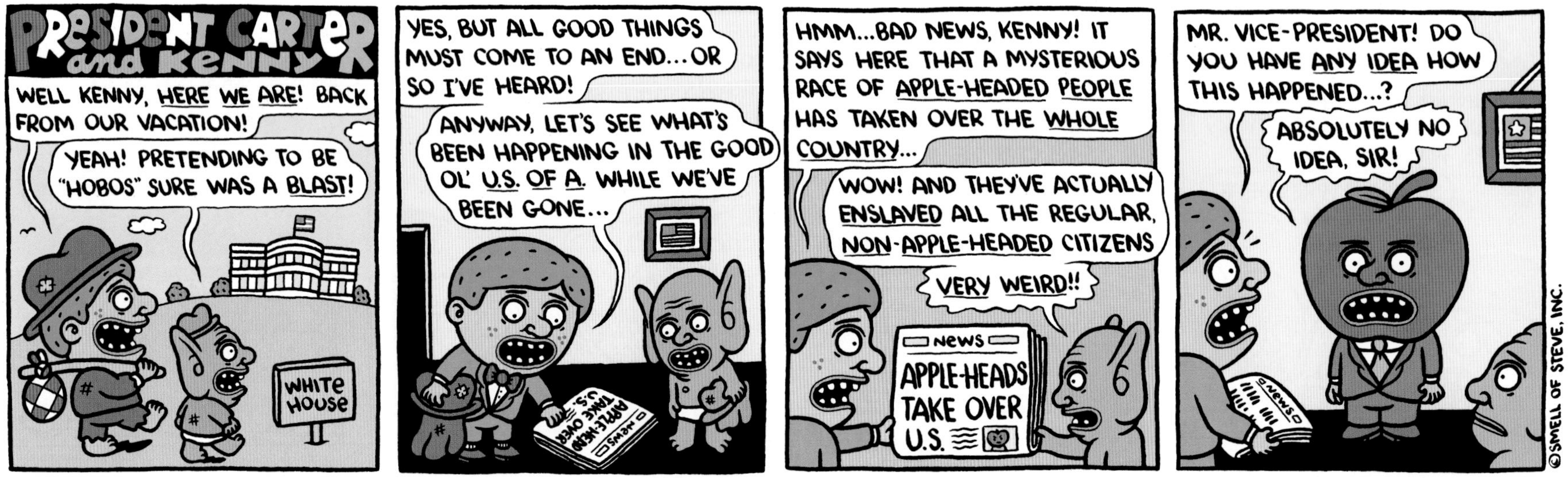
PRESIDENT CARTER and KENNY
WELL KENNY, HERE WE ARE! BACK FROM OUR VACATION!
YEAH! PRETENDING TO BE "HOBOS" SURE WAS A BLAST!
WHITE HOUSE
YES, BUT ALL GOOD THINGS MUST COME TO AN END... OR SO I'VE HEARD!
ANYWAY, LET'S SEE WHAT'S BEEN HAPPENING IN THE GOOD OL' U.S. OF A. WHILE WE'VE BEEN GONE...
HMM...BAD NEWS, KENNY! IT SAYS HERE THAT A MYSTERIOUS RACE OF APPLE-HEADED PEOPLE HAS TAKEN OVER THE WHOLE COUNTRY...
WOW! AND THEY'VE ACTUALLY ENSLAVED ALL THE REGULAR, NON-APPLE-HEADED CITIZENS
VERY WEIRD!!
NEWS
APPLE-HEADS TAKE OVER U.S.
MR. VICE-PRESIDENT! DO YOU HAVE ANY IDEA HOW THIS HAPPENED...?
ABSOLUTELY NO IDEA, SIR!
NEWS
©SMELL OF STEVE, INC.

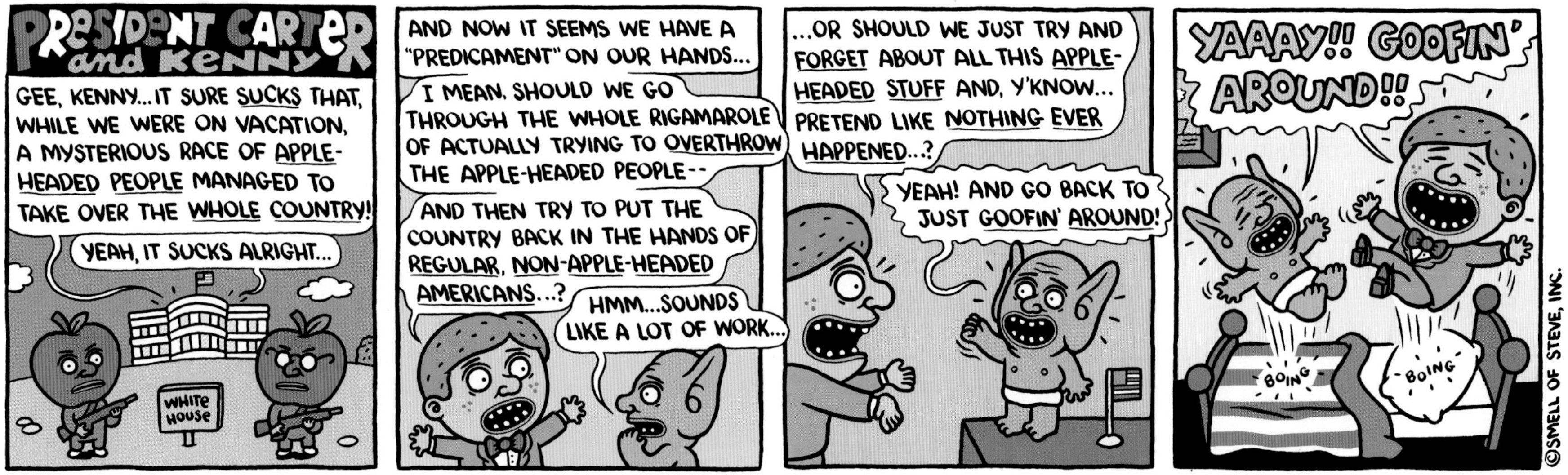
PRESIDENT CARTER and KENNY
GEE, KENNY... IT SURE SUCKS THAT, WHILE WE WERE ON VACATION, A MYSTERIOUS RACE OF APPLE-HEADED PEOPLE MANAGED TO TAKE OVER THE WHOLE COUNTRY!
YEAH, IT SUCKS ALRIGHT...
WHITE HOUSE
AND NOW IT SEEMS WE HAVE A "PREDICAMENT" ON OUR HANDS...
I MEAN, SHOULD WE GO THROUGH THE WHOLE RIGAMAROLE OF ACTUALLY TRYING TO OVERTHROW THE APPLE-HEADED PEOPLE--
AND THEN TRY TO PUT THE COUNTRY BACK IN THE HANDS OF REGULAR, NON-APPLE-HEADED AMERICANS...?
HMM...SOUNDS LIKE A LOT OF WORK...
...OR SHOULD WE JUST TRY AND FORGET ABOUT ALL THIS APPLE-HEADED STUFF AND, Y'KNOW... PRETEND LIKE NOTHING EVER HAPPENED...?
YEAH! AND GO BACK TO JUST GOOFIN' AROUND!
YAAAY!! GOOFIN' AROUND!!
BOING
BOING
©SMELL OF STEVE, INC.

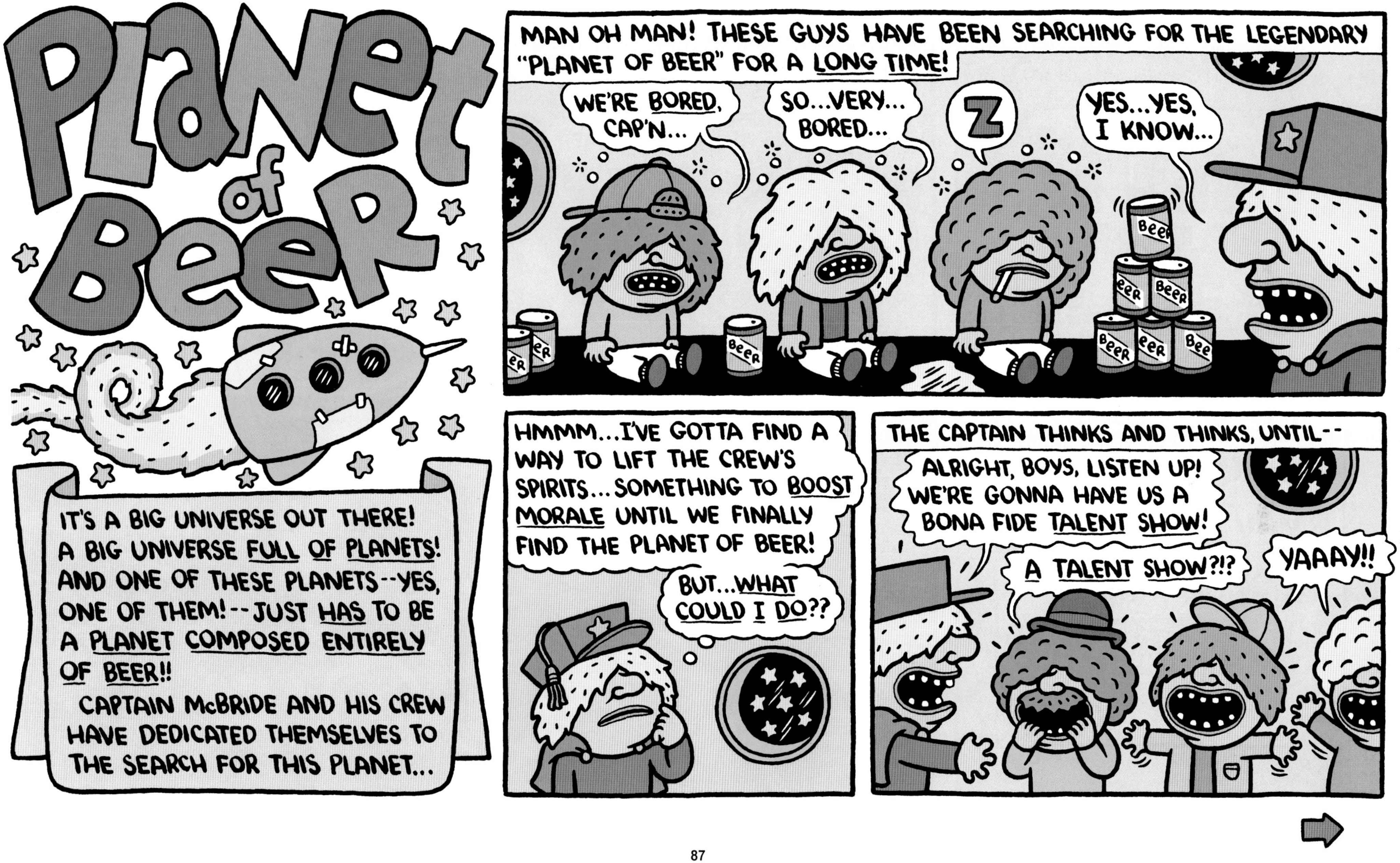
PLANET of BEER
IT'S A BIG UNIVERSE OUT THERE! A BIG UNIVERSE FULL OF PLANETS! AND ONE OF THESE PLANETS--YES, ONE OF THEM!--JUST HAS TO BE A PLANET COMPOSED ENTIRELY OF BEER!!
CAPTAIN McBRIDE AND HIS CREW HAVE DEDICATED THEMSELVES TO THE SEARCH FOR THIS PLANET...
MAN OH MAN! THESE GUYS HAVE BEEN SEARCHING FOR THE LEGENDARY "PLANET OF BEER" FOR A LONG TIME!
WE'RE BORED, CAP'N...
SO...VERY... BORED...
Z
YES...YES, I KNOW...
BEER
HMMM...I'VE GOTTA FIND A WAY TO LIFT THE CREW'S SPIRITS...SOMETHING TO BOOST MORALE UNTIL WE FINALLY FIND THE PLANET OF BEER!
BUT...WHAT COULD I DO??
THE CAPTAIN THINKS AND THINKS, UNTIL--
ALRIGHT, BOYS, LISTEN UP! WE'RE GONNA HAVE US A BONA FIDE TALENT SHOW!
A TALENT SHOW?!?
YAAAY!!

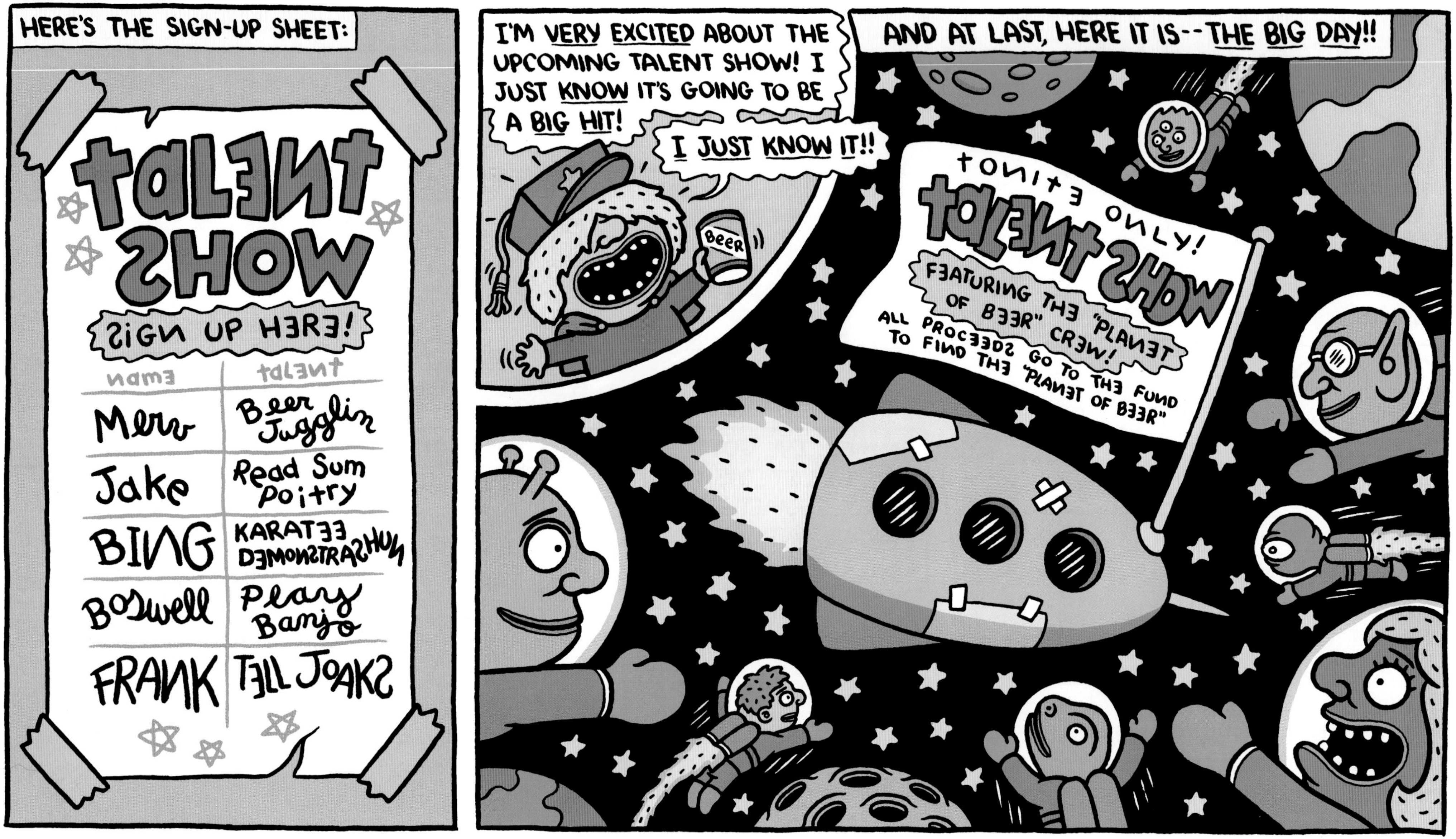
HERE'S THE SIGN-UP SHEET:
TALENT SHOW
SIGN UP HERE!
NAME | TALENT
Merv | Beer Jugglin
Jake | Read Sum Poitry
BING | KARATEE DEMONSTRASHUN
Boswell | Play Banjo
FRANK | TELL JOAKS
I'M VERY EXCITED ABOUT THE UPCOMING TALENT SHOW! I JUST KNOW IT'S GOING TO BE A BIG HIT!
I JUST KNOW IT!!
BEER
AND AT LAST, HERE IT IS--THE BIG DAY!!
TONITE ONLY!
TALENT SHOW
FEATURING THE "PLANET OF BEER" CREW!
ALL PROCEEDS GO TO THE FUND TO FIND THE "PLANET OF BEER"

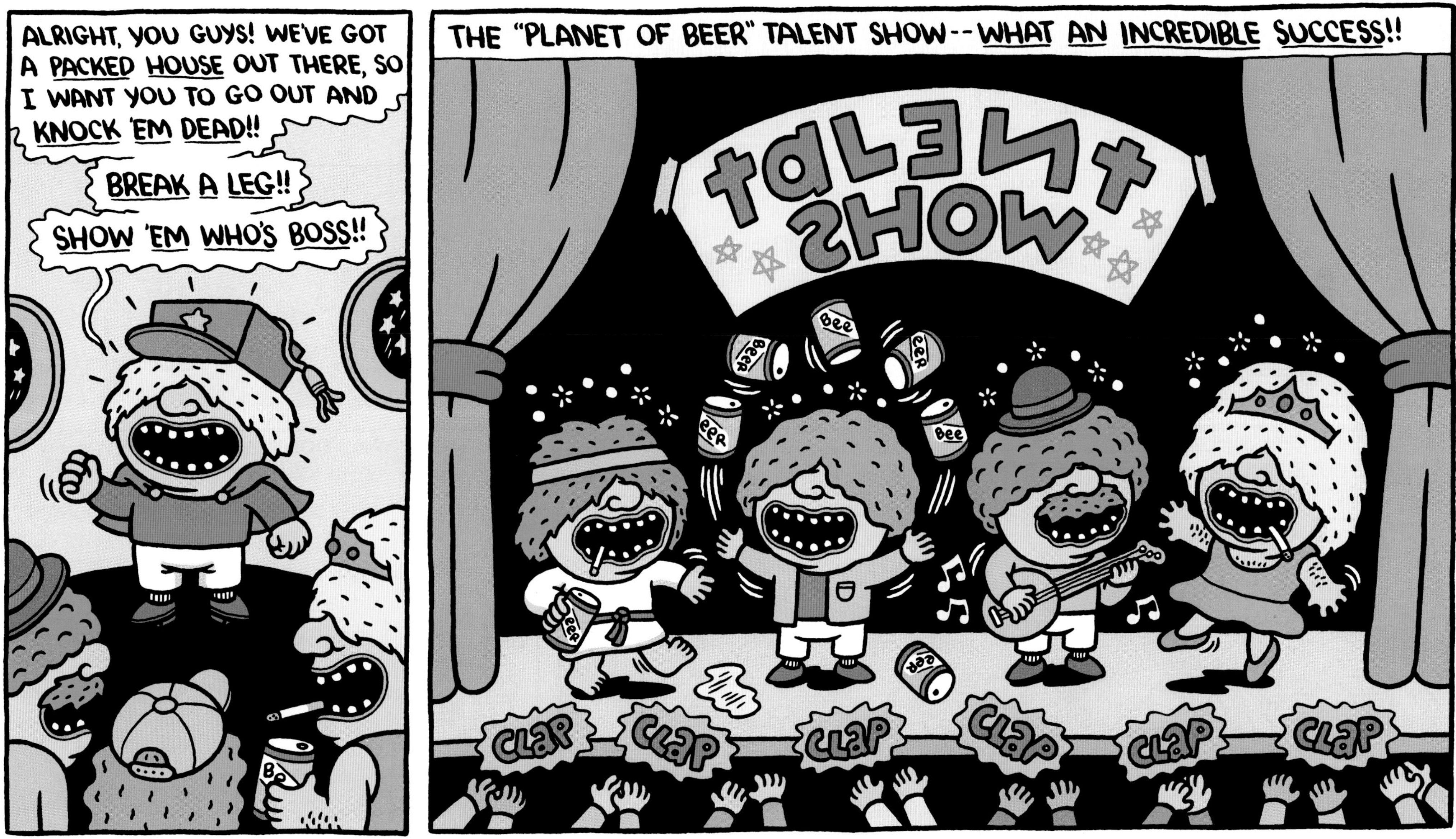
ALRIGHT, YOU GUYS! WE'VE GOT A PACKED HOUSE OUT THERE, SO I WANT YOU TO GO OUT AND KNOCK 'EM DEAD!!
BREAK A LEG!!
SHOW 'EM WHO'S BOSS!!
THE "PLANET OF BEER" TALENT SHOW--WHAT AN INCREDIBLE SUCCESS!!
CLAP
CLAP
CLAP
CLAP
CLAP
CLAP

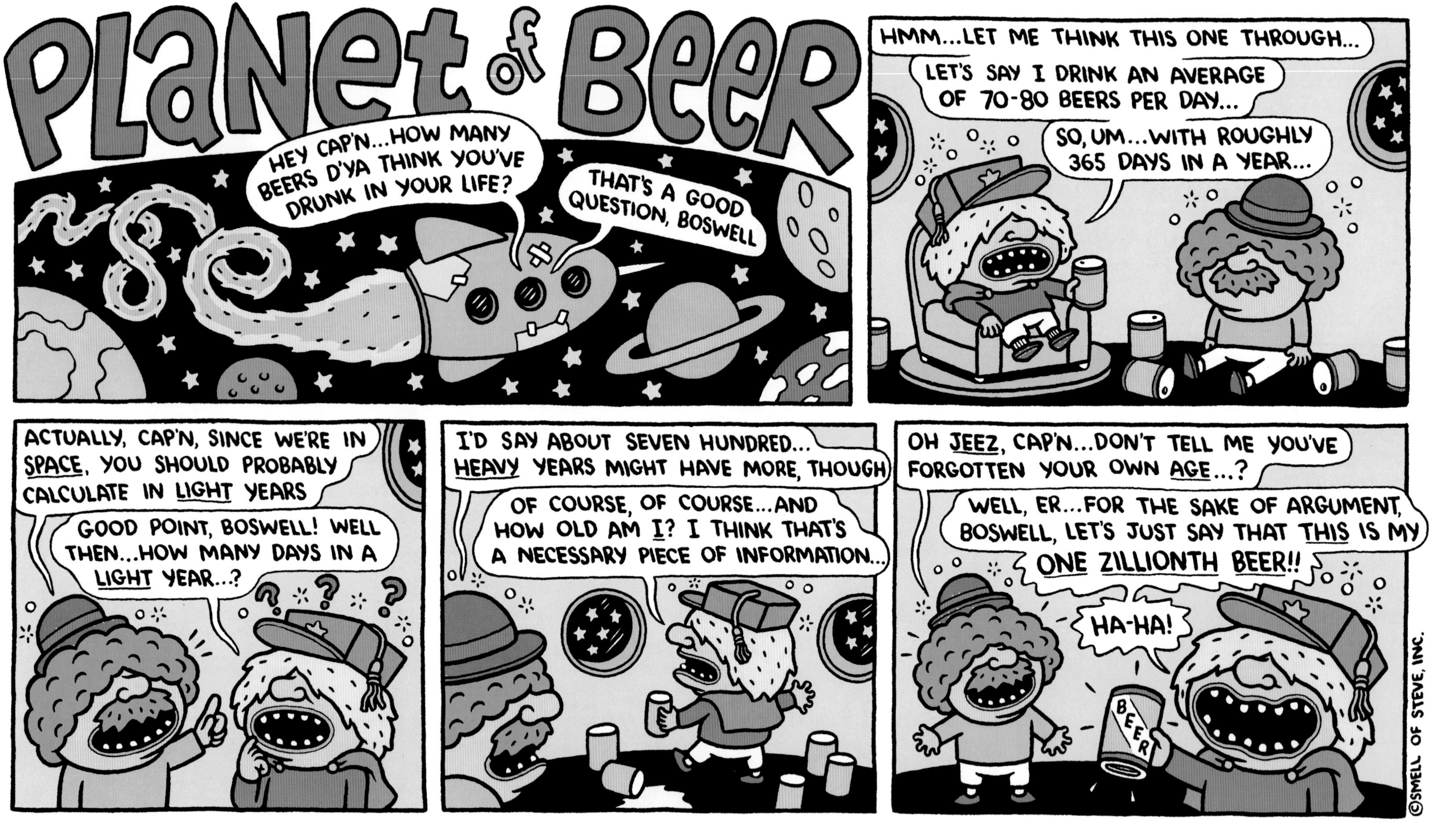
PLANET of BEER
HEY CAP'N...HOW MANY BEERS D'YA THINK YOU'VE DRUNK IN YOUR LIFE?
THAT'S A GOOD QUESTION, BOSWELL
HMM...LET ME THINK THIS ONE THROUGH...
LET'S SAY I DRINK AN AVERAGE OF 70-80 BEERS PER DAY...
SO, UM...WITH ROUGHLY 365 DAYS IN A YEAR...
ACTUALLY, CAP'N, SINCE WE'RE IN SPACE, YOU SHOULD PROBABLY CALCULATE IN LIGHT YEARS
GOOD POINT, BOSWELL! WELL THEN...HOW MANY DAYS IN A LIGHT YEAR...?
I'D SAY ABOUT SEVEN HUNDRED... HEAVY YEARS MIGHT HAVE MORE, THOUGH
OF COURSE, OF COURSE...AND HOW OLD AM I? I THINK THAT'S A NECESSARY PIECE OF INFORMATION...
OH JEEZ, CAP'N...DON'T TELL ME YOU'VE FORGOTTEN YOUR OWN AGE...?
WELL, ER...FOR THE SAKE OF ARGUMENT, BOSWELL, LET'S JUST SAY THAT THIS IS MY ONE ZILLIONTH BEER!!
HA-HA!
BEER
©SMELL OF STEVE, INC.

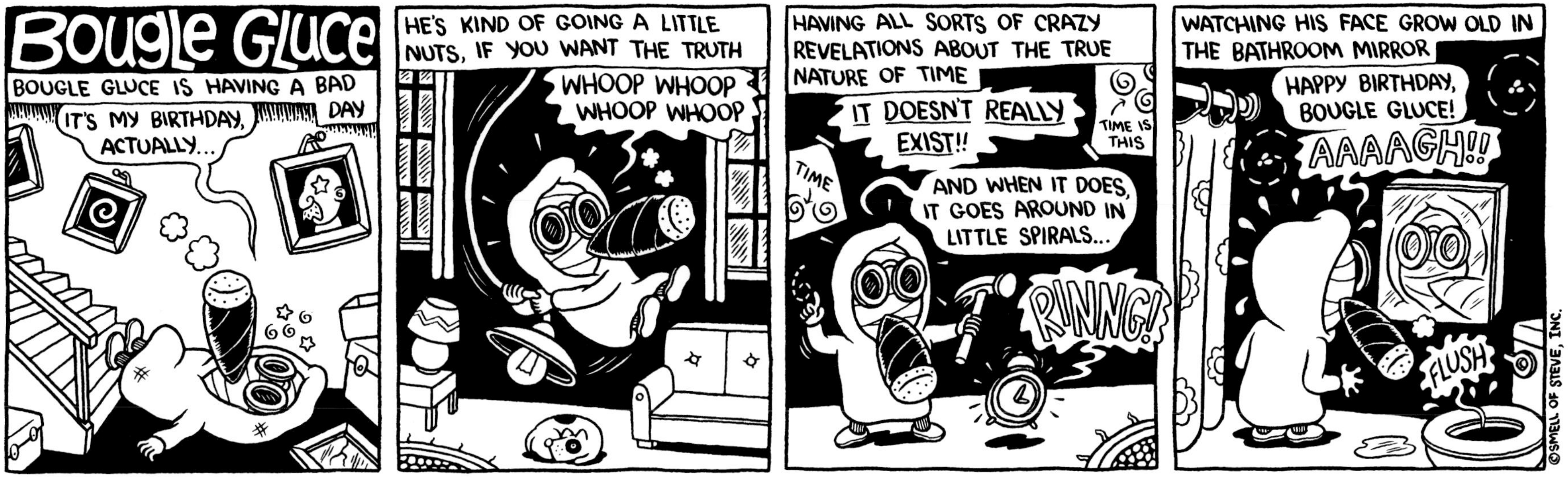
BOUGLE GLUCE
BOUGLE GLUCE IS HAVING A BAD DAY
IT'S MY BIRTHDAY, ACTUALLY...
HE'S KIND OF GOING A LITTLE NUTS, IF YOU WANT THE TRUTH
WHOOP WHOOP WHOOP WHOOP
HAVING ALL SORTS OF CRAZY REVELATIONS ABOUT THE TRUE NATURE OF TIME
IT DOESN'T REALLY EXIST!!
TIME IS THIS
TIME
AND WHEN IT DOES, IT GOES AROUND IN LITTLE SPIRALS...
RINNG!
WATCHING HIS FACE GROW OLD IN THE BATHROOM MIRROR
HAPPY BIRTHDAY, BOUGLE GLUCE!
AAAAGH!!
FLUSH
©SMELL OF STEVE, INC.

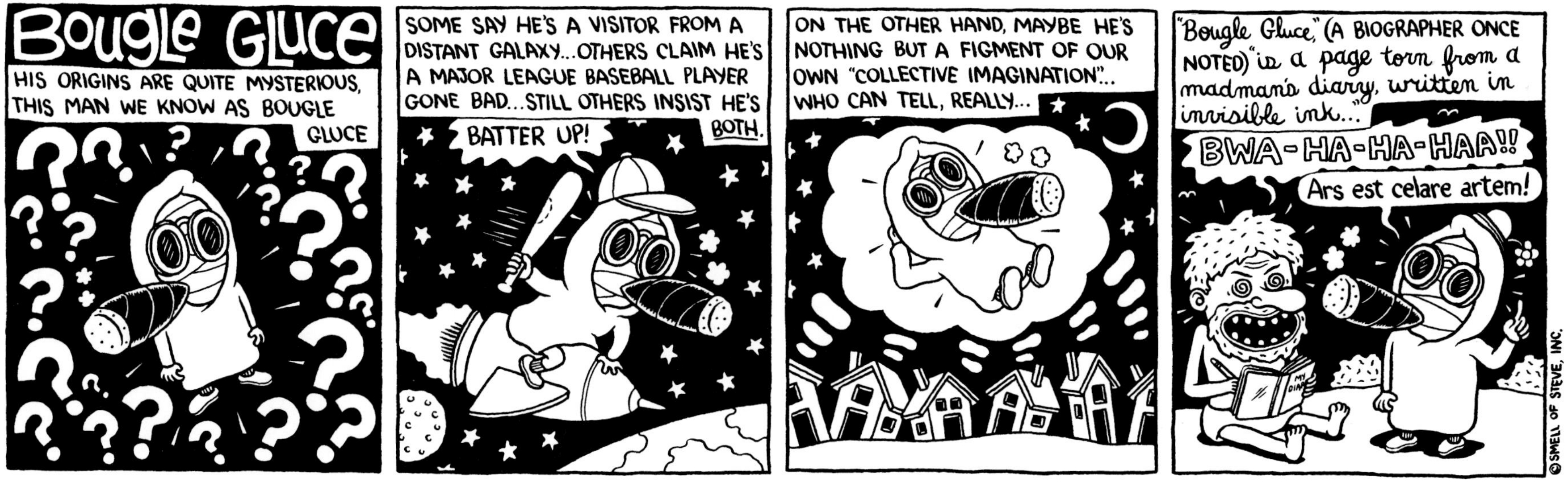
BOUGLE GLUCE
HIS ORIGINS ARE QUITE MYSTERIOUS, THIS MAN WE KNOW AS BOUGLE GLUCE
SOME SAY HE'S A VISITOR FROM A DISTANT GALAXY...OTHERS CLAIM HE'S A MAJOR LEAGUE BASEBALL PLAYER GONE BAD...STILL OTHERS INSIST HE'S BOTH.
BATTER UP!
ON THE OTHER HAND, MAYBE HE'S NOTHING BUT A FIGMENT OF OUR OWN "COLLECTIVE IMAGINATION"... WHO CAN TELL, REALLY...
"Bougle Gluce," (A BIOGRAPHER ONCE NOTED) "is a page torn from a madman's diary, written in invisible ink..."
BWA-HA-HA-HAA!!
Ars est celare artem!
©SMELL OF STEVE, INC.

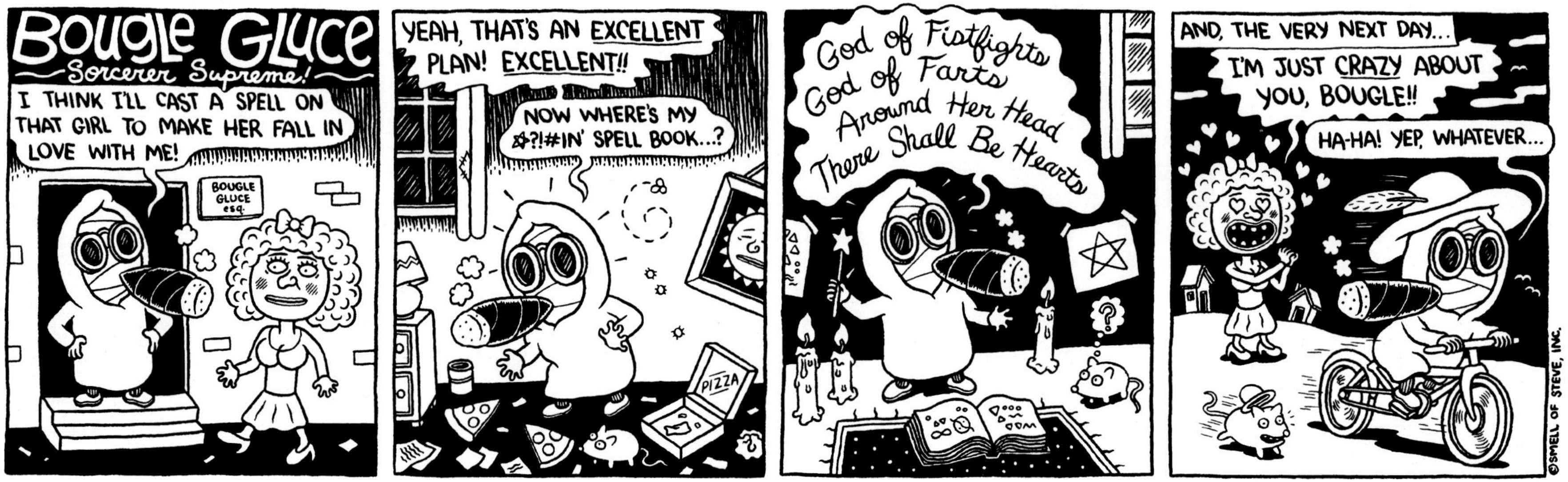
Bougle Gluce
Sorcerer Supreme!
I THINK I'LL CAST A SPELL ON THAT GIRL TO MAKE HER FALL IN LOVE WITH ME!
BOUGLE GLUCE esq.
YEAH, THAT'S AN EXCELLENT PLAN! EXCELLENT!!
NOW WHERE'S MY ✡?!#IN' SPELL BOOK...?
PIZZA
God of Fistfights
God of Farts
Around Her Head
There Shall Be Hearts
AND, THE VERY NEXT DAY...
I'M JUST CRAZY ABOUT YOU, BOUGLE!!
HA-HA! YEP, WHATEVER...
©SMELL OF STEVE, INC.

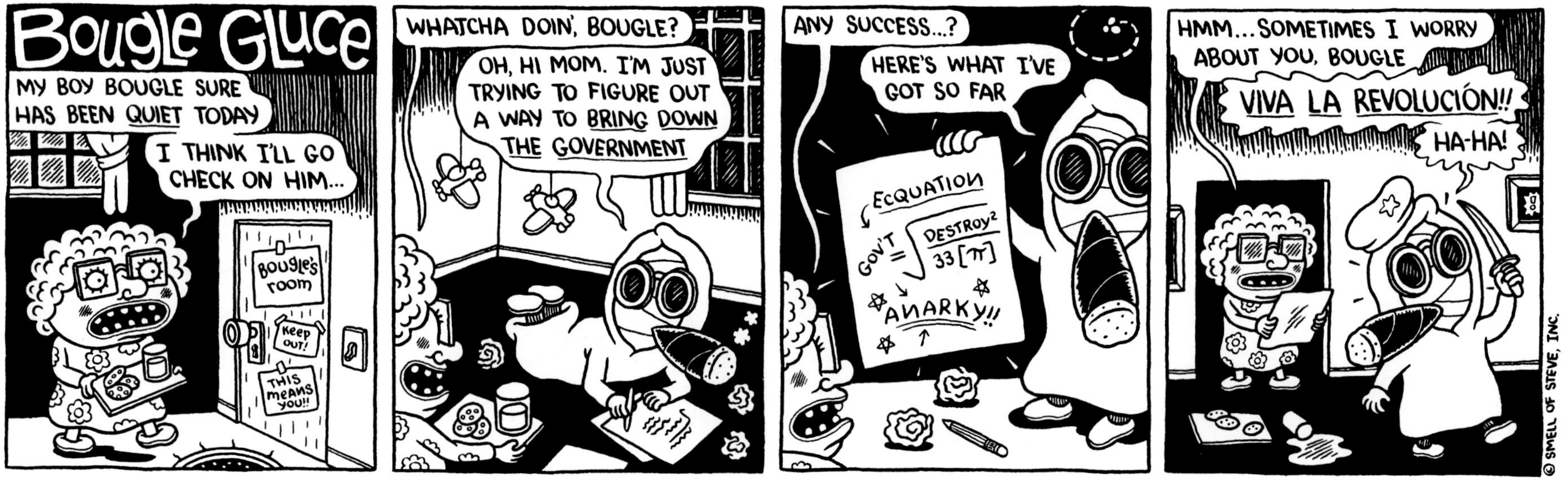
Bougle Gluce
MY BOY BOUGLE SURE HAS BEEN QUIET TODAY
I THINK I'LL GO CHECK ON HIM...
Bougle's room
Keep out!
THIS means you!!
WHATCHA DOIN', BOUGLE?
OH, HI MOM. I'M JUST TRYING TO FIGURE OUT A WAY TO BRING DOWN THE GOVERNMENT
ANY SUCCESS...?
HERE'S WHAT I'VE GOT SO FAR
ECQUATION
GOV'T = √(DESTROY² / 33 [π])
ANARKY!!
HMM... SOMETIMES I WORRY ABOUT YOU, BOUGLE
VIVA LA REVOLUCIÓN!!
HA-HA!
© SMELL OF STEVE, INC.

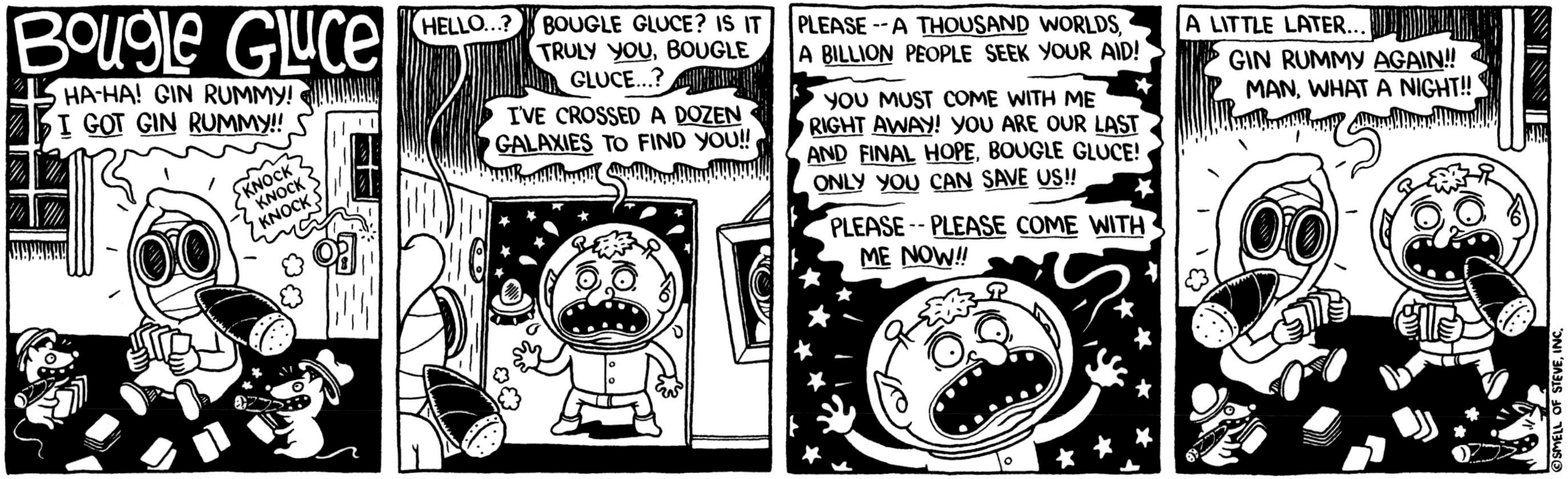
BOUGLE GLUCE
HA-HA! GIN RUMMY! I GOT GIN RUMMY!!
KNOCK KNOCK KNOCK
HELLO...?
BOUGLE GLUCE? IS IT TRULY YOU, BOUGLE GLUCE...?
I'VE CROSSED A DOZEN GALAXIES TO FIND YOU!!
PLEASE -- A THOUSAND WORLDS, A BILLION PEOPLE SEEK YOUR AID!
YOU MUST COME WITH ME RIGHT AWAY! YOU ARE OUR LAST AND FINAL HOPE, BOUGLE GLUCE! ONLY YOU CAN SAVE US!!
PLEASE -- PLEASE COME WITH ME NOW!!
A LITTLE LATER...
GIN RUMMY AGAIN!! MAN, WHAT A NIGHT!!
© SMELL OF STEVE, INC.

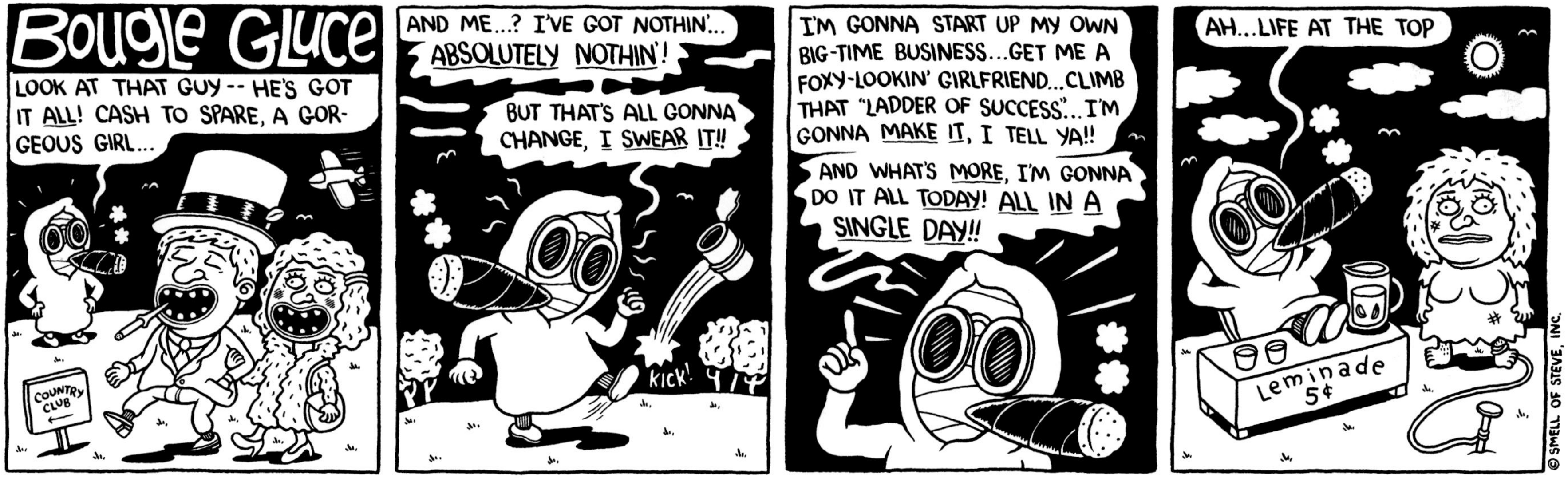
BOUGLE GLUCE
LOOK AT THAT GUY -- HE'S GOT IT ALL! CASH TO SPARE, A GORGEOUS GIRL...
COUNTRY CLUB
AND ME...? I'VE GOT NOTHIN'... ABSOLUTELY NOTHIN'!
BUT THAT'S ALL GONNA CHANGE, I SWEAR IT!!
KICK!
I'M GONNA START UP MY OWN BIG-TIME BUSINESS...GET ME A FOXY-LOOKIN' GIRLFRIEND...CLIMB THAT "LADDER OF SUCCESS"... I'M GONNA MAKE IT, I TELL YA!!
AND WHAT'S MORE, I'M GONNA DO IT ALL TODAY! ALL IN A SINGLE DAY!!
AH...LIFE AT THE TOP
Leminade 5¢
© SMELL OF STEVE, INC.

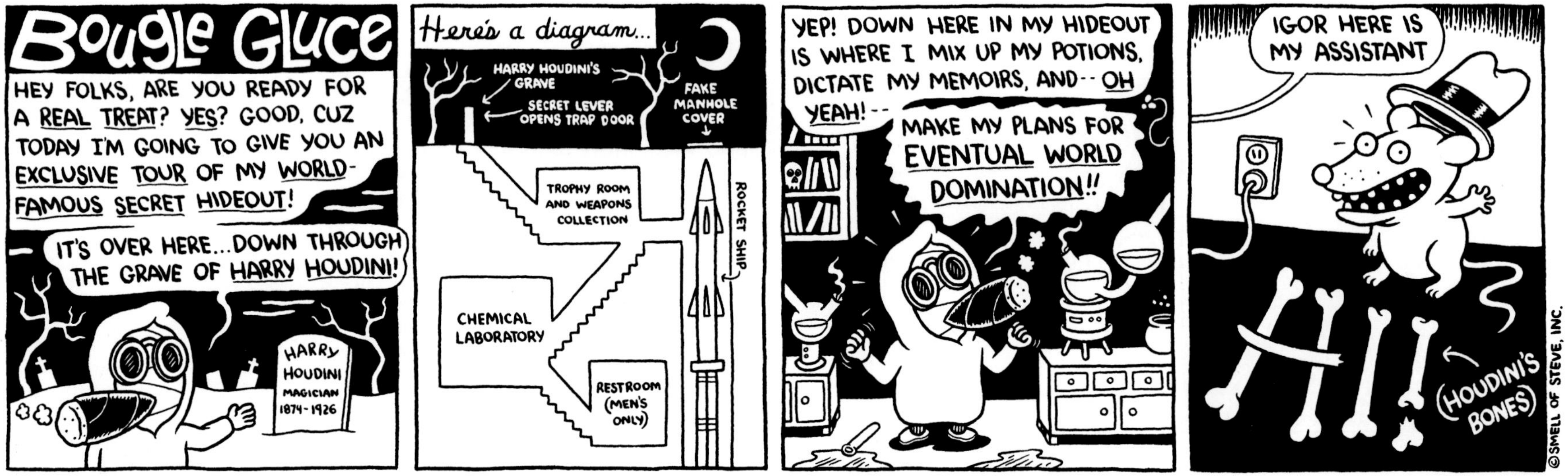

Bougle Gluce
HEY FOLKS, ARE YOU READY FOR A REAL TREAT? YES? GOOD, CUZ TODAY I'M GOING TO GIVE YOU AN EXCLUSIVE TOUR OF MY WORLD-FAMOUS SECRET HIDEOUT!
IT'S OVER HERE... DOWN THROUGH THE GRAVE OF HARRY HOUDINI!
HARRY HOUDINI MAGICIAN 1874-1926
Here's a diagram...
HARRY HOUDINI'S GRAVE
SECRET LEVER OPENS TRAP DOOR
FAKE MANHOLE COVER
TROPHY ROOM AND WEAPONS COLLECTION
ROCKET SHIP
CHEMICAL LABORATORY
RESTROOM (MEN'S ONLY)
YEP! DOWN HERE IN MY HIDEOUT IS WHERE I MIX UP MY POTIONS, DICTATE MY MEMOIRS, AND-- OH YEAH! --
MAKE MY PLANS FOR EVENTUAL WORLD DOMINATION!!
IGOR HERE IS MY ASSISTANT
(HOUDINI'S BONES)
©SMELL OF STEVE, INC.

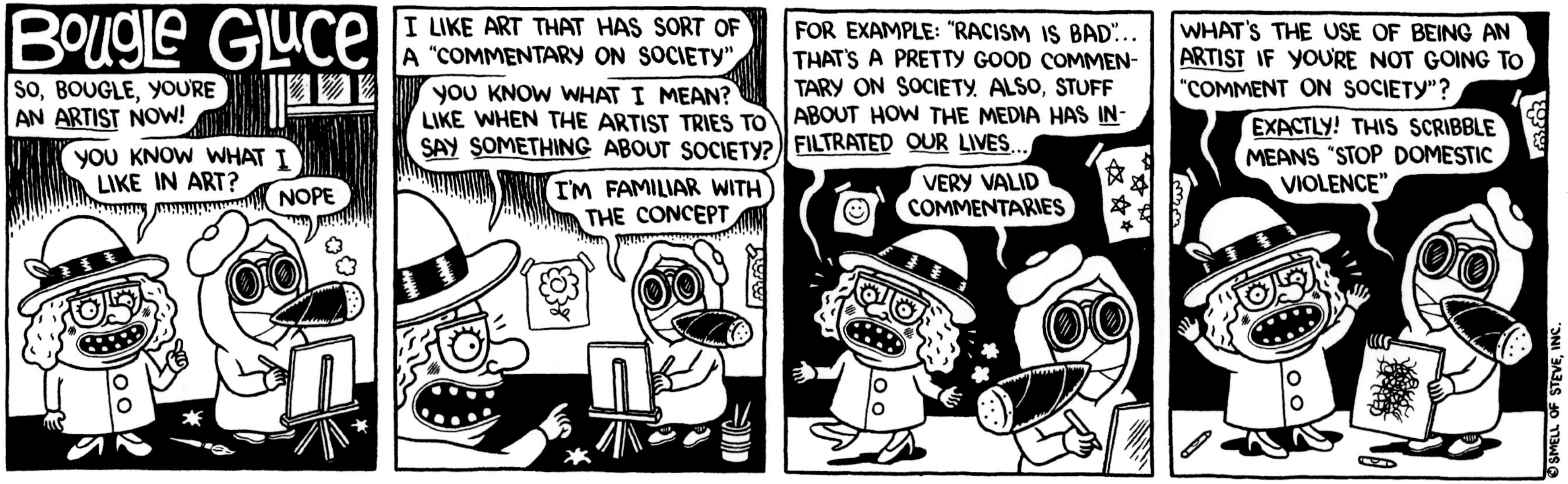

Bougle Gluce
SO, BOUGLE, YOU'RE AN ARTIST NOW!
YOU KNOW WHAT I LIKE IN ART?
NOPE
I LIKE ART THAT HAS SORT OF A "COMMENTARY ON SOCIETY"
YOU KNOW WHAT I MEAN? LIKE WHEN THE ARTIST TRIES TO SAY SOMETHING ABOUT SOCIETY?
I'M FAMILIAR WITH THE CONCEPT
FOR EXAMPLE: "RACISM IS BAD"... THAT'S A PRETTY GOOD COMMENTARY ON SOCIETY. ALSO, STUFF ABOUT HOW THE MEDIA HAS INFILTRATED OUR LIVES...
VERY VALID COMMENTARIES
WHAT'S THE USE OF BEING AN ARTIST IF YOU'RE NOT GOING TO "COMMENT ON SOCIETY"?
EXACTLY! THIS SCRIBBLE MEANS "STOP DOMESTIC VIOLENCE"
©SMELL OF STEVE, INC.

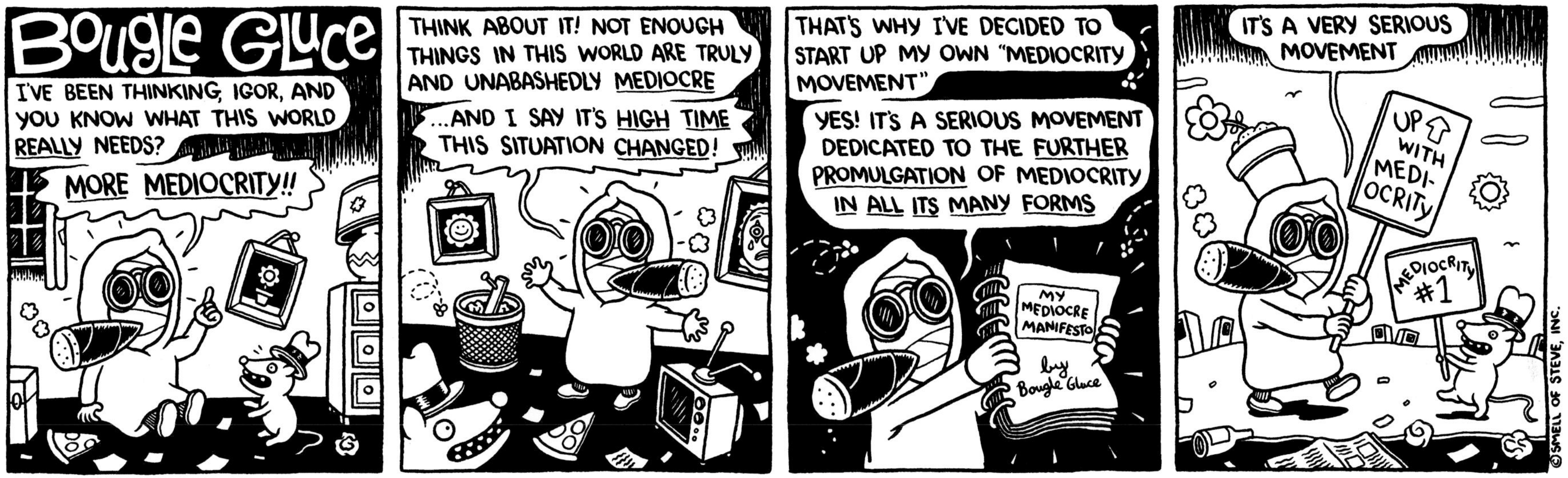
BOUGLE GLUCE
I'VE BEEN THINKING, IGOR, AND YOU KNOW WHAT THIS WORLD REALLY NEEDS?
MORE MEDIOCRITY!!
THINK ABOUT IT! NOT ENOUGH THINGS IN THIS WORLD ARE TRULY AND UNABASHEDLY MEDIOCRE
...AND I SAY IT'S HIGH TIME THIS SITUATION CHANGED!
THAT'S WHY I'VE DECIDED TO START UP MY OWN "MEDIOCRITY MOVEMENT"
YES! IT'S A SERIOUS MOVEMENT DEDICATED TO THE FURTHER PROMULGATION OF MEDIOCRITY IN ALL ITS MANY FORMS
MY MEDIOCRE MANIFESTO by Bougle Gluce
IT'S A VERY SERIOUS MOVEMENT
UP WITH MEDIOCRITY
MEDIOCRITY #1
©SMELL OF STEVE, INC.

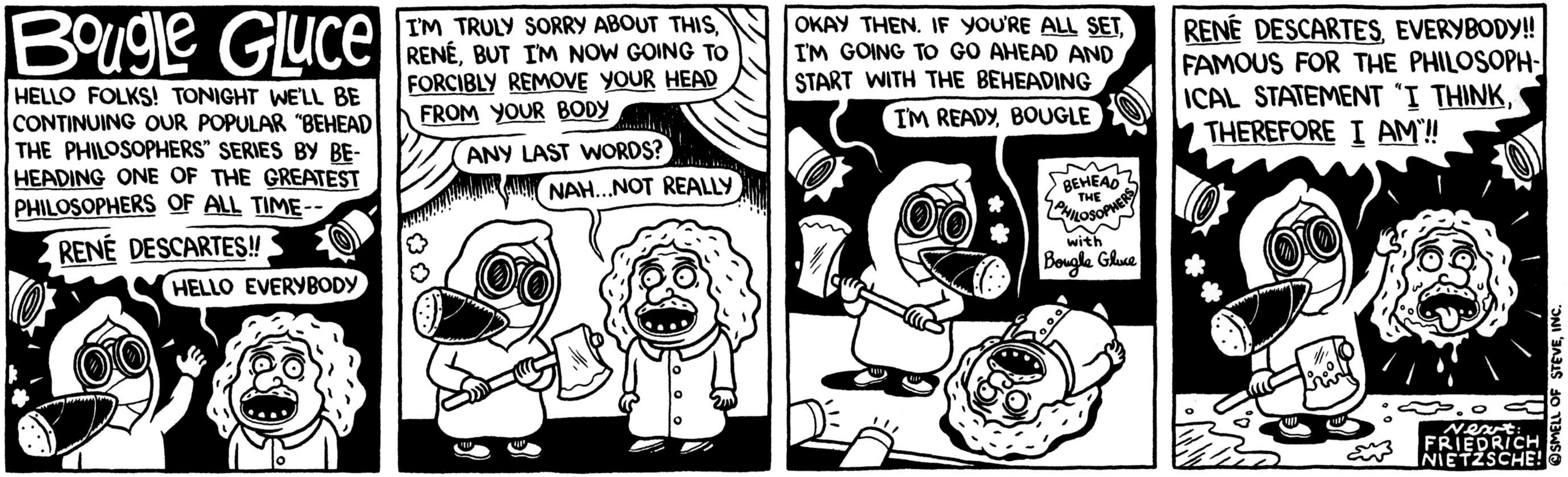
BOUGLE GLUCE
HELLO FOLKS! TONIGHT WE'LL BE CONTINUING OUR POPULAR "BEHEAD THE PHILOSOPHERS" SERIES BY BEHEADING ONE OF THE GREATEST PHILOSOPHERS OF ALL TIME--
RENÉ DESCARTES!!
HELLO EVERYBODY
I'M TRULY SORRY ABOUT THIS, RENÉ, BUT I'M NOW GOING TO FORCIBLY REMOVE YOUR HEAD FROM YOUR BODY
ANY LAST WORDS?
NAH...NOT REALLY
OKAY THEN. IF YOU'RE ALL SET, I'M GOING TO GO AHEAD AND START WITH THE BEHEADING
I'M READY, BOUGLE
BEHEAD THE PHILOSOPHERS with Bougle Gluce
RENÉ DESCARTES, EVERYBODY!! FAMOUS FOR THE PHILOSOPHICAL STATEMENT "I THINK, THEREFORE I AM"!!
Next: FRIEDRICH NIETZSCHE!
©SMELL OF STEVE, INC.

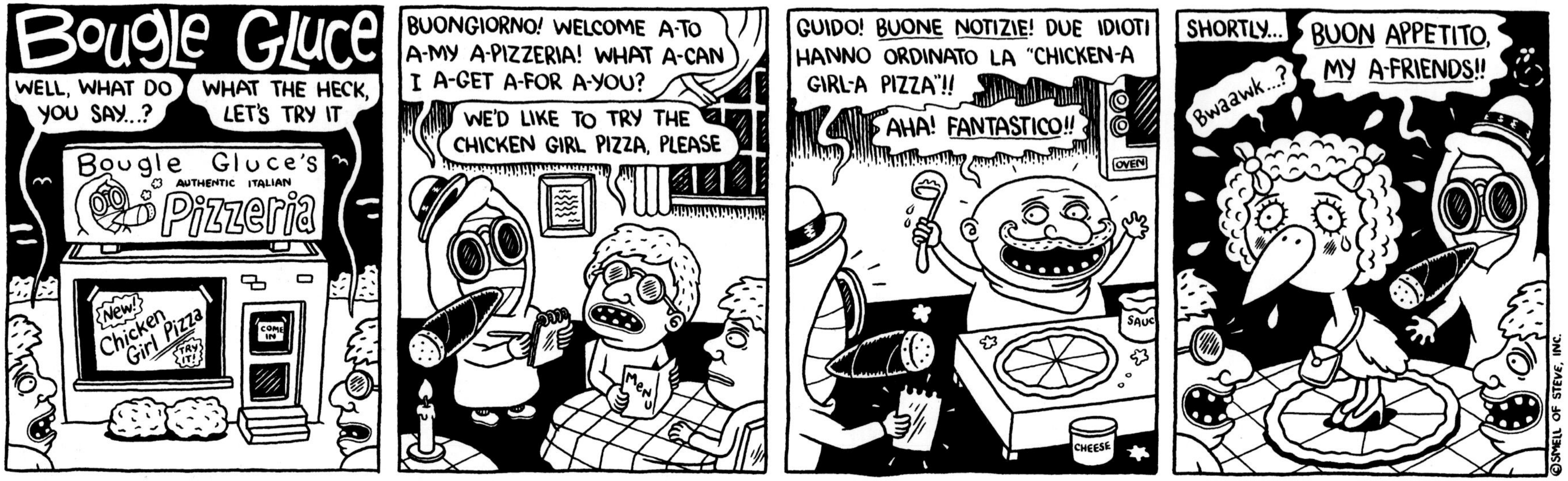
Bougle Gluce
WELL, WHAT DO YOU SAY...?
WHAT THE HECK, LET'S TRY IT
Bougle Gluce's AUTHENTIC ITALIAN Pizzeria
New! Chicken Girl Pizza TRY IT!
COME IN
BUONGIORNO! WELCOME A-TO A-MY A-PIZZERIA! WHAT A-CAN I A-GET A-FOR A-YOU?
WE'D LIKE TO TRY THE CHICKEN GIRL PIZZA, PLEASE
MENU
GUIDO! BUONE NOTIZIE! DUE IDIOTI HANNO ORDINATO LA "CHICKEN-A GIRL-A PIZZA"!!
AHA! FANTASTICO!!
OVEN
SAUC
CHEESE
SHORTLY...
BUON APPETITO, MY A-FRIENDS!!
Bwaawk...?
©SMELL OF STEVE, INC.

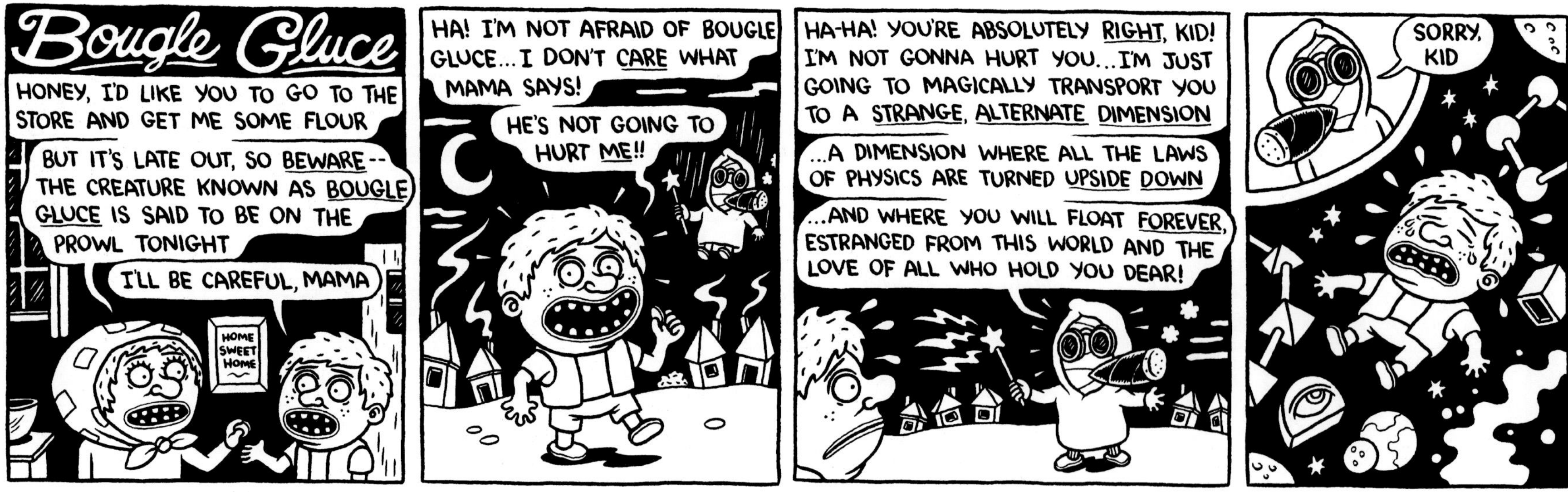
Bougle Gluce
HONEY, I'D LIKE YOU TO GO TO THE STORE AND GET ME SOME FLOUR
BUT IT'S LATE OUT, SO BEWARE-- THE CREATURE KNOWN AS BOUGLE GLUCE IS SAID TO BE ON THE PROWL TONIGHT
I'LL BE CAREFUL, MAMA
HOME SWEET HOME
HA! I'M NOT AFRAID OF BOUGLE GLUCE... I DON'T CARE WHAT MAMA SAYS!
HE'S NOT GOING TO HURT ME!!
HA-HA! YOU'RE ABSOLUTELY RIGHT, KID! I'M NOT GONNA HURT YOU... I'M JUST GOING TO MAGICALLY TRANSPORT YOU TO A STRANGE, ALTERNATE DIMENSION
...A DIMENSION WHERE ALL THE LAWS OF PHYSICS ARE TURNED UPSIDE DOWN
...AND WHERE YOU WILL FLOAT FOREVER, ESTRANGED FROM THIS WORLD AND THE LOVE OF ALL WHO HOLD YOU DEAR!
SORRY, KID
©SMELL OF STEVE, INC.

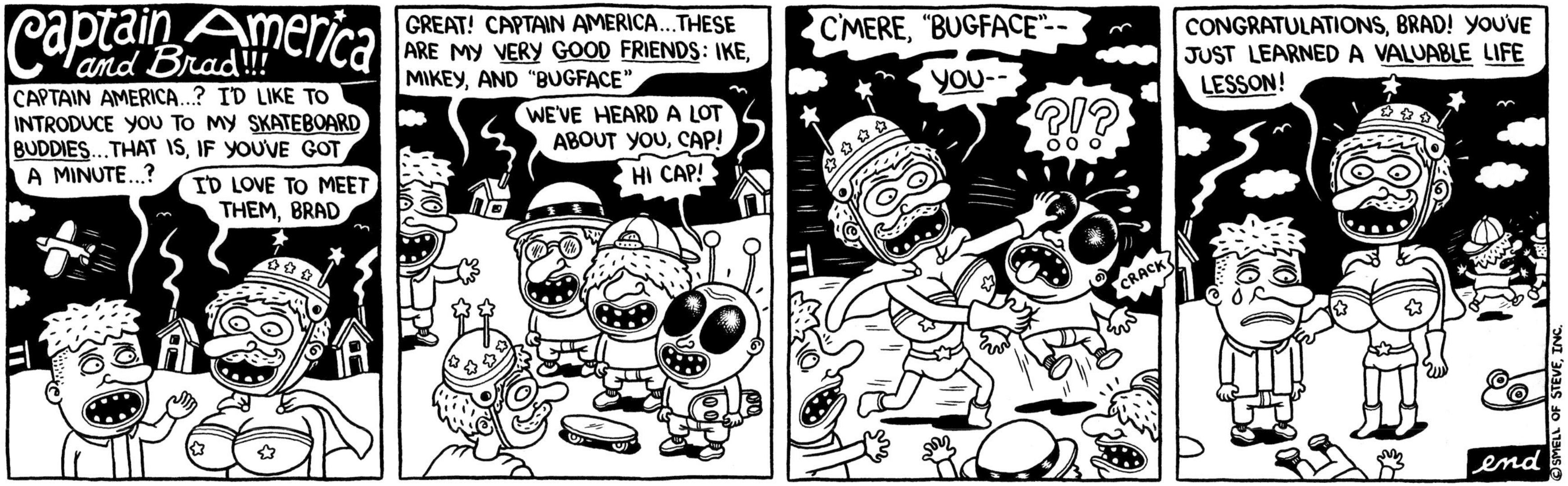
Captain America and Brad!!!
CAPTAIN AMERICA...? I'D LIKE TO INTRODUCE YOU TO MY SKATEBOARD BUDDIES...THAT IS, IF YOU'VE GOT A MINUTE...?
I'D LOVE TO MEET THEM, BRAD
GREAT! CAPTAIN AMERICA...THESE ARE MY VERY GOOD FRIENDS: IKE, MIKEY, AND "BUGFACE"
WE'VE HEARD A LOT ABOUT YOU, CAP!
HI CAP!
C'MERE, "BUGFACE"--
YOU--
?!?
CRACK
CONGRATULATIONS, BRAD! YOU'VE JUST LEARNED A VALUABLE LIFE LESSON!
end
©SMELL OF STEVE, INC.

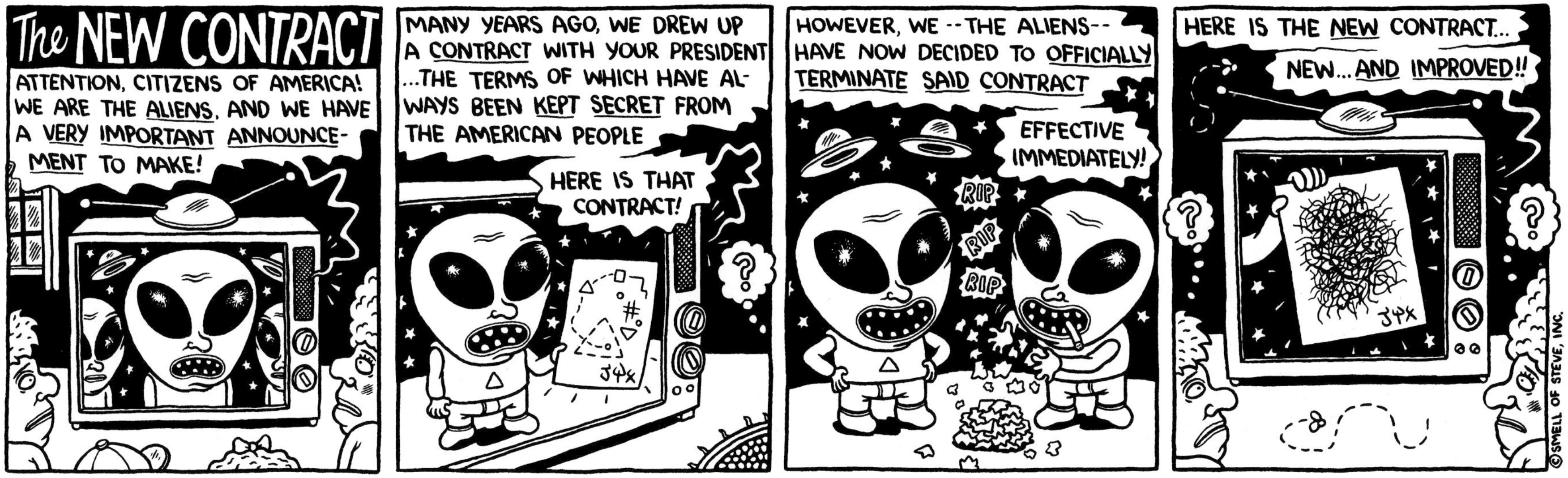
The NEW CONTRACT
ATTENTION, CITIZENS OF AMERICA! WE ARE THE ALIENS, AND WE HAVE A VERY IMPORTANT ANNOUNCE-MENT TO MAKE!
MANY YEARS AGO, WE DREW UP A CONTRACT WITH YOUR PRESIDENT ...THE TERMS OF WHICH HAVE AL-WAYS BEEN KEPT SECRET FROM THE AMERICAN PEOPLE
HERE IS THAT CONTRACT!
?
HOWEVER, WE --THE ALIENS-- HAVE NOW DECIDED TO OFFICIALLY TERMINATE SAID CONTRACT
EFFECTIVE IMMEDIATELY!
RIP
RIP
RIP
HERE IS THE NEW CONTRACT...
NEW...AND IMPROVED!!
?
?
©SMELL OF STEVE, INC.

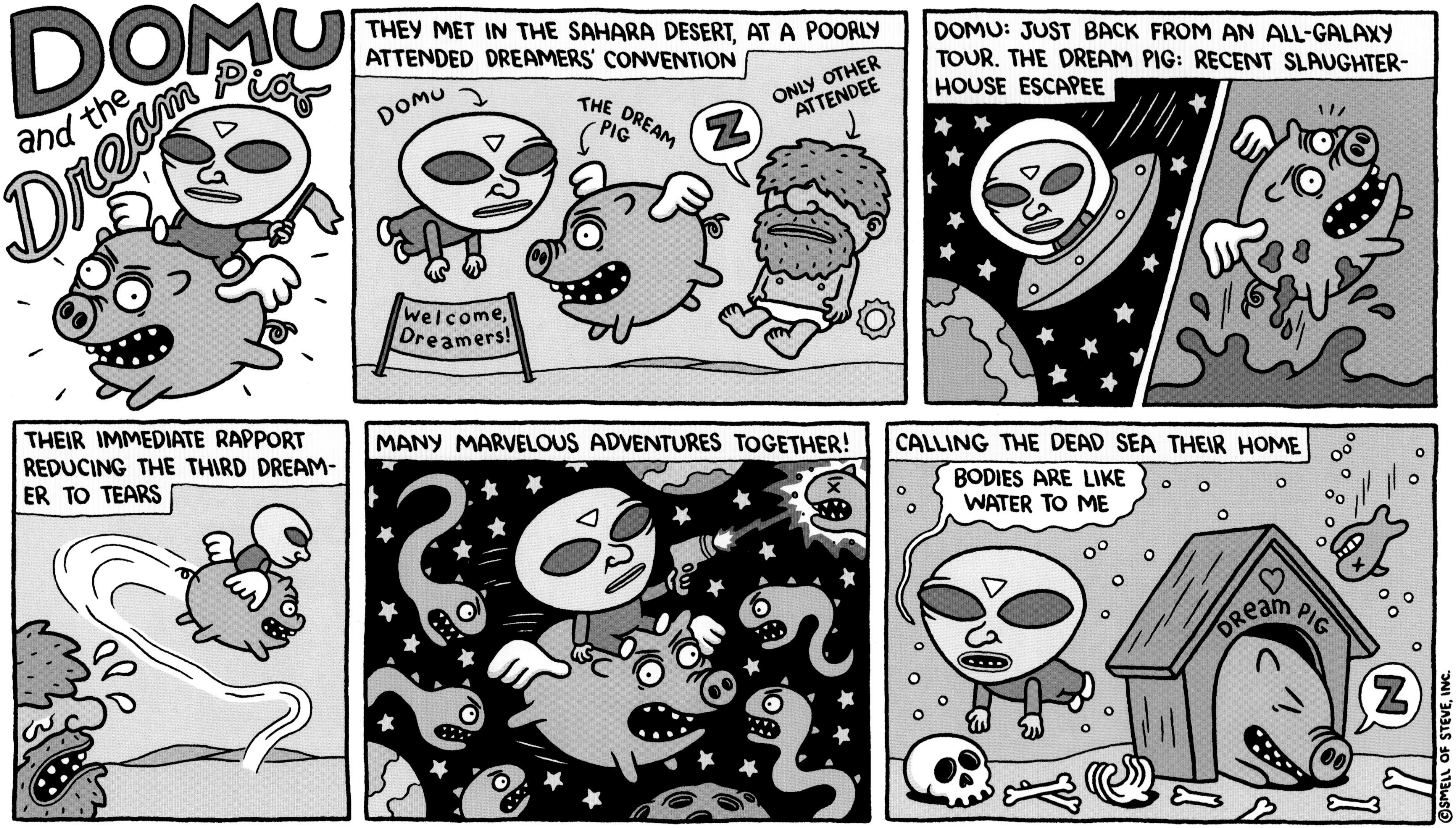
DOMU
and the
Dream Pig
THEY MET IN THE SAHARA DESERT, AT A POORLY ATTENDED DREAMERS' CONVENTION
DOMU
THE DREAM PIG
Z
ONLY OTHER ATTENDEE
Welcome, Dreamers!
DOMU: JUST BACK FROM AN ALL-GALAXY TOUR. THE DREAM PIG: RECENT SLAUGHTER-HOUSE ESCAPEE
THEIR IMMEDIATE RAPPORT REDUCING THE THIRD DREAMER TO TEARS
MANY MARVELOUS ADVENTURES TOGETHER!
CALLING THE DEAD SEA THEIR HOME
BODIES ARE LIKE WATER TO ME
DReam PIG
Z
©SMELL OF STEVE, INC.

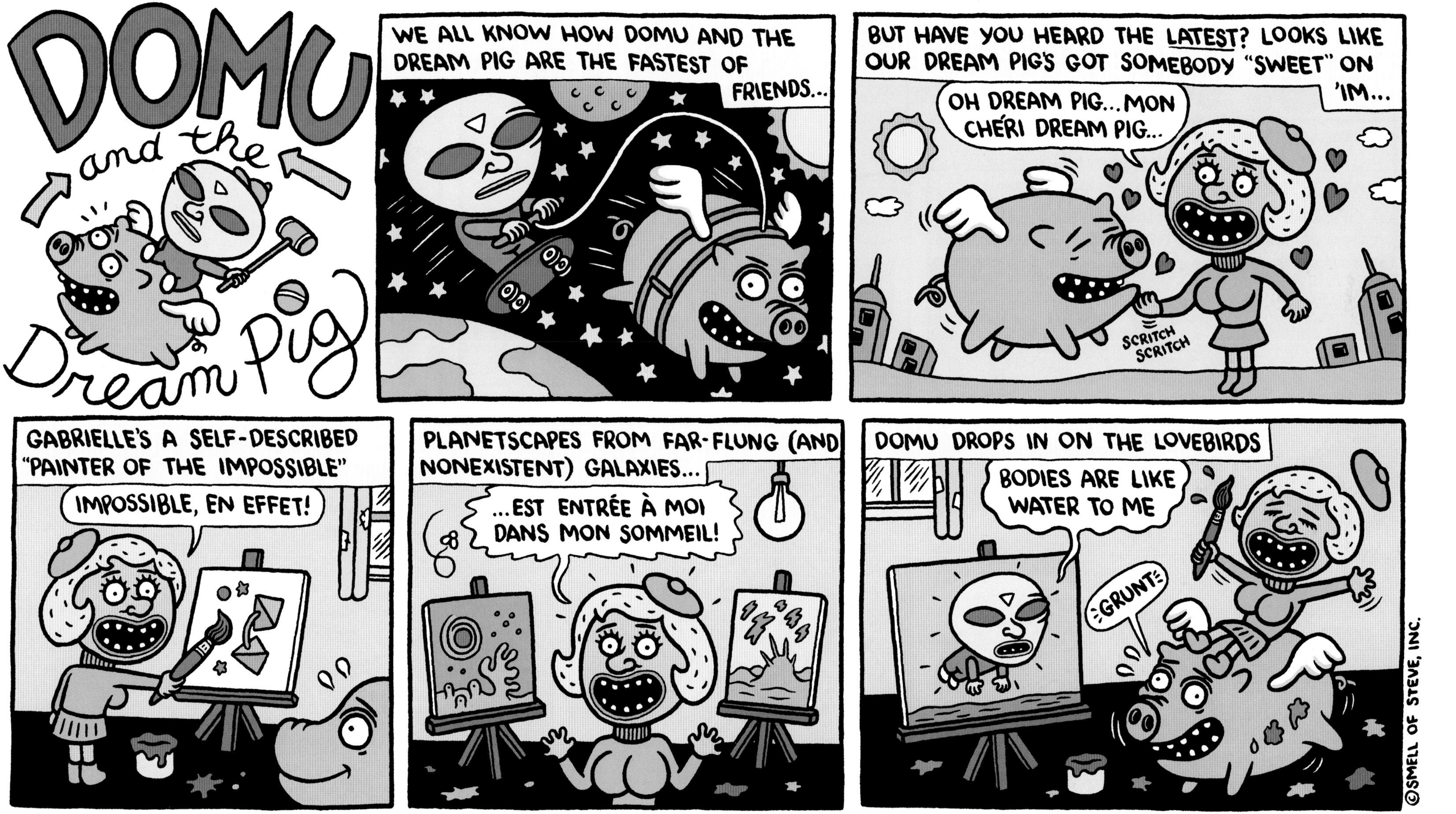
DOMU and the Dream Pig
WE ALL KNOW HOW DOMU AND THE DREAM PIG ARE THE FASTEST OF FRIENDS...
BUT HAVE YOU HEARD THE LATEST? LOOKS LIKE OUR DREAM PIG'S GOT SOMEBODY "SWEET" ON 'IM...
OH DREAM PIG... MON CHÉRI DREAM PIG...
SCRITCH SCRITCH
GABRIELLE'S A SELF-DESCRIBED "PAINTER OF THE IMPOSSIBLE"
IMPOSSIBLE, EN EFFET!
PLANETSCAPES FROM FAR-FLUNG (AND NONEXISTENT) GALAXIES...
...EST ENTRÉE À MOI DANS MON SOMMEIL!
DOMU DROPS IN ON THE LOVEBIRDS
BODIES ARE LIKE WATER TO ME
GRUNT
©SMELL OF STEVE, INC.

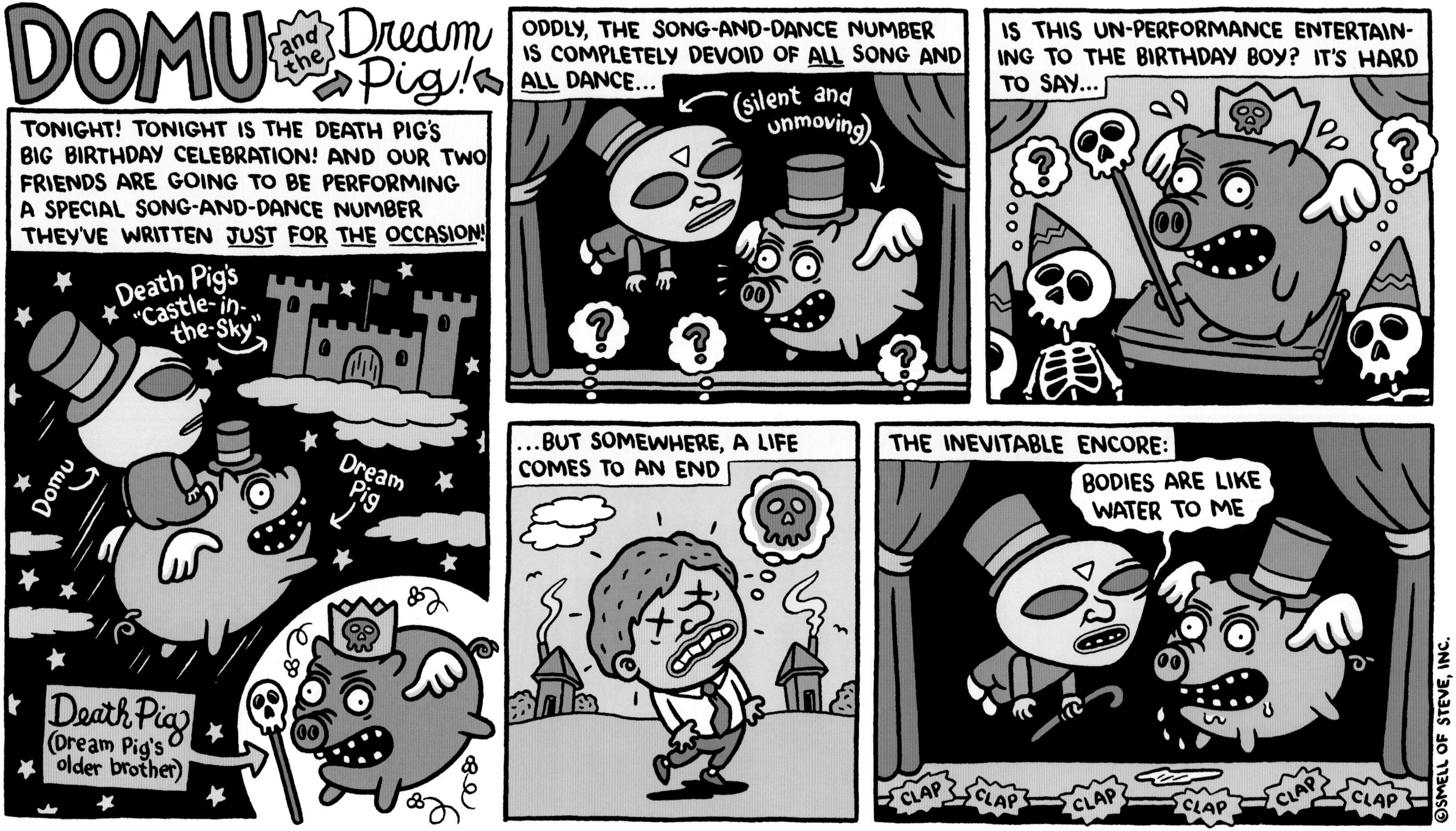
DOMU and the Dream Pig!
TONIGHT! TONIGHT IS THE DEATH PIG'S BIG BIRTHDAY CELEBRATION! AND OUR TWO FRIENDS ARE GOING TO BE PERFORMING A SPECIAL SONG-AND-DANCE NUMBER THEY'VE WRITTEN JUST FOR THE OCCASION!
Death Pig's "Castle-in-the-Sky"
Domu
Dream Pig
Death Pig (Dream Pig's older brother)
ODDLY, THE SONG-AND-DANCE NUMBER IS COMPLETELY DEVOID OF ALL SONG AND ALL DANCE...
(silent and unmoving)
IS THIS UN-PERFORMANCE ENTERTAINING TO THE BIRTHDAY BOY? IT'S HARD TO SAY...
...BUT SOMEWHERE, A LIFE COMES TO AN END
THE INEVITABLE ENCORE:
BODIES ARE LIKE WATER TO ME
CLAP CLAP CLAP CLAP CLAP CLAP
©SMELL OF STEVE, INC.

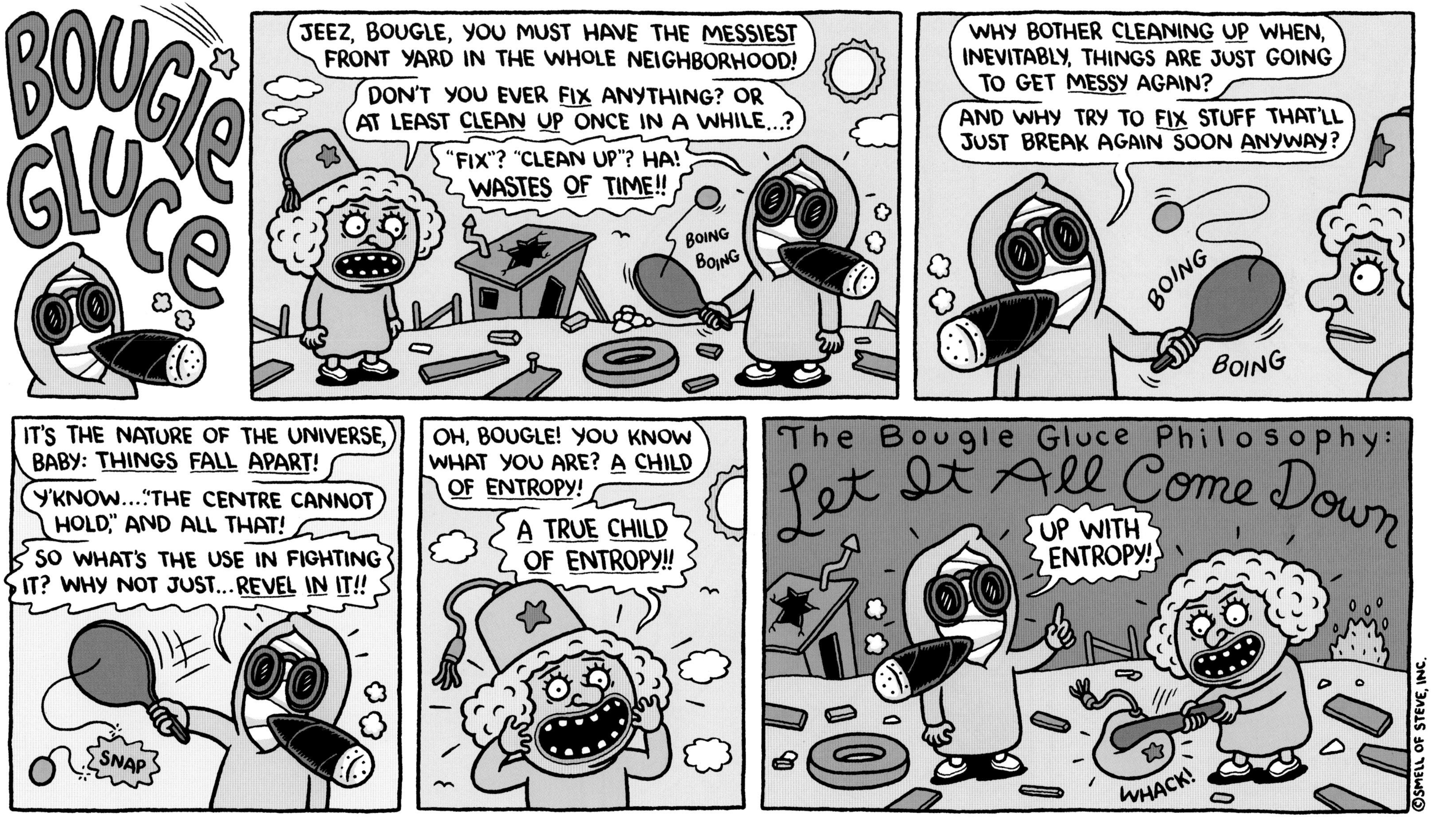
BOUGLE GLUCE
JEEZ, BOUGLE, YOU MUST HAVE THE MESSIEST FRONT YARD IN THE WHOLE NEIGHBORHOOD!
DON'T YOU EVER FIX ANYTHING? OR AT LEAST CLEAN UP ONCE IN A WHILE...?
"FIX"? "CLEAN UP"? HA! WASTES OF TIME!!
BOING BOING
WHY BOTHER CLEANING UP WHEN, INEVITABLY, THINGS ARE JUST GOING TO GET MESSY AGAIN?
AND WHY TRY TO FIX STUFF THAT'LL JUST BREAK AGAIN SOON ANYWAY?
BOING
BOING
IT'S THE NATURE OF THE UNIVERSE, BABY: THINGS FALL APART!
Y'KNOW..."THE CENTRE CANNOT HOLD," AND ALL THAT!
SO WHAT'S THE USE IN FIGHTING IT? WHY NOT JUST...REVEL IN IT!!
SNAP
OH, BOUGLE! YOU KNOW WHAT YOU ARE? A CHILD OF ENTROPY!
A TRUE CHILD OF ENTROPY!!
The Bougle Gluce Philosophy:
Let It All Come Down
UP WITH ENTROPY!
WHACK!
©SMELL OF STEVE, INC.

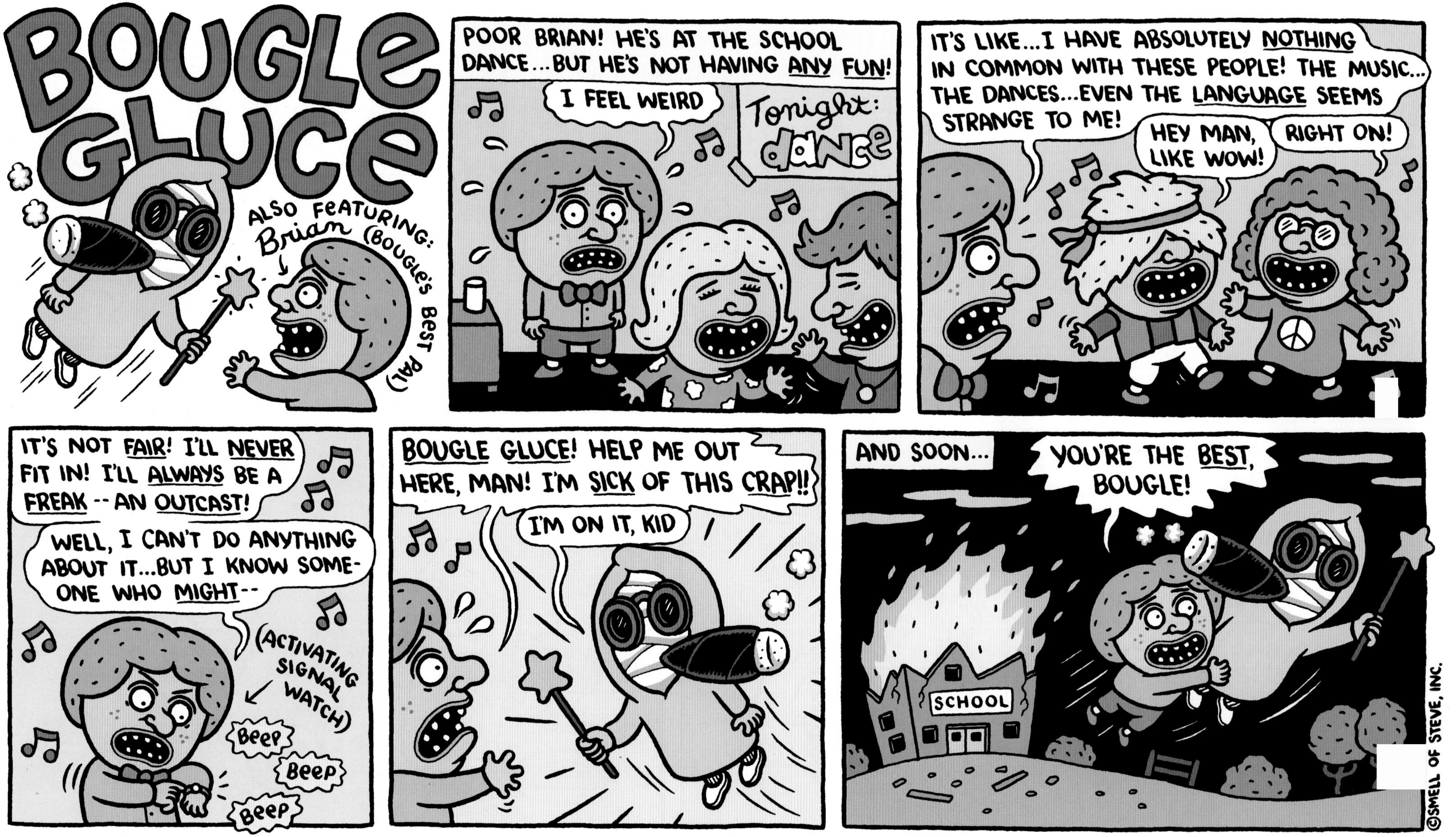
BOUGLE GLUCE
ALSO FEATURING: Brian (BOUGLE'S BEST PAL)
POOR BRIAN! HE'S AT THE SCHOOL DANCE...BUT HE'S NOT HAVING ANY FUN!
I FEEL WEIRD
Tonight: dance
IT'S LIKE...I HAVE ABSOLUTELY NOTHING IN COMMON WITH THESE PEOPLE! THE MUSIC... THE DANCES...EVEN THE LANGUAGE SEEMS STRANGE TO ME!
HEY MAN, LIKE WOW!
RIGHT ON!
IT'S NOT FAIR! I'LL NEVER FIT IN! I'LL ALWAYS BE A FREAK -- AN OUTCAST!
WELL, I CAN'T DO ANYTHING ABOUT IT...BUT I KNOW SOME-ONE WHO MIGHT--
(ACTIVATING SIGNAL WATCH)
BEEP
BEEP
BEEP
BOUGLE GLUCE! HELP ME OUT HERE, MAN! I'M SICK OF THIS CRAP!!
I'M ON IT, KID
AND SOON...
YOU'RE THE BEST, BOUGLE!
SCHOOL
©SMELL OF STEVE, INC.

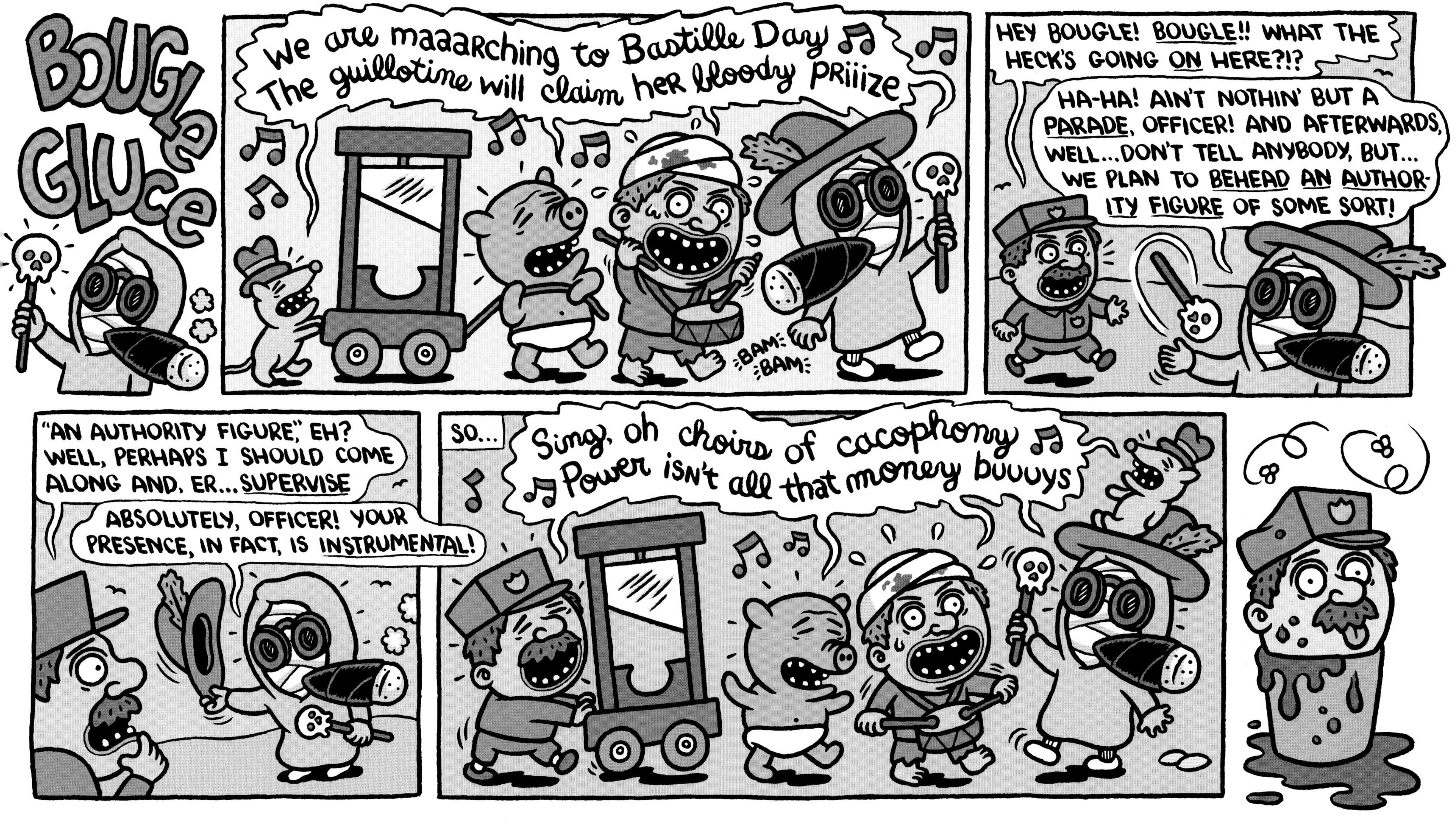
BOUGLE GLUCE
We are maaarching to Bastille Day
The guillotine will claim her bloody priiize
BAM BAM
HEY BOUGLE! BOUGLE!! WHAT THE HECK'S GOING ON HERE?!?
HA-HA! AIN'T NOTHIN' BUT A PARADE, OFFICER! AND AFTERWARDS, WELL...DON'T TELL ANYBODY, BUT... WE PLAN TO BEHEAD AN AUTHORITY FIGURE OF SOME SORT!
"AN AUTHORITY FIGURE," EH? WELL, PERHAPS I SHOULD COME ALONG AND, ER...SUPERVISE
ABSOLUTELY, OFFICER! YOUR PRESENCE, IN FACT, IS INSTRUMENTAL!
SO...
Sing, oh choirs of cacophony
Power isn't all that money buuuys

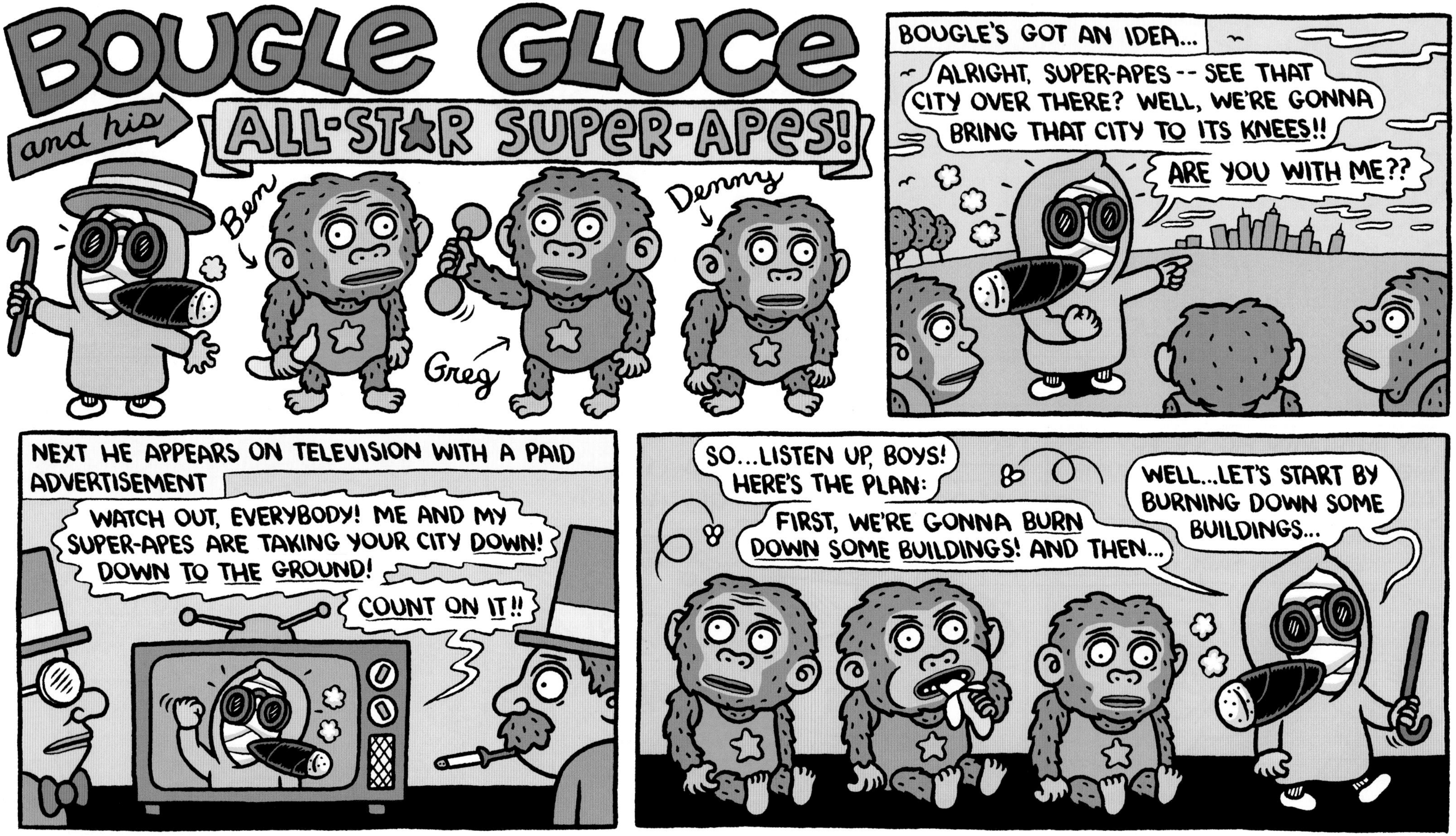
BOUGLE GLUCE
and his
ALL-STAR SUPER-APES!
Ben
Greg
Denny
BOUGLE'S GOT AN IDEA...
ALRIGHT, SUPER-APES -- SEE THAT CITY OVER THERE? WELL, WE'RE GONNA BRING THAT CITY TO ITS KNEES!!
ARE YOU WITH ME??
NEXT HE APPEARS ON TELEVISION WITH A PAID ADVERTISEMENT
WATCH OUT, EVERYBODY! ME AND MY SUPER-APES ARE TAKING YOUR CITY DOWN! DOWN TO THE GROUND!
COUNT ON IT!!
SO...LISTEN UP, BOYS! HERE'S THE PLAN:
FIRST, WE'RE GONNA BURN DOWN SOME BUILDINGS! AND THEN...
WELL...LET'S START BY BURNING DOWN SOME BUILDINGS...

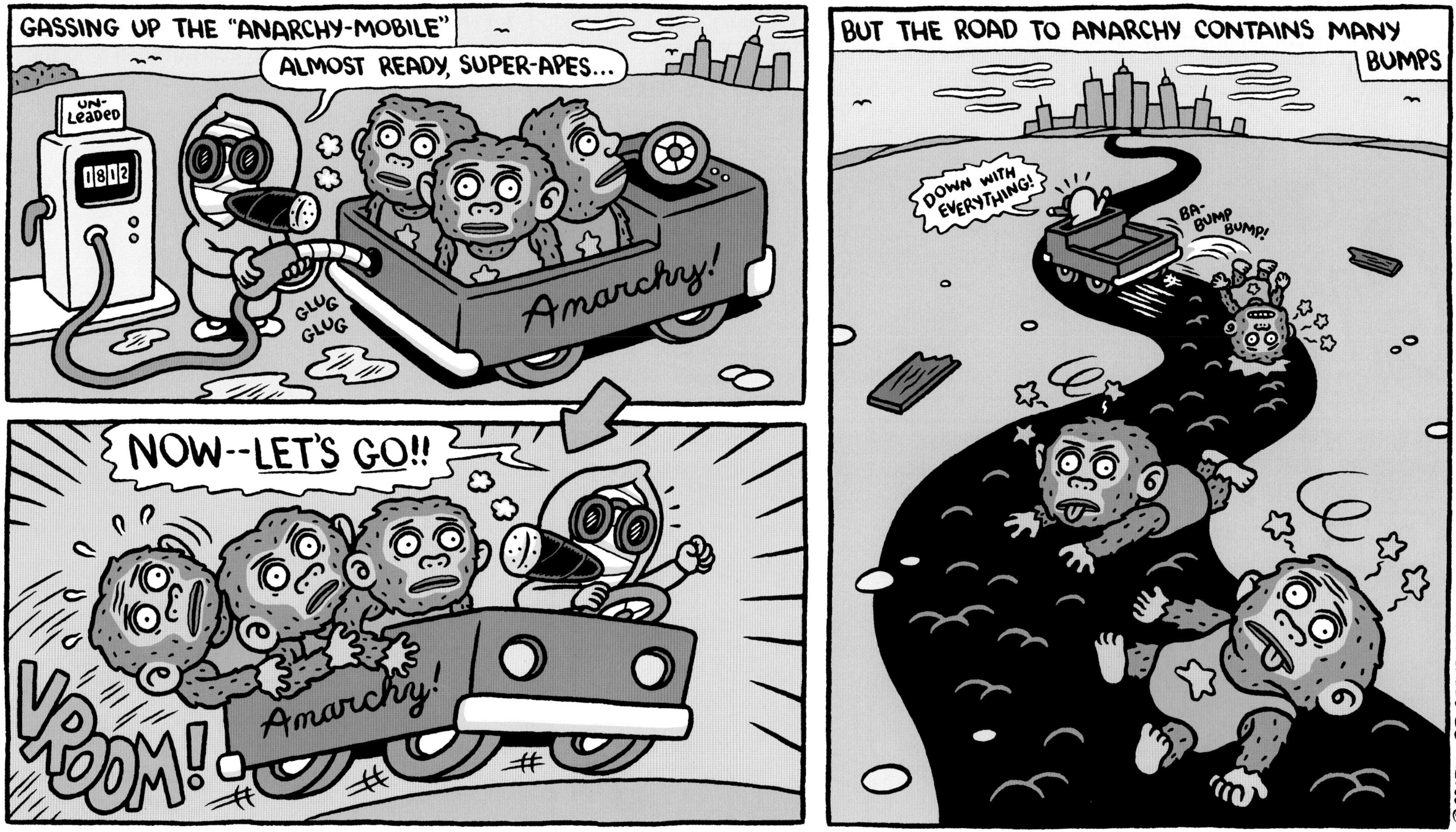

GASSING UP THE "ANARCHY-MOBILE"
ALMOST READY, SUPER-APES...
UN-LEADED
1812
GLUG GLUG
Anarchy!
NOW--LET'S GO!!
VROOM!
Anarchy!
BUT THE ROAD TO ANARCHY CONTAINS MANY BUMPS
DOWN WITH EVERYTHING!
BA-BUMP BUMP!

©SMELL OF STEVE, INC.

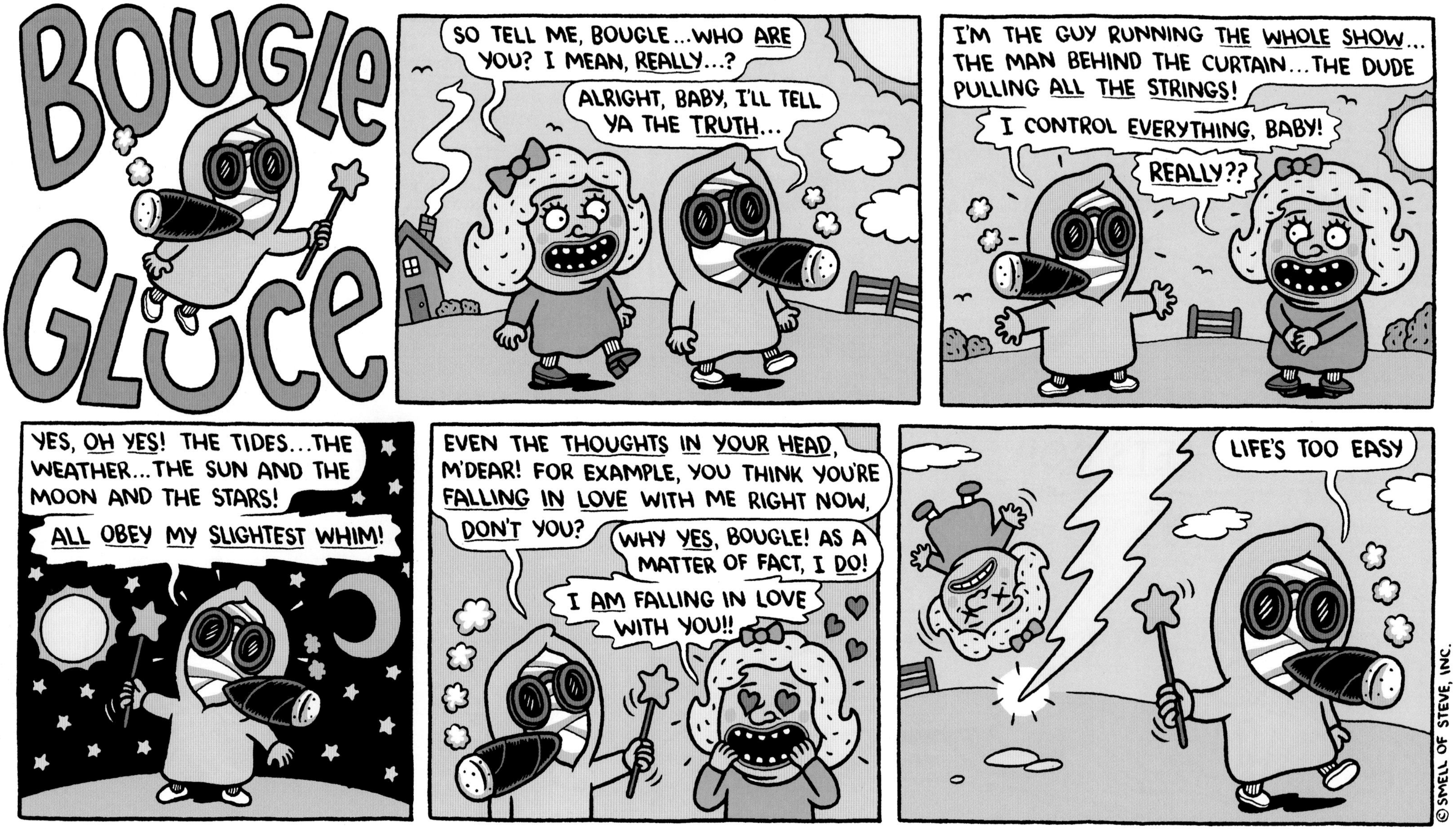
BOUGLE GLUCE
SO TELL ME, BOUGLE...WHO ARE YOU? I MEAN, REALLY...?
ALRIGHT, BABY, I'LL TELL YA THE TRUTH...
I'M THE GUY RUNNING THE WHOLE SHOW... THE MAN BEHIND THE CURTAIN...THE DUDE PULLING ALL THE STRINGS!
I CONTROL EVERYTHING, BABY!
REALLY??
YES, OH YES! THE TIDES...THE WEATHER...THE SUN AND THE MOON AND THE STARS!
ALL OBEY MY SLIGHTEST WHIM!
EVEN THE THOUGHTS IN YOUR HEAD, M'DEAR! FOR EXAMPLE, YOU THINK YOU'RE FALLING IN LOVE WITH ME RIGHT NOW, DON'T YOU?
WHY YES, BOUGLE! AS A MATTER OF FACT, I DO!
I AM FALLING IN LOVE WITH YOU!!
LIFE'S TOO EASY
©SMELL OF STEVE, INC.

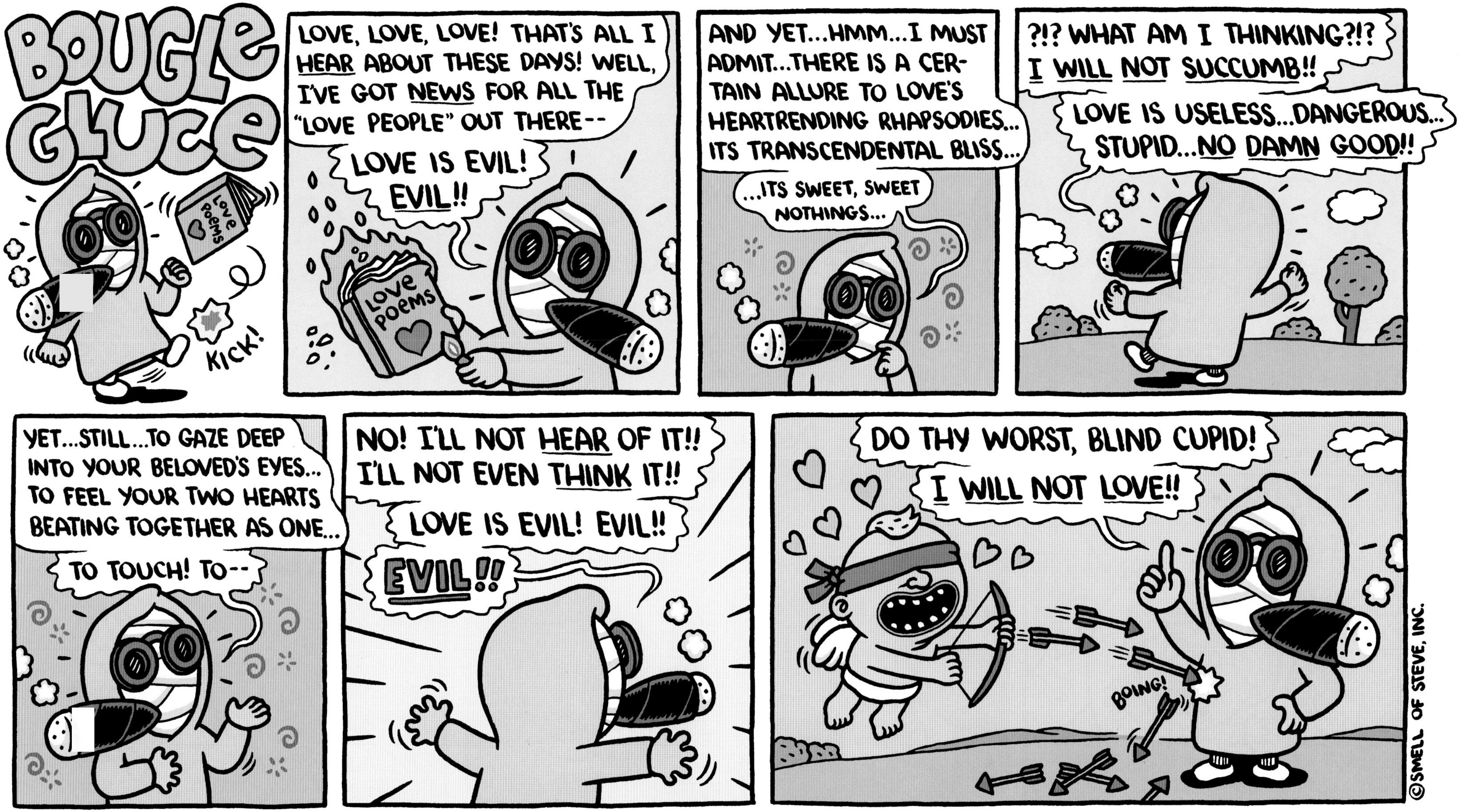
BOUGLE GLUCE
LOVE POEMS
KICK!
LOVE, LOVE, LOVE! THAT'S ALL I HEAR ABOUT THESE DAYS! WELL, I'VE GOT NEWS FOR ALL THE "LOVE PEOPLE" OUT THERE--
LOVE IS EVIL! EVIL!!
LOVE POEMS
AND YET...HMM...I MUST ADMIT...THERE IS A CERTAIN ALLURE TO LOVE'S HEARTRENDING RHAPSODIES... ITS TRANSCENDENTAL BLISS...
...ITS SWEET, SWEET NOTHINGS...
?!? WHAT AM I THINKING?!? I WILL NOT SUCCUMB!!
LOVE IS USELESS...DANGEROUS... STUPID...NO DAMN GOOD!!
YET...STILL...TO GAZE DEEP INTO YOUR BELOVED'S EYES... TO FEEL YOUR TWO HEARTS BEATING TOGETHER AS ONE...
TO TOUCH! TO--
NO! I'LL NOT HEAR OF IT!! I'LL NOT EVEN THINK IT!!
LOVE IS EVIL! EVIL!!
EVIL!!
DO THY WORST, BLIND CUPID!
I WILL NOT LOVE!!
BOING!
©SMELL OF STEVE, INC.

DOMU and the DREAM PIG

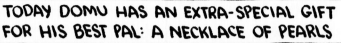
TODAY DOMU HAS AN EXTRA-SPECIAL GIFT FOR HIS BEST PAL: A NECKLACE OF PEARLS

SUCH A SPECIAL NECKLACE! EACH PEARL CONTAINING THE SOUL OF A CAPTURED CHILD

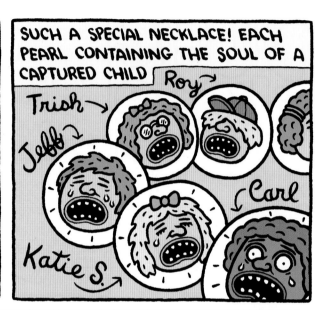

Trish →
Roy →
Jeff →
Katie S. →
Carl

HERE'S YOUNG BRIAN, WHO WAS ONE OF THE LAST TO BE TAKEN

HELP! LET ME OUT!

HELP!!

(*The night Domu came for him*)

BODIES ARE LIKE WATER TO ME

THE DREAM PIG LOVES HIS WONDERFUL NEW GIFT

HELP HELP HELP HELP HELP HELP

© SMELL OF STEVE, INC.

108

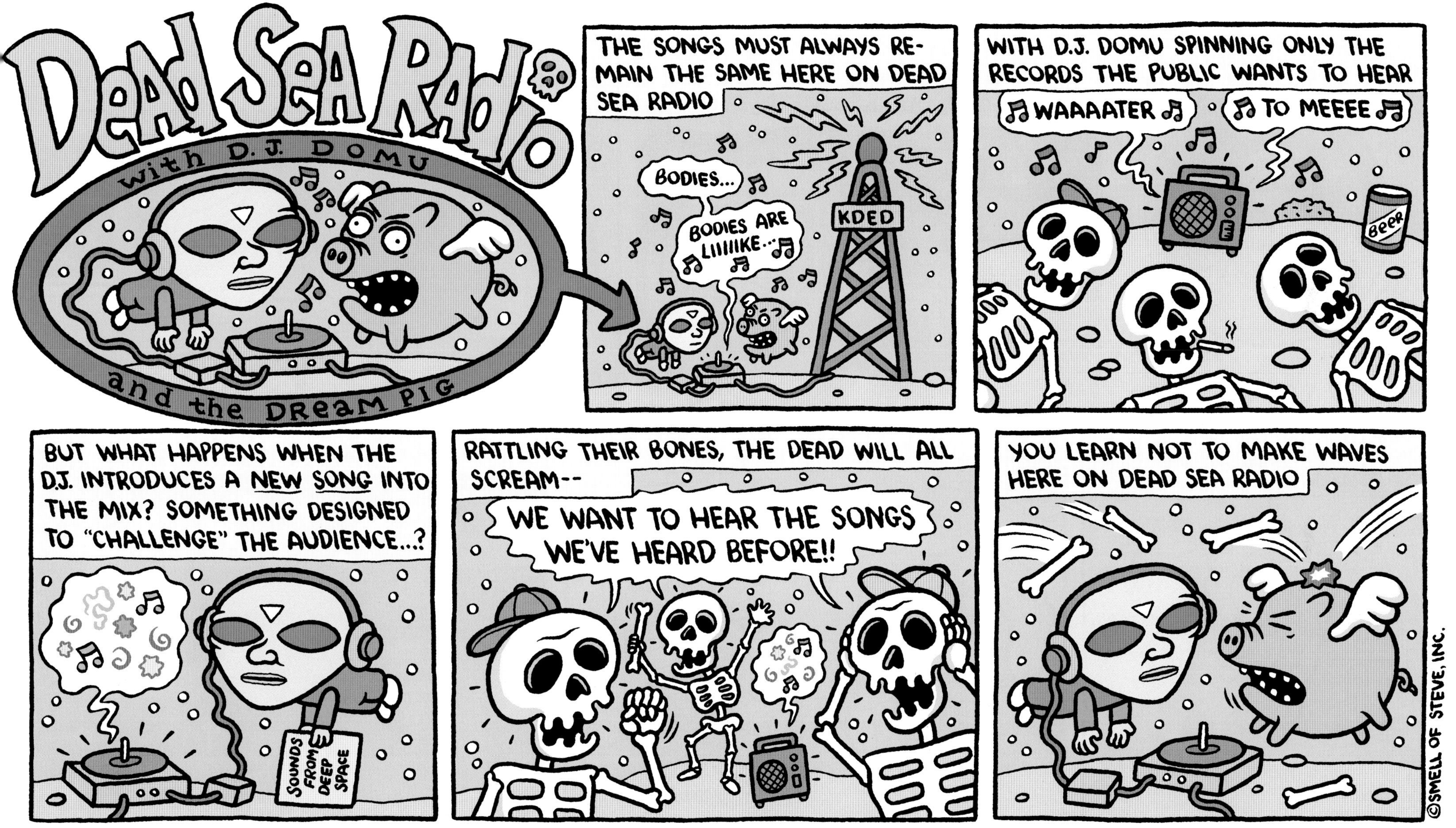
DEAD SEA RADIO
with D.J. DOMU
and the DREAM PIG
THE SONGS MUST ALWAYS RE-MAIN THE SAME HERE ON DEAD SEA RADIO
BODIES...
BODIES ARE LIIIIIKE...
KDED
WITH D.J. DOMU SPINNING ONLY THE RECORDS THE PUBLIC WANTS TO HEAR
WAAAAATER
TO MEEEE
BEER
BUT WHAT HAPPENS WHEN THE D.J. INTRODUCES A NEW SONG INTO THE MIX? SOMETHING DESIGNED TO "CHALLENGE" THE AUDIENCE...?
SOUNDS FROM DEEP SPACE
RATTLING THEIR BONES, THE DEAD WILL ALL SCREAM--
WE WANT TO HEAR THE SONGS WE'VE HEARD BEFORE!!
YOU LEARN NOT TO MAKE WAVES HERE ON DEAD SEA RADIO
©SMELL OF STEVE, INC.

THE TOWER

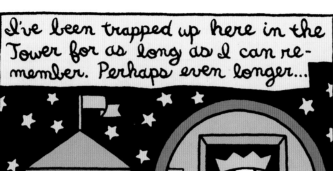
I've been trapped up here in the Tower for as long as I can remember. Perhaps even longer...

I do my best to keep busy, though. Once every seven days I sit down and carefully spell out my Message (it's always the same Message)

Help me I'm trapped in the

and send it flying down to the town below

What a ridiculous waste of time

I'll never get out of this place

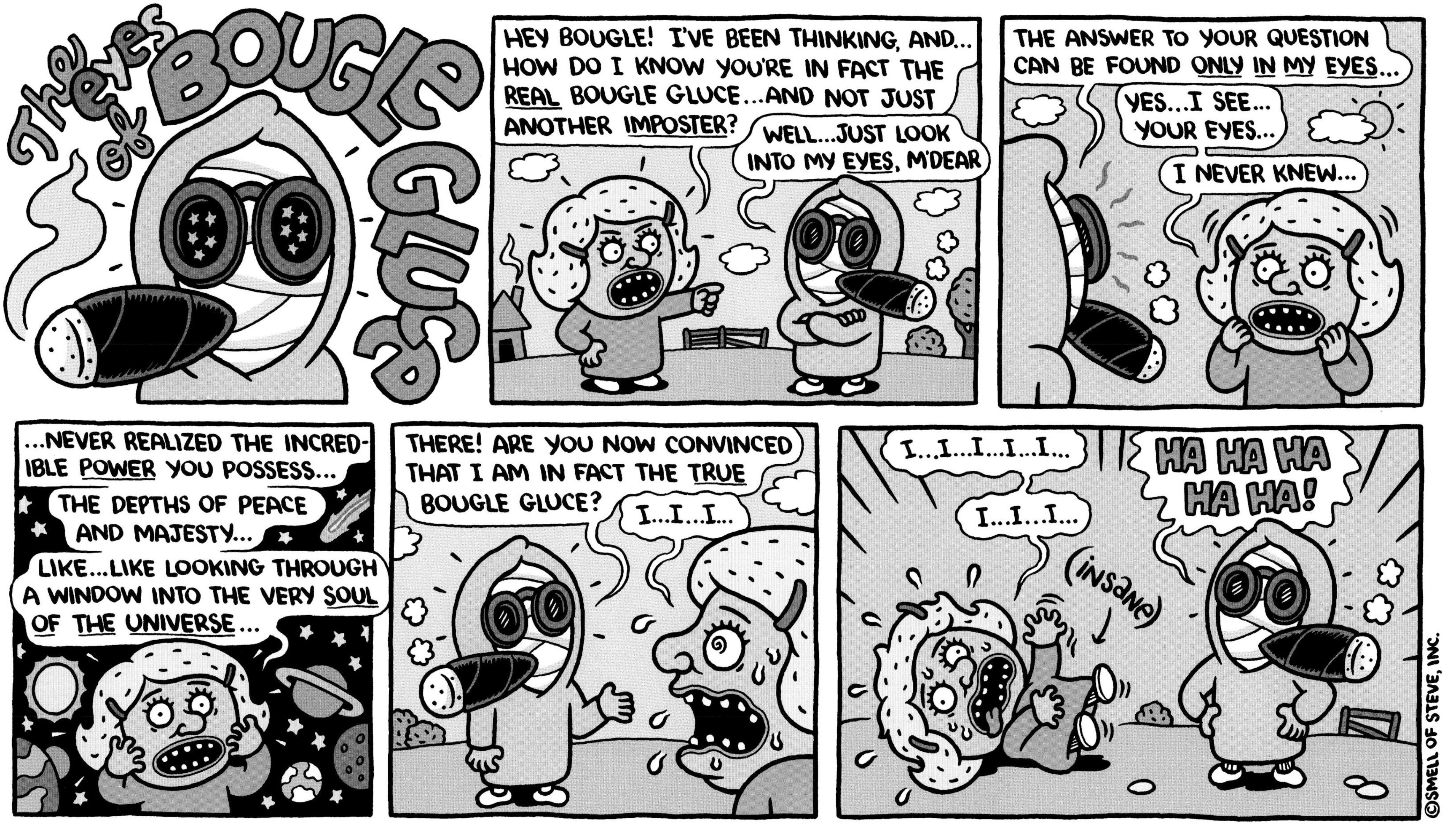

The Eyes of BOUGLE GLUCE
HEY BOUGLE! I'VE BEEN THINKING, AND... HOW DO I KNOW YOU'RE IN FACT THE REAL BOUGLE GLUCE...AND NOT JUST ANOTHER IMPOSTER?
WELL...JUST LOOK INTO MY EYES, M'DEAR
THE ANSWER TO YOUR QUESTION CAN BE FOUND ONLY IN MY EYES...
YES...I SEE... YOUR EYES...
I NEVER KNEW...
...NEVER REALIZED THE INCREDIBLE POWER YOU POSSESS...
THE DEPTHS OF PEACE AND MAJESTY...
LIKE...LIKE LOOKING THROUGH A WINDOW INTO THE VERY SOUL OF THE UNIVERSE...
THERE! ARE YOU NOW CONVINCED THAT I AM IN FACT THE TRUE BOUGLE GLUCE?
I...I...I...
I...I...I...I...I...
I...I...I...
(insane)
HA HA HA HA HA!
©SMELL OF STEVE, INC.

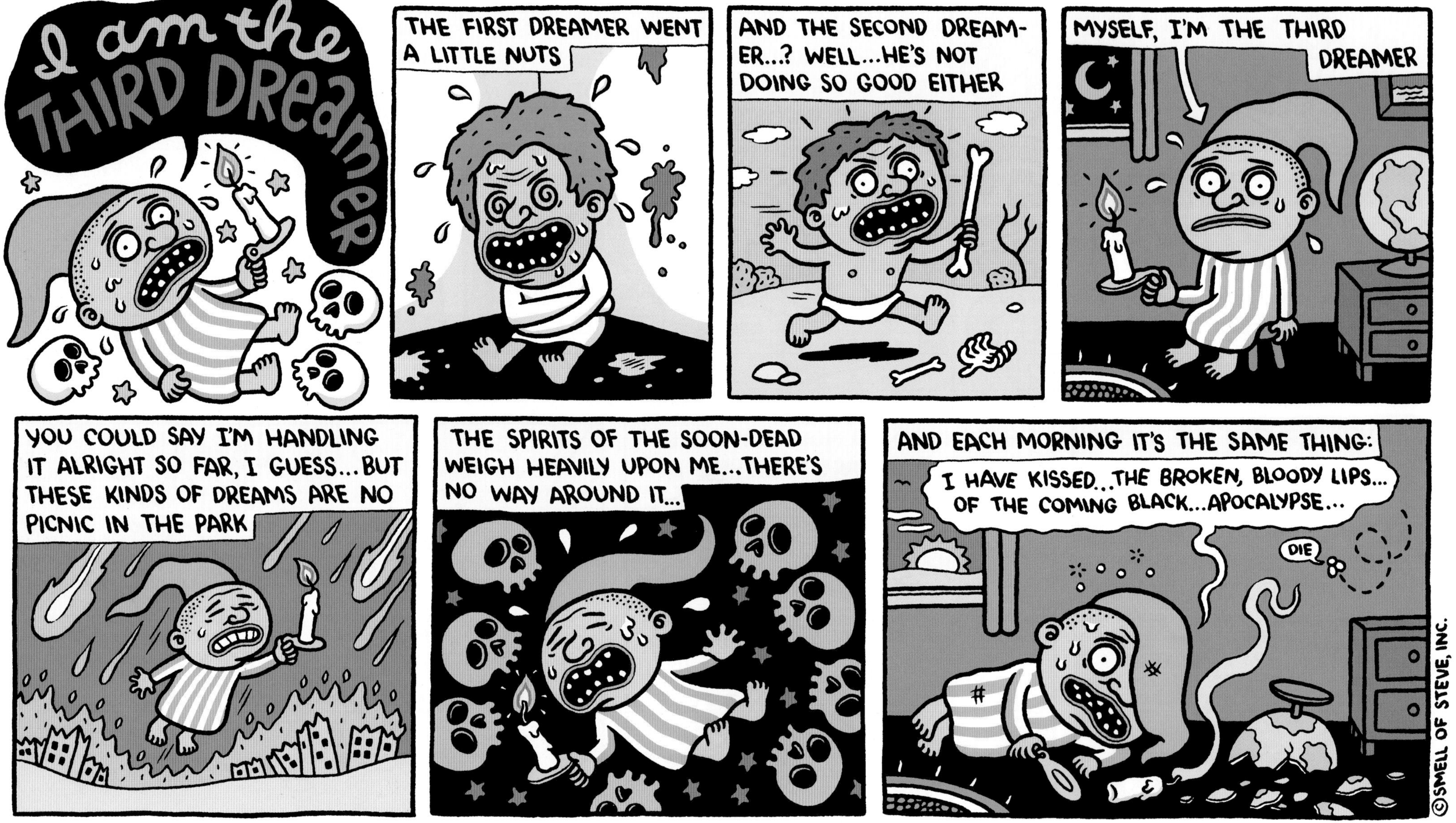
I am the THIRD DREAMER
THE FIRST DREAMER WENT A LITTLE NUTS
AND THE SECOND DREAMER...? WELL...HE'S NOT DOING SO GOOD EITHER
MYSELF, I'M THE THIRD DREAMER
YOU COULD SAY I'M HANDLING IT ALRIGHT SO FAR, I GUESS... BUT THESE KINDS OF DREAMS ARE NO PICNIC IN THE PARK
THE SPIRITS OF THE SOON-DEAD WEIGH HEAVILY UPON ME... THERE'S NO WAY AROUND IT...
AND EACH MORNING IT'S THE SAME THING:
I HAVE KISSED...THE BROKEN, BLOODY LIPS... OF THE COMING BLACK...APOCALYPSE...
DIE
©SMELL OF STEVE, INC.

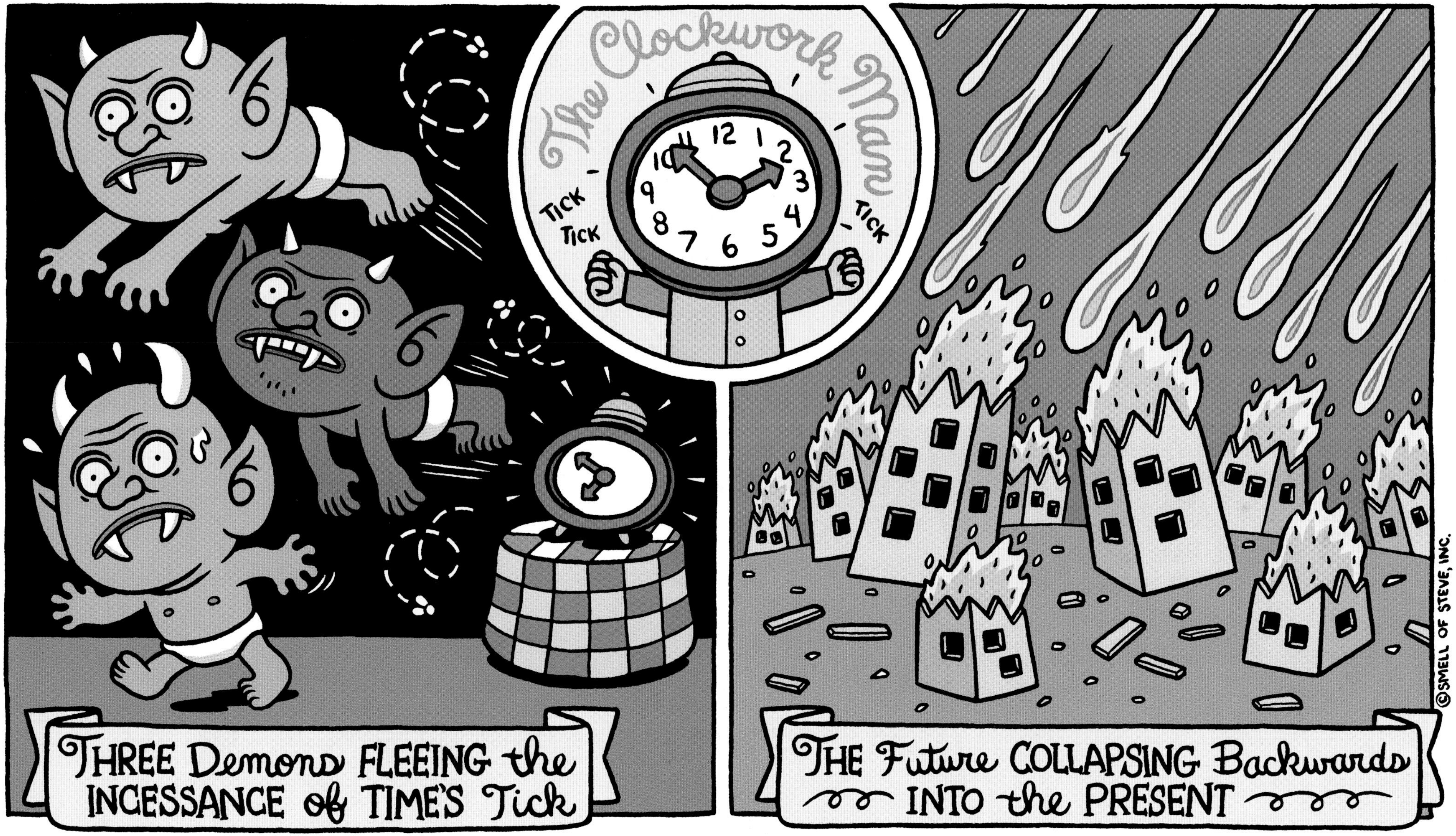
The Clockwork Man
TICK
TICK
TICK
THREE Demons FLEEING the INCESSANCE of TIME'S Tick
THE Future COLLAPSING Backwards INTO the PRESENT
©SMELL OF STEVE, INC.

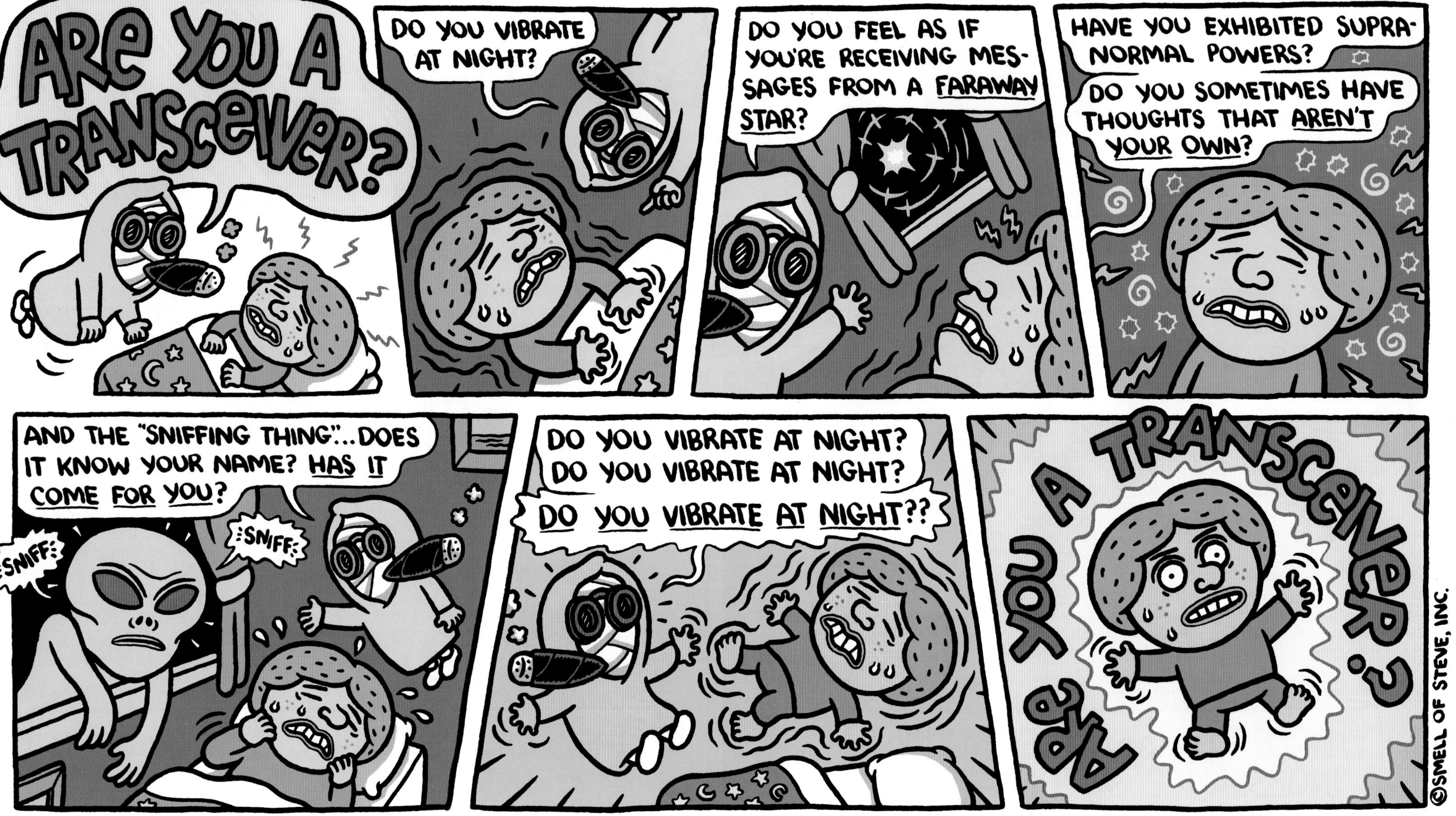

ARE YOU A TRANSCEIVER?
DO YOU VIBRATE AT NIGHT?
DO YOU FEEL AS IF YOU'RE RECEIVING MESSAGES FROM A FARAWAY STAR?
HAVE YOU EXHIBITED SUPRANORMAL POWERS?
DO YOU SOMETIMES HAVE THOUGHTS THAT AREN'T YOUR OWN?
AND THE "SNIFFING THING"... DOES IT KNOW YOUR NAME? HAS IT COME FOR YOU?
SNIFF
SNIFF
DO YOU VIBRATE AT NIGHT? DO YOU VIBRATE AT NIGHT?
DO YOU VIBRATE AT NIGHT??
ARE YOU A TRANSCEIVER?
©SMELL OF STEVE, INC.

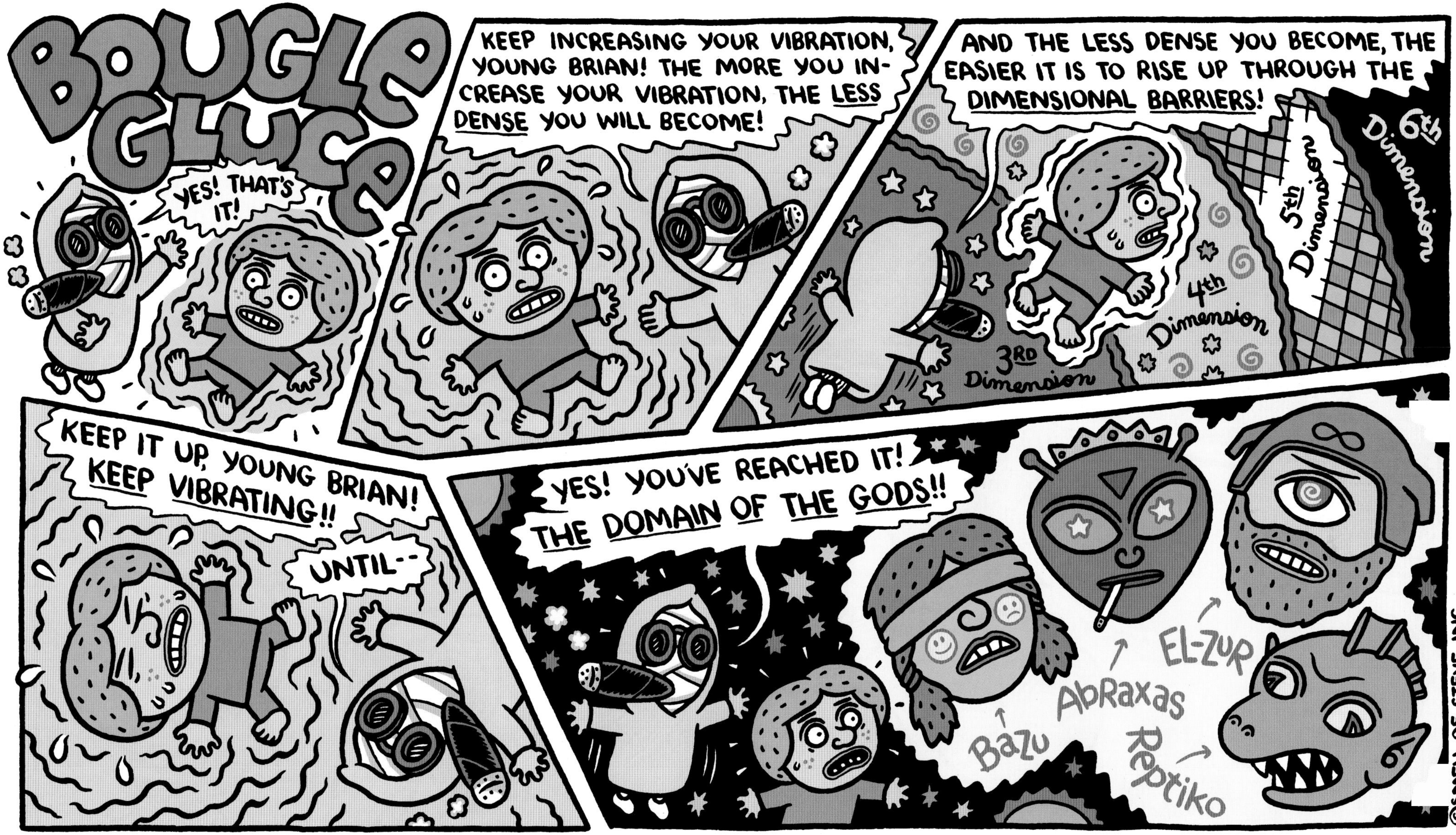
BOUGLE GLUCE
YES! THAT'S IT!
KEEP INCREASING YOUR VIBRATION, YOUNG BRIAN! THE MORE YOU INCREASE YOUR VIBRATION, THE LESS DENSE YOU WILL BECOME!
AND THE LESS DENSE YOU BECOME, THE EASIER IT IS TO RISE UP THROUGH THE DIMENSIONAL BARRIERS!
6th Dimension
5th Dimension
4th Dimension
3RD Dimension
KEEP IT UP, YOUNG BRIAN! KEEP VIBRATING!!
UNTIL--
YES! YOU'VE REACHED IT! THE DOMAIN OF THE GODS!!
Bazu
Abraxas
EL-ZUR
Reptiko
©SMELL OF STEVE, INC.

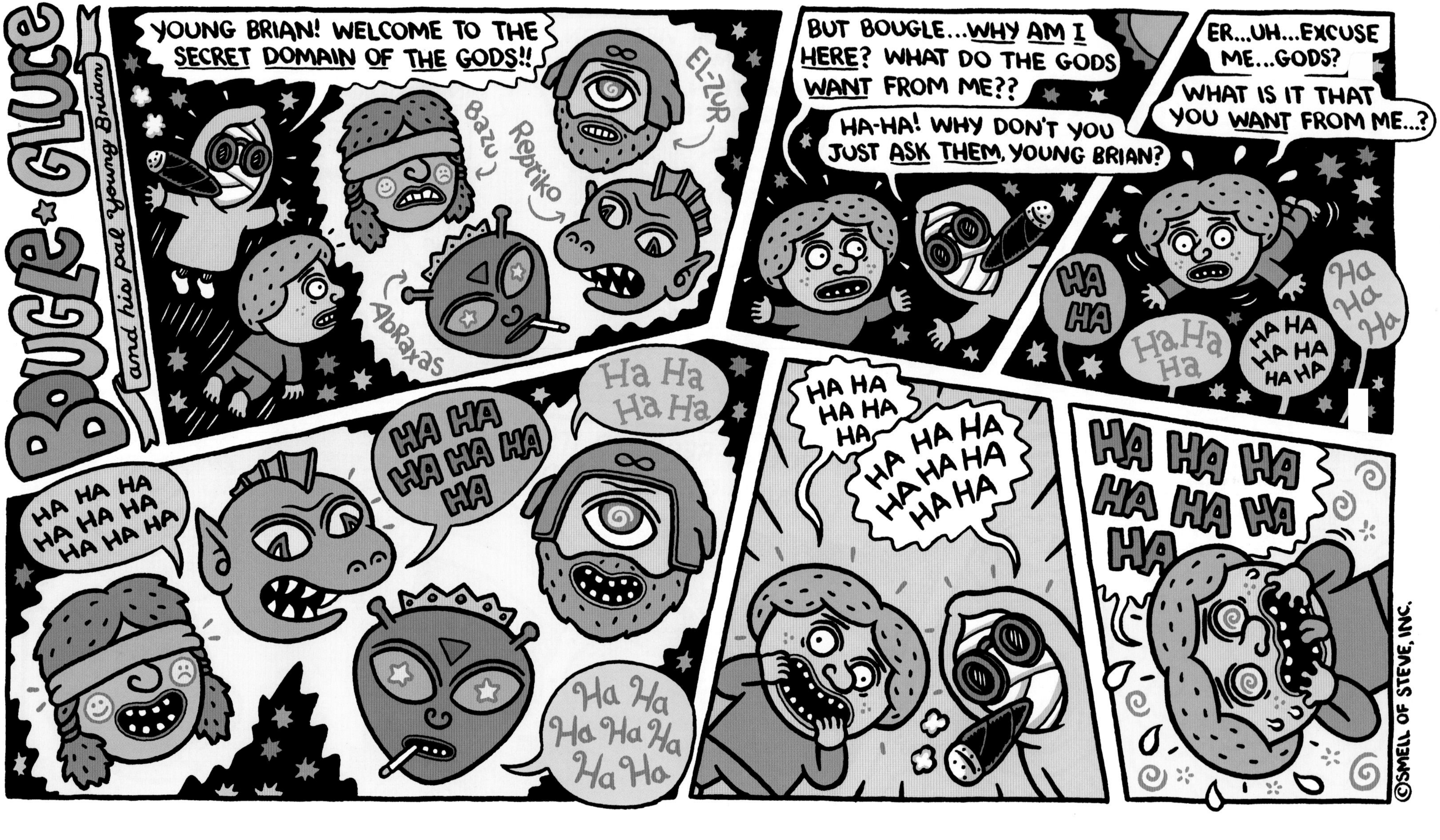

BOUGLE·GLUE
and his pal Young Brian
YOUNG BRIAN! WELCOME TO THE SECRET DOMAIN OF THE GODS!!
Bazu
Reptiko
EL-ZUR
Abraxas
BUT BOUGLE...WHY AM I HERE? WHAT DO THE GODS WANT FROM ME??
HA-HA! WHY DON'T YOU JUST ASK THEM, YOUNG BRIAN?
ER...UH...EXCUSE ME...GODS?
WHAT IS IT THAT YOU WANT FROM ME...?
HA HA
Ha Ha Ha
HA HA HA HA HA HA
Ha Ha Ha
HA HA HA HA HA HA HA HA
HA HA HA HA HA HA HA
Ha Ha Ha Ha
Ha Ha Ha Ha Ha Ha Ha
HA HA HA HA HA
HA HA HA HA HA HA HA HA
HA HA HA HA HA HA HA
©SMELL OF STEVE, INC.

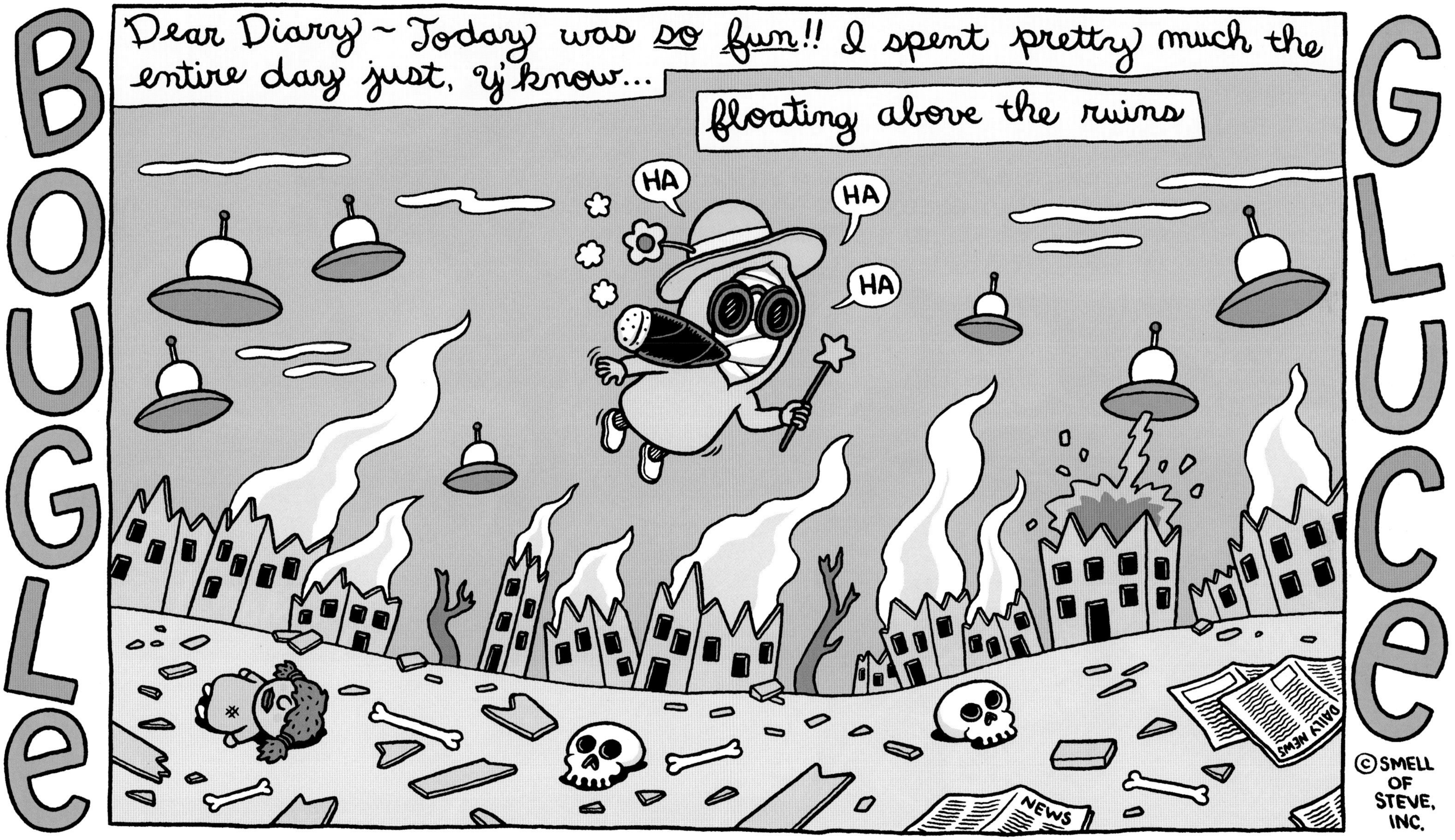
BOUGLe
GLUCe
Dear Diary ~ Today was so fun!! I spent pretty much the entire day just, y'know...
floating above the ruins
HA
HA
HA
DAILY NEWS
NEWS
©SMELL OF STEVE, INC.

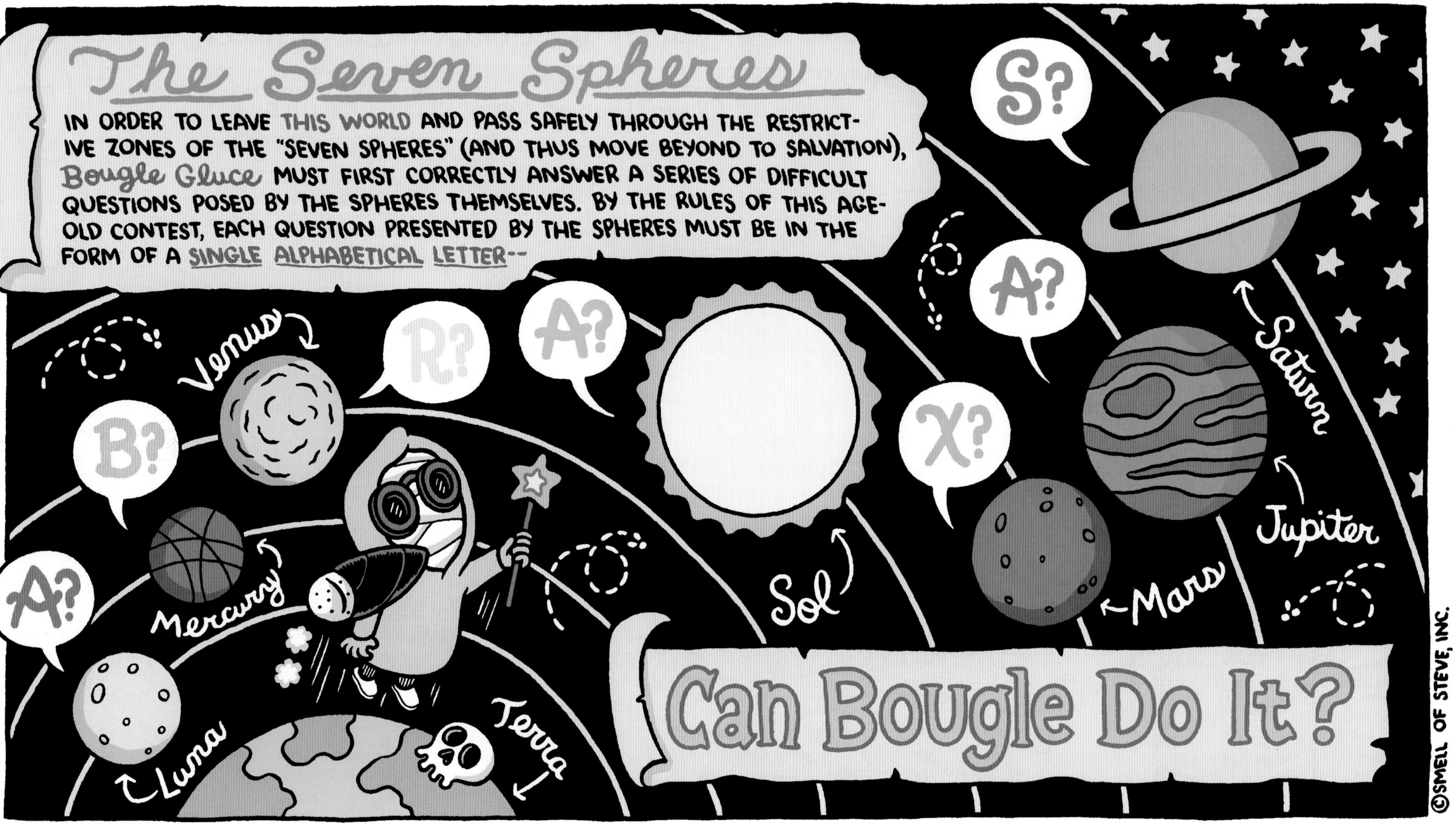

The Seven Spheres
IN ORDER TO LEAVE THIS WORLD AND PASS SAFELY THROUGH THE RESTRICTIVE ZONES OF THE "SEVEN SPHERES" (AND THUS MOVE BEYOND TO SALVATION), Bougle Gluce MUST FIRST CORRECTLY ANSWER A SERIES OF DIFFICULT QUESTIONS POSED BY THE SPHERES THEMSELVES. BY THE RULES OF THIS AGE-OLD CONTEST, EACH QUESTION PRESENTED BY THE SPHERES MUST BE IN THE FORM OF A SINGLE ALPHABETICAL LETTER--
A?
B?
R?
A?
X?
A?
S?
Luna
Mercury
Venus
Terra
Sol
Mars
Jupiter
Saturn
Can Bougle Do It?
©SMELL OF STEVE, INC.

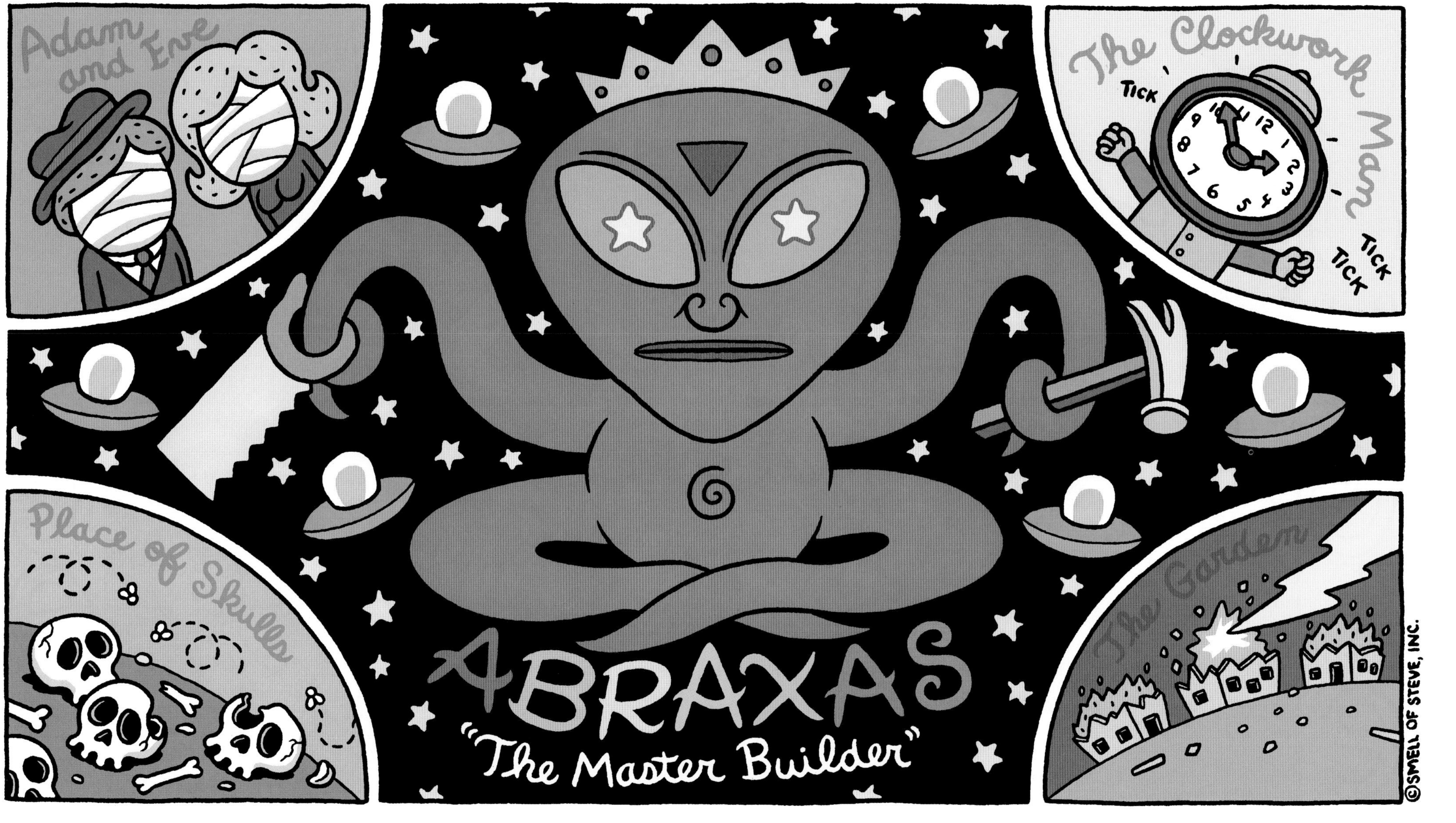
Adam and Eve
The Clockwork Man
TICK
TICK
TICK
Place of Skulls
The Garden
ABRAXAS
"The Master Builder"
©SMELL OF STEVE, INC.

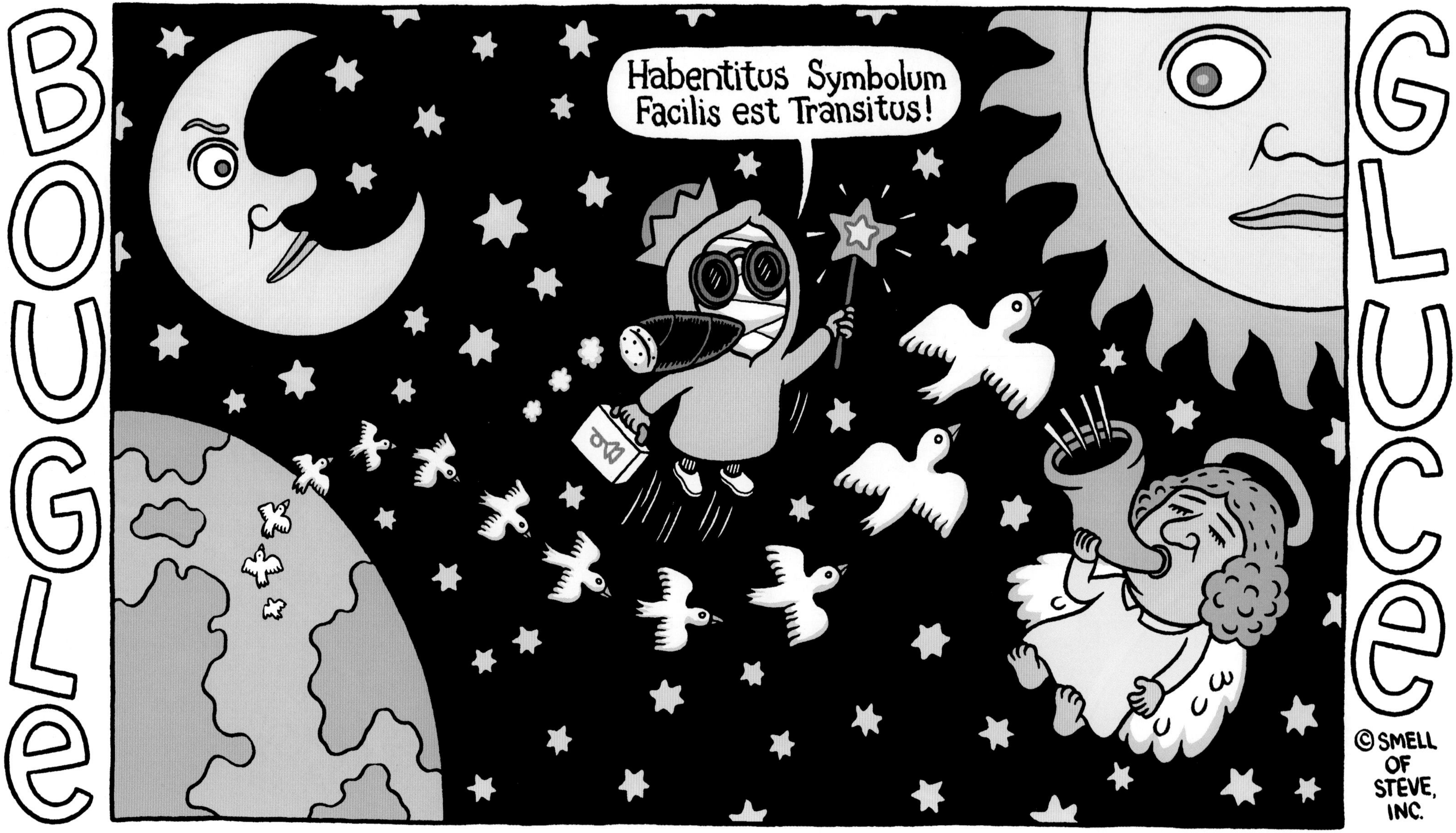
BOUGLe
GLUCe
Habentitus Symbolum Facilis est Transitus!
©SMELL OF STEVE, INC.

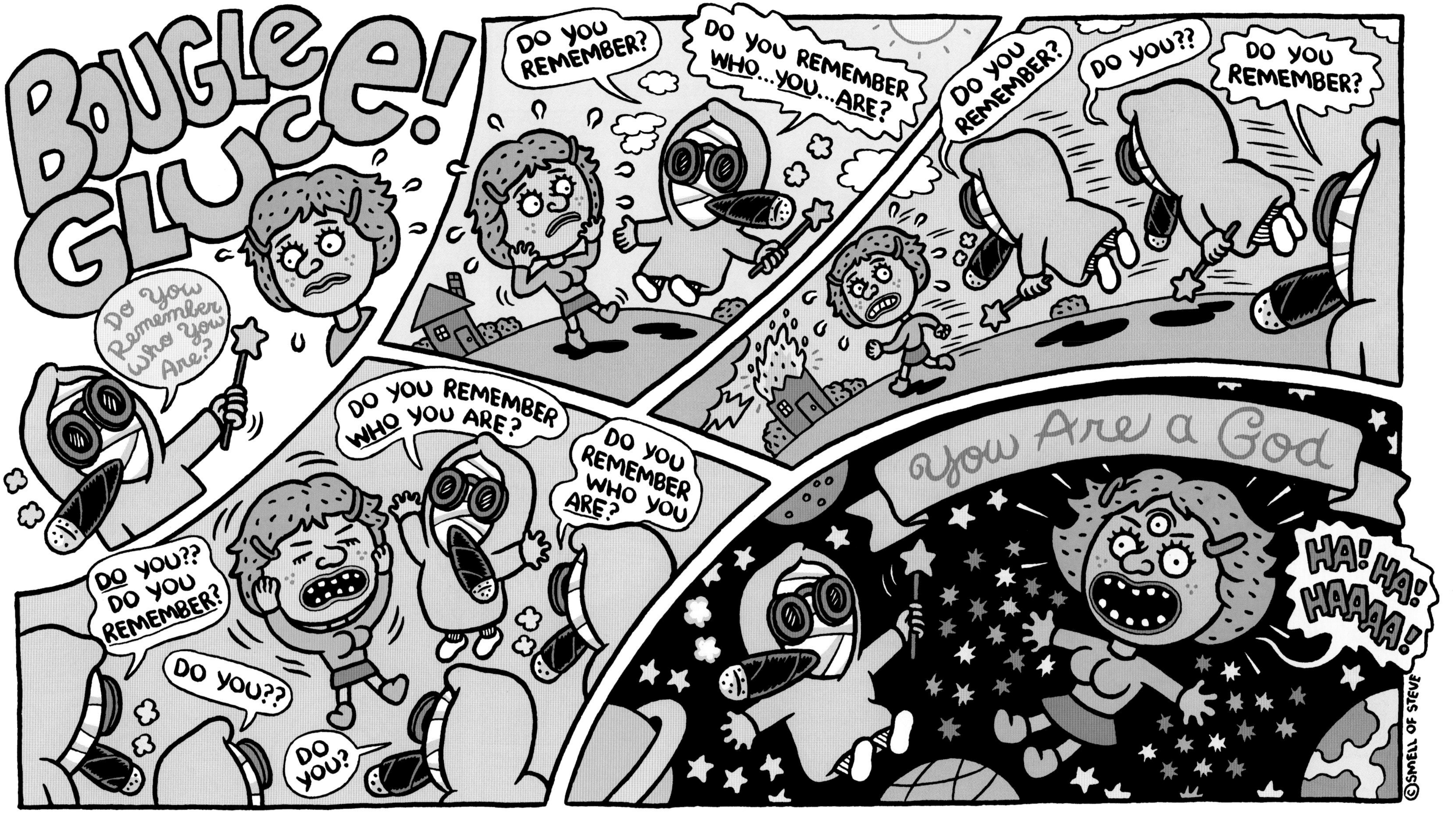
BOUGLEE! GLUCE!
Do You Remember Who You Are?
DO YOU REMEMBER?
DO YOU REMEMBER WHO...YOU...ARE?
DO YOU REMEMBER?
DO YOU??
DO YOU REMEMBER?
DO YOU REMEMBER WHO YOU ARE?
DO YOU REMEMBER WHO YOU ARE?
DO YOU?? DO YOU REMEMBER?
DO YOU??
DO YOU?
You Are a God
HA! HA! HAAAA!
©SMELL OF STEVE

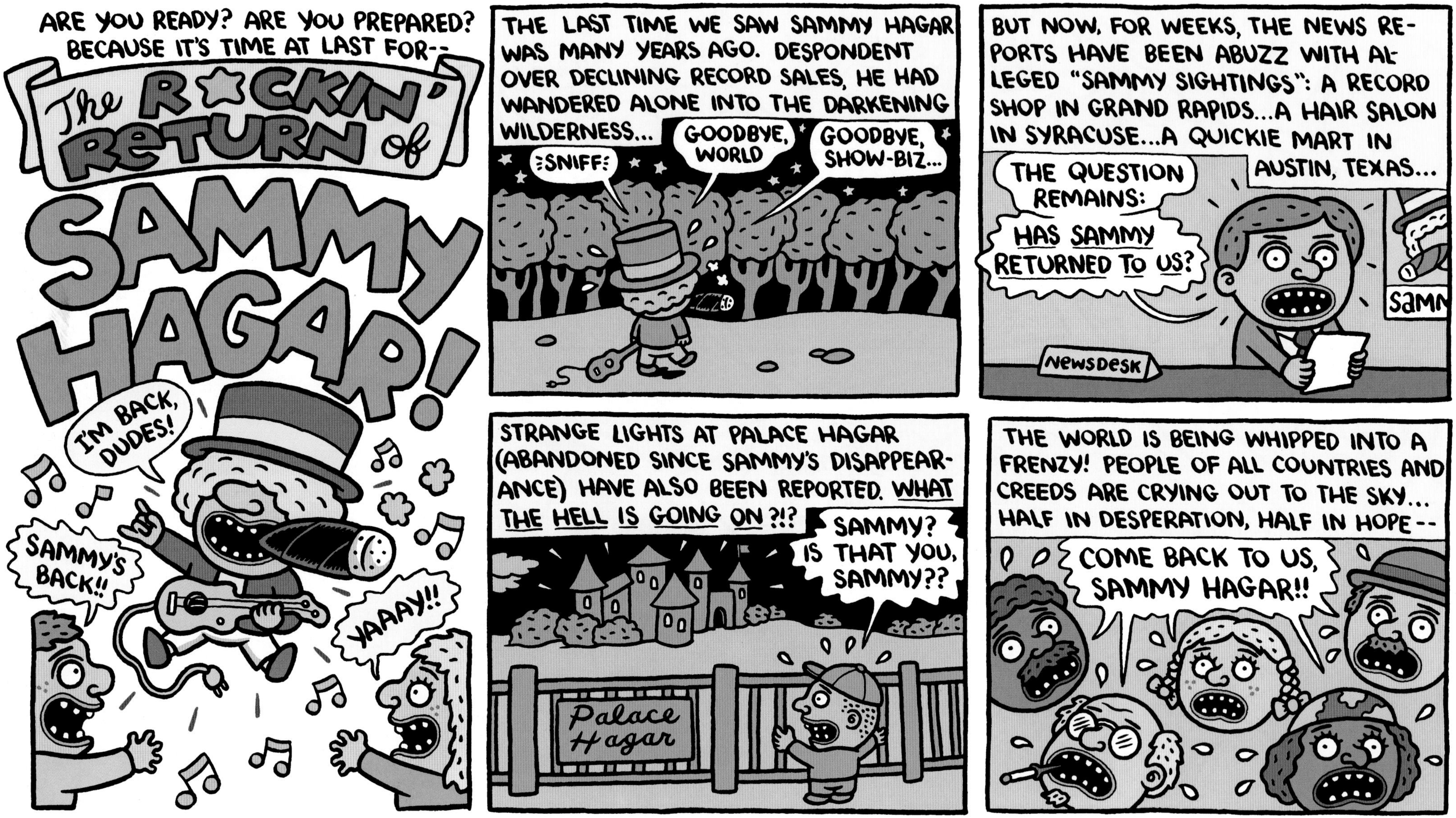
ARE YOU READY? ARE YOU PREPARED? BECAUSE IT'S TIME AT LAST FOR--
The ROCKIN' RETURN of
SAMMY HAGAR!
I'M BACK, DUDES!
SAMMY'S BACK!!
YAAAY!!
THE LAST TIME WE SAW SAMMY HAGAR WAS MANY YEARS AGO. DESPONDENT OVER DECLINING RECORD SALES, HE HAD WANDERED ALONE INTO THE DARKENING WILDERNESS...
SNIFF
GOODBYE, WORLD
GOODBYE, SHOW-BIZ...
BUT NOW, FOR WEEKS, THE NEWS REPORTS HAVE BEEN ABUZZ WITH ALLEGED "SAMMY SIGHTINGS": A RECORD SHOP IN GRAND RAPIDS...A HAIR SALON IN SYRACUSE...A QUICKIE MART IN AUSTIN, TEXAS...
THE QUESTION REMAINS:
HAS SAMMY RETURNED TO US?
NEWSDESK
SAMM
STRANGE LIGHTS AT PALACE HAGAR (ABANDONED SINCE SAMMY'S DISAPPEARANCE) HAVE ALSO BEEN REPORTED. WHAT THE HELL IS GOING ON?!?
SAMMY? IS THAT YOU, SAMMY??
Palace Hagar
THE WORLD IS BEING WHIPPED INTO A FRENZY! PEOPLE OF ALL COUNTRIES AND CREEDS ARE CRYING OUT TO THE SKY... HALF IN DESPERATION, HALF IN HOPE--
COME BACK TO US, SAMMY HAGAR!!

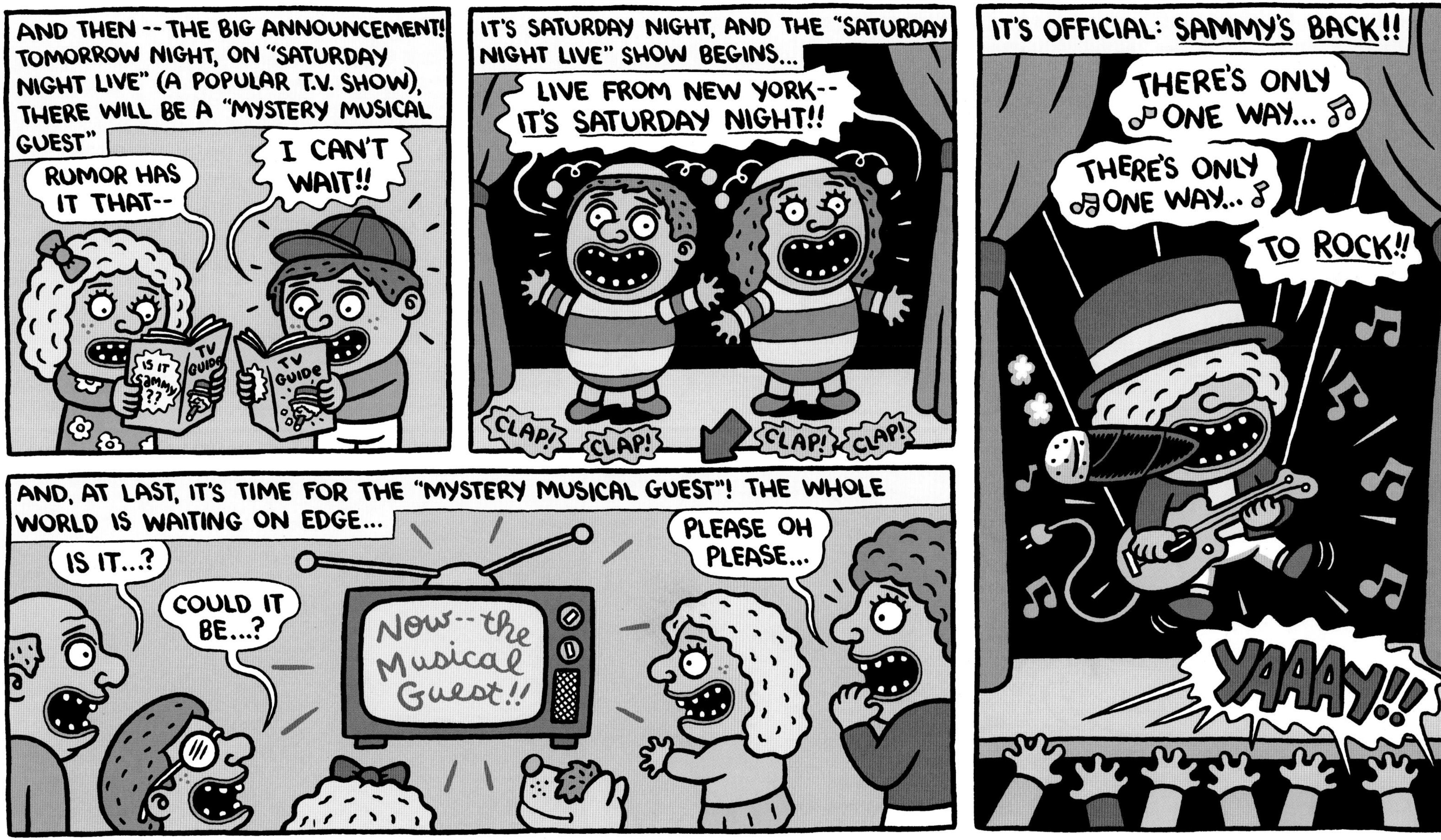
AND THEN -- THE BIG ANNOUNCEMENT! TOMORROW NIGHT, ON "SATURDAY NIGHT LIVE" (A POPULAR T.V. SHOW), THERE WILL BE A "MYSTERY MUSICAL GUEST"
RUMOR HAS IT THAT--
I CAN'T WAIT!!
TV GUIDE
IS IT SAMMY ??
TV GUIDE
IT'S SATURDAY NIGHT, AND THE "SATURDAY NIGHT LIVE" SHOW BEGINS...
LIVE FROM NEW YORK-- IT'S SATURDAY NIGHT!!
CLAP! CLAP! CLAP! CLAP!
AND, AT LAST, IT'S TIME FOR THE "MYSTERY MUSICAL GUEST"! THE WHOLE WORLD IS WAITING ON EDGE...
IS IT...?
COULD IT BE...?
Now--the Musical Guest!!
PLEASE OH PLEASE...
IT'S OFFICIAL: SAMMY'S BACK!!
THERE'S ONLY ONE WAY...
THERE'S ONLY ONE WAY...
TO ROCK!!
YAAAY!!

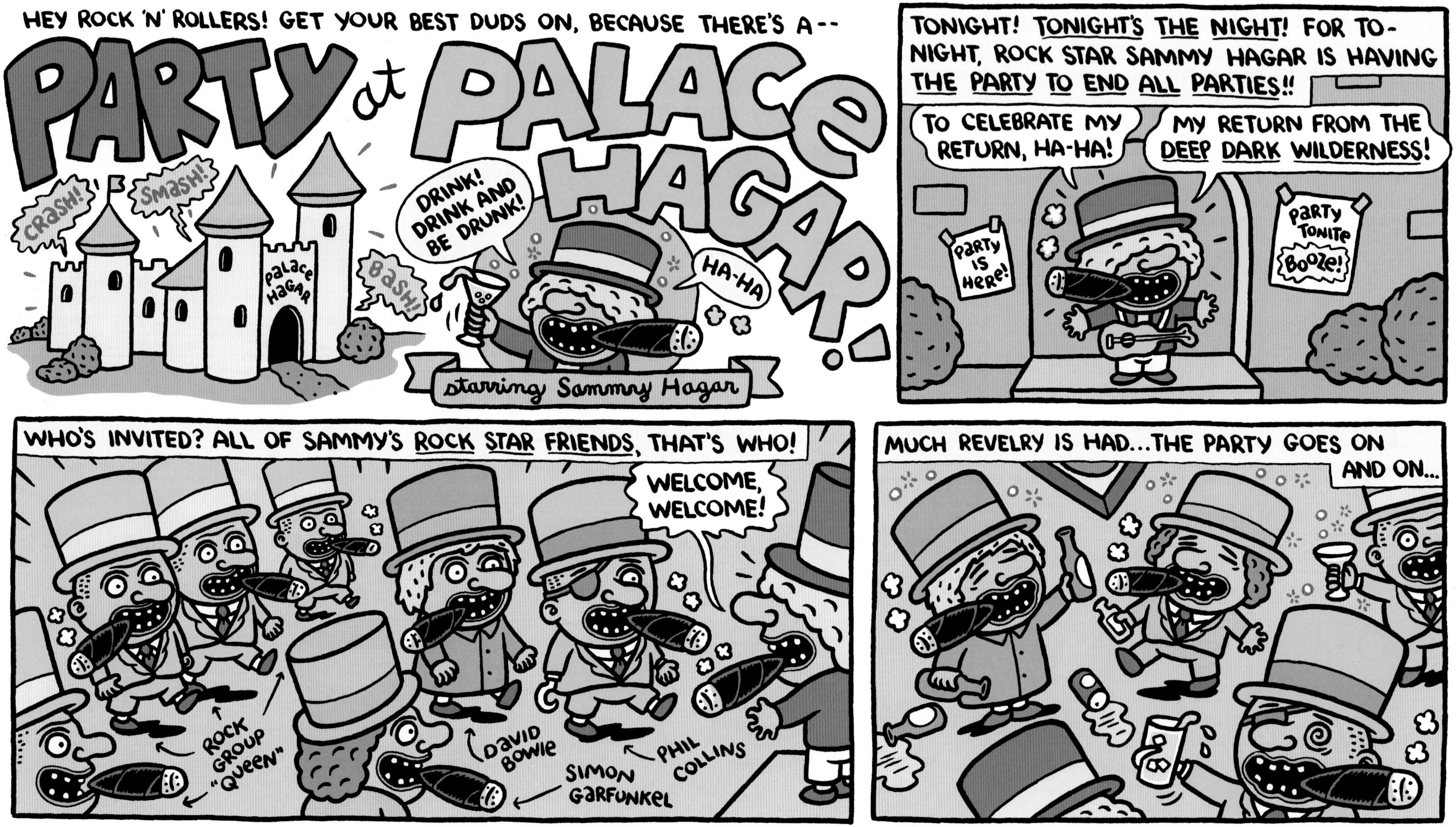

HEY ROCK 'N' ROLLERS! GET YOUR BEST DUDS ON, BECAUSE THERE'S A--
PARTY at PALACE HAGAR!
CRASH!
SMASH!
BASH!
PALACE HAGAR
DRINK! DRINK AND BE DRUNK!
HA-HA
starring Sammy Hagar
TONIGHT! TONIGHT'S THE NIGHT! FOR TO-NIGHT, ROCK STAR SAMMY HAGAR IS HAVING THE PARTY TO END ALL PARTIES!!
TO CELEBRATE MY RETURN, HA-HA!
MY RETURN FROM THE DEEP DARK WILDERNESS!
PARTY IS HERE!
PARTY TONITE BOOZE!
WHO'S INVITED? ALL OF SAMMY'S ROCK STAR FRIENDS, THAT'S WHO!
WELCOME, WELCOME!
ROCK GROUP "QUEEN"
DAVID BOWIE
SIMON GARFUNKEL
PHIL COLLINS
MUCH REVELRY IS HAD...THE PARTY GOES ON AND ON...

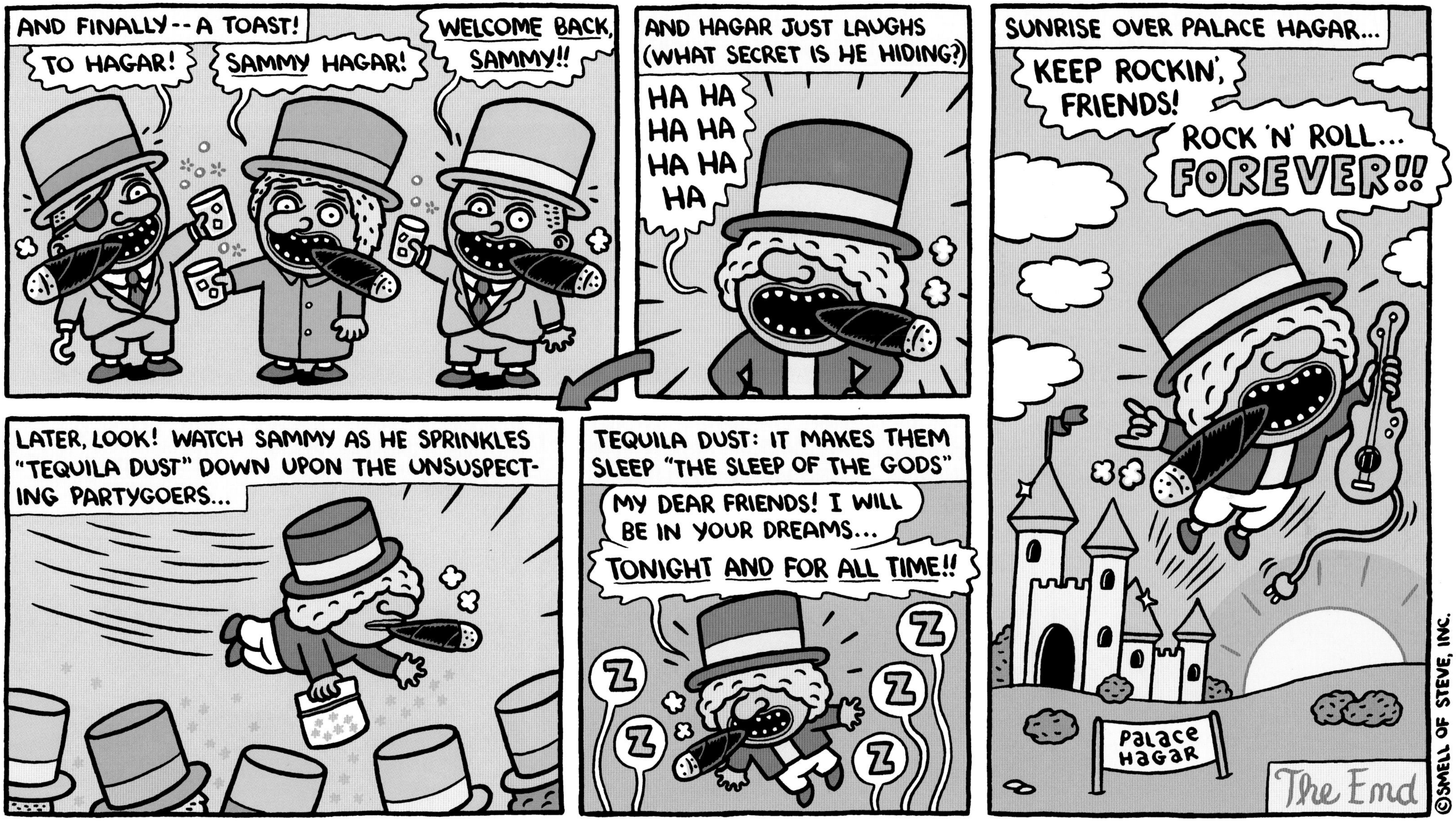
AND FINALLY--A TOAST!
TO HAGAR!
SAMMY HAGAR!
WELCOME BACK, SAMMY!!
AND HAGAR JUST LAUGHS (WHAT SECRET IS HE HIDING?)
HA HA HA HA HA HA HA
SUNRISE OVER PALACE HAGAR...
KEEP ROCKIN', FRIENDS!
ROCK 'N' ROLL... FOREVER!!
LATER, LOOK! WATCH SAMMY AS HE SPRINKLES "TEQUILA DUST" DOWN UPON THE UNSUSPECT-ING PARTYGOERS...
TEQUILA DUST: IT MAKES THEM SLEEP "THE SLEEP OF THE GODS"
MY DEAR FRIENDS! I WILL BE IN YOUR DREAMS...
TONIGHT AND FOR ALL TIME!!
Z
Z
Z
Z
Palace Hagar
The End
©SMELL OF STEVE, INC.

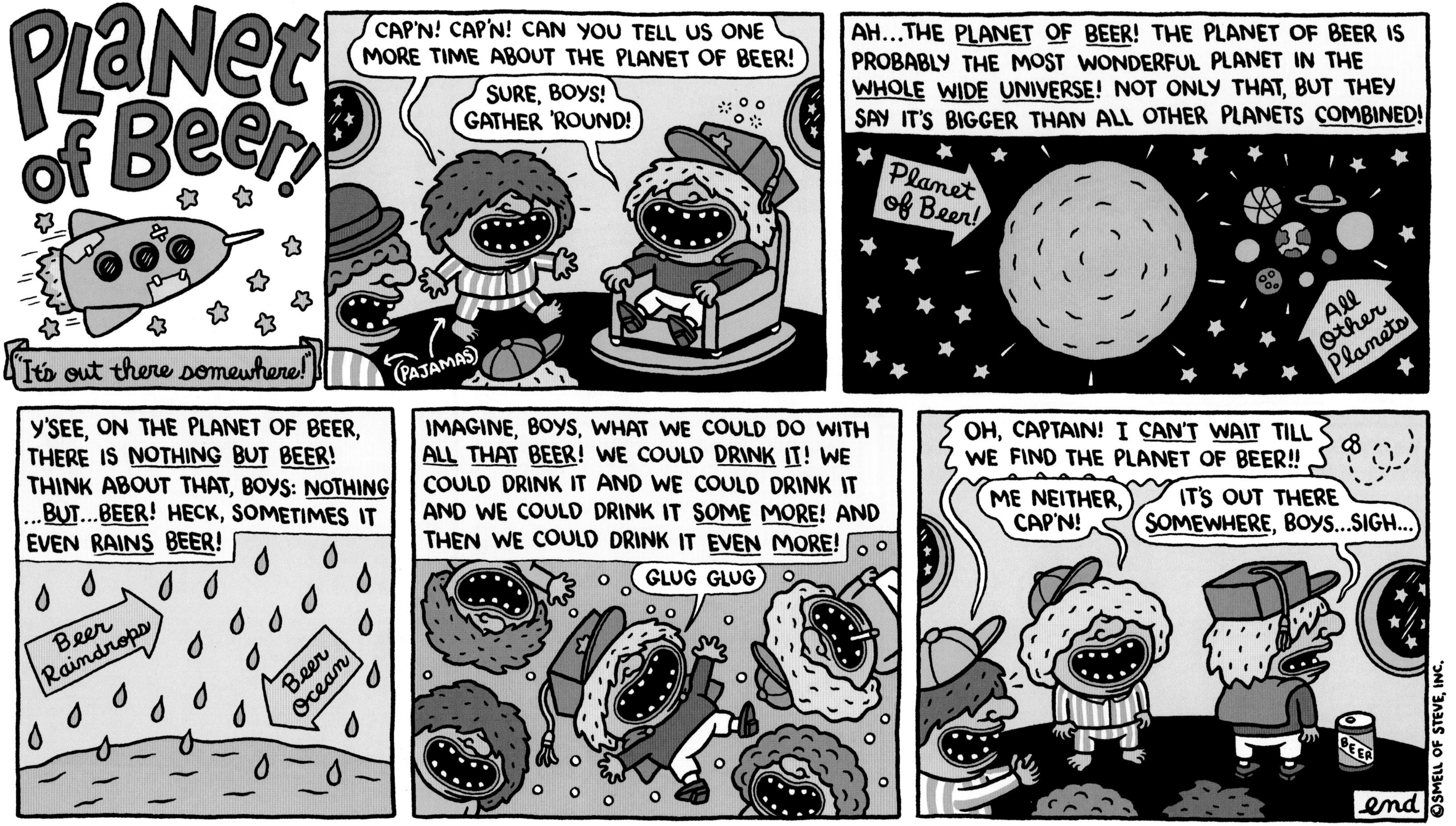
PLANET of BEER!
"It's out there somewhere!"
CAP'N! CAP'N! CAN YOU TELL US ONE MORE TIME ABOUT THE PLANET OF BEER!
SURE, BOYS! GATHER 'ROUND!
(PAJAMAS)
AH...THE PLANET OF BEER! THE PLANET OF BEER IS PROBABLY THE MOST WONDERFUL PLANET IN THE WHOLE WIDE UNIVERSE! NOT ONLY THAT, BUT THEY SAY IT'S BIGGER THAN ALL OTHER PLANETS COMBINED!
Planet of Beer!
All Other Planets
Y'SEE, ON THE PLANET OF BEER, THERE IS NOTHING BUT BEER! THINK ABOUT THAT, BOYS: NOTHING ...BUT...BEER! HECK, SOMETIMES IT EVEN RAINS BEER!
Beer Raindrops
Beer Ocean
IMAGINE, BOYS, WHAT WE COULD DO WITH ALL THAT BEER! WE COULD DRINK IT! WE COULD DRINK IT AND WE COULD DRINK IT AND WE COULD DRINK IT SOME MORE! AND THEN WE COULD DRINK IT EVEN MORE!
GLUG GLUG
OH, CAPTAIN! I CAN'T WAIT TILL WE FIND THE PLANET OF BEER!!
ME NEITHER, CAP'N!
IT'S OUT THERE SOMEWHERE, BOYS...SIGH...
BEER
end
©SMELL OF STEVE, INC.

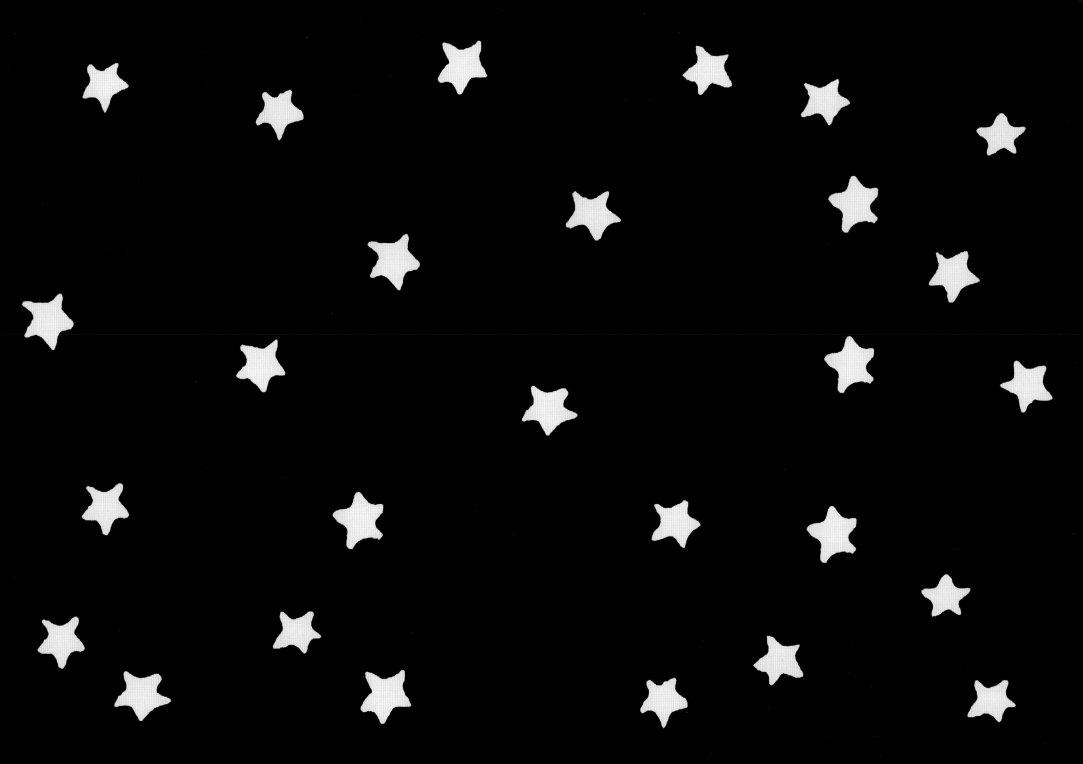

Hey, did you hear something? A giant SUCKING sound, perhaps . . . ?
That, my friend, was the sound of a big bunch of

DIDN'T-MAKE-IT-INTO-THE-BOOK

Smell of Steve™ comic strips getting sucked down HERE, into the . . .

Smell of Steve™ BLACK HOLE!

FLYMAN AND BERNIE! MY FIRST (AND BEST) COMIC STRIP CHARACTERS

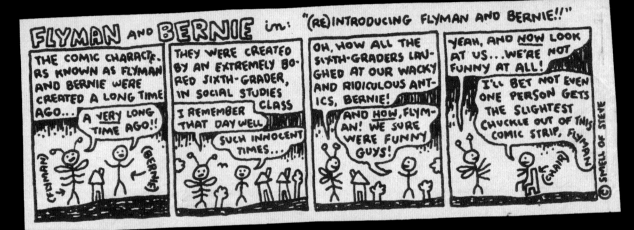

FLYMAN AND BERNIE in: "(RE)INTRODUCING FLYMAN AND BERNIE!!"
THE COMIC CHARACTERS KNOWN AS FLYMAN AND BERNIE WERE CREATED A LONG TIME AGO...
A VERY LONG TIME AGO!!
(FLYMAN)
(BERNIE)
THEY WERE CREATED BY AN EXTREMELY BORED SIXTH-GRADER, IN SOCIAL STUDIES CLASS
I REMEMBER THAT DAY WELL
SUCH INNOCENT TIMES...
OH, HOW ALL THE SIXTH-GRADERS LAUGHED AT OUR WACKY AND RIDICULOUS ANTICS, BERNIE!
AND HOW, FLYMAN! WE SURE WERE FUNNY GUYS!
YEAH, AND NOW LOOK AT US...WE'RE NOT FUNNY AT ALL!
I'LL BET NOT EVEN ONE PERSON GETS THE SLIGHTEST CHUCKLE OUT OF THIS COMIC STRIP, FLYMAN
(CHAIR)
© SMELL OF STEVE

SMELL OF STEVE, INC.
"Planet of Beer!"
CAPTAIN'S LOG: This is the starship "Galactica." I am the captain of this ship.
ZOOM!
GALACTICA
Here's my crew. Good people, all of them. Solid people. Strong people. Excellent people to have along with you on a mission such as this.
DOES ANYBODY KNOW OUR COORDINATES?
And what is our mission? To seek out the legendary Planet of Beer!!
THIS IS THE "PLANET OF BEER"
IT MAY OR MAY NOT ACTUALLY EXIST
THE CAP'N
PLANET OF BEER
BEER
I am the driving force behind this search.
HEY...WHERE'S MY LIGHTER?
PLANET... OF...BEER...
cont.
©1998 SMELL OF STEVE, INC.

THE VERY FIRST P.O.B. STRIP. NOTE THE STAR TREK-IAN SPACESHIP INEXPLICABLY NAMED "GALACTICA"

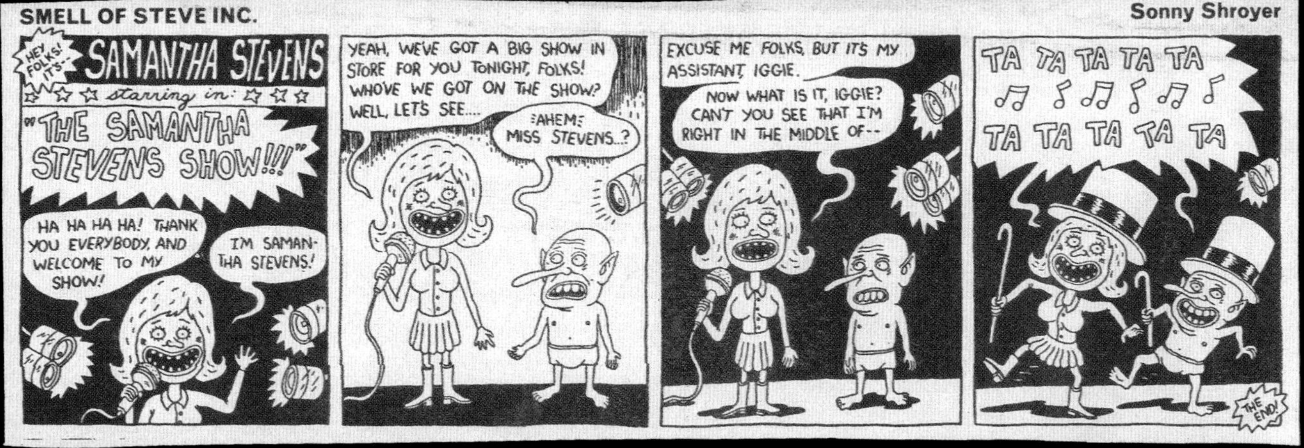
SMELL OF STEVE INC.
Sonny Shroyer
HEY FOLKS! IT'S
SAMANTHA STEVENS
starring in:
"THE SAMANTHA STEVENS SHOW!!!"
HA HA HA HA! THANK YOU EVERYBODY, AND WELCOME TO MY SHOW!
I'M SAMANTHA STEVENS!
YEAH, WE'VE GOT A BIG SHOW IN STORE FOR YOU TONIGHT, FOLKS! WHO'VE WE GOT ON THE SHOW? WELL, LET'S SEE....
AHEM MISS STEVENS..?
EXCUSE ME FOLKS, BUT IT'S MY ASSISTANT, IGGIE.
NOW WHAT IS IT, IGGIE? CAN'T YOU SEE THAT I'M RIGHT IN THE MIDDLE OF--
TA TA TA TA TA
TA TA TA TA TA
THE END!

VERY EARLY S.O.S. (I DON'T "GET" IT EITHER)

A TRAGIC, TRUE STORY. I DON'T THINK POOR MANNY EVER GOT THOSE SHIRTS BACK...

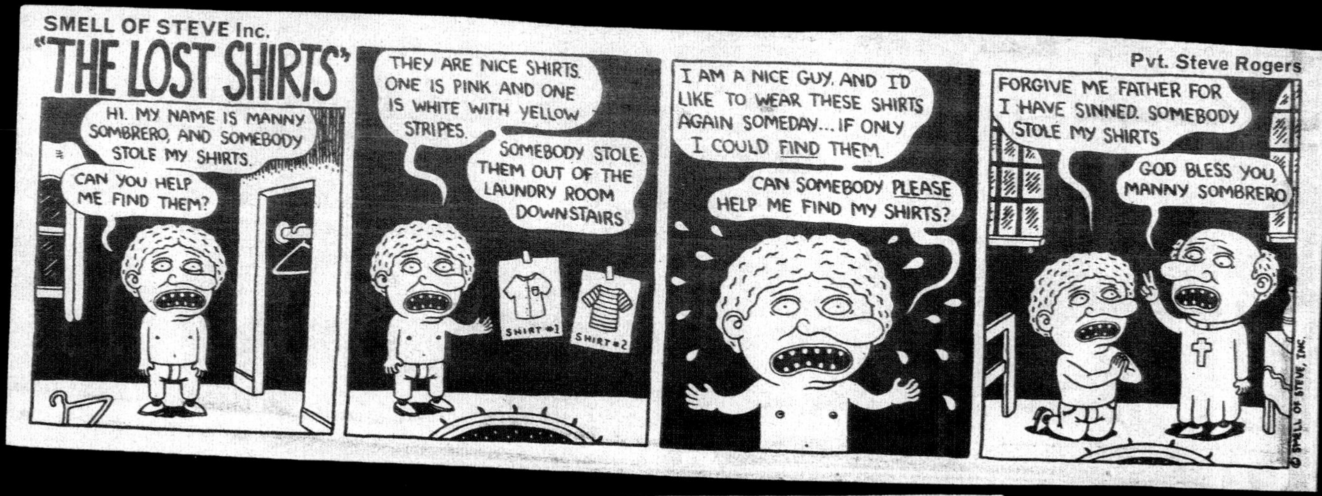
SMELL OF STEVE Inc.
"THE LOST SHIRTS"
Pvt. Steve Rogers
HI. MY NAME IS MANNY SOMBRERO, AND SOMEBODY STOLE MY SHIRTS.
CAN YOU HELP ME FIND THEM?
THEY ARE NICE SHIRTS. ONE IS PINK AND ONE IS WHITE WITH YELLOW STRIPES.
SOMEBODY STOLE THEM OUT OF THE LAUNDRY ROOM DOWNSTAIRS
SHIRT #1
SHIRT #2
I AM A NICE GUY, AND I'D LIKE TO WEAR THESE SHIRTS AGAIN SOMEDAY... IF ONLY I COULD FIND THEM.
CAN SOMEBODY PLEASE HELP ME FIND MY SHIRTS?
FORGIVE ME FATHER FOR I HAVE SINNED. SOMEBODY STOLE MY SHIRTS
GOD BLESS YOU, MANNY SOMBRERO
© SMELL OF STEVE, INC.

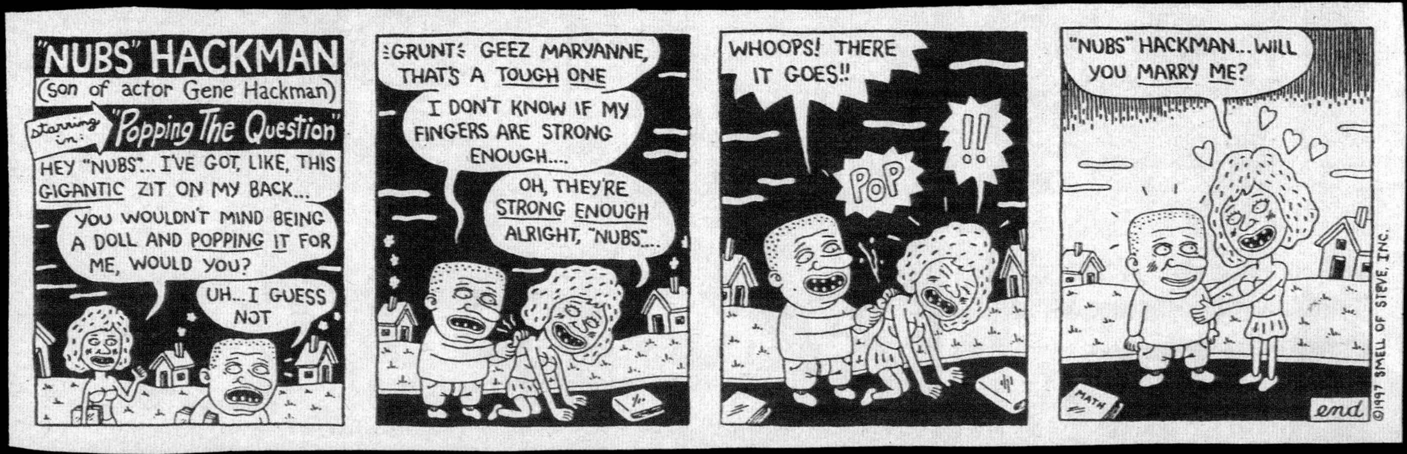
"NUBS" HACKMAN
(son of actor Gene Hackman)
starring in: "Popping The Question"
HEY "NUBS"... I'VE GOT, LIKE, THIS GIGANTIC ZIT ON MY BACK...
YOU WOULDN'T MIND BEING A DOLL AND POPPING IT FOR ME, WOULD YOU?
UH... I GUESS NOT
GRUNT GEEZ MARYANNE, THAT'S A TOUGH ONE
I DON'T KNOW IF MY FINGERS ARE STRONG ENOUGH....
OH, THEY'RE STRONG ENOUGH ALRIGHT, "NUBS"...
WHOOPS! THERE IT GOES!!
POP
!!
©1997 SMELL OF STEVE, INC.
"NUBS" HACKMAN... WILL YOU MARRY ME?
MATH
end

GENE HACKMAN: STAR OF MANY CRAPPY MOVIES. "NUBS" HACKMAN: STAR OF MANY CRAPPY COMIC STRIPS.

BASED ON AN ACTUAL CONVERSA- TIO[redacted]MES AND LI[redacted]SES HAVE BE[redacted]TERED SO[redacted]WHAT)

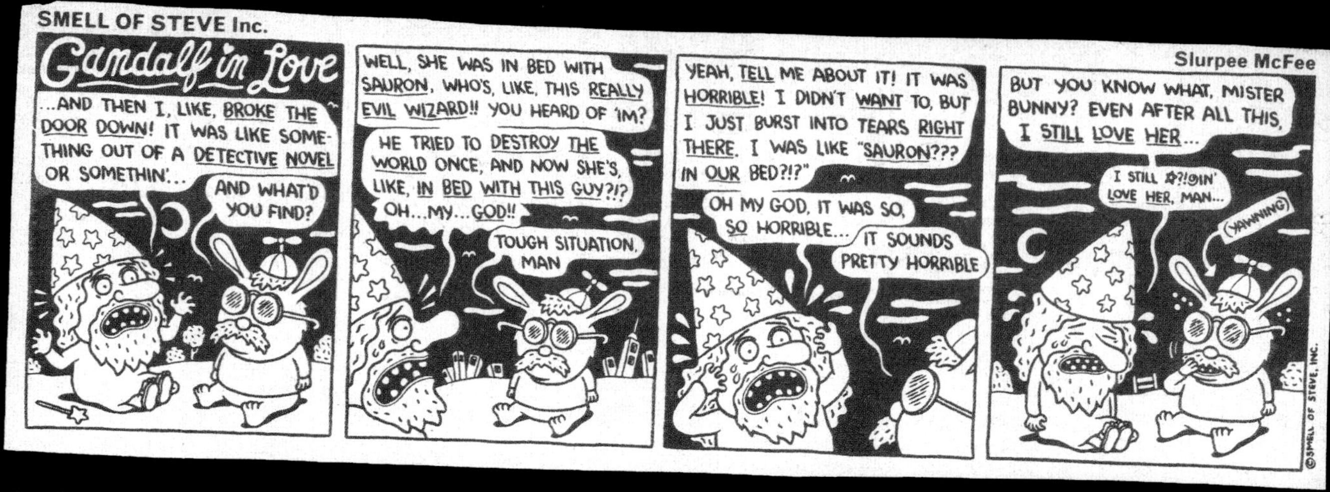
SMELL OF STEVE Inc.
Gandalf in Love
Slurpee McFee
...AND THEN I, LIKE, BROKE THE DOOR DOWN! IT WAS LIKE SOMETHING OUT OF A DETECTIVE NOVEL OR SOMETHIN'...
AND WHAT'D YOU FIND?
WELL, SHE WAS IN BED WITH SAURON, WHO'S, LIKE, THIS REALLY EVIL WIZARD!! YOU HEARD OF 'IM?
HE TRIED TO DESTROY THE WORLD ONCE, AND NOW SHE'S, LIKE, IN BED WITH THIS GUY?!? OH...MY...GOD!!
TOUGH SITUATION, MAN
YEAH, TELL ME ABOUT IT! IT WAS HORRIBLE! I DIDN'T WANT TO, BUT I JUST BURST INTO TEARS RIGHT THERE. I WAS LIKE "SAURON??? IN OUR BED?!?"
OH MY GOD, IT WAS SO, SO HORRIBLE...
IT SOUNDS PRETTY HORRIBLE
BUT YOU KNOW WHAT, MISTER BUNNY? EVEN AFTER ALL THIS, I STILL LOVE HER...
I STILL #?!@IN' LOVE HER, MAN...
(YAWNING)
©SMELL OF STEVE, INC.

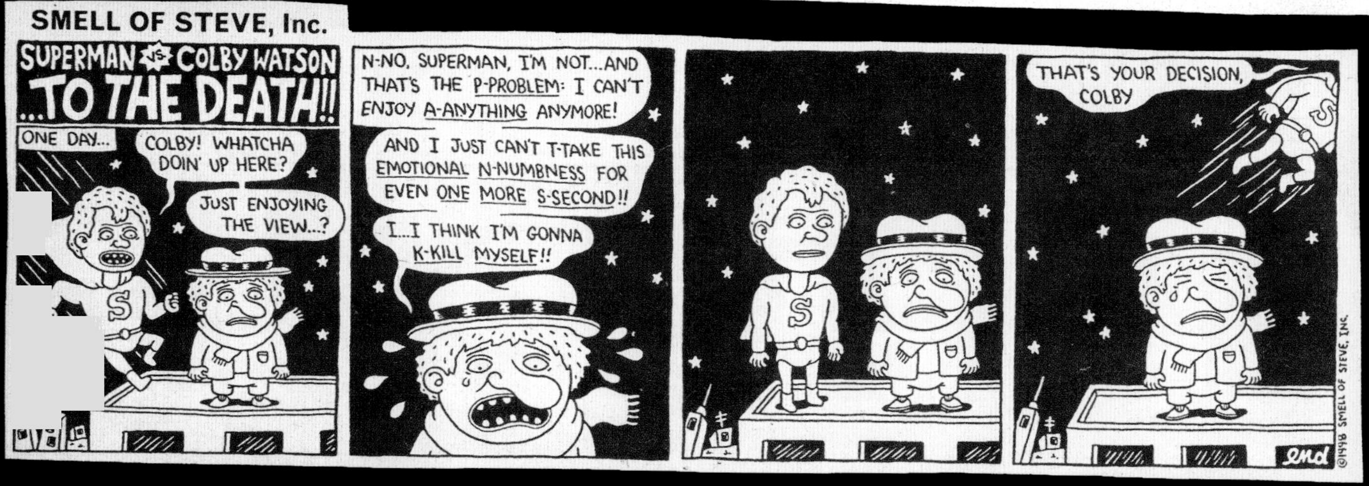
SMELL OF STEVE, Inc.
SUPERMAN VS COLBY WATSON ...TO THE DEATH!!
ONE DAY...
COLBY! WHATCHA DOIN' UP HERE?
JUST ENJOYING THE VIEW...?
N-NO, SUPERMAN, I'M NOT...AND THAT'S THE P-PROBLEM: I CAN'T ENJOY A-ANYTHING ANYMORE!
AND I JUST CAN'T T-TAKE THIS EMOTIONAL N-NUMBNESS FOR EVEN ONE MORE S-SECOND!!
I...I THINK I'M GONNA K-KILL MYSELF!!
THAT'S YOUR DECISION, COLBY
end
©1998 SMELL OF STEVE, INC.

MY OLD ROOMMATE COLBY WATSON WASN'T TOO HAPPY ABOUT THIS ONE

WAS ACTUALLY SUPPOSED TO GO I[redacted]HE BOOK, B[redacted] FORGOT A[redacted]OUT IT.

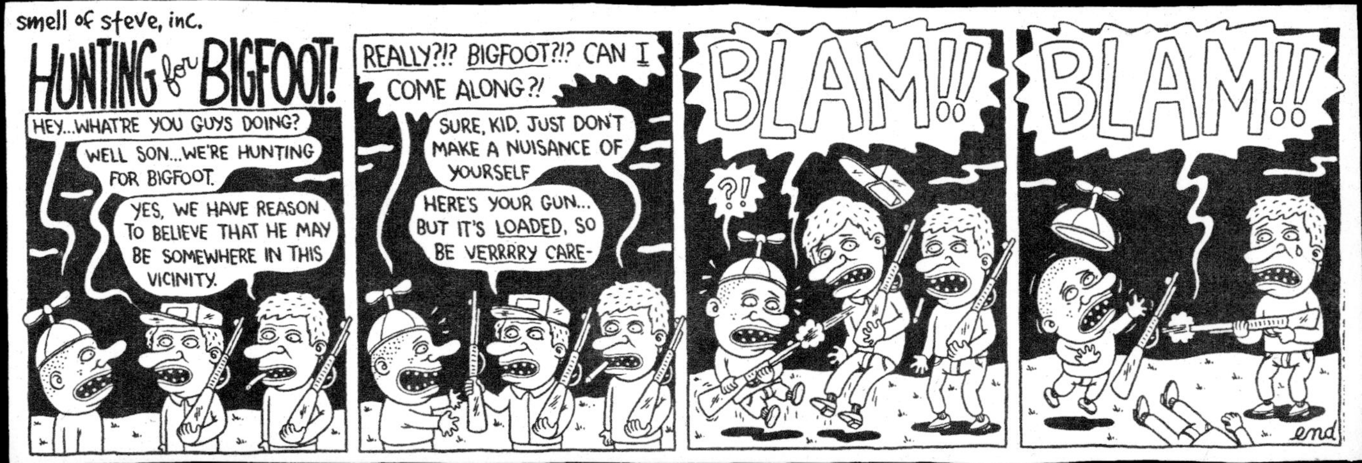
smell of steve, inc.
HUNTING for BIGFOOT!
HEY...WHAT'RE YOU GUYS DOING?
WELL SON...WE'RE HUNTING FOR BIGFOOT.
YES, WE HAVE REASON TO BELIEVE THAT HE MAY BE SOMEWHERE IN THIS VICINITY.
REALLY?!? BIGFOOT?!? CAN I COME ALONG?!
SURE, KID. JUST DON'T MAKE A NUISANCE OF YOURSELF
HERE'S YOUR GUN... BUT IT'S LOADED, SO BE VERRRRY CARE-
BLAM!!
?!
BLAM!!
end

A continuation of the "story" that leaves off on page 67 (well...with a few episodes missing in between).

My Fonzie epics were especially hated by many readers ...which is why I decided to include lots of 'em in this volume. ☺

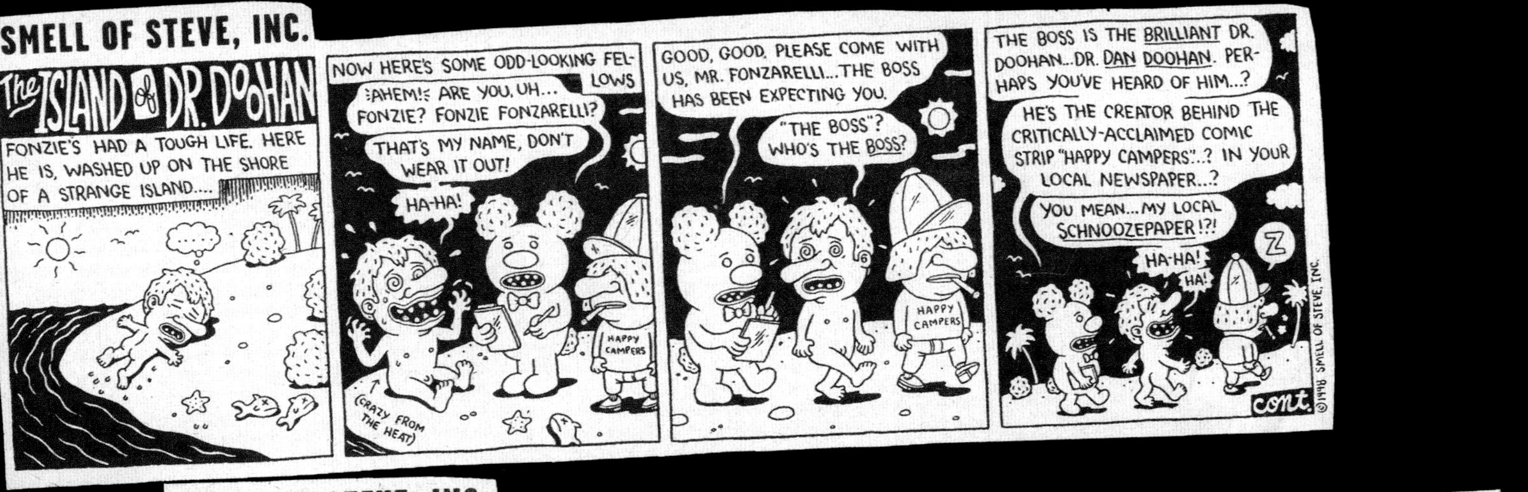
SMELL OF STEVE, INC.
The ISLAND of DR. DOOHAN
FONZIE'S HAD A TOUGH LIFE. HERE HE IS, WASHED UP ON THE SHORE OF A STRANGE ISLAND....
NOW HERE'S SOME ODD-LOOKING FELLOWS
:AHEM!: ARE YOU, UH... FONZIE? FONZIE FONZARELLI?
THAT'S MY NAME, DON'T WEAR IT OUT!
HA-HA!
(CRAZY FROM THE HEAT)
HAPPY CAMPERS
GOOD, GOOD. PLEASE COME WITH US, MR. FONZARELLI... THE BOSS HAS BEEN EXPECTING YOU.
"THE BOSS"? WHO'S THE BOSS?
HAPPY CAMPERS
THE BOSS IS THE BRILLIANT DR. DOOHAN...DR. DAN DOOHAN. PERHAPS YOU'VE HEARD OF HIM...?
HE'S THE CREATOR BEHIND THE CRITICALLY-ACCLAIMED COMIC STRIP "HAPPY CAMPERS"...? IN YOUR LOCAL NEWSPAPER...?
YOU MEAN...MY LOCAL SCHNOOZEPAPER!?!
HA-HA! HA!
Z
©1998 SMELL OF STEVE, INC.
cont.

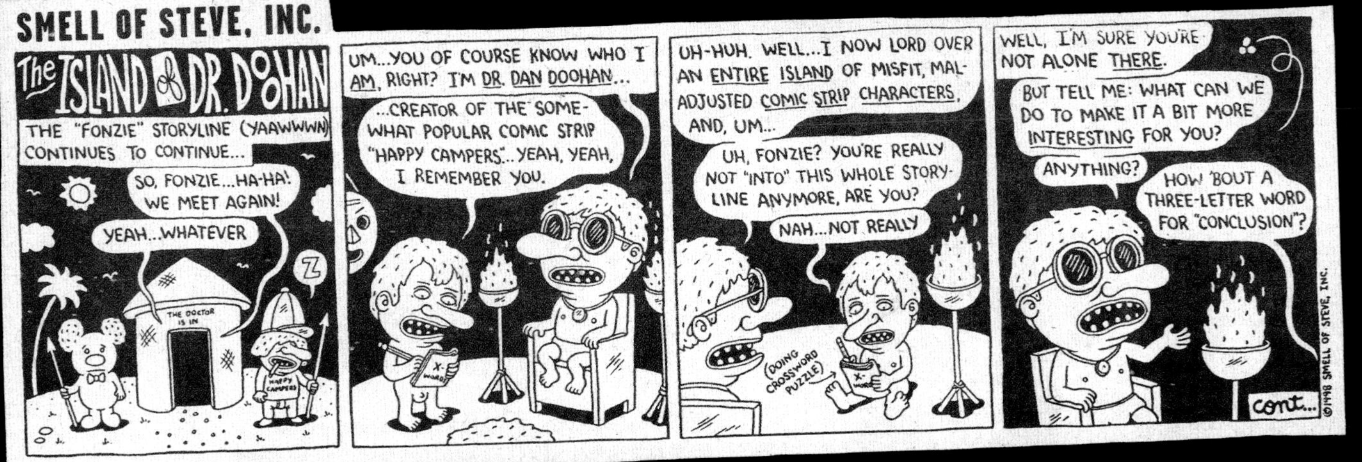
SMELL OF STEVE, INC.
The ISLAND of DR. DOOHAN
THE "FONZIE" STORYLINE (YAAWWWN) CONTINUES TO CONTINUE...
SO, FONZIE...HA-HA! WE MEET AGAIN!
YEAH...WHATEVER
THE DOCTOR IS IN
Z
UM...YOU OF COURSE KNOW WHO I AM, RIGHT? I'M DR. DAN DOOHAN...
...CREATOR OF THE SOMEWHAT POPULAR COMIC STRIP "HAPPY CAMPERS"...YEAH, YEAH, I REMEMBER YOU.
UH-HUH. WELL...I NOW LORD OVER AN ENTIRE ISLAND OF MISFIT, MALADJUSTED COMIC STRIP CHARACTERS, AND, UM...
UH, FONZIE? YOU'RE REALLY NOT "INTO" THIS WHOLE STORYLINE ANYMORE, ARE YOU?
NAH...NOT REALLY
(DOING CROSSWORD PUZZLE)
WELL, I'M SURE YOU'RE NOT ALONE THERE.
BUT TELL ME: WHAT CAN WE DO TO MAKE IT A BIT MORE INTERESTING FOR YOU?
ANYTHING?
HOW 'BOUT A THREE-LETTER WORD FOR "CONCLUSION"?
cont...
©1998 SMELL OF STEVE, INC.

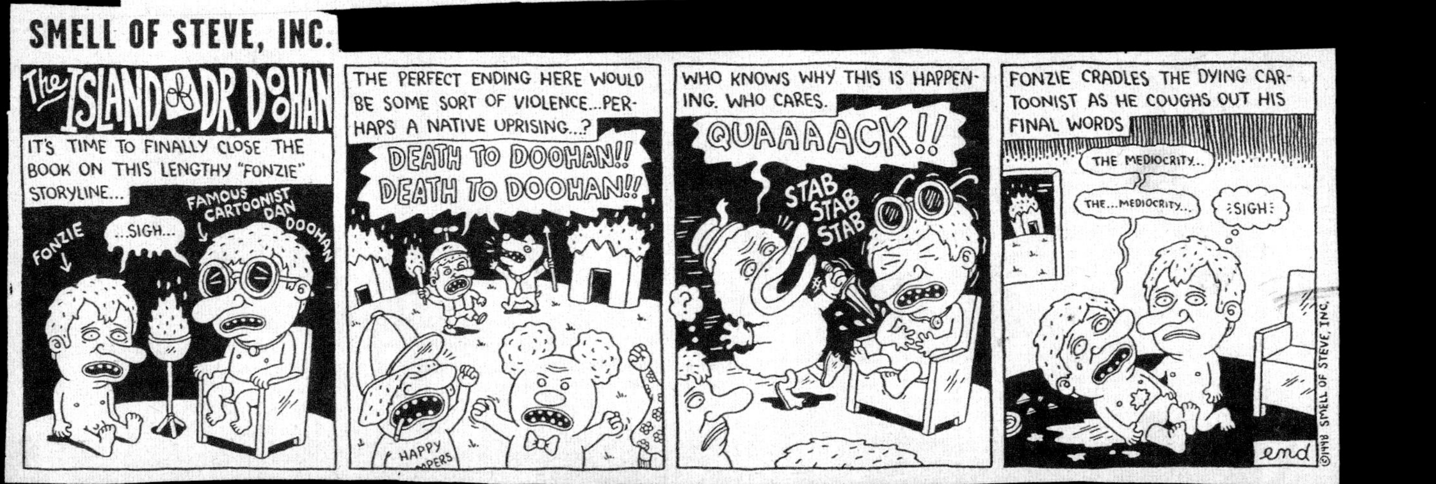
SMELL OF STEVE, INC.
The ISLAND of DR. DOOHAN
IT'S TIME TO FINALLY CLOSE THE BOOK ON THIS LENGTHY "FONZIE" STORYLINE...
FONZIE
...SIGH...
FAMOUS CARTOONIST DAN DOOHAN
THE PERFECT ENDING HERE WOULD BE SOME SORT OF VIOLENCE...PERHAPS A NATIVE UPRISING...?
DEATH TO DOOHAN!! DEATH TO DOOHAN!!
WHO KNOWS WHY THIS IS HAPPENING. WHO CARES.
QUAAAACK!!
STAB STAB STAB
FONZIE CRADLES THE DYING CARTOONIST AS HE COUGHS OUT HIS FINAL WORDS
THE MEDIOCRITY...
THE...MEDIOCRITY...
:SIGH:
end
©1998 SMELL OF STEVE, INC.

MICHAEL KEATON AS A WORLD-FAMOUS FLATULENT MATH TEXTBOOK

(SOMETIMES THINGS GET TAKEN FURTHER THAN ANYONE REALLY WANTS TO GO...)

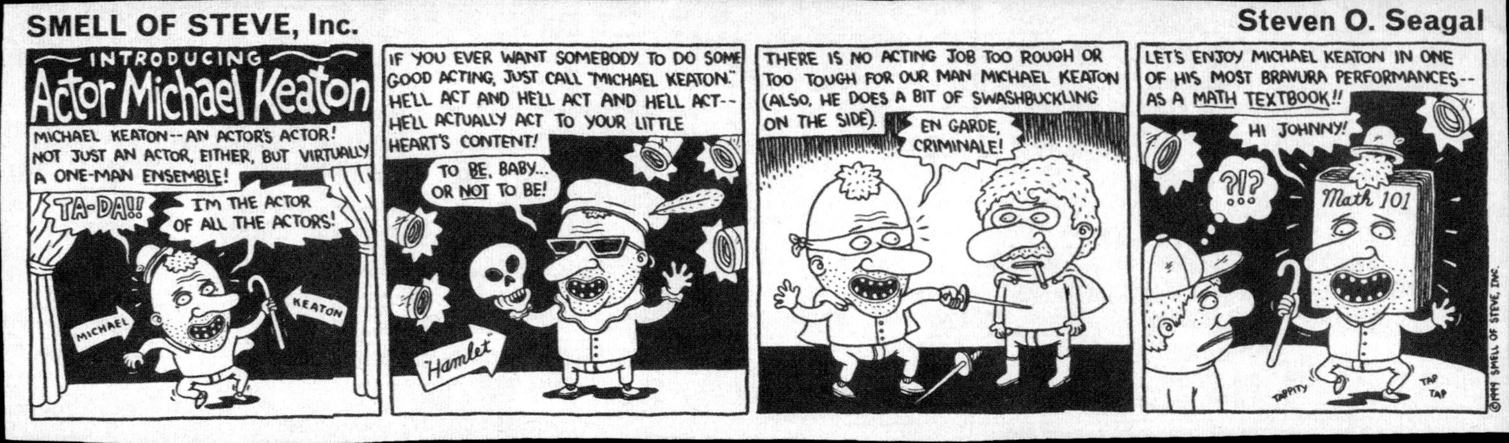
SMELL OF STEVE, Inc.
Steven O. Seagal
INTRODUCING
Actor Michael Keaton
MICHAEL KEATON--AN ACTOR'S ACTOR! NOT JUST AN ACTOR, EITHER, BUT VIRTUALLY A ONE-MAN ENSEMBLE!
TA-DA!!
I'M THE ACTOR OF ALL THE ACTORS!
MICHAEL
KEATON
IF YOU EVER WANT SOMEBODY TO DO SOME GOOD ACTING, JUST CALL "MICHAEL KEATON." HE'LL ACT AND HE'LL ACT AND HE'LL ACT--HE'LL ACTUALLY ACT TO YOUR LITTLE HEART'S CONTENT!
TO BE, BABY... OR NOT TO BE!
"Hamlet"
THERE IS NO ACTING JOB TOO ROUGH OR TOO TOUGH FOR OUR MAN MICHAEL KEATON (ALSO, HE DOES A BIT OF SWASHBUCKLING ON THE SIDE).
EN GARDE, CRIMINALE!
LET'S ENJOY MICHAEL KEATON IN ONE OF HIS MOST BRAVURA PERFORMANCES--AS A MATH TEXTBOOK!!
HI JOHNNY!
?!?
Math 101
TAPPITY
TAP TAP
©1999 SMELL OF STEVE, INC.

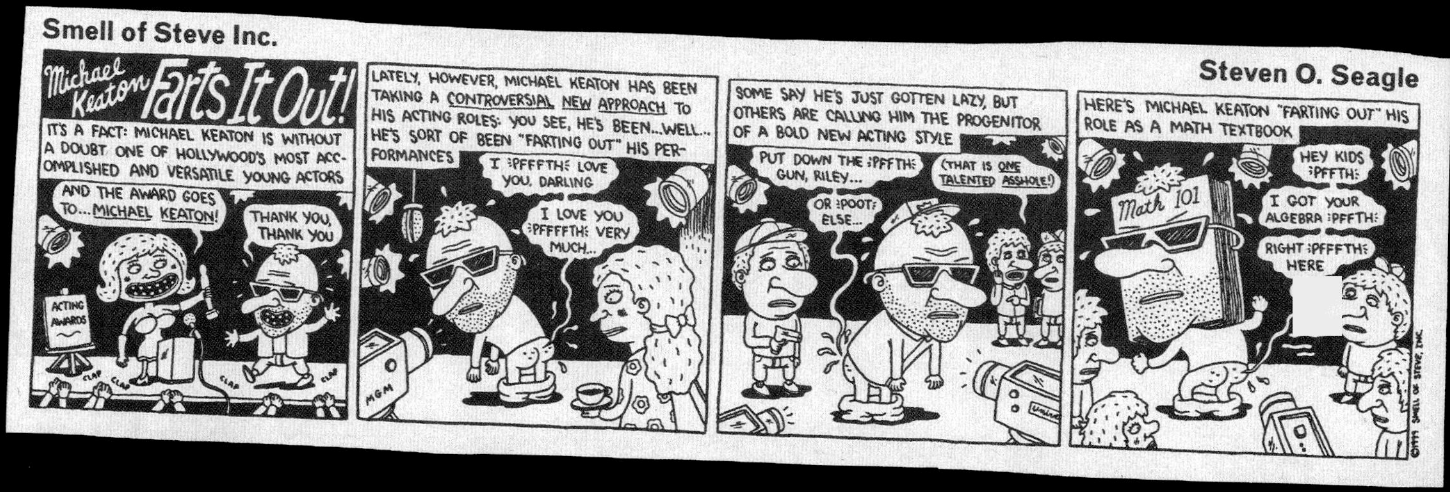
Smell of Steve Inc.
Steven O. Seagle
Michael Keaton Farts It Out!
IT'S A FACT: MICHAEL KEATON IS WITHOUT A DOUBT ONE OF HOLLYWOOD'S MOST ACCOMPLISHED AND VERSATILE YOUNG ACTORS
AND THE AWARD GOES TO...MICHAEL KEATON!
THANK YOU, THANK YOU
ACTING AWARDS
CLAP
CLAP
CLAP
CLAP
LATELY, HOWEVER, MICHAEL KEATON HAS BEEN TAKING A CONTROVERSIAL NEW APPROACH TO HIS ACTING ROLES: YOU SEE, HE'S BEEN...WELL... HE'S SORT OF BEEN "FARTING OUT" HIS PERFORMANCES
I :PFFFTH: LOVE YOU, DARLING
I LOVE YOU :PFFFFTH: VERY MUCH...
MGM
SOME SAY HE'S JUST GOTTEN LAZY, BUT OTHERS ARE CALLING HIM THE PROGENITOR OF A BOLD NEW ACTING STYLE
PUT DOWN THE :PFFTH: GUN, RILEY...
OR :POOT: ELSE...
(THAT IS ONE TALENTED ASSHOLE!)
HERE'S MICHAEL KEATON "FARTING OUT" HIS ROLE AS A MATH TEXTBOOK
HEY KIDS :PFFTH:
I GOT YOUR ALGEBRA :PFFTH:
RIGHT :PFFFTH: HERE
Math 101
©1999 SMELL OF STEVE, INC.

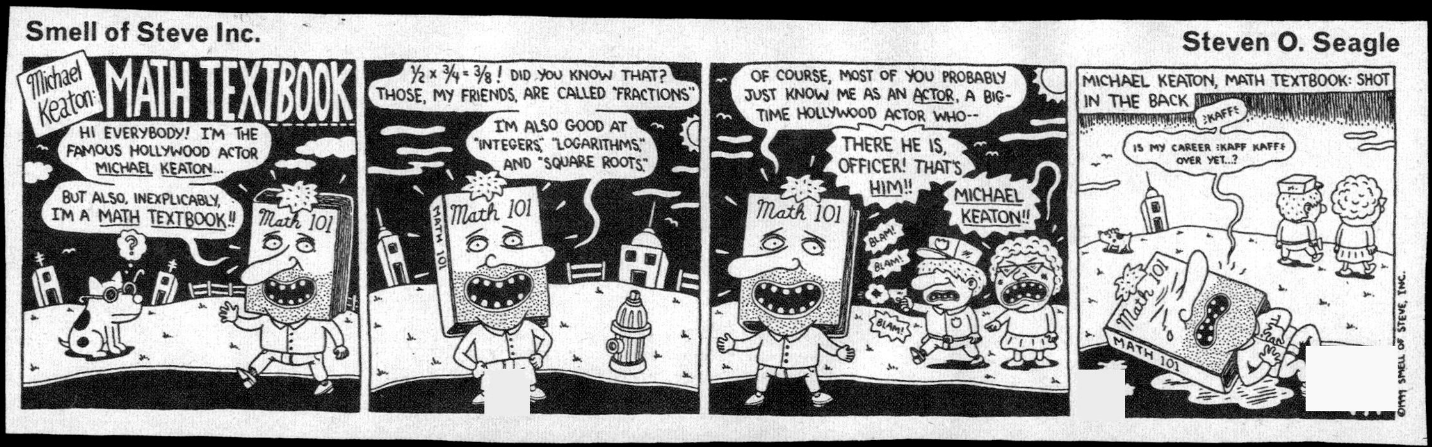
Smell of Steve Inc.
Steven O. Seagle
Michael Keaton: MATH TEXTBOOK
HI EVERYBODY! I'M THE FAMOUS HOLLYWOOD ACTOR MICHAEL KEATON...
BUT ALSO, INEXPLICABLY, I'M A MATH TEXTBOOK!!
?
Math 101
1/2 x 3/4 = 3/8! DID YOU KNOW THAT? THOSE, MY FRIENDS, ARE CALLED "FRACTIONS"
I'M ALSO GOOD AT "INTEGERS," "LOGARITHMS," AND "SQUARE ROOTS."
MATH 101
OF COURSE, MOST OF YOU PROBABLY JUST KNOW ME AS AN ACTOR, A BIG-TIME HOLLYWOOD ACTOR WHO--
THERE HE IS, OFFICER! THAT'S HIM!!
MICHAEL KEATON!!
BLAM!
BLAM!
BLAM!
MICHAEL KEATON, MATH TEXTBOOK: SHOT IN THE BACK
:KAFF:
IS MY CAREER :KAFF KAFF: OVER YET...?
MATH 101
©1999 SMELL OF STEVE, INC.

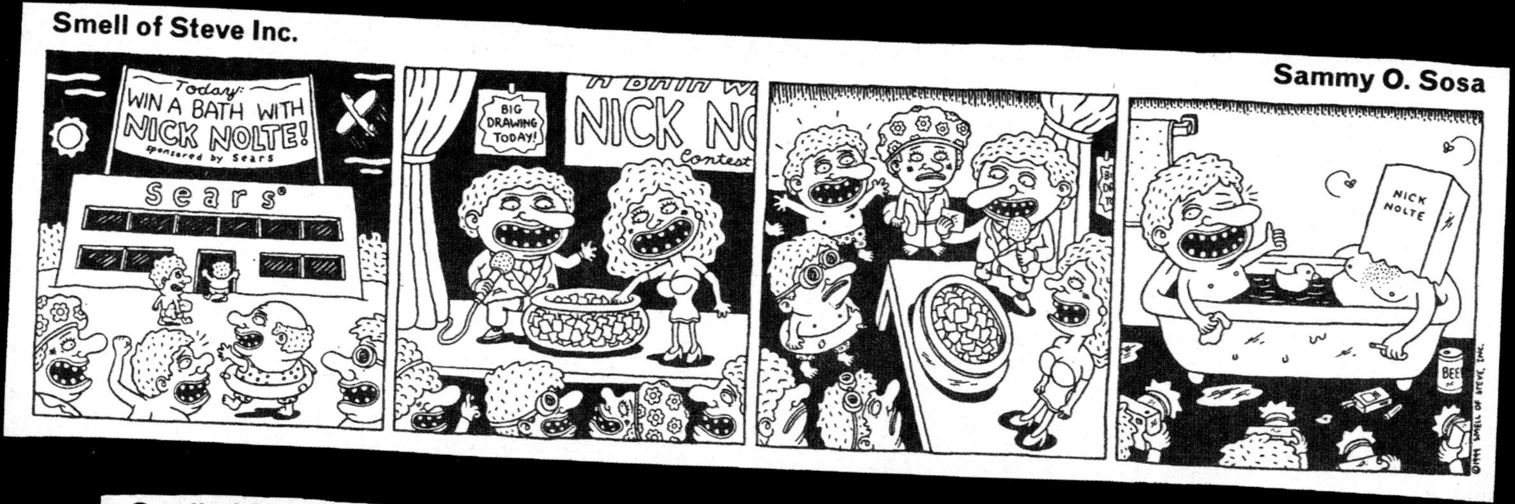
Smell of Steve Inc.
Sammy O. Sosa
Today: WIN A BATH WITH NICK NOLTE!
sponsored by Sears
Sears
BIG DRAWING TODAY!
NICK NO
Contest
NICK NOLTE
©1999 SMELL OF STEVE, INC.

every ARTIST goes THROUGH A NICK NOLTE PHASE AT SOME POINT

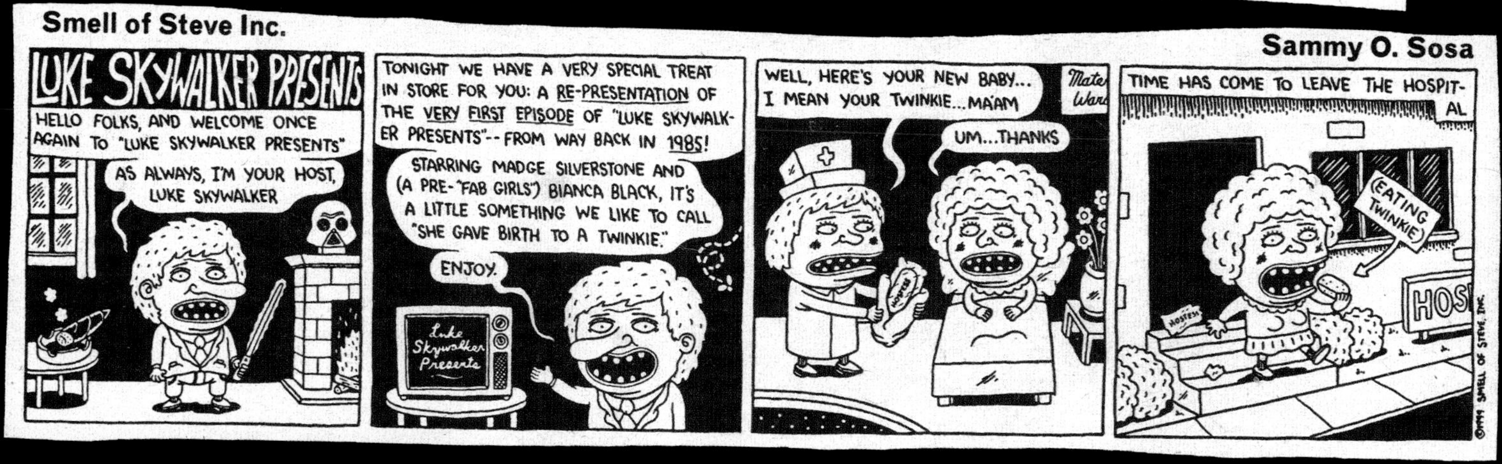
Smell of Steve Inc.
Sammy O. Sosa
LUKE SKYWALKER PRESENTS
HELLO FOLKS, AND WELCOME ONCE AGAIN TO "LUKE SKYWALKER PRESENTS"
AS ALWAYS, I'M YOUR HOST, LUKE SKYWALKER
TONIGHT WE HAVE A VERY SPECIAL TREAT IN STORE FOR YOU: A RE-PRESENTATION OF THE VERY FIRST EPISODE OF "LUKE SKYWALKER PRESENTS"-- FROM WAY BACK IN 1985!
STARRING MADGE SILVERSTONE AND (A PRE-"FAB GIRLS") BIANCA BLACK, IT'S A LITTLE SOMETHING WE LIKE TO CALL "SHE GAVE BIRTH TO A TWINKIE."
ENJOY.
Luke Skywalker Presents
WELL, HERE'S YOUR NEW BABY... I MEAN YOUR TWINKIE... MA'AM
UM... THANKS
TIME HAS COME TO LEAVE THE HOSPITAL
EATING TWINKIE
HOS
HOSTESS
©1999 SMELL OF STEVE, INC.

← ???

BASED, SADLY, ON AN ACTUAL CONVERSATION

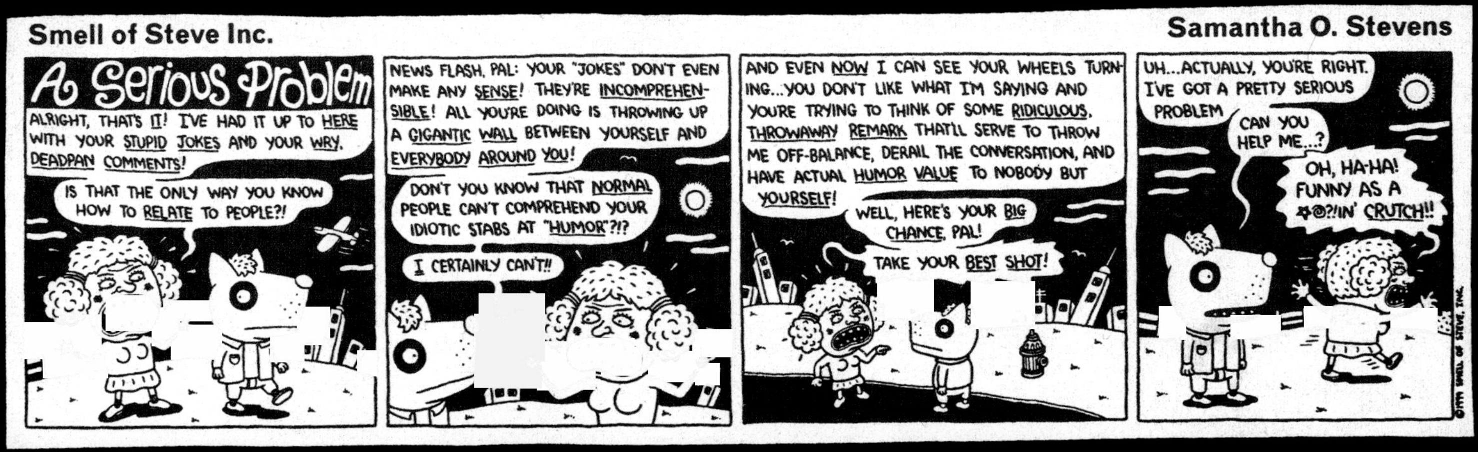
Smell of Steve Inc.
Samantha O. Stevens
A Serious Problem
ALRIGHT, THAT'S IT! I'VE HAD IT UP TO HERE WITH YOUR STUPID JOKES AND YOUR WRY, DEADPAN COMMENTS!
IS THAT THE ONLY WAY YOU KNOW HOW TO RELATE TO PEOPLE?!
NEWS FLASH, PAL: YOUR "JOKES" DON'T EVEN MAKE ANY SENSE! THEY'RE INCOMPREHENSIBLE! ALL YOU'RE DOING IS THROWING UP A GIGANTIC WALL BETWEEN YOURSELF AND EVERYBODY AROUND YOU!
DON'T YOU KNOW THAT NORMAL PEOPLE CAN'T COMPREHEND YOUR IDIOTIC STABS AT "HUMOR"?!?
I CERTAINLY CAN'T!!
AND EVEN NOW I CAN SEE YOUR WHEELS TURNING... YOU DON'T LIKE WHAT I'M SAYING AND YOU'RE TRYING TO THINK OF SOME RIDICULOUS, THROWAWAY REMARK THAT'LL SERVE TO THROW ME OFF-BALANCE, DERAIL THE CONVERSATION, AND HAVE ACTUAL HUMOR VALUE TO NOBODY BUT YOURSELF!
WELL, HERE'S YOUR BIG CHANCE, PAL!
TAKE YOUR BEST SHOT!
UH... ACTUALLY, YOU'RE RIGHT. I'VE GOT A PRETTY SERIOUS PROBLEM
CAN YOU HELP ME...?
OH, HA-HA! FUNNY AS A ✲@?!IN' CRUTCH!!
©1999 SMELL OF STEVE, INC.

AGAINST MY BETTER JUDGEMENT, I ONCE DREW AN ENTIRE COMIC BOOK FEATURING THIS PHIL COLLINS CHARACTER →

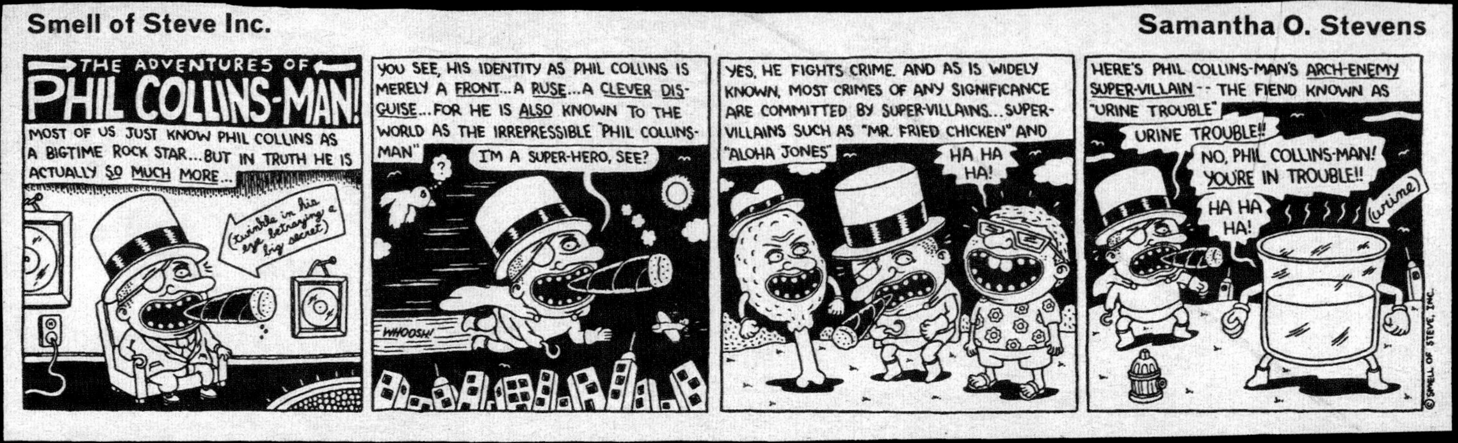

Smell of Steve Inc.
Samantha O. Stevens
THE ADVENTURES OF PHIL COLLINS-MAN!
MOST OF US JUST KNOW PHIL COLLINS AS A BIGTIME ROCK STAR... BUT IN TRUTH HE IS ACTUALLY SO MUCH MORE...
twinkle in his eye betraying a big secret
YOU SEE, HIS IDENTITY AS PHIL COLLINS IS MERELY A FRONT... A RUSE... A CLEVER DISGUISE... FOR HE IS ALSO KNOWN TO THE WORLD AS THE IRREPRESSIBLE "PHIL COLLINS-MAN"
I'M A SUPER-HERO, SEE?
WHOOSH!
YES, HE FIGHTS CRIME. AND AS IS WIDELY KNOWN, MOST CRIMES OF ANY SIGNIFICANCE ARE COMMITTED BY SUPER-VILLAINS... SUPER-VILLAINS SUCH AS "MR. FRIED CHICKEN" AND "ALOHA JONES"
HA HA HA!
HERE'S PHIL COLLINS-MAN'S ARCH-ENEMY SUPER-VILLAIN -- THE FIEND KNOWN AS "URINE TROUBLE"
URINE TROUBLE!!
NO, PHIL COLLINS-MAN! YOU'RE IN TROUBLE!!
HA HA HA!
(urine)
© SMELL OF STEVE, INC.

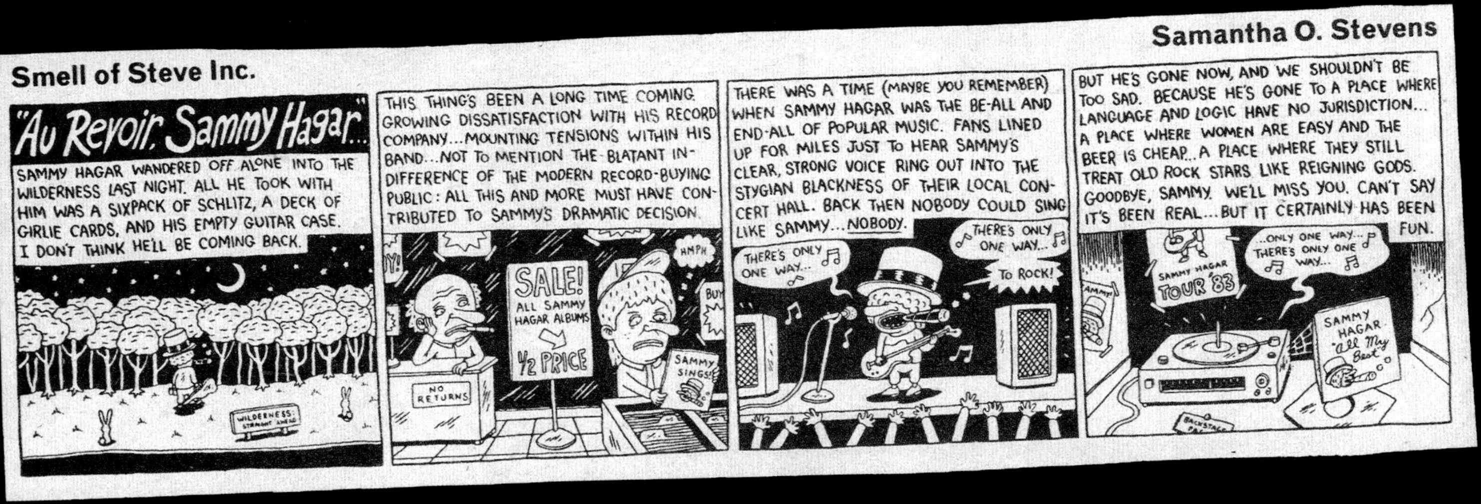

Samantha O. Stevens
Smell of Steve Inc.
"Au Revoir, Sammy Hagar..."
SAMMY HAGAR WANDERED OFF ALONE INTO THE WILDERNESS LAST NIGHT. ALL HE TOOK WITH HIM WAS A SIXPACK OF SCHLITZ, A DECK OF GIRLIE CARDS, AND HIS EMPTY GUITAR CASE. I DON'T THINK HE'LL BE COMING BACK.
WILDERNESS:
THIS THING'S BEEN A LONG TIME COMING. GROWING DISSATISFACTION WITH HIS RECORD COMPANY... MOUNTING TENSIONS WITHIN HIS BAND... NOT TO MENTION THE BLATANT INDIFFERENCE OF THE MODERN RECORD-BUYING PUBLIC: ALL THIS AND MORE MUST HAVE CONTRIBUTED TO SAMMY'S DRAMATIC DECISION.
HMPH
SALE! ALL SAMMY HAGAR ALBUMS ½ PRICE
NO RETURNS
SAMMY SINGS!
THERE WAS A TIME (MAYBE YOU REMEMBER) WHEN SAMMY HAGAR WAS THE BE-ALL AND END-ALL OF POPULAR MUSIC. FANS LINED UP FOR MILES JUST TO HEAR SAMMY'S CLEAR, STRONG VOICE RING OUT INTO THE STYGIAN BLACKNESS OF THEIR LOCAL CONCERT HALL. BACK THEN NOBODY COULD SING LIKE SAMMY... NOBODY.
THERE'S ONLY ONE WAY...
THERE'S ONLY ONE WAY...
TO ROCK!
BUT HE'S GONE NOW, AND WE SHOULDN'T BE TOO SAD. BECAUSE HE'S GONE TO A PLACE WHERE LANGUAGE AND LOGIC HAVE NO JURISDICTION... A PLACE WHERE WOMEN ARE EASY AND THE BEER IS CHEAP... A PLACE WHERE THEY STILL TREAT OLD ROCK STARS LIKE REIGNING GODS. GOODBYE, SAMMY. WE'LL MISS YOU. CAN'T SAY IT'S BEEN REAL... BUT IT CERTAINLY HAS BEEN FUN.
SAMMY HAGAR TOUR '83
...ONLY ONE WAY... THERE'S ONLY ONE WAY...
SAMMY HAGAR "All My Best"

← DON'T WORRY... SAMMY CAME BACK! (see pages 138-141)

THANKS! ★ LIZ ★ MOM and DAD ★ CAROLYN ★ MATT ★ STEFANO ★ STEVE ★ GREG ★ JASON ★ S. STEEN ★ D. LASKY ★ CANNED HAMM ★ ELLSWORTH ★ PAULUS ★ SHANNON ★ SHAWNA ★ ED B. ★ SAL ★ J. MACLEOD ★ R. GARWIG

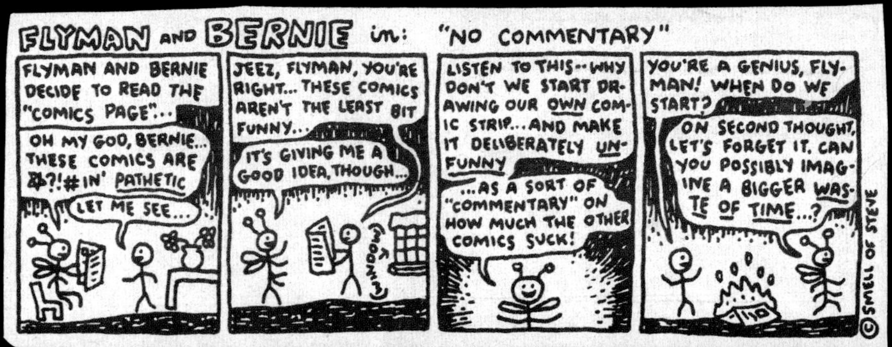

FLYMAN AND BERNIE in: "NO COMMENTARY"
FLYMAN AND BERNIE DECIDE TO READ THE "COMICS PAGE"...
OH MY GOD, BERNIE... THESE COMICS ARE #?!#IN' PATHETIC
LET ME SEE...
JEEZ, FLYMAN, YOU'RE RIGHT... THESE COMICS AREN'T THE LEAST BIT FUNNY...
IT'S GIVING ME A GOOD IDEA, THOUGH...
LISTEN TO THIS -- WHY DON'T WE START DRAWING OUR OWN COMIC STRIP... AND MAKE IT DELIBERATELY UNFUNNY
...AS A SORT OF "COMMENTARY" ON HOW MUCH THE OTHER COMICS SUCK!
YOU'RE A GENIUS, FLYMAN! WHEN DO WE START?
ON SECOND THOUGHT, LET'S FORGET IT. CAN YOU POSSIBLY IMAGINE A BIGGER WASTE OF TIME...?
© SMELL OF STEVE

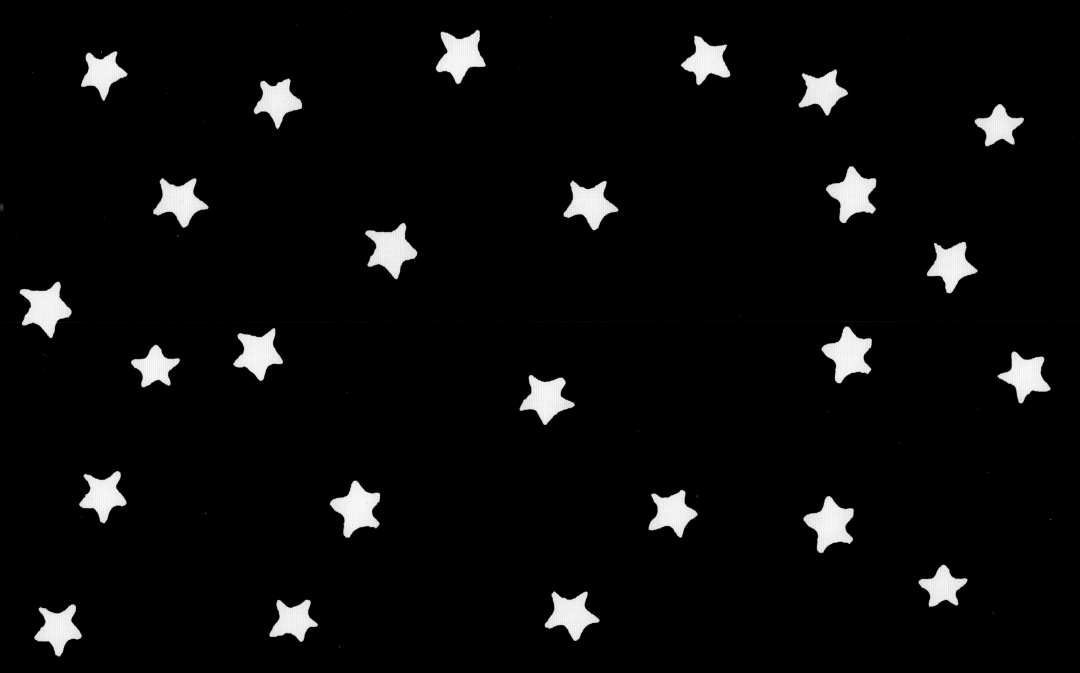

PUBLISHER Mike Richardson • **EXECUTIVE VICE PRESIDENT** Neil Hankerson • **CHIEF FINANCIAL OFFICER** Tom Weddle • **VICE PRESIDENT OF PUBLISHING** Randy Stradley • **VICE PRESIDENT OF BUSINESS DEVELOPMENT** Michael Martens • **VICE PRESIDENT OF MARKETING, SALES, AND LICENSING** Anita Nelson • **VICE PRESIDENT OF PRODUCT DEVELOPMENT** David Scroggy • **VICE PRESIDENT OF INFORMATION TECHNOLOGY** Dale LaFountain **DIRECTOR OF PURCHASING** Darlene Vogel • **GENERAL COUNSEL** Ken Lizzi • **EDITORIAL DIRECTOR** Davey Estrada • **SENIOR MANAGING EDITOR** Scott Allie • **SENIOR BOOKS EDITOR, DARK HORSE BOOKS** Chris Warner **SENIOR BOOKS EDITOR, M PRESS/DH PRESS** Robert Simpson • **EXECUTIVE EDITOR** Diana Schutz • **DIRECTOR OF DESIGN AND PRODUCTION** Cary Grazzini • **ART DIRECTOR** Lia Ribacchi • **DIRECTOR OF SCHEDULING** Cara Niece

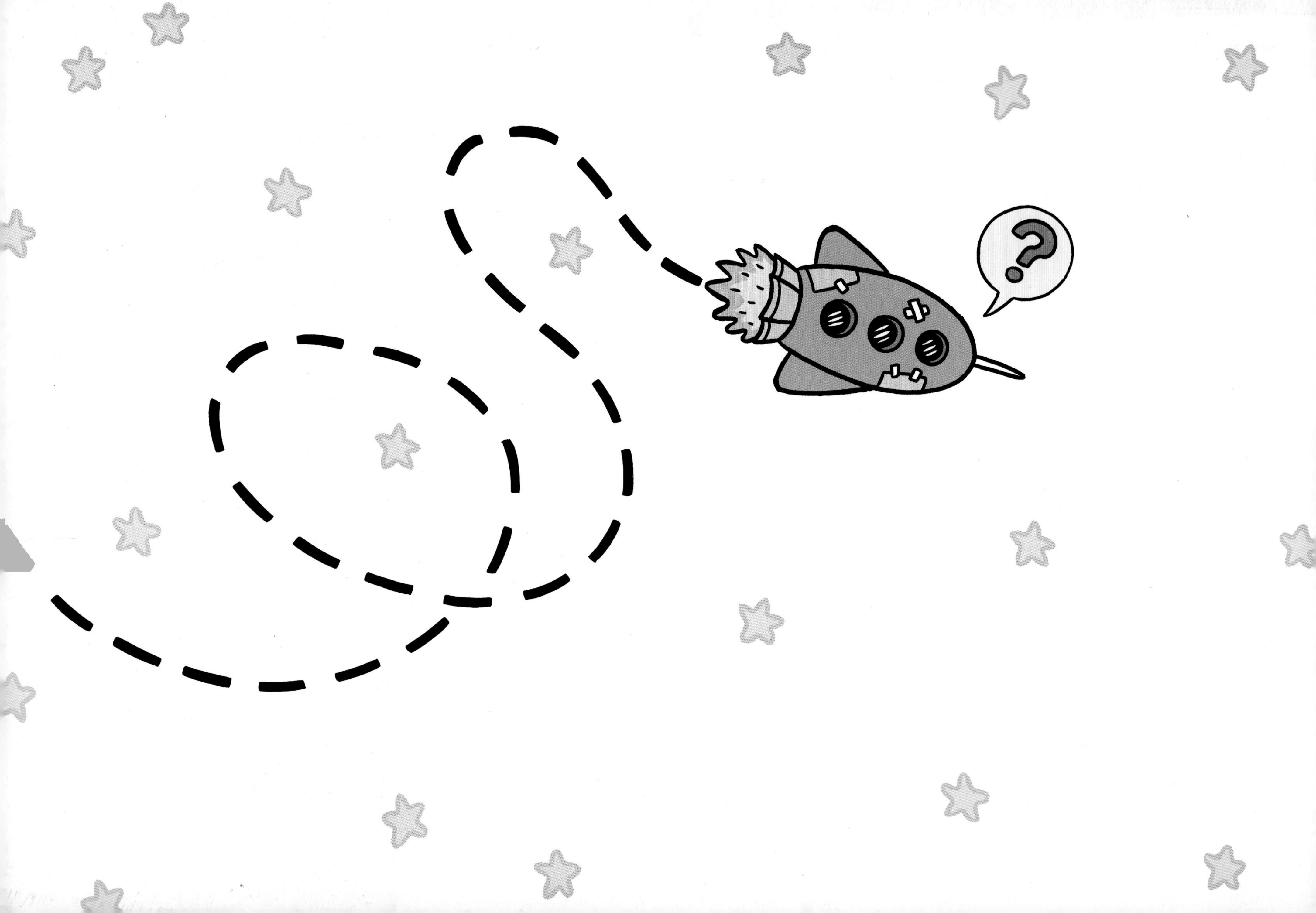
?